OECD Reviews of Regulatory Reform

Regulatory Reform
in Greece

OECD

ORGANISATION FOR ECONOMIC CO-OPERATION AND DEVELOPMENT

ORGANISATION FOR ECONOMIC CO-OPERATION AND DEVELOPMENT

Pursuant to Article 1 of the Convention signed in Paris on 14th December 1960, and which came into force on 30th September 1961, the Organisation for Economic Co-operation and Development (OECD) shall promote policies designed:

- to achieve the highest sustainable economic growth and employment and a rising standard of living in Member countries, while maintaining financial stability, and thus to contribute to the development of the world economy;
- to contribute to sound economic expansion in Member as well as non-member countries in the process of economic development; and
- to contribute to the expansion of world trade on a multilateral, non-discriminatory basis in accordance with international obligations.

The original Member countries of the OECD are Austria, Belgium, Canada, Denmark, France, Germany, Greece, Iceland, Ireland, Italy, Luxembourg, the Netherlands, Norway, Portugal, Spain, Sweden, Switzerland, Turkey, the United Kingdom and the United States. The following countries became Members subsequently through accession at the dates indicated hereafter: Japan (28th April 1964), Finland (28th January 1969), Australia (7th June 1971), New Zealand (29th May 1973), Mexico (18th May 1994), the Czech Republic (21st December 1995), Hungary (7th May 1996), Poland (22nd November 1996), Korea (12th December 1996) and the Slovak Republic (14th December 2000). The Commission of the European Communities takes part in the work of the OECD (Article 13 of the OECD Convention).

Publié en français sous le titre:
LA RÉFORME DE LA RÉGLEMENTATION EN GRÈCE

FOREWORD

The OECD Review of Regulatory Reform in Greece is one of a series of country reports carried out under the OECD's Regulatory Reform Programme, launched in 1998 in response to a mandate by OECD Ministers.

The Regulatory Reform Programme is aimed at helping governments improve regulatory quality – that is, reforming regulations which raise unnecessary obstacles to competition, innovation and growth, while ensuring that regulations efficiently serve important social objectives.

The Programme is part of a broader effort at the OECD to support sustained economic development, job creation and good governance. It fits with other initiatives such as our annual country economic surveys; the Jobs Strategy; the OECD Principles of Corporate Governance; and the fight against corruption, hard-core cartels and harmful tax competition.

Drawing on the analysis and recommendations of good regulatory practices contained in the 1997 OECD *Report to Ministers on Regulatory Reform*, the Regulatory Reform Programme is a multi-disciplinary process of in-depth country reviews, based on self-assessment and on peer evaluation by several OECD committees.

The country Reviews are not comprehensive, but, rather, targeted at key reform areas. Each Review has the same structure, including three thematic chapters on the quality of regulatory institutions and government processes; competition policy and enforcement; and the enhancement of market openness through regulatory reform. Each Review also contains chapters on sectors such as electricity and telecommunications, and an assessment of the macroeconomic context for reform in the country under review.

The country Reviews benefited from a process of extensive consultations with a wide range of government officials (including elected officials) from the country reviewed, business and trade union representatives, consumer groups, and academic experts from many backgrounds.

These Reviews demonstrate clearly that in many areas, a well-structured and implemented programme of regulatory reform has brought lower prices and more choice for consumers, helped stimulate innovation, investment, and new industries, and thereby aided in boosting economic growth and overall job creation. Comprehensive regulatory reforms have produced results more quickly than piece-meal approaches; and such reforms over the longer-term helped countries to adjust more quickly and easily to changing circumstances and external shocks. At the same time, a balanced reform programme must take into account important social concerns. Adjustment costs in some sectors have been painful, although experience shows that these costs can be reduced if reform is accompanied by supportive policies, including active labour market policies, to cushion adjustment.

While reducing and reforming regulations is a key element of a broad programme of regulatory reform, country experience also shows that in a more competitive and efficient market, new regulations and institutions are sometimes necessary to assure that private anticompetitive behaviour does not delay or block the benefits of reform and that health, environmental and consumer protection is assured. In countries pursuing reform, which is often difficult and opposed by vested interests, sustained and consistent political leadership is an essential element of successful reform efforts, and transparent and informed public dialogue on the benefits and costs of reform is necessary for building and maintaining broad public support for reform.

The policy options presented in the Reviews may pose challenges for each country concerned, but they do not ignore wide differences between national cultures, legal and institutional traditions and economic circumstances. The in-depth nature of the Reviews and the efforts made to consult with a wide range of stakeholders reflect the emphasis placed by the OECD on ensuring that the policy options presented are relevant and attainable within the specific context and policy priorities of each country reviewed.

The OECD Reviews of Regulatory Reform are published on the responsibility of the Secretary-General of the OECD, but their policy options and accompanying analysis reflect input and commentary provided during peer review by all 30 OECD Member countries and the European Commission and during consultations with other interested parties.

The Secretariat would like to express its gratitude for the support of the Government of Greece, for the OECD Regulatory Reform Programme and its consistent co-operation during the review process. It also would like to thank the many OECD committee and country delegates, representatives from the OECD's Trade Union Advisory Committee (TUAC) and Business and Industry Advisory Committee (BIAC), and other experts whose comments and suggestions were essential to this report.

ACKNOWLEDGEMENTS

This series of Reviews of Regulatory Reform in OECD countries was completed under the responsibility of Deputy Secretary-General **Sally Shelton-Colby**. The Review of Greece reflects contributions from many sources, including the Government of Greece. Major contributions were also made by the Committees of the OECD, representatives of Member governments, and members of the Business and Industry Advisory Committee (BIAC) and the Trade Union Advisory Committee (TUAC), as well as other groups. This report was peer reviewed on 22 March 2001 in the OECD's Ad Hoc Multidisciplinary Group on Regulatory Reform.

In the OECD Secretariat, the following people contributed substantially to the review of Greece: the former **Head of Programme on Regulatory Reform** and lead drafter: Scott H. Jacobs; **Document preparation**: Jennifer Stein; **Economics Department**: Chapter 1 was principally prepared by a consultant, Alexander Sarris, Department of Economics, University of Athens, and in the OECD Secretariat, Peter Hoeller, and benefited from work by Giuseppe Nicoletti on regulatory indicators; **Public Management Service**: Cesar Córdova-Novion, and Martin Stokie, Department of Treasure and Finance, Melbourne, Australia, on secondment to the OECD; **Trade Directorate**: Evdokia Moïsé, Anthony Kleitz; **Directorate for Financial, Fiscal and Enterprise Affairs**: Patricia Heriard-Dubreuil, Bernard J. Phillips, Sally Van Siclen, Michael Wise; **Directorate for Science, Technology, and Industry**: Dimitri Ypsilanti and Natasha Constantelou of the National Technical University of Athens; **General Secretariat**: Steve Cutts. The current Head of the Programme on Regulatory Reform is Rolf Alter.

TABLE OF CONTENTS

Part I

List of Boxes

List of Tables

List of Figures

Part II

Part I

OECD REVIEW
OF REGULATORY REFORM
IN GREECE

EXECUTIVE SUMMARY

In the mid-1990s, for the first time in post-war history, Greek strategies for economic development shifted markedly to reliance on market forces rather than on state-managed growth. Economic management in the 20 years after 1974 had led to a downward spiral in economic performance, ultimately resulting in crisis and discrediting the traditionally interventionist and regulatory role of the Greek State in the economy. Today, during a period of economic resurgence in Greece, combined with political and macroeconomic stability, there are new opportunities for much-needed reforms. The many significant reforms underway reforms are accelerating structural adjustment, creating a new economy that is more flexible and competitive in regional and global markets. The major challenges over the next few years will be to systematically unwind the extensive state involvement in the economy, to discourage entrenched habits of rent-seeking, and to ensure the sustainability of strong growth at low inflation through the establishment of regulatory policy regimes and institutions that support investment, innovation, and vigorous competition. In future, the strengths of Greek entrepreneurship – clearly demonstrated by the thriving SME informal sector of the post-war years – will become the driving force of the modern Greek economy.

Yet Greece lags other OECD countries in regulatory reforms, and still suffers from the high costs of poor regulation in some areas and too little pro-market regulation in others, such as the liberalizing utility sectors. Long traditions of political intervention and protection of economic actors are difficult to reverse, but a pro-reform consensus is emerging. The confluence of positive elements – growing social consensus for reform, macroeconomic and political stability, and healthy economic growth that will ease the pain of transition – suggest that the next few years will be decisive years of reform in Greece.

Chapter 1. The macroeconomic context for regulatory reform. Macroeconomic reforms and EMU membership establish a basis for continued strong growth, and provide a good opportunity for Greece to push forward with deeper supply-side reforms. Greece's state-led development strategy based on import substitution and credit allocation produced strong growth until 1974, but left a legacy of corporatism and extensive state collaboration with powerful private firms, and fostered the growth of a very large informal sector. Economic performance deteriorated sharply after 1974, in the midst of historic political change and international economic turbulence. A vicious cycle emerged as weaker enterprises required more state support, and as a faltering economy was used to justify more controls. As a result, though there were some improvements in social policy, in many respects Greece ended the 1980s in worse shape than it began.

Genuine reforms were launched in the 1990s with important changes to financial and labour market regulations, some product market liberalisation, and initial steps in state reform. The corner was turned in the mid-1990s, when a package of EU-related reforms boosted growth and investment. Since then, Greece has made progress in converging with the rest of Europe. Market liberalisation has proceeded the furthest in the financial sector. Today, while the Greek economy is on track to continued solid growth, a high priority should be placed on further supply-side reforms to hold down inflation and take full advantage of opportunities. Public enterprises create costly economy-wide distortions, and continuation of privatisation is a high priority. In the telecommunications sector, services and prices have improved after reform, but energy reforms lag. Simplification of the tax system has improved transparency and tax revenues, but major reform is necessary to establish a level playing field for enterprises. Reducing red tape and regulatory uncertainties for firms should boost potential growth. Distortions and disincentives in public sector performance continue to reduce the certainty and efficiency of the general regulatory environment. Many concrete steps can be taken to raise potential output growth. The focus should be on comprehensive reforms that create vigorous market competition through regulatory and institutional reforms.

Chapter 2. Government capacity to assure high quality regulation. Further improvement of public governance in Greece – no less than a reinvention of the relationship between the public administration and the market – is needed for the success of regulatory reform. A cultural tradition within the public service of mistrust of market forces has led to over-regulation and rent-seeking. Basic reforms of the Greek civil service are needed to create the capacity for an efficient and transparent regulatory system including strengthening the professionalism and accountability of the public administration and improving policy coordination. A government-wide strategy for regulatory quality and a framework of quality standards should be adopted and made effective through new institutions to protect the quality of domestic regulations. Despite recent improvements, regulatory transparency in Greece lags behind other OECD countries. Use of regulatory impact analysis can improve understanding of costs and benefits of regulatory actions within the Greek public administration, and guide the appropriate use of regulation and should be accompanied by periodic reviews of the need for existing regulations. Poor compliance practices, too, undermine the competitiveness of law-abiding firms. Decentralisation is bringing regulatory decisions closer to the citizens, but regulatory quality controls should be strengthened in local governments. Independent sectoral regulators are needed to promote market competition in newly privatised markets. Useful steps are already underway. In parallel with the acceleration of regulatory reform in the 1990s, the Greek government launched a series of reforms to improve the efficiency and effectiveness of its public administration. In April 2000, the Prime Minister announced that his government will improve client service, complete decentralisation, and reduce the substantial administrative burdens hindering investment.

Chapter 3. The role of competition policy in regulatory reform. In Greece, recognition of the key role of effective competition policy has been slow to emerge. In a business and policy culture that has been characterised by extensive state regulation, direct control of prices, and substantial state-owned enterprises, competition policy has not been a high priority. In late 2000, Greece took positive steps to strengthen the competition agency, but EU reforms may require further steps. Underlying many problems is a lack of resources and skills in the Competition Committee and its secretariat, which, in combination with low thresholds for merger notification that have wasted available resources, has weakened enforcement against costly competition abuses. The rules for horizontal agreements are adequate, but have been disused due to lack of resources. The Competition Committee has been too dependent on a ministry that was not committed to market competition. Consumer protection policy has no clear connection to competition policy goals, and application is left principally to private action.

Chapter 4. Enhancing market openness through regulatory reform. Greece is pursuing market opening policies which are important for a small country dependent on trade, but Greece has a poor record in attracting foreign investment. Greece has integrated several of the OECD's efficient regulation principles into domestic regulations, but falls short on transparency in rulemaking, avoidance of unnecessary trade restrictiveness, and application of competition principles. The discretionary character of public consultation has reduced market confidence among foreign parties while the one-stop shop for foreign investors is of uncertain value. Market openness is further reduced by regulatory complexity and inefficient administration. Public procurement is formally open, but in practice problems still arise. Measures to ensure non-discrimination should concentrate on the services sectors. The absence of prior assessment of regulatory impact on the economy raises the risk of unduly trade-restrictive regulation. Greece ranks high on use of internationally harmonised standards and is advanced in recognition of equivalence of other countries' regulatory measures, but institutions for accreditation should be strengthened.

Chapter 5. Regulatory reform in electricity, domestic ferries, and trucking. Greece has taken many of the steps needed to improve the performance of its electricity sector, but the package is not yet complete. Electricity prices are at OECD averages, but these prices mask inefficiencies and distortions that reduce job creation and economic growth. The integrated structure of the Greek electricity sector is the largest barrier to market competition. Further clarity about the role of the state and the market will improve both market confidence and the performance of PPC, and more attention is needed to market access to open the markets to new entrants. Resources and regulatory powers must be placed in a regulatory body, independent of Ministry and the regulated companies. The domestic ferry sector is crucial in Greece and historically has been highly regulated. Reforms are now underway to improve the regulatory framework. As part of these reforms, regulatory institutions should be modernised so that producers do not have undue influence. Economic regulation should be eased, so that the companies make choices about commercial operations in response to consumer wishes and developments in the marketplace. As producers make more commercial decisions, the Ministry should ensure that the regulatory framework is transparent, accountable, and pro-competition. Several regulatory reforms would increase efficiency and reduce the costs of ferry service, such as a focus on service to islands rather than to routes, extending competitive tendering for unprofitable routes, and freeing up fares over competitive routes. With reform, service can be maintained to all designated islands, but at lower cost while employment can be increased by more competition. The Greek regulatory regime for trucking is not sustainable, but very recent steps were taken to begin a process of major reform.

Chapter 6. Regulatory reform in the telecommunications industry. Greece reformed its telecommunications sector later than most OECD countries, and competition is relatively undeveloped With the right reforms, though, Greece could quickly build a transparent and neutral regulatory framework based on sound economic principles. Compliance with important requirements of the EC derogation have been considerably delayed. Due to these and other delays in implementing the regulatory framework, essential regulatory safeguards are still missing. Regulation of entry and licensing is unnecessarily burdensome, and discourages market entry. Greece is taking positive action to open access to the local loop, but a lack of alternate infrastructure will slow competition. In parallel with adding new pro-competition regulations, the arduous task of continual streamlining of the regulatory regime must go on.

Chapter 7. Conclusions and policy options for regulatory reform. Under the spur of intensifying European competition and seizing the opportunity of a stable political and macroeconomic environment, Greece has launched itself on the road to market liberalisation. This road, trod later in Greece than in most European countries, is necessary to fuel the sustainable economic growth that will create jobs and drive convergence with other European countries. Now that the vicious economic cycle of the previous twenty years, from 1974 to 1994, has been broken, Greece is moving further and faster on microeconomic reforms than at any time in the post-war period. Sustained and consistent reforms over the next few years will do much to bring Greek regulatory practices up to OECD good practices and build valuable credibility in the market for Greek reforms.

Most Greeks will benefit from regulatory reform. Indeed, the benefits of further regulatory reform for Greece are likely to be higher than for most OECD countries. Yet the resistance of many protected groups to change, despite recent changes in attitudes, will continue to be hard to overcome. Major steps recommended in this report include:

- *Speed up and improve the implementation of regulatory reform by enhancing accountability in the central government for regulatory quality, and by promoting tools for regulatory quality throughout the public administration.* Regulatory reform would be faster and more effective with a government-wide policy on the objectives and tools of reform, backed up by a ministerial-level committee that is supported by an expert unit on regulatory reform. A step by step programme for regulatory impact analysis is key, in order to introduce better regulatory and non-regulatory instruments that will improve policy results.

- *Improve regulatory transparency through more systematic use of public consultation, continued clarification of procurement criteria, communication to affected members of the public, and codification.* A mandatory public consultation requirement, based on objective criteria, would substantially improve regulatory quality and transparency. Ongoing efforts for improving the clarity of pre-selection and award criteria for public procurement should be actively pursued. Informal and occasional initiatives to display information on the Internet should be formalised and applied in a systematic manner across the administration. Greece should aim to prepare an inventory of all laws, including subordinate regulations.

— *Intensify efforts to reduce administrative barriers to businesses by establishing a central registry of administrative procedures and licences, considering the "silence is consent" rule, and initiating a comprehensive review to determine how to reduce burdens.* Administrative burdens, and in particular business licences and permits are among the most important barriers to Greek entrepreneurs and to market entry.

— *To combat regulatory inflation and update older regulations, review and evaluate existing regulations and paperwork.* Regulatory inflation is undermining the integrity of the Greek regulatory system. Although this is a very large task, efforts should be made to develop a rolling, systematic process of codification and evaluation of existing laws and other regulations.

— *Encourage greater co-ordination between local government and the central administration by i) defining clearly relevant regulatory competencies for each level of government, ii) providing resources, people, and financing for delivery of services that those competencies dictate, and iii) assisting in the development of management capacities for quality regulation at all levels of administration.* The decentralisation process undertaken since the mid-1990s has enhanced local government capacities and competencies. As decentralisation proceeds, other countries' experiences show that intensive efforts are needed to safeguard regulatory quality at sub-national levels.

— *Improve mechanisms within the administration to produce quality outcomes for the citizens through further reform of the civil service.* The culture of the Greek public administration is gradually moving away from legalism and formalism to focus on results. Elements of further reform could include performance-based management focussed on policy results, pay incentives for public servants, greater flexibility within the public administration, and enhanced co-ordination and co-operation between ministries.

— *Following the new competition law of August 2000, take further steps to strengthen the capacities, expand the role, and target the priorities of the Competition Committee.* Competition policy should be strengthened by expanding resources, bolstering independence, targeting merger reviews, emphasising horizontal abuses, wider advocacy powers for the competition authority with its participation in de-monopolisation policies, and ensuring that market openness issues are considered.

— *Promote market openness by reducing discrimination in domestic regulation and encouraging the use of international standards and quality certification.* Constraints on entry into regulated service markets should be assessed and eliminated unless they can be clearly justified as the best way to obtain legitimate public policy goals. Quality control and certification should gain more prominence in the business culture if the Greek market is to benefit fully from international standards.

— *Complete privatisation of structurally competitive services and industries.* Public enterprises account for 6% of employment and 27% of investment, yet almost all public enterprises are poorly managed and inefficient.

— *In the electricity sector, develop effective competition in generation and supply, develop regulatory institutions that promote investment, efficiency, and competition, improve the corporate governance of PPC to a fully commercial basis, and evaluate the state of the electricity sector, after some time, with a view to further reform.*

— *The newest telecommunications law made much progress, but essential regulatory safeguards should be established to lay the foundation for the Greek information society by ensuring full competition in the market.* Recent moves to create an independent regulatory body are welcome, because they are of prime importance in Greece to ensure transparent and non-discriminatory regulations. Regulation of prices through government authorisation is not appropriate for current competitive circumstances. Assuring interconnection to the incumbent's public switched telephone network is a key competitive safeguard, and, likewise, local loop competition will not be able to develop effectively unless number portability and pre-selection are assured. The government needs to establish a transparent universal service funding mechanism. In order to simplify and streamline regulations

Greece could immediately adopt a class licensing system that relies on simple authorisation for market entry. Finally, it is important that the incumbent be allowed to act independently in the market without undue interference from the government, its major shareholder.

Chapter 1

REGULATORY REFORM IN GREECE

INTRODUCTION

In the mid-1990s, for the first time in post-war history, Greek strategies for economic development shifted markedly to reliance on market forces rather than on state-managed growth. Economic management in the 20 years after 1974 had led to a downward spiral in economic performance, ultimately resulting in crisis and discrediting the traditionally interventionist and regulatory role of the Greek state in the economy. The change to market solutions was illustrated in mid-2000, when the government explained that "the State should no longer get involved in the operation of private enterprises, and neither [should it] pretend to be a businessman."[1]

Today, during a period of economic resurgence in Greece, there are new opportunities for much-needed reforms.

Today, during a period of economic resurgence in Greece, combined with political and macroeconomic stability, there are new opportunities for much-needed reforms. Reforms are accelerating structural adjustment, creating a new economy that is more flexible and competitive in regional and global markets. Major challenges over the next few years will be to systematically unwind the extensive state involvement in the economy, to discourage entrenched habits of rent-seeking, and to ensure the sustainability of strong growth at low inflation through the establishment of regulatory policy regimes and institutions that support investment, innovation, and vigorous competition. In future, the strengths of Greek entrepreneurship – clearly demonstrated by the thriving SME informal sector of the post-war years – will become the driving force of the new Greek economy.

Regulatory reform emerged in the wake of macroeconomic reforms, and by the late 1990s many significant reforms were underway.

Regulatory reform emerged gradually in the 1990s in the wake of extensive macroeconomic reforms carried out in response to changing external pressures. In particular, regulatory reform developed due to the demands of EU membership, though Greece has moved more slowly than other EU members to take advantage of the opportunities offered by the European Single Market. Transposition of EU directives has had a positive influence on the market orientation of Greek regulatory regimes. However, implementing the *acquis communautaire* has been difficult in terms of content and speed. Greece sought derogations that delayed important reforms and the benefits for Greek consumers and workers that reforms would have brought. In the latest EU Scoreboard, Greece has the highest deficit of directives yet to be transposed.[2]

By the mid-1990s, a virtuous circle was taking shape: sound macroeconomic policy created economic growth that eased the real or perceived costs of structural reforms, while structural reforms further boosted growth and improved macroeconomic performance.

Structural reforms in Greece can be classified into three phases. First were deep and fast reforms in a few sectors, beginning with banking; that phase was still in process in early 2001. In the next phase, market principles are being introduced into the utility sectors, beginning in the mid-1990s. Finally, a challenge already accepted by political leadership is modernisation of the public sector. Since the mid-1990s, the pace of reform has accelerated with the drive to qualify for membership in the euro area, as it became recognised that microeconomic problems were constraining the benefits of successful macroeconomic reforms. A virtuous circle was at hand: sound macroeconomic policy had created the economic growth that eased the costs of structural reforms, while structural reforms further boosted growth and improved macroeconomic performance.

A wide range of regulatory reforms are currently underway, including liberalisation of government-owned enterprises, of utilities such as transport, energy, and communications, as well as some non-utility sectors. Competition has developed in the financial sector, and most big banks are now private (although the largest bank is still state-controlled). Successful reform of the financial and securities sectors provides both an example and foundation for further reform. Privatisation has advanced far in the many sectors where major firms were under direct or indirect government control. Market-opening initiatives in standards and customs have improved trade and investment opportunities. Reform of public services and public sector efficiency is changing the institutional landscape, illustrated by de-politicisation and decentralisation initiatives, and an important new commitment to competition policy was adopted in late 2000.

Yet Greece lags other OECD countries in regulatory reforms, and still suffers from the high costs of poor regulation.

Yet Greece still lags in regulatory reform and market liberalisation. Many markets continue to be protected, poorly regulated, and inefficient.

Among OECD countries, however, Greece still lags in regulatory reform, market liberalisation, and market openness. The structural reforms of the past ten years include major steps in the right direction, but many markets continue to be protected, poorly regulated, and inefficient. The style of governance, institutional infrastructure, and policy frameworks has been slow to adapt and modernise (Clogg, 1992). Excessive state intervention in many forms still distorts market functioning, while insufficient regulation to enhance competition and protect consumer interests prevails in sectors such as electricity, transport, and communications. SMEs are also hit hard by poor regulation, driving many of them out of the formal sector altogether. There is excessive protection of "insiders", while outsiders incur substantial costs of operation and entry. This restrains business activity in general and investment in particular.

Despite the move to competition principles as the constitution of the new economic strategy, the lack of a clear conception of competition policy in Greece and its objectives, combined with weak institutions, has made competition policy ineffective as a framework for market-oriented reforms. A new law adopted in August 2000 improved the effectiveness and priorities of competition policy by boosting staff and strengthening the competition agency and over time should help bring Greece up to OECD standards in this area.

Given the success in macroeconomic adjustment, the attention of Greek policy makers should now turn to vigorous pursuit of structural reforms.

Simultaneous reforms in policies, public institutions and administrative practices are needed to accelerate and complete reforms already underway. Adoption of laws and regulations to conform to EU standards has already boosted potential economic growth. Large macroeconomic imbalances have been brought under control, so decision-making is now taking place in a stable macroeconomic environment. Given the success in macroeconomic adjustment, the attention of Greek policy makers should now turn to the vigorous pursuit of structural reforms.

Box 1.1.   What is regulation and regulatory reform?

There is no generally accepted definition of regulation applicable to the very different regulatory systems in OECD countries. In the OECD work, regulation refers to the diverse set of instruments by which governments set requirements on enterprises and citizens. Regulations include laws, formal and informal orders and subordinate rules issued by all levels of government, and rules issued by non-governmental or self-regulatory bodies to whom governments have delegated regulatory powers. Regulations fall into three categories:

- *Economic regulations* intervene directly in market decisions such as pricing, competition, market entry, or exit. Reform aims to increase economic efficiency by reducing barriers to competition and innovation, often through deregulation and use of efficiency-promoting regulation, and by improving regulatory frameworks for market functioning and prudential oversight.

- *Social regulations* protect public interests such as health, safety, the environment, and social cohesion. The economic effects of social regulations may be secondary concerns or even unexpected, but can be substantial. Reform aims to verify that regulation is needed, and to design regulatory and other instruments, such as market incentives and goal-based approaches, that are more flexible, simpler, and more effective at lower cost.

- *Administrative regulations* are paperwork and administrative formalities – so-called "red tape" – through which governments collect information and intervene in individual economic decisions. They can have substantial impacts on private sector performance. Reform aims at eliminating those no longer needed, streamlining and simplifying those that are needed, and improving the transparency of application.

Regulatory reform is used in the OECD work to refer to changes that improve regulatory quality, that is, enhance the performance, cost-effectiveness, or legal quality of regulations and related government formalities. Reform can mean revision of a single regulation, the scrapping and rebuilding of an entire regulatory regime and its institutions, or improvement of processes for making regulations and managing reform. Deregulation is a subset of regulatory reform and refers to complete or partial elimination of regulation in a sector to improve economic performance.

Source: OECD (1997), OECD *Report on Regulatory Reform*, Paris.

Long traditions of political intervention and protection of economic actors are difficult to reverse, but a pro-reform consensus is emerging.

Traditions of state intervention, clientelism, and protection in Greece have slowed reform and increased its political costs.

Progress in regulatory reform in Greece has been more difficult than in many OECD countries. Because structural reforms run counter to long traditions of state intervention, political clientelism, and economic protection, reforms have been slow and have entailed considerable political costs. Beginning with the first Greek monarchs in 1832, Greece "became locked in a centralised system which has continued throughout its modern history'and has always been a cause of slow-moving and creaking governmental machinery."[3] Political instability, which continued from Greece's independence in the 1820s until the 1970s, further undermined the development of a stable policy environment and a neutral and professional public administration. As Chapter 2 indicates, only in the 1990s have substantial steps been taken to create modern administrative capacities for effective governance.

As a result, interlocking interests between public and private sectors have been difficult to unravel. During the whole of the 1990s, there was considerable opposition by entrenched insiders in the public and private sectors to structural reforms such as privatisation of state-owned enterprises and liberalization of monopolies.

Today, a new Greek consensus seems to be emerging in the government and the general public that faster and deeper liberalisation and other structural reforms are needed to maintain strong growth with lower inflation and rapidly reduce the income gap with the other EU countries. It is notable that, during the elections of Spring 2000, structural reforms were promoted by both major parties. Meanwhile a younger generation, often educated abroad, is bringing new ideas as advisors, lobbyists, and entrepreneurs. Greek and foreign entrepreneurs alike are pushing aggressively for new opportunities to invest and enter markets.

The next few years will be decisive years of reform in Greece.

The confluence of positive elements – growing social consensus for reform, macroeconomic and political stability, and healthy economic growth that will ease the pain of transition – suggest that the next few years will be decisive years of reform in Greece.

THE MACROECONOMIC CONTEXT FOR SECTORAL REGULATORY REFORM

Macroeconomic reforms and EMU membership establish a basis for continued strong growth, and provide a good opportunity for Greece to push forward with deeper supply-side reforms.

Macroeconomic reform has restored confidence in the capacities of the government to establish the policy environment for market-led growth.

The economic resurgence of Greece in the 1990s has been largely a story of macroeconomic reform that has restored confidence in the capacities of the government to establish the policy environment for market-led growth. Supply side reforms, such as regulatory improvements, have received less attention, however, and inefficient regulatory policies and ineffective competition policies continue to reduce the benefits of a sound macroeconomic environment.

Structural reforms should be easier to implement in the next phase of reform because, over the past five years, economic performance in Greece has greatly improved. Annual GDP growth surpassed the EU average, while inflation and government deficits declined sufficiently to secure membership in the euro area. In June 2000, following a positive opinion by the European Commission and the EU Council of economic and finance ministers (Ecofin) on Greece's application to join the European Economic and Monetary Union (EMU), the European Council endorsed Greek membership.

A large productivity gap remains with respect to the EU average, but is declining, while unemployment was at end-2000 the second highest in the OECD.

These are substantial successes, though in some respects Greek economic performance continues to lag that of the best performing OECD countries.[4] A large productivity gap remains with respect to the EU average, but is declining. Growth has been characterised by capital deepening and improved labour productivity, but unemployment has drifted up and was at end-2000 the second highest in the OECD. Rapid growth is likely to continue over the next few years, spurred by public and private investment induced by continued large capital transfers under the EU's third Community Support Framework (CSF), by the prospect of low inflation and low interest rates following EMU membership in early 2001, and by preparations for the 2004 Olympic games. Solid growth should reduce the transition costs of adjustment, and provides a good opportunity for Greece to push forward with substantial supply-side reforms.

Greece's state-led development strategy based on import substitution and credit allocation produced strong growth until 1974...

From 1954 until 1973, the Greek economy recorded one of the fastest average GDP growth rates in the world.

From 1954 until 1973 the Greek economy expanded by 7%, recording one of the fastest average GDP growth rates in the world. Fast growth was combined with low inflation and low balance of payment deficits. Due to substantial out-migration, the per-capita growth rate was even higher.

The industrial policy of the pre-1974 period was largely one of import substitution. Extensive protection of traditional labour-intensive industries induced growth and employment in manufacturing. Growth was stimulated also by state allocation of long and short-term credit, which was until 1982 centrally controlled by a Currency Committee. Overall, the institutions and regulatory regimes established at the time, such as the 1952 constitution and subsequent tax laws, were very favourable for private investors, though workers fared less well due to the suppression of labour rights. Participation of the Greek drachma in the Bretton Woods system damped inflationary expectations. Fiscal policy aimed at low levels of public consumption, high rates of public investment, and balanced budgets. Labour market policy guaranteed that labour costs would not increase above productivity gains. Wage discipline was enforced by the authoritarian dictatorial regime that was in power from 1967 till 1974, which suppressed the unions. During this period, unit labour costs in Greece relative to the European Community declined by more than 30%, and the share of labour in value-added also declined.[5]

...but left a legacy of corporatism and extensive state collaboration with powerful private firms, and fostered the growth of a very large informal sector.

...but Greece's pre-1974 economic policies planted the seeds of economic decline.

As has been seen in other heavily interventionist development strategies, Greece's pre-1974 economic policies planted the seeds of economic decline. The *"country's post-war 'miracle' can be said to have been intimately linked with the emergence of a ubiquitous, overinterventionist, overregulating, paternalistic and protectionist state"*.[6] The Greek economic system of the time has been characterised as state corporatism.[7] Private investment incentives were coupled with substantial interlocking interests between state financial institutions that controlled the bulk of credit, and those few families who controlled a large share of traditional industries. This created close connections between the public and private sectors of the economy that partly explain the difficulty of structural reforms today. Moreover, due to equity ownership by state-owned banks, public control of firms, especially larger ones, was extensive, and invited frequent political intervention into enterprise decisions.

A dual industrial structure developed in Greece: an "official" and highly regulated sector in product, credit and labour markets, and an extensive "informal" and unincorporated sector that was mostly unregulated.

The state preference for large enterprises fostered a dual industrial structure in Greece. An "official" sector evolved in product, credit and labour markets. This sector, either private or public in ownership, was highly regulated in resource allocation and decision making. The effectiveness and application of regulations on pricing, taxation and subsidisation, protection from competition, hiring and firing, credit extension, and so forth were negotiated bilaterally between enterprises and public authorities. Budget constraints were soft for most large firms, resulting in high levels of debt. Meanwhile, an extensive "informal" and unincorporated sector developed, mostly consisting of small-scale industrial, commercial and service firms, that possessed little or no negotiating power in the political sphere and banking system, but that was competitive in relevant markets. Estimates based on a Social Accounting Matrix (SAM) of Greece for 1984 show that the informal sector accounted for about 45% of GDP.

Greek regulation tended to be highly discretionary and non-transparent, and distorted market forces.

The Greek public administration developed a highly discretionary and non-transparent regulatory style in this period. The principal industrial policy tool was the selective application of a large number of rules and exemptions that applied to investment activity, financing, production and trade. Price controls, selective protection coupled with credit rationing, and subsidies were the most commonly used instruments. The combination of state policy with lobbying by special interests created a variety of market conditions applying to different sectors of economic activity. In this regulatory environment, market forces were muted, distorted, or contravened entirely.

Economic performance deteriorated sharply after 1974, in the midst of historic political change and international economic turbulence.

In the 1970s, changing domestic and international conditions placed severe pressures on the rigid and highly-regulated Greek economy, and Greece entered a period of crisis management in the midst of democratisation.

Changing domestic and international conditions placed severe pressures on the rigid and highly-regulated Greek economy. Economic policy from 1974 until 1985 can be characterised as crisis management in the midst of democratisation. The political change of 1974 coincided with the first oil crisis. The labour unions and working population demanded redistributive measures that had been largely suppressed during the dictatorship, at the same time that two successive oil shocks would have required a restrictive policy stance to dampen inflation. In response, the government increased taxes and public spending. The result was stagflation, a significant drop in public investment, and a large increase in transfer payments.[8] At the same time, real wages increased above productivity gains, which reduced profits.

Economic performance deteriorated sharply.

After 1974, and until 1985, economic performance deteriorated sharply. Annual output growth averaged 2%, inflation averaged 18%, and the external deficit as a share of GDP doubled. On virtually all dimensions, economic performance dropped below the EU average. The economic slowdown can be attributed almost entirely to two factors: a decline in the pace of capital accumulation, and a decline in productivity.[9]

The size of the state grew rapidly...

Meanwhile, state spending grew rapidly. Intensified political competition put upward pressure on public expenditures. Following the elections in 1980, the primary deficit jumped from 0.5% of GDP in 1980 to 7% in 1981. Expenditure surged primarily due to extensive hiring in the public sector, and substantial increases in wage and non-wage benefits, though public wages did not significantly lag private sector wages. Subsidies to ailing enterprises also increased.

...and between 1980 and 1985, government spending rose by more than 10 percentage points of GDP, the steepest rise recorded in the OECD area.

The size of the state sector continued to increase in 1982 to 1985 at a time of major political changes. A socialist government assumed power for the first time after World War II, and Greece joined the European Community (EEC). Economic policy continued to focus on redistribution. Current expenditure increased at the expense of public investment, though sizeable EEC transfers partly offset the large decline in domestic savings. Between 1980 and 1985, government outlays increased by more than 10 percentage points of GDP, the steepest rise recorded in the OECD area.

State interventions into an increasingly troubled private sector, combined with wage awards that exceeded productivity, slowed economic adjustment at the same time that market opening in the EEC required faster adjustment.

Many large firms that had grown rapidly in the pre-1974 environment became "problematic" but were not allowed to close.

In an environment of slowing growth, many large firms that had grown rapidly in the favourable pre-1974 environment became "problematic." They were not allowed to close, however, due to a policy of preserving jobs. Rather, they were effectively nationalised as their assets were acquired by state-owned banks. To preserve employment, the Currency Committee allocated credit to many of

21

the ailing large corporations, both private and public, diverting credit from the rest of the economy.

The government of the early 1980s introduced structural changes that affected the public sector, the labour market, and consequently the private sector. In the public sector, policies to reduce corruption and patronage in the civil service were good steps (but later had unintended side effects). Automatic, seniority-based promotions were introduced, and salary differences among different grades were suppressed, reducing incentives for good performance. Simultaneously, stronger labour unions in the public sector induced wage increases that were higher than in the private sector. The public sector wage settlements were signals for large subsequent wage increases in the private sector, resulting in a profit-squeeze. Labour markets were made more rigid by, for instance, laws that limited lay-offs.

Trade performance deteriorated as support to non-tradable sectors induced a large trade deficit. EEC entry, which was accompanied by large transfers especially to farmers, allowed easy financing of these deficits, but led to an appreciation of the real exchange rate, and accelerated the relative decline of sectors producing export goods. This led to stagnation of production in industrial sectors. Furthermore, the productivity and profitability of investments declined, in response to the distortions that were introduced.[10]

The administrative allocation of credit kept many inefficient private firms alive, and squeezed the rest of the private sector, especially smaller firms.

EEC entry and the ensuing trade liberalisation further squeezed profits and the profitability of investment. This triggered more state interventions that drew the state more deeply into the economy. In 1982, the government attempted to counter the profit-squeeze by subsidising the cost of private investment projects at rates that depended on location and sector.[11] Moreover, the government's desire to stem unemployment increases led to credit policies, implemented by state-owned banks, that limited bankruptcies of large private firms. At the same time, the overall level of loanable funds declined, because of the rise of public sector deficits. Thus, the administrative allocation of credit kept many inefficient private firms alive, and squeezed the rest of the private sector, especially smaller firms. An industry reconstruction corporation, set up in 1983 to manage the take-over of ailing private corporations by the public sector, was accompanied by discussion of yet more nationalisations.

A vicious cycle had emerged as weaker enterprises required more state support, and as a faltering economy was used to justify more controls.

The accumulation of debts of inefficient private firms led to further increases in subsidies and higher budget deficits.

A vicious cycle had emerged. The accumulation of debts of inefficient private firms led to further increases in subsidies and higher budget deficits. Attempts at macroeconomic stabilisation later in the 1980s failed, and defensive regulatory controls continued to increase. Despite strong GDP growth, public sector borrowing reached 22% of GDP in 1989. Growing tax evasion and delays in tax collection reduced public revenues, while public expenditures remained high. Inflationary pressures built up, which prompted the authorities to freeze administered prices in sectors controlled by public enterprises.

Greece paid a large price for the poor economic and budgetary policies of the 1980s, and in many respects ended the decade in worse shape than it began.

By the end of the 1980s, economic conditions in Greece were drastically worse than at the beginning.

By the end of the 1980s, economic conditions in Greece were drastically worse than at the beginning, despite some improvements in social policy. The annual average rate of GDP growth during the decade was 1.0% (compared to 3.2% in the EU area). Average annual growth in labour productivity was only 0.6%, while total fixed investment fell by 1.6% annually. At the same time, average annual inflation in Greece was 20.1%, compared to 5.2% in the EU.[12]

The public sector was in bad financial shape. The number of pensioners and the average pension rose rapidly during the decade. The ratio of pensions to GDP rose from 7% to 15% of GDP by the end of the decade. The number of employed people per pensioner fell from 2.8 in 1979 to 2 in 1989, and the deficit of the pension system rose from 1% of GDP in 1980 to 9% in 1989. Government debt, as a share of GDP, increased from 32% in 1981 to 100% by 1989. Meanwhile, growth in other social expenditures, such as education, and health, was curtailed because outlays on pensions skyrocketed.

Private sector performance was reduced by the interventionist, distorting, and unstable policy environment...

Private sector performance was hard hit by the interventionist, distorting, and unstable policy environment. Frequent policy changes over the decade had raised investment risks and reduced market confidence. Coupled with poor infrastructure development (an inadequate road network and substandard communications), this resulted in a very low level of foreign direct investment, which, with low national savings, led to low overall investment. The credit squeeze, stricter labour market policies, and tax increases had strong negative effects especially on smaller firms. Such firms increasingly evaded official controls.

...as policies during the 1980s attempted to conserve an outdated industrial structure.

Policies during the decade conserved an outdated industrial structure, and induced substantial substitution of capital for labour in response to sharply rising labour costs. Despite protectionist measures, import penetration increased due to trade liberalisation following EEC entry. Yet the share of intra-industry trade in total trade in 1990 was by far the lowest in Europe and increased only a little, while the quality of Greek manufactured exports relative to the quality of manufactured imports declined substantially.[13]

Genuine reforms were launched in the 1990s with important changes to financial and labour market regulations, some product market liberalisation, and initial steps in state reform.

A turn-around began in the early 1990s, with reforms of the banking sector.

Between 1990 and 1993, substantial reforms were initiated, and some earlier policies were reversed under a Medium Term Adjustment Program. Financial liberalisation, begun in the mid-1980s during the stabilisation program, intensified after 1990 due to plans to create a single European currency, and the possible entry

23

of the drachma into the Exchange Rate Mechanism (ERM). The banks' obligatory investment in government paper was reduced from 40% in 1990 to 15% in 1992, and eliminated in 1993. This forced the public sector, which traditionally had privileged access to scarce financial resources, to compete on equal terms with the private sector for funds. The obligation of banks to earmark funds for loans to small and medium sized enterprises was abolished. Moreover, consumer credit was largely liberalised in 1992, and interest rates were freed, while controls on foreign capital transactions were liberalised in 1993.

Labour market policy became somewhat less interventionist, and wage bargaining has been conducted since 1991 without government interference. Some labour market rules were revised, such as the lifting of impediments to part-time work, the reduction of off-season allowances for construction workers, and the lengthening of the contribution period that gives right to a pension.

Liberalisation began in several product markets.

Several product markets were liberalised. Price and profit margin controls were abolished for many products, the bakery trade was deregulated, pricing of standard petroleum products was liberalised, shopping hours for retail outlets were freed, parts of the telecommunication market were opened to competition including the cellular mobile market, and the monopoly of Olympic Airways in domestic flights was lifted.

Privatisation began slowly.

A start was made in reorganising the public sector to reduce state control over the economy and improve finances. Some publicly-owned companies were privatised and non-viable firms owned by state banks or other state entities were liquidated. However, implementation was slow as the commercial value of many companies was low, the stock market climate was not favourable, and privatisation procedures were cumbersome and unclear. There was considerable reluctance and opposition within state agencies to relinquish control of companies, and strong opposition by workers. By end-1992, employment in the wider public sector was reduced by 18 000 people, with a large share accounted for by the privatisation of the Athens Bus Company (8 000 people). Steps were taken to improve tax collection, but were not effective. Important changes were introduced in the pension system for public employees. However, the goal of reducing public sector employment by 10% by 1993 was not achieved, and measures to improve the efficiency of public service delivery were not adopted.

The corner was turned in the mid-1990s, when a package of EU-related reforms boosted growth and investment. Since then, Greece has made progress in converging with the rest of Europe.

Sustained and deep reform in Greece finally took off in the mid-1990s, mostly driven by EU-wide liberalisation initiatives and convergence programmes.

Sustained policy reform was carried out largely within the framework of European integration (see Box 1.2). Since the early 1990s, the European single market programme has driven liberalisation. At the same time, policy continued to aim at EMU entry, focusing on fiscal consolidation, reducing inflation via the hard drachma policy, and restraint of civil servant wages to moderate private sector wage demands. These policies were laid out in the first Convergence Program (for 1993-98), the government's policy blue print for joining European Economic and Monetary Union. Under the second Community Support Framework (CSF), up to 70% of public investment was co-financed by the EU, and EU investment funds accounted for more than 40% of public investment expenditure.

1996-2000 witnessed strong GDP growth, above the EU average, and the 2001 budget could yield a surplus for the first time in several decades.

The reform policies proved largely successful. The period 1996-2000 witnessed strong GDP growth, above the EU average, a considerable decline in inflation, and a continuous reduction in public debt as a share of GDP. In 1996-2000, real GDP grew by almost 1% above the EU average. Inflation fell from 8.2% in 1996 to 2.4% in 2000, even though it has risen again due to the oil price hike and the effective depreciation of the drachma. The public sector deficit declined from 7.4% of GDP in 1996 to 0.8% of GDP in 2000, and the 2001 budget could yield a surplus for the first time in several decades.

Good growth performance was led largely by investment growth, which was stimulated by continued capital inflows from the EU, primarily for infrastructure development. The upturn was also due to other factors. First, the confidence of the private sector was bolstered by the prospect of Greece joining EMU soon. Second, efforts to liberalise some markets created a feeling of irreversibility, opened opportunities for fresh investments, and lowered production costs. Finally, considerable improvements in infrastructure, especially in telecommunications, and transport, reduced the "distance" between Greece and its markets.

Unemployment, however, is still a problem

Unemployment, nevertheless, has risen despite increases in employment. Between 1996 and 1999 the unemployment rate rose from 10.3% to 11.7%, while at the same time in the EU the unemployment rate declined from 10.9% to 9.4%. The increase in Greece largely reflects increasing labour force participation, especially by women, the legalisation of immigrants and a pick-up in labour productivity. More recently, strong growth reduced unemployment to 11.2% by mid-2000.

Today, the Greek economy is on track to continued solid growth. A high priority should be placed on supply-side reforms to hold down inflation and take full advantage of opportunities.

Short-term growth prospects are very favourable (OECD, Economic Outlook, No. 68), despite the deterioration in the international climate. Exports should decelerate, but domestic demand should remain strong. Household consumption should be boosted by job creation, low interest rates and brimming consumer confidence that should outweigh the negative effects of oil price hikes. Capital spending is also likely to rise substantially. Hence, output growth could remain at around 4% in 2001, and rise by somewhat more in 2002. This should allow a decline in the unemployment rate. Inflation is projected to peak at the end of 2000, but could remain close to 2 ¾% in 2001. However, underlying inflation is likely to drift up further over the projection period.

Faster, wider, and deeper regulatory reforms would help hold down inflationary pressures in future...

Accelerating, widening, and deepening regulatory reforms will help to hold down inflation while stimulating growth. In recent years, disinflation was driven by tight macroeconomic policies and by income policies geared to wage moderation. Looking ahead, however, these factors may operate differently:

– First, while the two-year wage agreement of May 2000 implies another moderate central wage increase, it includes a catch-up clause for 2002, if average inflation is higher than anticipated in 2001. Moreover, wage drift has become sizeable in some fast-growing sectors.

Box 1.2. External factors affecting Greek economic policy in the 1990s

Several major external factors have conditioned regulatory policy and the performance of the Greek economy over the last decade:

The need to abide by the rules of the EU single market program (SMP) has been key to progress. The legal framework, launched in 1985 and mostly completed by 1992, has spurred most liberalisation measures in Greece. Greece's record in adopting measures is, however, below average, thus delaying gains from reforms. The EU's Single Market Scoreboard of November 2000 shows that Greece is the country with the highest backlog of non-transposed directives. Moreover, Greece has been granted many derogations from the timely implementation of single market directives.

The Maastricht criteria pertaining to macroeconomic targets that must be fulfilled for membership in the euro area have stimulated monetary and fiscal discipline.

Large injections of EU funds in support of adjustments under two successive Community Support Frameworks (CSFs) have driven large increases in public investment. Like the first CSF, the second CSF, between 1994 and 1999, accounted for about 30% of total public investment, and almost 50% in the last years. Total capital infusions into Greece from the second CSF amounted to about 2.5% of GDP annually. In addition, current transfers (mostly agriculture-related subsidies due to the CAP), accounted for another 2.5% of GDP. In other words, over the last decade, total EU transfers benefiting Greece have been close to 5% of GDP, an enormous external stimulus.

The growth stimulus from this large external injection of resources has been considerable. Simulations to evaluate the second CSF suggest that the net contribution of the second CSF was about 0.6% of GDP annually. Its major contribution seems to have been on the demand side, with investment in 1999 estimated to have been 25% larger under the CSF than without.[1] Employment is estimated to have been 2.3% higher in 1999 compared to the no-CSF scenario. There would have been no employment growth without the CSF. The effect could have been even stronger had there not been significant lags in the implementation of projects. By end 1998, one year before the end of the second CSF, only 55% of the funds had been absorbed. Given that the bulk of the second CSF involved funds for improving infrastructure, human capital development, and the modernisation of enterprises, the lag in absorption and implementation has probably held back growth. Moreover, the majority of public works were completed late and had substantial quality problems. This is largely due to the inefficiency of the public administration in designing, implementing and monitoring the construction of public works. The backlog was swiftly reduced at the end of the implementation period, which probably contributed to more rapid growth in 1999 and 2000.

In the context of the EU's foreign trade policy, tariff trade barriers have fallen further with the conclusion of the Uruguay Round. However, tariffs on textile and steel still remain high and the high level of agricultural protection in the EU has not declined, despite efforts to reform the Common Agricultural Policy.

---

1. Most investment stimulus seems to have come from public investment, estimated to have been 54% larger in 1999 due to the CSF. Private investment in 1999, in turn, is estimated to have been only 15% larger than without the CSF.

– Second, fiscal policy was restrictive until 1999, but then shifted into neutral gear in 2000. The fiscal stance is likely to remain broadly neutral in 2001 and 2002, though strong growth should ensure a further improvement in the budget balance.

– Third, while the hard drachma policy and the maintenance of high interest rates in recent years were instrumental in taming inflationary pressures, monetary policy has eased substantially. Moreover, liquidity of the banking system will rise between January 2001 and July 2002, when the Bank of Greece will gradually release banks' required reserve holdings that are in excess of their current reserve requirements, following the reduction in the ratio from 12 to 2% from July 2000. The short-run effect of the monetary policy easing could be smaller than in Ireland, Portugal or Spain prior to joining the EMU, because Greek households are large net creditors. But with indebtedness low and financial markets evolving quickly, there is considerable room for leverage for both households and enterprises. Demand could receive a sizeable boost over an extended period. The relatively rapid expansion of credit, which is currently running at a rate close to 17%, the upward drift in underlying inflation and a widening current account deficit highlight overheating risks.

...supporting government projections of lower inflation under its stability programme.

The government's December 2000 Stability Programme projects average output growth of somewhat more than 5% between 2001 and 2004, accompanied by receding inflation. Investment, boosted by the third Community Support Framework would be the most buoyant component of GDP. The government balance is projected to move to a surplus of 2% of GDP in 2003 and 2004, while government debt would decline to 84% of GDP.

ECONOMIC IMPACTS OF SECTORAL REGULATORY REFORM

In 1998, Greece ranked 20th among 21 OECD countries in the restrictiveness of product market regulations.

Economic performance is undermined by the fact that decades of state intervention and a late start in market liberalisation compared to other OECD countries has left Greece with a heavy burden of inefficient regulation. The OECD's indicators on product market regulation show that, in 1998, Greece ranked 20th among 21 OECD countries in the overall restrictiveness of product market regulations (Figure 1.1). Regulatory interventions in 1998 were particularly heavy with respect to state controls and economic regulation.

During the 1990s, the government attempted to increase the pace of structural reform in several areas, with uneven success:

– The pace of privatisation accelerated significantly in 1998 and 1999. Privatisation receipts amounted to 4% of GDP in 1999. Progress slowed in 2000 due to elections, adverse market conditions, and preparatory measures for deeper reforms. In the meantime, the government has announced a new privatisation plan that includes the sale of minority (and in some cases, majority) stakes, and tenders for managing the operations of another 12 enterprises.

– The freeing up of the telecommunications sector is well advanced, though behind other OECD countries (see Chapter 6). Voice telephony has been liberalised since January 2001. By contrast, little progress has been made in liberalising the energy sector. While Greek legislation has been brought in line with the relevant EU directives, competitive pressures are likely to remain low.

– Competition policy (see Chapter 3) has been ineffective so far, but a law in 2000 should strengthen competition policy institutions.

– Plans to reform pension and health care systems, major government expenditures, were postponed, and measures to improve labour market flexibility have been timid so far.

– Tax compliance has improved, but the tax burden is distributed unevenly and base-broadening could reduce tax rates on both capital and labour.[14]

Box 1.3. **Key structural problems in the Greek economy**

The Greek economy exhibits a number of costly structural problems, such as institutional and regulatory frameworks that prevent speedy adjustments to external changes and market signals. Major structural problems include:

– *Inefficient regulatory regimes in key sectors*. The reforms that have been made to date have not yet tackled the fundamental underlying structural problems with respect to regulation. Product market liberalisation, wherever attempted, such as in the banking and telecommunications sectors, has resulted in considerable improvements in efficiency, lower prices for consumers, and increased employment. Substantial gains could be reaped by liberalising other sectors still highly constrained by administrative barriers to entry, and the remaining public monopolies.

– *Public enterprises*. Currently, 50 publicly-owned enterprises employ about 6% of employees and account for about 22% of all investment. Their products account for 7% of the CPI basket and their financing needs have imposed a heavy burden on public debt. The ten largest public enterprises are monopolies or oligopolies in telecommunications, energy, and transport. Inadequate management, inflexible labour arrangements, high labour costs, and delays in modernisation have resulted in poor performance and significant product market distortions, and have raised the cost of inputs for other sectors.

– *Ineffective competition policy*. Competition policy has played a minor role in raising competitive pressures. The Competition Committee does not have the capacity to deal with competition problems arising from efforts to protect inefficient state-owned enterprises, and has been unable to undertake systematic investigations of sectors that show significant competition problems. The Committee does not have the power to deal with potential distortions due to subsidies, while the ministry that formerly set its budget has supported "gentlemen's agreements" among firms to constrain price increases to meet the Maastricht inflation criterion. As Chapter 3 notes, recognising the need to strengthen the role of the Competition Committee, a recent law aims to correct several of the shortcomings in the operation of the Competition Committee.

> Key structural problems in the Greek economy (*cont.*)
>
> – *Public administration performance*. This is a high priority for reform, as it influences almost every aspect of the Greek economy. The capacity to develop and implement high quality regulatory regimes depends on the efficiency of the administration. Unfortunately, low salaries, inadequate incentives, and rigid labour regulations have lowered the capacity of the Greek administration.
>
> – A *relatively rigid labour market environment*. Long term unemployment has risen independently of the business cycle, suggesting a rise in the structural rate of unemployment. The labour market in Greece is dual and segmented with about half of the employed being in formal dependent employment, while the rest is self-employed, or in the underground economy. About 25% of the employees in the formal sector are in the public sector or in public enterprises. The formal labour market is characterised by slow adjustment, largely due to the institutional and regulatory framework of the labour market, in particular the high cost of labour dismissals, and other aspects of employment protection legislation (EPL). The most recent OECD comparative analysis of EPL, revealed that, among 21 OECD countries, Greece has the 20th most stringent EPL (see Table in Box 1.5). The rigidity of the public sector labour market spills over to the private sector and adversely affects employment.
>
> – *The social security and pension system*. In 1999, the total spending for social security, including pensions, health care, unemployment insurance, etc. amounted to 19.7% of GDP. The introduction of generous pension measures during 1978-85 resulted in a surge of pension expenditures from 6% of GDP in the mid-1970s to 13.2% of GDP in 1999. Simulations by the OECD suggest that the present value of net pension outlays (gross outlays minus revenues from contributions) is 196% of 1994 GDP, a ratio that is among the highest in the OECD. Public health expenditures have gradually risen to 5% of GDP, without major improvements in the level of service. Both of these are areas of critical importance where structural reforms are urgently needed. The authorities have commissioned a major study, to be submitted in April 2001, examining the financial prospects of the pension system and evaluating various options for reform. The government expects that pension reform will be in place in September 2001.
>
> – *State-controlled banks*. Despite considerable liberalisation of the financial sector, state-controlled banks accounted for 45% of deposits and credits in 2000 (down from 60% in 1995). Due to competition, however, and the restructuring of portfolios of several banks, their performance has improved, despite market share losses. Nevertheless, a considerable effort is needed to raise their performance to private sector standards.

Public enterprises have created costly economy-wide distortions. Continuation of the privatisation programme is a high priority.

Public enterprises account for 6% of employment and 27% of investment, yet almost all public enterprises are inefficient. This imposes a heavy burden on sustainable economic growth. Product market reforms such as sectoral regulatory reforms are intimately linked to privatisation and reform of public enterprises, as the latter are monopolies in key utility industries.

Unprofitable, inefficient public firms continue to be supported to the detriment of viable private firms.

Continued reform of public enterprises is necessary, for several reasons. First, their inefficient performance results in high costs for their products and services that penalise downstream firms that purchase their products. Second, the privileged position of

29

employees in these firms has led to wage pressures and generous benefits that push up the demands and reservation wages in the private sector, with negative impacts on overall employment. Third, their deficits burden the budget, necessitating higher tax rates, or crowding out social spending. Fourth, their commercial behaviour has burdened many private firms competing with public enterprises. Many arrears of public enterprises to other firms in the public sector are not paid or partially paid (such as electricity and communications bills). This gives public enterprises an unfair advantage over private-sector competitors. The consequence is that unprofitable, inefficient public firms continue to be supported to the detriment of viable private firms.

Some progress has been made. The Greek convergence program for 1999-2002 shows that the state currently controls no companies involved in the production of goods, except three defense enterprises. The IRO that controlled public enterprises involved in goods production is being wound down. Concerning public monopolies in utilities, the state has yet to sell more than 49% of any public utility, as private majority stakes are forbidden by law. The government recently decided, however, to lift the upper limit on private ownership of one public utility, the OTE (see Box 1.4 for the pace of privatisation).

In the telecommunications sector, services and prices have improved after reform, but energy reforms lag.

In the telecommunications sector, reforms that started in the early 1990s have led to substantial improvements in services and lower prices.

In the telecommunications sector, reforms that started in the early 1990s have led to substantial improvements in services and lower prices. As Chapter 6 points out, the incumbent firm, the cellular mobile sector with three market participants has had vigorous competition and telephone prices fell steeply in recent years as OTE rebalanced prices in view of the 1 January 2001 opening of the voice market to competition and indirect international competition. Internet access prices have converged to the OECD average. In January 2001, the Greek fixed telephony market was opened to competition, which should further increase competition. The government plans to conclude strategic alliances for OTE as well as ELTA (the national post office).

In the water industry, the Athens and Salonica water and sewage companies are to be privatised after being split into two parts each, namely land and plant management separated from service provision.

The electricity market, a monopoly of the Public Power Corporation (PPC), is to be partly liberalised in February 2001, as discussed in Chapter 5. In preparation, the regulatory framework for the electricity market has been re-organised, and a new Energy Regulatory Authority established. However, the key constraint for new electricity generation companies is access to fuel, and not much competition is likely to emerge. Barriers to entry are substantial because of the vertical integration of PPC and the geographic and technical isolation of the Greek network.

Box 1.4.   Recent and envisioned privatisations of state owned enterprises in Greece

Period April 1998-December 1999

Public enterprise	Type of reform	Date completed
1. Bank of Macedonia-Thrace	Privatisation	April 1998
2. General Bank	Privatisation	April 1998
3. Hellenic Petroleum Corp (ELPE)	First sale of stock	June 1998
4. Bank of Crete	Privatisation	June 1998
5. Bank of Central Greece	Privatisation	July 1998
6. Greek Telecommunications Org. (OTE)	Third sale of stock	November 1998
7. Athens Stock Exchange (XAA)	Sale of stock	November 1998
8. Ionian Bank	Privatisation	March 1999
9. Olympic Catering	First sale of stock	April 1999
10. OTE	Fourth sale of stock	July 1999
11. Duty Free Shops (KAE)	Partial privatisation	August 1999
12. Olympic Catering	Second sale of stock	August 1999
13. Hellenic Petroleum	Second sale of stock	December 1999
14. Hellenic Bank for Industrial Development (ETVA)	Sale of stock	December 1999
15. Athens Water and Sewerage Corp. (EYDAP)	Sale of stock	December 1999
16. Public Natural Gas Co. (DEPA)	Partial privatisation	December 1999

Program of new privatisations and sales of stock for 2000 and 2001

1. Commercial Bank of Greece	Strategic alliance	October 2000
2. Athens Stock Exchange (XAA)	Sale of stock	June 2000
3. Hellenic Aerospace Industry (EAV)	Partial privatisation	Postponed
4. AEDIK (Corinth Canal Co.)	Concession contract	March 2001
5. Olympic Airlines	Privatisation	
6. COSMOTE	Sale of stock	September 2000
7. Hellenic Post (ELTA)	Strategic alliance	
8. ODIE (Horse Racing Org.)	Concession contract	Postponed
9. OPAP (football lotteries)	Sale of stock	April 2001
10. Thessaloniki Port Authority (OLTh)	Sale of stock	
11. Agricultural Bank of Greece (ATE)	Sale of stock	December 2000
12. OTE	Strategic alliance	
13. International Fair of Thessaloniki	Partial privatisation	
14. Thessaloniki Water and Sewerage Corp. (EYATh)	Sale of stock	
15. Public Power Corporation	Sale of stock	
16. Pireas Port Authority (OLP)	Sale of stock	
17. ETVA	Privatisation	
18. Hellenic Vehicle Industry (ELVO)	Partial privatisation	August 2000

Market liberalisation has proceeded the furthest in the financial sector.

In the financial sector, which has seen the largest dose of liberalisation, competition and economies of scale have induced mergers and restructuring. The largest bank, the National Bank of Greece (NBG) has written off all non-performing debt. The Commercial Bank of Greece has increased its capital through the sale of Ionian Bank, and is seeking a strategic partner. Privatisation is planned in 2001, and has already begun with the sale of a minority share (6%) to the French bank Credit Agricole. The two largest specialised banks in the public sector – the Hellenic Bank for Industrial Development (ETVA) and the Agricultural Bank of Greece (ATE) – have been slower in restructuring because of the large number of bad loans, and unprofitable companies in their portfolios. However, both banks now meet capital adequacy requirements.

Deregulation seems to have enhanced the growth of banks and increased employment.

Deregulation has improved the performance of the banking sector. According to a study by the Hellenic Bank Association, deregulation has enhanced the growth of banks, and has increased employment.[15] The negative impact of structural changes on employment (introduction of new technologies, mergers and acquisitions, and introduction of the euro) are estimated to have been small. However, the operating cost to income ratio in the banking sector is still considerably above the EU average.

Financial liberalisation has had positive impacts on the Athens Stock Exchange (ASE) which exhibited spectacular growth in market capitalisation, the number of account holders, and financial returns. This has provided wider opportunities for private firms to raise capital and restructure. Despite significant fluctuations in stock market prices since 1998, due largely to the thinness of the market, the improvement in the regulatory framework, such as the dematerialization of securities and rules on information disclosure, enhanced confidence and investor safety. A new stock market for small and medium-sized enterprises has begun to operate, which should provide opportunities for smaller companies to raise capital.

Simplification of the tax system has improved transparency and tax revenues, but major reform is necessary to establish a level playing field for enterprises.

In past years, the Greek tax system seemed drawn from Byzantine traditions, but considerable effort is being made to improve its efficiency and transparency.

In past years, the Greek tax system seemed drawn from Byzantine traditions. Numerous tax changes over many years had been implemented in a piecemeal fashion, contributing to a complex and non-transparent tax system that performed poorly. Considerable effort is being made to better inform the public about tax laws, procedures, and forms. A telephone hotline and the Internet have been used to this end. The Ministry of Finance is collaborating with the US Internal Revenue Service to improve tax administration and collection. Considerable effort has gone into computerising tax administration and a recently-created unit on economic crimes (SDOE) is being strengthened with IT tools. Successful steps in recent years to raise tax compliance have been reflected in strong revenue growth. The efficiency of several taxes (cost of collection versus revenue) has been studied, as has the need for many (around 1 000) taxes that are not part of the general budget, but are collected by third parties and directly spent by various entities.[16] Elimination and consolidation of many of these taxes began in the 2001 budget.

Nevertheless, the tax system continues to create major and costly distortions.

Nevertheless, the tax system continues to create major and costly distortions. These distortions are not related to the overall level of taxation, which is not high by international comparisons, but are due to poor application of tax policies and to the uneven distribution of the tax burden. First, tax laws change frequently, creating an environment of uncertainty for investment. Second, firms are subject to auditing for 7 years after tax returns are filed, after which their books are automatically closed. The law stipulates that all firms must be audited for each period, but as there are many small firms and not enough tax officials, the law is impossible to apply. The consequence is that, each year, hundreds of thousands of cases of incomplete past audits approach the period of expiration. So as not to lose tax revenue, the government often invites firms to compromise by paying a smaller share of the potential tax liability when the end of the seven-year period approaches. This establishes incentives for firms to avoid paying taxes on time to benefit from delayed audits and amnesties. This also penalises law-abiding firms by conferring a cost advantage on firms that do not obey the laws.

The government has indicated that it plans to introduce wide-ranging tax reforms in 2002. Numerous options exist to widen the tax bases and address the uneven distribution of the tax burden (OECD, 2000). Taxation of self-employed is low, for instance, while social security contribution rates are very high, which partly explains the very high number of self-employed in Greece. A wide range of tax incentives for the business sector should be re-assessed and streamlined. Such incentives complicate tax administration and increase compliance costs. Tax incentives should be granted only in the few areas where market failures are likely to exist.

Reducing red tape and regulatory uncertainties for firms should boost potential growth...

Business and citizens dealing with the administration complain about...

As described in Chapter 2, the complaints of most entities that deal with the public administration are:

...numerous formalities...

– There are too many administrative procedures for transactions and licenses,

...lack of coordination...

– Formalities are dispersed over several ministries or other public entities,

...long delays...

– There are long delays in the response of the public administration in issuing documents or certificates, and

...uncertainties.

– There is sometimes considerable discretion in the interpretation of particular laws and regulations, as well as selective enforcement.

Table 1.1. Sectoral regulatory reform in Greece by early 2001

Industry	Rationale and industry structure	Recent reforms	Price regulation	Regulation of entry and exit	Other regulations that affect competition	Mandated changes in industry structure	Future reforms needed
Air transport	Until the 1990s, Olympic Airways was Greece's only domestic carrier and ground handler. Participation of other carriers for charter cargo and taxi flights was allowed in 1991. Airports are state owned.	The third EU liberalization package (EU Directive 96/67) in 1996 introduced a common aviation area in the EU, with uniform requirements for entry, market structure and fares. Greece implemented it in 1998 and issued several regulations on ground handling.	Airfares are mostly free, but the state intervenes in cases of "too high" or "too low" fares. Before 1996, prices for ground handling were not regulated. Now prices are discussed between a managing body of the airport, an airport users committee, and the firm providing ground handling services.	Regulations govern ground handlers' entry and exit. Similarly for domestic airlines.	None	None	Completion of privatisation of Olympic Airways
Coastal shipping ferries	The Ministry of Merchant Marine (MMM) tightly regulates the sector. Specific vessel licences are granted by the MMM for specified itineraries. There are only three major companies, with a fringe of smaller firms.	The EU Directive on liberalising marine transport dating from 1992 is to be implemented earlier than the scheduled date of implementation, which was 2004. At the beginning of 1999, cabotage restrictions were lifted on EU-flagged vessels of over 650 tons.	Fares are set by the MMM.	Very strict, as licensing is in force. The current licensing system prevents the entry of more high-speed vessels. Licenses are not issued on demand, and are difficult to obtain.	Services to unprofitable routes are bundled with itineraries to profitable island routes. Many regulations govern the hotel aspects of ships and employment.	None mandated. Protection of domestic companies will be lost due to the enactment of liberalizing EU legislation. This will result in market-driven restructuring in the sector.	Transparency of licensing should be improved. Routes should be unbundled, a hub and spoke system developed, licences tendered, and fares liberalized. Safety standards should be maintained in competitive markets.
Road transport-trucking	A considerable number of trucks exist, mostly for own account transport. Third party transport trucks are less than 5% of the total fleet. Licenses are issued at prefectorial and national levels. Licenses for own account transport are not transferable.	In 1992, bilateral transit services were liberalized in the EU, and in 1998 national or "cabotage" markets were liberalized in the EU.	Maximum and minimum prices are regulated by law for intra and inter prefectorial transport.	A licensing system is in place. Entry standards are harmonized among EU members, but interpretations differ. The number of permits for third party transport is fixed.			
	A single state-owned company (PPC) is vertically integrated in all aspects of the electricity sector, except for system operation. Some industrial companies generate 2% of electricity, largely consumed by them with the rest sold to PPC.	Law 2773/99 of December 1999 removed the prohibition on entry into electricity generation. In mid-2000, an Energy Regulatory Authority was established to regulate the sector. PPC is to separate accounts for four electricity activities (lignite mining, generation, transmission, and distribution). In February 2001, 30% of the electricity market will be open to competition.	Prices are regulated by the Minister for Development, including prices of electricity sold to PPC. Price regulations are not based on rate of return or efficiency incentives. PPC has not been run as a profit making entity.	Barriers remain high. Barriers include access to fuel, transmission and distribution, high switching costs for potential customers and low PPC prices to large industrial customers.	Access to fuel is the major obstacle to electricity generation. Natural gas is monopolized by a state company and will not be deregulated until 2003.	30% of the electricity market must be liberalized by 2001, growing to 35% in 2003. Large customers can choose supplier. A System Transmission Operator is to be established in 2000.	Licensing and price regulations should be removed, while maintaining and strengthening safety standards. Non-discriminatory access to transmission and distribution is needed. Access prices must be subject to independent regulation.

Sectoral regulatory reform in Greece by early 2001 (cont.)

Industry	Rationale and industry structure	Recent reforms	Price regulation	Regulation of entry and exit	Other regulations that affect competition	Mandated changes in industry structure	Future reforms needed
Telecommunications	Before 1980, a public monopoly was held by OTE in all telecommunication services. Since 1990, a gradual liberalization has occurred, and the market for voice communications opened to competition on 1 January 2001.	In 1990, value added and mobile telephony services were deregulated. In 1994 all telecommunication services were liberalized except voice telephony. Full liberalization took place on 1 January 2001. A regulatory authority, the National Telecommunications Commission was established in 1995.	Prices are largely determined in the market. For OTE, which is designated as having significant market power, pricing is subject to principles of transparency, cost orientation and non-discrimination. Mobile telephony companies cannot charge customers lower tariffs than the OTE's highest long distance rates.	Since 1999, laws adapted to EU standards dictate the terms of entry, renewal of licenses, etc.		None mandated, but the mandated liberalization of voice telephony in 2001 will increase the number of companies.	Greek legislation needs to further adapt to EU laws. For instance, number portability needs to be introduced without delay.
Postal communications	Until 1998, ELTA held a monopoly in postal services. Since 1985, private companies have entered courier services (initially international but later also domestic). Until 1997, these services were provided under the general commercial law.	In 1998, a framework law adapted Greek legislation to EU Directive 97/67 and operation of courier companies was included in the general communications licensing regime.	Courier-services prices are free. Prices of normal postal services must abide by general principles (transparency, cost basis, etc.). Since 1998, prices are freely determined by ELTA.	Specific laws govern conditions for issuing licenses to operate postal service companies. General permits are needed to provide liberalized services, and a special license to provide full range services.	None	None are foreseen at present.	
Banking and Finance	Before 1987, banking was dominated by public sector banks, and the Bank of Greece set interest rate and administrative regulations. The banking system was used to finance the public sector deficit, and negative real interest rates prevailed.	In the late 1980s, interest rates were liberalized, credit controls and interest rate subsidies were reduced, government bond sales to the public were introduced, and the stock exchange law was modernized. In 1992, a law incorporating EU banking directives was adopted, and by 1994 liberalization of banking was complete. Dematerialization of securities, improvement of disclosure rules and a better regulatory framework were introduced in the 1990s, and a securities and exchange commission was instituted to oversee the stock exchange. Capital movements were liberalised in late 1990s.	Prices for banking and financial products are free.	Entry of banks is regulated by the Bank of Greece. For finance companies, the securities and exchange commission as well as the Bank of Greece regulate entry under specific laws.	Minimum capital requirements exist for banks and finance companies.		Further modernisation of the regulatory regime for the stock market.

Table 1.2. Potential impacts of sectoral regulatory reform in Greece

Industry	Industry structure and competition	Industry profits	Output, price, relative prices	Service or product quality and innovations	Sectoral wages and unemployment	Efficiency, productivity and costs
Air transport	After the reforms, 14 airline companies and 8 air taxi companies currently operate in Greece. Several new ground handling companies have entered in several airports	Several new airlines have invested and expanded domestically and internationally. Some rationalization has occurred, with a merger between two private airlines	Domestic competition has intensified, fares have been deregulated and have become lower.	Service has considerably improved. The number of flights in several domestic and foreign routes increased.	Employment in the industry increased as a result of new entrants. Employment within Olympic has declined.	Efficiency of service provision has improved.
Coastal shipping/ferries	There have been many mergers in recent years. The three largest companies bought many smaller ones. The Adriatic routes are more competitive than the Aegean routes, a reflection of the more regulated Aegean routes.	Profits have improved for the major companies that are listed in the Athens Stock Exchange.	Sales have increased for the sector, but prices have not declined as they are controlled.	Several high-speed ferries have been introduced that have cut travel times. On the other hand the total number of ships seems to have declined. On the Adriatic routes competition has led to service improvement and price declines.	There seems to be a decline in employment with simultaneous increase in wages.	Recent mergers seem to have led to efficiency gains.
Road transport-trucking	Considerable recent entry of internationally based trucking firms into Greek domestic market.	Competition has led to profit declines.	Because of non-issuance of third party permits, own account transport is growing. This is inefficient.	Lack of issuance of new licenses has led to upgrading in size of existing truck fleet.		
Electric power	Transmission and distribution are monopolized by PPC. The system operator is 51 percent state-owned, and at present 49 percent by PPC.	PPC profits are low, and return on equity is far below normal for the industry.	Industrial prices are low, and household prices are average compared to other European IEA countries. Input prices are distorted and cross-subsidization occurs.	Service quality is variable.	Sectoral wages are higher than in other industries, and employment is excessive.	Efficiency is rather low.
Telecommunications	Three companies (OTE and two private ones) are operating in mobile telephony. OTE has lost its monopoly of voice telecommunications in early 2001. About 240 companies provide a variety of services (leased lines, internet access, etc.)	Profits of both OTE as well as the two other private companies have been very high. Profits of other service providers have increased and this is manifested by the fast increase in the number of companies.	The market for mobile services has grown very fast. Currently telecommunications comprises 4% of GDP. Prices have fallen considerably, especially in last three years, and are at or below OECD average.	Non-competing services of OTE have improved tremendously along with mobile telephony services. The number of mainlines has almost doubled since 1985. Several new products have been introduced, and the time delay or installing a new fixed telephone by OTE has declined from a period of 81 months in 1990 to only five days in 1999. The percentage of faults repaired within 24 hours has increased from 57% in 1993 to 91% in 1999. The volume of complaints with OTE has declined significantly.	While OTE employment has declined, the sector has seen employment expansion as private firms have expanded their activities and capacity.	The decrease in prices along with rising profits manifests increasing levels of efficiency both for OTE as well as the private sector companies. OTE's labor productivity has increased considerably since 1995.

Potential impacts of sectoral regulatory reform in Greece (*Cont.*)

Industry	Industry structure and competition	Industry profits	Output, price, relative prices	Service or product quality and innovations	Sectoral wages and unemployment	Efficiency, productivity and costs
Postal sector	The number of postal service companies that currently operate in Greece is 167, compared to one before 1985.	Considerable expansion of the number and range of services of postal service companies is consistent with profit increases.	The output of the sector has considerably expanded, and prices have generally fallen. The market for courier services has doubled in the last five years. Despite increased competition, ELTA sales grew by 20% in 1999.	Service provision has generally improved, especially for non-standard courier services.	Sectoral employment has stayed roughly constant. Employment is expected to increase with the introduction of new services.	
Banking and finance	Privatisations of public banks, mergers and entry of new banks have enhanced competition. The market share of publicly controlled banks has declined. A large number of specialized private firms offer a wide variety of financial services.	Profitability has risen considerably in recent years.	The volume of financial services has increased, prices have declined.	Technical innovation such as increased automation has led to considerable service provision improvement, and the variety of products has expanded.	Banking employment has declined, but the entry of a variety of private companies offering financial services has enhanced overall sector employment. Salaries for skilled personnel have increased rapidly.	Considerable efficiency gains have been obtained in the financial service sector, labor productivity has increased and costs have declined.

As a result, the Greek private sector incurs substantially higher costs in setting up and operating a company compared with other countries.

The Greek private sector incurs substantially higher costs in setting up and operating a company compared with other countries. For instance, it takes 1 to 5 months to start a trading company in Greece, compared to a few days in OECD countries with a lenient regulatory regime, and the period is even longer for industrial concerns. Business surveys estimate that more than 10% of an entrepreneur's time is spent on administrative formalities, while the cost of complying with tax regulations is 2 to 5% of gross profits. Such burdensome rules and regulations invite corruption, as firms try to find ways to speed up the procedures, and avoid regulations.

Chapter 2 describes the major efforts underway in Greece – including decentralisation, compilation of citizens' guides, simplification of forms, and Internet access to forms – to reduce the burdens of red tape and inefficient bureaucracy for citizens and firms. An interesting development is the establishment of compensation committees for citizens that lose through bureaucratic delays. The relevant law provides for compensation of up to GRD 200 000 for losses incurred.

Box 1.5. Labour market reforms should be a high priority in Greece

Despite recent changes in labour laws that have improved market flexibility, Greek labour laws are too restrictive. Considerable flexibility is needed in the more competitive environment that has been created by the abolition of barriers within the EU. As noted and shown in the table below, the most recent OECD comparative analysis of EPL revealed that, among 21 OECD countries, Greece has the 20th most stringent EPL (see Table below).

There are many examples of ineffective or restrictive labour laws. Greek labour laws allow maximum overtime of only 15 hours per semester, but this is frequently violated. Similarly, labour laws allow part-time employment, but frequently part-timers are obliged to work much longer hours for the same pay. Greece still has the lowest share of part-time employees in the OECD (about 6%). Another example is the stipulation that 8% of jobs in all firms must be reserved for the handicapped in full-time permanent jobs. These people are chosen by special committees outside the firms. This policy has been applied in the public enterprise sector, where 30 000 handicapped have been absorbed in the last few years. Application of this rule in the private sector has been delayed because of strong resistance by private firms who demand the right to choose these people themselves. A year-2000 law prescribes that the maximum number of people that can be fired each month is 4 for companies that employed, at the beginning of the month, 20-200 workers and 2-3% of the labour force for larger companies, with the condition that the maximum number will never exceed 30 workers.

Frequent violations of the laws are possible because many small enterprises are difficult to monitor. Inadequate policing confers cost advantages on firms that violate the laws, and render less competitive the law-abiding firms. As a result, the laxity of enforcement obliges many firms in the formal economy to find ways to evade the laws as well. One way that has become common in the last decade is to employ illegal immigrants. Since many small enterprises employ illegal immigrants to avoid paying social security contributions, formal sector firms have found it convenient to outsource some labour-intensive activities to small sub-contractors, who in turn employ illegals, and can offer their products and services at lower cost. Employment in the formal sector is thus curtailed, and the informal sector grows.

Labour market policy has changed under the National Action Plan (NAPs) for employment for 1999 and subsequent NAPs, in favour of more training, a better job placement system, better professional orientation for new entrants in the labour market, tax incentives for enterprises, local employment pacts, and others.

Severity of EPL in OECD countries

	Overall degree of EPL in 1998		EPL for regular contracts in 1998	EPL for temporary contracts in 1998	Overall index of EPL in 1990	Change in the score of EPL between 1990 and 1998
	Rank	Score	Rank	Rank	Rank	Score in 98-score in 90
United States	1	0.2	1	1	1	0.0
United Kingdom	2	0.5	2	1	2	0.0
Canada	3	0.6	4	1	3	0.0
Ireland	4	1.0	8	1	5	0.0
New Zealand	5	1.0	6	5	4	0.0
Australia	6	1.1	3	6	6	0.0
Switzerland	7	1.3	5	6	7	0.0
Denmark	8	1.5	9	6	10	0.0
Belgium	9	2.1	7	15	13	0.0
Finland	10	2.1	10	11	8	−0.3
Netherlands	11	2.4	20	9	14	0.1
Austria	12	2.4	14	12	9	0.0
Sweden	13	2.4	17	10	16	−0.1
Japan	14	2.6	19	13	11	0.5
Germany	15	2.8	18	14	17	0.1
Norway	16	2.9	15	16	15	0.0
France	17	3.1	11	19	12	0.1
Spain	18	3.2	13	20	19	−1.0
Italy	19	3.3	16	18	20	0.0
Greece	**20**	**3.5**	**12**	**21**	**18**	**−0.2**
Portugal	21	3.7	21	17	21	−0.6

Note: The scores are from 0 to 6 with 0 denoting the lowest degree of EPL and 6 the highest.
Source: Nicoletti, Scarpetta, and O. Boylaud (1999).

Further reform is needed, however, as Greek employment protection legislation (EPL) is still very stringent by international standards.

Lack of flexibility in the formal labour market, coupled with considerable flexibility in the uncontrolled informal labour market, have induced substantial employment of illegal immigrants, and the expansion of activities in the underground economy. The situation cannot be corrected by policing the underground economy. Changes to the rules governing the formal labour market are necessary. As discussed in the 2000 OECD Economic Survey of Greece, the government submitted in late 2000 a draft law on labour market reform. Proposals to lower EPL and tackle the few remaining impediments to part-time employment are steps in the right direction. The government has also proposed to raise the mandatory premium for overtime work. Alternatively, the government proposal allows for the annualisation of working time, if the employer and employees agree, while at the same time cutting the effective work week from 40 to 38 hours. This approach would raise labour cost and could reduce labour supply, if not offset by additional labour market measures.

Concerning the other key rigidities, EPL will remain very restrictive. The minimum wage is likely to constitute a barrier to labour market entry for young people and women, unemployment for both being especially high. This is why employment subsidies and proposed cuts in employer's social security contribution rates target both of these groups, lowering the labour cost to the employer. From 2000 onwards, the government pays part of employee contributions to the social security system for minimum wage earners. This measure is largely redistributive, but will stimulate labour supply and also improve incentives to work in the formal economy. The same is true for the "making work pay" measures for part-time workers. These measures should be combined with improvements in education, as there is mismatch between private sector demands and the skills of graduates of public higher education institutions.

Distortions and disincentives in public sector performance continue to reduce the certainty and efficiency of the general regulatory environment.

Fiscal consolidation efforts may have undermined efforts to increase professionalism in the civil service.

It is ironic that fiscal consolidation efforts may have induced more regulations, corruption, and inefficiency. This is because public sector pay restraint, along with the fact that differences in salaries between the highest and lowest civil service grades are small, have undermined efforts to increase professionalism in the civil service, as Chapter 2 notes. Employees, especially those with responsibilities, regard their salaries as insufficient remuneration, and adjust their effort. Second, the system has encouraged rent-seeking to supplement incomes. While rent seeking has always existed in some parts of the civil service, private sector operators indicate that it may have actually increased in recent years, partly as a response to low public sector salaries and lack of a reward system.

At the same time, the regulatory framework imposed by the European Union has increased the workload for many ministries.

At the same time, the regulatory framework imposed by the European Union has increased the workload for many ministries. The increased work load should have been rewarded by rising salaries, at least for those that bear more responsibilities, or with other non-wage benefits. However, the current system of remuneration in the civil service does not allow differential treatment of employees or offices performing at higher levels. Neither does it allow for bonuses or other rewards. The consequence is that the quality of regulatory enforcement has suffered, and hence uncertainty about the rules of the game has become larger. Studies suggest that this has serious negative implications for growth,[17] and undermines the longer-term reputation of the Greek government in assuring a level playing field for market entrants.

In several areas, the difficulties facing the public administration in carrying out tasks imposed by the new regulatory frameworks, and under the pressure of tight time schedules imposed by EU rules, have been recognised. In these cases, parallel and privately-controlled administrative mechanisms have been created to do work normally done by public sector entities, but with better incentives and outside the bureaucratic restrictions of civil service. Examples are several monitoring and evaluation entities created in the context of the second CSF. The impression of some high level ministry officials, however, is that these parallel mechanisms have not performed as expected, have created considerable rivalry problems with the civil service, and may not be sustainable.

ANTICIPATED EFFECTS OF FURTHER REGULATORY REFORM

Benefits to Greek consumers, workers, and producers of further regulatory reforms are likely to be considerable.

The benefits to Greek consumers, workers, and producers of further regulatory reforms are likely to be considerable, though estimates are subject to much uncertainty. Inflationary pressures due to strong domestic demand can be countered by regulatory reforms that will lead to efficiency gains and cost reductions in key intermediate inputs. Experience in other countries has shown that broad regulatory reform, along with supportive macroeconomic and labour market policies can provide an appropriate framework for improving competition and the business environment. A more business-friendly climate will in turn stimulate activity, which would allow the absorption of the high number of unemployed, and to enhance technological adaptation and restructuring. Greek entrepreneurs have proved in the past, both within Greece, but also in the international context, that given the proper framework and opportunities, they are ready to grasp new opportunities.

The total income gain from regulatory reform could be 9-11% of GDP.

Using a method pioneered in the 1997 OECD Report on Regulatory Reform, the 1998 OECD Survey of Greece estimated the potential gains from ambitious but not unprecedented liberalisation of several product markets. Major efficiency gains would result in lower costs. Falling intermediate input prices would have significant wider effects. Some prices would fall, notably telecommunications services and petroleum, but others would increase to come closer to the costs of fulfilling public service obligations. The need for infrastructure investment would increase capital costs, but innovation, in telecommunications and electric power, would reduce costs and prices. Most static price reductions appear to result from greater competition in the petroleum, electric power, and especially telecommunications sectors. When dynamic longer-term effects are considered, the OECD model predicts a cumulative output increase of 5-7% of GDP. Considering the significance of higher quality products and a better budget balance, the total income gain could be 9-11% of GDP (OECD, 1998).

For this report, the assumptions utilised for the 1998 OECD simulations with respect to product market liberalisation and the impact on prices (mainly in energy, transport and communications), were used with a dynamic general equilibrium (CGE) model of the Greek economy to simulate the potential impact of regulatory reforms.[18] The results indicate that, compared to the baseline scenario, liberalisation increases GDP by 1 and 1.5 percentage points for each of the simulated years. Cumulated over the simulation period, this implies a potential gain of more than 10% of GDP. This is close to the earlier OECD calculations made with a different approach.

Considerable additional gains can be obtained by reforming the public sector...

These calculations have focused only on heavily-regulated product market sectors. However, considerable additional gains can be obtained by reforming the public sector itself. As noted, surveys suggest that entrepreneurs devote considerable time to dealing with bureaucracy. The same is true of most citizens, with the consequence that substantial resources are wasted. Other gains can be expected from reduced rent seeking and corruption as well as better use of public labour resources but it is difficult to make empirical estimates.[19] They would, nevertheless appear to be sizeable.

...and by liberalising other sectors still highly constrained by administrative barriers to entry, and public monopolies.

Recent positive developments in the Greek economy are a good start towards stronger growth and faster convergence. But these gains are still far below the growth performance that could be achieved with a better regulatory and administrative framework. The reforms that have been undertaken so far have not as yet touched on many fundamental underlying regulatory problems.

Product market liberalisation, where it was attempted, such as in the banking and telecommunications sectors, considerably improved efficiency, lowered prices for consumers and increased employment. Substantial further gains can be reaped by liberalising other sectors still highly constrained by administrative barriers to entry, and public monopolies.

Fundamental problems in public administration, that have not as yet been the object of reform, have created severe distortions in the private sector, and have retarded investment and growth. These distortions and the resulting inefficiencies will become more acute and costly as the requirements imposed on the public administration grow because of the increased regulatory requirements due to deep integration in Europe and to a more competitive international economic environment. Substantial transfers from the EU in successive CSFs have improved performance, but are likely to shrink in the medium and long run, which makes the case for regulatory reform even more urgent.

Today, it appears that a window of opportunity exists for sorely needed changes in the regulatory framework.

The private sector, under increasing pressure from trade liberalisation in the EU's internal market, has begun to adapt. However, the regulatory framework and the entrenched position of insider firms and unions have imposed extra burdens that will be difficult to diminish unless further reforms are undertaken. Given the continuity of structural reform policies under the re-elected government, the need to become more flexible after the introduction of the euro, greater public awareness of the need for regulatory reforms, and the improved economic climate, it appears that a window of opportunity exists for radical but sorely needed changes in the regulatory framework.

Many concrete steps can be taken to raise potential output growth. The focus should be on comprehensive reforms that create vigorous market competition through regulatory and institutional reforms.

The challenge is not only privatisation, but also the creation of a long-term regulatory and institutional environment supportive of genuine competition.

The challenges of regulatory reform are daunting. Table 1.1 and Chapter 7 of this report list many additional reforms in product markets that will improve the prospects for sustainable economic growth. The challenge is not only privatisation, but also the creation of a long-term regulatory and institutional environment supportive of genuine competition. This is a more difficult agenda, even involving cultural changes in public and private sectors, but one that will produce the efficiency and innovation gains needed in Greece. Privatisation is, in other words, only a part of the overall reform strategy needed.

Privatisation itself faces substantial difficulties.

Privatisation itself faces substantial difficulties, despite the fact that the current position of the government supports privatisation of public enterprises. The strong resistance of firms and labour unions against full privatisation, and the difficulty of inducing good management in monopolistic public sector enterprises, suggests that in the short run it will be important to allow competition by lowering barriers to entry. Competition will lessen the monopoly power of insiders, and will permit a wider range of services to be provided to consumers. Licensing procedures should be made more transparent, with auctions replacing administrative decisions. A good example of distortions that may arise is the coastal shipping industry, where non-transparent licensing of various routes has resulted in monopolistic market structures, as explained in Chapter 5.

The reform package must also include the wider policy environment: labour market rules, public sector performance, and the investment climate.

In Greece, the bulk of skilled workers is employed in the relatively less productive public sector.

Labour market rigidities, coupled in Greece with an unbalanced structure of employment, have contributed to the mediocre growth performance. A major factor to propel growth is human capital but, in Greece, the bulk of skilled workers is employed in the relatively less productive public sector. According to estimates based on a Social Accounting Matrix for Greece,[20] 14% of total employed have higher education. Of the "highly skilled" employees, 30% are employed in public administration, and another 30% in health and education, which are largely public. An additional 16% are employed in market service sectors that includes several public or publicly controlled enterprises like banks or insurance companies. Thus, about 65% of the well educated are employed in the wider public sector. The share of skilled non-manual workers in total employment in primarily private sectors like manufacturing is very small, lower than 10% for most sectors.

These statistics imply that on the one hand the bulk of production is intensively using low skilled labour, and on the other that the bulk of skilled labour is employed in the public sector. The rigidities and the lack of flexibility in the public sector labour market could thus have affected adversely the adjustment and modernisation of the private sector. Furthermore, inadequate incentives for skilled workers in the public sector imply an under-utilisation of their skills, and a misallocation of the most productive resource in the economy. Moreover, there is significant job mismatch in the private sector. Firms have difficulties finding skilled labour.

In public administration, as Chapter 2 explains, the initiatives of the last few years have not yet touched the roots of the basic problem of public sector inefficiency.

A major challenge for future years will be to establish greater credibility of the policy regime for foreign investors.

A major challenge for future years, as discussed in Chapter 4, will be to establish greater credibility of the policy regime for foreign investors. One of the major problems that investors face in Greece is the instability of policies such as tax policies, environmental policies, etc. There are two major aspects to the credibility issue. The first is that microeconomic policy should be governed by rules rather than discretion. In other words, a prospective investor should know the rules governing investment, and these rules should remain for a reasonable period of time. Any changes should be pre-announced, and, if changed, enough time should be given to private sector entities for consultation and adaptation. The second aspect of credibility is that all entities should be treated the same way. The history of policy and politics in Greece suggests that often more lenient treatment is given to certain insider firms or groups, relative to outsiders. This implies that substantial capital is normally invested by firms and entrepreneurs to acquire the status of an "insider". This is an invisible form of investment, but valuable. It is more difficult for foreign investors to become "insiders" without a heavy investment in "insider capital". This partly explains why foreign investment is so low in Greece, and why it has mainly been in the form of acquiring existing firms.

Figure 1.1. **Comparativee indicators of product market regulation in OECD Countries, end-1997 Overall regulatory approaches**[1]

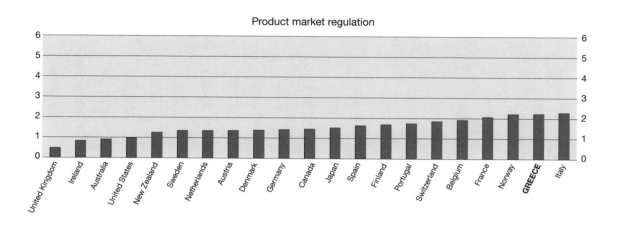

Product market regulation

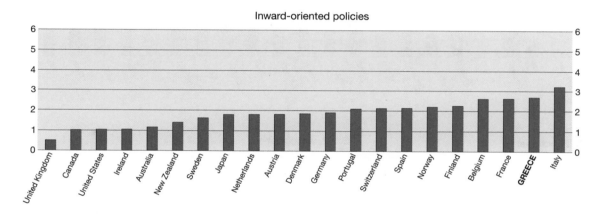

Inward-oriented policies

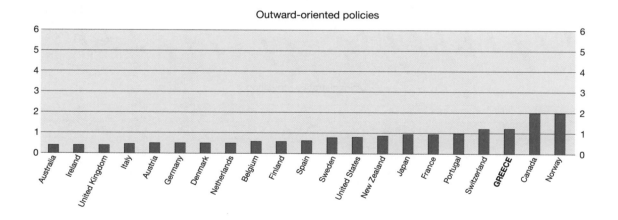

Outward-oriented policies

1. The scale of indicators is 0-6 from least to most restrictive.
Source: OECD.

Figure 1.1.   **Comparativee indicators of product market regulation in OECD Countries, end-1997** *(Cont).*
Overall regulatory approaches[1]

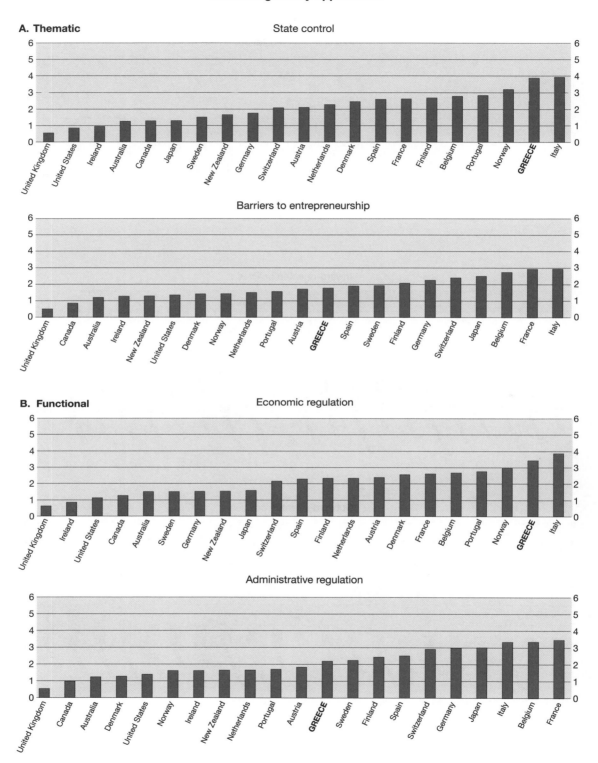

A. Thematic

State control

Barriers to entrepreneurship

B. Functional

Economic regulation

Administrative regulation

1.   The scale of indicators is 0-6 from least to most restrictive.

Source: OECD.

Chapter 2

GOVERNMENT CAPACITY TO ASSURE
HIGH QUALITY REGULATION

Reinvention of the relationship between the public administration and the market is needed for the success of regulatory reform.

Further improvement of public governance in Greece – no less than a reinvention of the relationship between the public administration and the market – is needed for the success of regulatory reform. Useful steps are already underway. In parallel with the acceleration of regulatory reform in the 1990s, the Greek government launched a series of reforms to improve the efficiency and effectiveness of its public administration. In April 2000, the Prime Minister announced that his government will improve client service, complete decentralisation, and reduce the substantial administrative burdens hindering investment.[21] A number of reforms were subsequently launched.

This is an urgent agenda. External pressures have moved faster than domestic reforms, and over the years a gap opened between, on the one hand, new social and economic demands and opportunities, and, on the other hand, the capacities of the Greek public sector to perform roles compatible with those new needs. The public administration does not yet have the incentives, institutions, capacities, and culture to develop and implement high quality regulatory regimes compatible with a more open and competition-based economy.

The Greek public service is not large, but administrative practices favour rent-seeking, clientelism, legalism, and formalism.

Regulatory regimes in Greece tend to be interventionist, costly, rigid, and focussed on details rather than results. Productivity and efficiency in the public sector are low. The Greek public service is not large compared to those of other European countries[22] (though it is growing quickly[23]) but for decades its administrative practices favoured rent-seeking, clientelism, legalism and formalism instead of market competition and policy efficiency. These characteristics directly reduce regulatory quality. The absence in the Greek public administration of a broad regulatory reform strategy, of the use of regulatory impact assessments, and of systematic public consultation such as a notice and comment process is in contrast to practices recommended by the OECD and adopted by many OECD countries. Recent progress in these areas is welcome, and such initiatives should be speedily and vigorously of implementation.

Box 2.1.   Managing regulatory quality in Greece

Ensuring regulatory transparency:

- In Greece, most consultation and transparency practices are not set by law. The most prominent consultative mechanism is the tripartite Economic and Social Committee, representing employers and businessmen; employees and civil servants; and citizens, local authorities, independent professions.

- In recent years, ministries have set up advisory committees and organised ad hoc meetings to discuss with interested parties important drafts. Ministries have discretion to appoint and invite participants, though.

- Many new regulations are published in the *Official Gazette*, available electronically. The Greek "Permanent Code of Legislation" is to be computerised by early 2001.

- One-stop shops have been set up at regional levels for services of social security, agricultural development, and commerce. It is intended that the programme be extended to all prefectures in 2001. A special one-stop shop for foreign investors called ELKE has operated since 1996 to provide information.

- Internet-based initiatives, such as ARIADNE, provide information on formalities to the general public.

Promoting regulatory reform and quality within the administration

- Individual ministries are responsible for the substantive aspects of regulations and their performance. For Presidential Decrees, the independent Council of State controls legality and quality of drafting.

- Programmes to reduce administrative burdens were launched recently. In 1998, a programme called "Quality for the Citizen" was developed to simplify administrative procedures and formalities. In 2000, a more comprehensive programme called "*Politeia*", which aims to improve the quality of services, was begun. Among its main aims are the recruitment of trained personnel who support reforms, development of new technologies and adoption of modern techniques of administrative control to improve transparency and eliminate corruption, adoption of modern financial management means for the public service based on benefit-cost analysis and comparative measurement of service and employee effectiveness, and reduction of administrative procedures which impose burdens on business and citizens etc.

Adopting explicit standards for regulatory quality

- Except for an experimental programme organised in the Ministry of National Economy, the government has not defined criteria for good regulation. The Ministry of Interior has set up a task force to develop such criteria, based on OECD recommendations.

Assessing regulatory impacts

- The only systematic assessment previous to enacting a new law or subordinate regulation concerns the assessment by the Ministry of Finance of potential impacts on the public budget.

Toward accountable and results-oriented regulation

- Since early 1990s, a programme to depolitise the civil service through a central recruitment agency has raised professional and ethic standards across the government.

- The decentralisation of regulatory powers to regional and local governments is reducing time and improving responsiveness at local level.

A cultural tradition within the public service of mistrust of market forces has led to over-regulation and rent-seeking.

There is a mistrust of competitive forces as tools for better motivation of public and private sector activity.

At bottom is a cultural problem that can be described as a lingering mistrust of incentives and competitive forces as tools for better motivation of public and private sector activity. Bureaucratic and centralised solutions are usually preferred, leading to widespread regulatory failures.

This has resulted in over-regulation of the private sphere, and is matched by over-regulation of the civil service by politicians. This two-edged polynomia has stifled creativity and dynamism through the public administration and society. Mistrust of markets and incentives creates a situation whereby policy failures and poor economic performance, rather than being analysed and corrected by actions that restore incentives, give way to even more regulation through tighter administrative controls. These in turn can be badly implemented due to lack of personnel, proper incentives and the incapacity of those entities entrusted with enforcement, with the consequence that more inefficiencies arise, and then more controls and regulations are implemented, resulting in a vicious cycle. This is the same vicious cycle seen in other OECD countries with highly legalistic administrative cultures, such as the United States, but Greece does not have the US cultures of transparency and market friendliness to offset the costs of excessive and inefficient regulation.

Regulatory reform based on transparency, client service, and market functioning can help restore trust in the state.

Regulatory reform based on principles of transparency, client service, and market functioning should be perceived as a strategy to cut the Gordian knot of distrust and restore effective relations and confidence among the state, the market, and civil society.

Mistrust is exacerbated by a culture of rent-seeking. There is a tendency by some public administration entities, such as those involved in licensing and allocation of public resources, to create red tape as a means to create rents. The best way to avoid rent seeking is to abolish or reduce requirements for licenses, and to use market mechanisms such as auctions to allocate scarce public resources.

An even more important issue is the quality rather than the number of regulations.

An even more important issue, though, is the quality rather than the number of regulations. If new regulations are poorly designed and implemented, they reduce social welfare and waste investment. Adequate quality control mechanisms are needed inside the public administration to ensure that new laws and other regulations will actually contribute to Greek social and economic progress.

Basic reforms of the Greek civil service are needed to create the capacity for an efficient and transparent regulatory system...

Greece must confront a number of entrenched obstacles and traditions in existing administrative and legal practices at national and subnational levels,[24] including skills, incentives for public sector employment, and accountability.

...including strengthening the professionalism and accountability of the public administration...

Policy coherence, co-ordination, and implementation are weakened by continuous political oversight and intervention.

Institutions for policy coherence, co-ordination, and implementation are weakened by a tradition of continuous political oversight and intervention. Close links between the top levels of the public administration and the political parties contribute to hierarchical structures that concentrate decision-making powers at the highest levels, slow response times, reduce flexibility, create bottlenecks, and reduce the accountability of lower level managers.

Upgrading the neutral competence of the civil service to reduce patronage and political influence has been a high priority. In 1994, Greece introduced a new recruitment and promotion process for public servants that was aimed at reducing clientelism and politicisation, and increasing technical capacities.[25] A centralised recruiting agency, ASEP, operates as an independent agency in charge of organising recruitment in the public service. To assure independence, its governance body is appointed by Parliament.

There have been clear successes in de-politicising the recruitment process...

ASEP was a clear success in de-politicising the recruitment process, formerly tainted by clientelism and favouritism in a highly politicised environment. The ASEP experience showed that centralised co-ordination, high professional standards, and consistent application of policy can increase trust and confidence in the public service in the public and in political spheres. But ASEP had unanticipated side-effects. The centralised recruiting system increased rigidities and made it more difficult to recruit skilled staff in a timely manner for specialised positions, for example, for staffing sectoral regulators. It also made difficult the tailoring of pay to performance and labour markets,[26] leading to a mismatch between human skills and tasks, and a lack of incentives for better performance. Resolving such problems is urgent because the market and regulatory environment at the international level is more complex and changing more quickly today. Positive reforms to ASEP were recently made. Procedures for recruiting skilled staff were speeded up by Law 2839/2000, which transferred some aspects of recruiting procedures to the public organisations concerned, while leaving final control of results to ASEP.

...but now more hiring flexibility is necessary for parts of the government competing directly with the private sector for specialised skills

To grant greater flexibility to parts of the government competing more directly with the private sector for specialised skills, such as the Capital Market Commission, the Committee for the Protection of Private Citizen Data, the Central Bank, the Ombudsman, and State-owned enterprises have been exempted. The competition policy authority has been partially exempted from the most rigid recruiting rules and can pay staff according to market prices. These exemptions are also needed by sectoral regulators who require market-valued skills.

...and improving policy coordination.

Policy co-ordination on regulatory actions could be improved. The rulemaking process remains legalistic, with few quality controls on regulatory design and impact. Important elements of rulemaking procedures are left to informal administrative traditions and the discretion of ministries. Within the public administration, inter-ministerial communication on draft legislation is limited to "competent" ministries, which compounds the fragmented or "silo" effect of policy. As in most OECD countries, subordinate regulations must be authorised by a higher-level law or regulation, but administrative processes for developing subordinate regulations mostly lack any check of economic impacts or policy results.

A government-wide strategy for regulatory quality and a framework of quality standards should be adopted...

A government-wide policy and implementation strategy for regulatory quality is needed, sustained by determined political will in the face of strong opposition.

Resolving these challenges will require a clear, government-wide policy and implementation strategy for regulatory quality, sustained by determined political will in the face of strong opposition. A range of new programmes and initiatives is required to improve regulatory quality. Awareness among stakeholders and the broad public of the importance, benefits, and costs of such a programme will be a powerful ally in overcoming obstacles from vested interests inside the public administration, as well as interests outside of the administration.

The 1997 OECD *Report on Regulatory Reform* recommends that countries adopt at the political level broad programmes of regulatory reform that establish clear objectives and frameworks for implementation.[27] Greece has launched a series of initiatives to improve its regulatory practices. Yet current reform initiatives do not represent a coherent or complete programme of regulatory quality improvement, and are not a sufficient programme to contribute significantly to economic performance. An explicit policy on quality of regulation, with the institutions to carry it out, would boost the benefits of reform for Greece.

A noteworthy action by the Prime Minister was the commissioning in 1998 of a series of reports on, among other things, the Quality of the Public Administration.[28] This report, known as the Spraos Report, recognises that problems exist within the Greek regulatory framework relating to quantity, cost of regulation, quality, and democratic legitimacy. The Spraos Report recommended the adoption of the 1995 OECD *Council Recommendation on Improving the Quality of Government Regulation*. The Report advocated the establishment of an agency to co-ordinate regulatory reform across government, with authority to express opinions on the quality of new regulations, such as legislation, Presidential Decrees, and ministerial decisions. Further, the report recommended that this agency should prepare a report to be tabled before Parliament on issues relating to regulatory quality. Since the publication of the Spraos Report, the government has reacted positively to its recommendations, and has adopted at least three.

Development of explicit and measurable government-wide criteria for making decisions on whether and how to regulate would help ensure that reform principles are applied equally by all ministries.

As a fundamental element of a new regulatory reform policy, the Greek government should develop more explicit and measurable government-wide criteria, for making decisions as to whether and how to regulate, and support those principles with written guidance to ministries. This would help ensure that reform principles are applied equally to new and old regulations, by all ministries. The

OECD recommends as a key principle that regulations should "produce benefits that justify costs, considering the distribution of effects across society." This principle is referred to in various countries as the "proportionality" principle or, in a more rigorous and quantitative form, as the benefit-cost test. This test is the preferred method for considering regulatory impacts because it aims to produce public policy that meets the criterion of being "socially optimal" (*i.e.*, maximising welfare).[29] Greece will need to strengthen, step-by-step, capacities for regulatory impact analysis to apply the benefit-cost test.

...and made effective through new institutions to protect the quality of domestic regulations.

Mechanisms for managing and tracking reform inside the administration are needed to keep reform on schedule and to avoid a recurrence of over-regulation. It is often difficult for ministries to reform themselves, given countervailing pressures, and maintaining consistency and systematic approaches across the entire administration is necessary if reform is to be broad-based. This requires the allocation of specific responsibilities and powers to agencies at the centre of government.

As yet, no body in the Greek administration is charged with monitoring and promoting a programme of regulatory reform and quality improvements.

As in many OECD countries, Greece emphasises the responsibility of individual ministries for reform performance within their areas of responsibility. Co-ordination of reform in Greece is carried out by inter-ministerial commissions and a few independent bodies that rely on legal controls and peer pressure. As yet, no dedicated body

---

Box 2.2. Self-assessment of regulatory reform in Greece

A recent self-assessment of regulatory quality by the Ministry of the National Economy has notable lessons. This pilot programme, begun in July 1999, systematically reviewed all regulations made over the last five years within the ministry. The 1995 OECD *Council Recommendation on Improving the Quality of Government Regulation* was used as a guiding principle to assess the quality of the regulations. The six month assessment involved the establishment of a regulatory reform group, composed of senior officers from different divisions within the ministry, who prepared the first inventory of all regulations including legislation, presidential and ministerial decisions.[1]

The review is an attempt to systematically assess regulatory quality within the Ministry of the National Economy. The lessons learned suggest that its design could be improved. The review lacks, for example, an independent and rigorous assessment of the impacts of regulations, the key information needed to test regulatory quality, and instead begins with qualitative statements about what the laws require. In fact, the review concluded that all legislation, Presidential Decrees, and ministerial decisions within the Ministry are effective and necessary. The only negative conclusion was that more could have been done to improve ELKE, the one-stop-shop investment promotion agency. Without independent input, self-assessment rarely yields highly critical conclusions and provides grounds for the argument that regulatory reform should be co-ordinated by a central agency or at arms-length of the ministries being reviewed.

1. Manolas Nikiforos' working group for the study of regulation (2000). Ministry of National Economy. The review examined 17 pieces of legislation, 12 Presidential Decrees, and 100 Ministerial Orders.

in the Greek administration is charged with monitoring and promoting a programme of regulatory reform and quality improvements.

For Presidential Decrees, the independent Council of State is charged with responsibility for controlling the legality and the quality of drafting.[30] In carrying out its functions, some observers indicate that its high technical standards have won a reputation as a tough guardian of legality. Indeed, in a kind of "institution-shopping," some ministers have opted to prepare a legislative amendment or ministerial decision to avoid the rigorous scrutiny of the Council of State.[31] For ministerial decisions, the responsible ministry prepares and publishes the measure according to the authorising law. They are controlled by a special commission of the Prime Minister's Office for their legality and by the Ministry of Finance for their budgetary impacts.

Despite recent improvements, regulatory transparency in Greece lags behind other OECD countries.

Reforms are promoting more transparent, open, and consultative procedures, but Greece still lags behind in improving regulatory transparency.

From ancient times, the Greeks have set the global benchmark for vigorous public debate and discussion on policy issues. In Greece, a growing number of reforms are promoting more transparent, open, and consultative procedures for making regulations. At the same time, though, long-standing practices continue to hinder openness and participation by the public in Greek regulatory development. Compared to other OECD countries, Greece is lagging behind in improving regulatory transparency.

Relations between the state and civil society have long been fairly blurred in Greece. Decades of patronage relationships between the state and civil society have turned the special interests of various social groups into one of the most pervasive factors in policy making but at the same time have seriously undermined the position of civil society as an independent entity.[32] As they were able to obtain information or advance their interests through informal avenues, the most influential civil society groups did not feel compelled to push the state for greater transparency and accountability. This state of affairs has not only born potential for capture but has also *de facto* excluded "outsiders". It has further fostered a climate of distrust within civil society as regards the reliability and probity of the administration.[33] However, in recent years, a more mature Greek democracy has gradually allowed market forces to play a greater role in the economy while favouring more open participation of civil society in the policymaking process. Both trends bode well for a progressive reinforcement of transparency.

The lack of a systematic and transparent public consultation mechanism reduces the quality of Greek regulation.

Except in the case of social partnership mechanisms in specific policy areas, public consultation in Greece is not formalised, and is left to the discretion of individual ministers or senior officials. Consultation is particularly rare for subordinate regulation, such as ministerial decisions, circulars and Presidential Decrees. The lack of a systematic and transparent public consultation mechanism reduces the quality of Greek regulation in several ways, by:

– Increasing the vulnerability of the public sector to capture and undue influence by particular interests;

– Weakening ministerial accountability for decisions;

– Causing regulatory failures due to inadequate information about the problem and the real-world impacts of decisions;

– Reducing government credibility and the legitimacy of government action.

The most prominent consultative mechanism is the tripartite Economic and Social Committee (ESC).[34] It was formed in 1994 to represent interest groups in Greece: employers and businessmen as one group; employees and civil servants as another; and citizens, local authorities, independent professions as the third. In addition, many advisory committees exist. Since 1994 the Ministry of Development consults consumer associations on issues related to consumer welfare via the National Consumer Association Council.[35] Some ministries organise *ad hoc* meetings to discuss drafts with interested parties. In such cases, the ministry itself chooses the participants. A consultation mechanism on the reform of the administration, established in Law 2839/2000, is the National Council for Administrative Reform, where administrative reform proposals are discussed by representatives of social and financial institutions, labour unions, scientific institutions, and the Greek Parliament.

Box 2.3.   **Transparency of regulatory systems in selected OECD countries**[1]

Based on self-assessment, this broad synthetic indicator is a relative measure of the openness of the regulation-making and regulatory review system. It ranks more highly national regulatory systems that provide for unrestricted public access to consultation processes, access to regulation through electronic and other publication requirements, access to regulatory impact analysis, and participation in reviews of existing regulation. It also ranks more highly those programmes with easy access to licence information, which tends to favour unitary over federal states. Greece scores below the EU, the OECD, and G7 averages. This is due to the fact that Greece does not publish its forward plans for regulation, public consultation does not occur for all regulatory proposals, and impact assessment is not required.

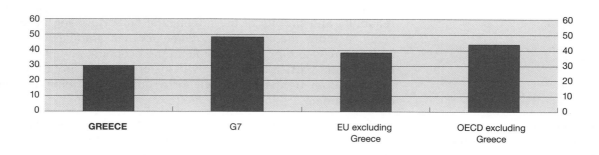

1.   The indicators used here are part of a dataset under construction as a contribution to the OECD Secretariat's horizontal work programme on regulatory reform. They are based in part on a survey of all OECD countries carried out in March-April 1998.

Source: Public Management Service, OECD (1999).

A wide variety of forms of consultation can be developed, but notice and comment processes are the most open form of consultation.

A government-wide policy on the use of consultation in making and amending regulations is key to improving regulatory quality. A wide variety of forms of consultation can be developed, but notice and comment processes are the most open form of consultation. It will be important to ensure that ministries carry out any new procedures systematically and consistently, that draft regulations are published early enough to allow meaningful public review, and that ministries actually respond to public comments, even if to explain why comments were not accepted.

Transparency requires that the administration effectively communicates the existence and content of all regulations to the public, and that enforcement policies be clear and equitable. In Greece, new regulations are published in the Official Gazette, which is available electronically.[36] The Greek "Permanent Code of Legislation" is to be computerised by early 2001. But there is no requirement to publish the internal circulars that instruct civil servants on how to implement regulations such as permits and licenses, and hence it can be difficult for businesses and citizens to understand how such requirements will be implemented. Mexico resolved a similar problem through a programme that created a central registry of formalities. The Mexican registry has positive security, that is no licence, permit or other formality can be enforced unless it is on the registry. No licence can be placed on the registry unless checked by an independent assessor against minimum quality criteria. The register is available through the Internet.[37]

Use of regulatory impact analysis can improve understanding of costs and benefits of regulatory actions within the Greek public administration, and guide the appropriate use of regulation…

The Greek private sector faces a maze of regulations, paperwork, and unnecessary controls…

Partly due to the administrative culture of controls on private behaviour and to an extreme risk aversion among civil servants, Greek regulations for the private sector are detailed and costly. There is a maze of regulations, paperwork, and unnecessary controls. To help correct these kinds of situations, the 1995 OECD *Recommendation on Improving the Quality of Government Regulation* emphasised the role of regulatory impact analysis (RIA) in systematically ensuring that the need for regulation is justified, and that the most efficient and effective policy options are chosen.

…in part because policy officials do not base decisions on an assessment of the costs and benefits of proposed regulations, such as impacts on economic activity.

Greece is drawing closer to adoption of a formal requirement to undertake regulatory impact analysis, due to the work of an interministerial committee created by the Public Administration Ministry in 2001 that is considering the OECD's recommendations, including those on RIA.[38] There is as yet no requirement to undertake RIA, and its lack has been a major gap in Greece's regulatory quality controls.[39] Policy officials do not base decisions on an assessment of the costs and benefits of proposed government actions, such as impacts on economic activity. While draft laws are accompanied by a Justification Report,[40] which describes the objective of the proposed measure, a justification report is neither empirical nor analytical, and is not required for subordinate regulation, Presidential Decrees, nor ministerial decisions. The Ministry of Finance provides a budget impact assessment for bills and amendments of laws, but this covers only a fraction of the total costs of most regulations, and is sufficient to assess regulatory costs. In moving to market-led growth in which the economy is fully integrated with Europe, a better RIA system is critical in ensuring that government actions are consistent with market-oriented principles of quality regulation.

A number of steps should be taken in Greece to enhance the use of RIA in the Greek public administration, in both the short and medium term, to meet OECD standards.

- An explicit policy at the highest levels of government could be the first step, as there is already recognition that RIA should be undertaken by the administration.[41] The Greek Parliament, as in Italy, could promote the use of RIA.

- A technical unit should be established at the centre of government with the technical capacities and the clout and credibility to enforce the RIA discipline.

- It is vital that the Greek RIA programme include from the outset a prolonged investment in training, guidance and a central help desk.

- A RIA programme in Greece should be based on quantitative assessment and methodologies that assure consistency and objectivity. The benefit-cost principle should be at the heart of the RIA programme.

- The public, and especially those affected by regulations, can provide the data necessary to complete RIA, and can check the feasibility of proposals, the alternatives considered, and the acceptance of the proposed regulation. Greece could formalise public consultation and at the same time improve rapidly the quality of RIAs – and foster accountability for regulators – by requiring that RIA be published through a 'notice and comment' mechanism. Greece is participating in the EU system of test panels where randomly selected firms evaluate the potential costs of a proposed regulation, and this could be expanded domestically.[42]

…and should be accompanied by periodic reviews of the need for existing regulations.

Since 1974, there has not been any major systematic review of regulations.

Since 1974, when Greece re-established democratic processes, there has been, except for a few specific areas such as transport and pensions, little systematic review of regulations. The review of rules has mostly been left to individual ministries, who have responsibility for updating and adapting their laws, including adopting EU directives. The main instrument for review is the codification of laws, which is painfully long and has a focus on clarity rather than on adapting the laws to modern circumstances. Tools like sunsetting or mandatory periodic reviews are absent from the Greek legal tradition. As a result, Greece's regulatory system is rigid and regulatory costs are unnecessarily high and increasing over time, with compliance lower than desired and confidence in the regulatory structure is undermined.

Poor compliance practices, too, undermine the competitiveness of law-abiding firms.

Greece faces important challenges in improving the application of and compliance with regulations.

In establishing a level playing field for the market, Greece faces important challenges in improving the application of and compliance with regulations. A study on implementation of EU directives on water quality concluded that "taking a broader perspective, the [compliance and implementation problems] tend[ed] to discredit rules and regulations, to encourage de facto situations and to undermine the development of a civic culture or respect for law and order".[43] A recent report indicated that regulatory transparency has been reduced due to "... overlapping laws and confusion in their application. Foreign companies consider the complexity of government regulations and procedures – and their inconsistent implementation by the Greek civil administration – to be the greatest impediment to operating in Greece".[44] Chapter I notes that taxation of private firms is another case. Regulations require auditing of all firms because of equity considerations, but the consequence is the opposite of what is intended: efficient and honest firms are penalised, while inefficient and dishonest firms escape sanctions. Evidence related to the large informal sector suggests a serious problem with regulatory compliance among SMEs.

The roots of the problem are varied. Together with historic relations and mistrust between citizens and the state, they include poorly designed regulations, overly complex regulatory regimes, lack of communication and co-ordination between ministries; scarcity of resources to enforce regulations; and delays in establishing enforcement institutions.[45] In the absence of RIA, there is a lack of consideration, at the development stage of a regulation, of the ability of citizens and entrepreneurs to comply.

A key issue is excessive regulatory discretion arising from broad interpretative powers provided to regulators.

A key issue is excessive regulatory discretion arising from broad interpretative powers provided to regulators. There are few external controls on implementation of subordinate legislation and administrative procedures regulating inspections and formalities such as licences and permits.[46] Unaccountable discretion may create opportunities for unethical behaviour at the delivery and service phase of public administration, such as licence applications, government approvals, and tax matters.[47] Since rigid implementation of poor regulations would greatly increase unnecessary regulatory costs in Greece, controls on discretion should proceed in parallel with improvements to regulatory flexibility and cost-efficiency.

Recent initiatives such as the Code of Administrative Procedure, the Civil Service Code, and the new Ombudsman are welcome steps, and will need to be strictly enforced.

Steps to improve compliance include the full range of quality procedures aimed at improving regulatory transparency, efficiency, and simplicity. Strict controls are needed on inconsistent application of the law by public servants, and clear rules and regulations governing business inspection and the authorisation processes (*i.e.* licences and permits).[48] Recent initiatives such as the Code of

Administrative Procedure (which regulates administrative procedures in terms of time limits for acting on citizens' cases and administrative appeal mechanisms), the Civil Service Code (which establishes anti-corruption mechanisms), and the new Ombudsman are welcome steps, and will need to be strictly enforced.

A critical aspect for their success will be the willingness of the judiciary to critically review administrative actions. Administrative justice is provided by administrative courts and by the Council of State as the Supreme Court.[49] The system is accepted as fair and effective. However, as in many OECD countries, the administration of justice in Greece is slow and expensive, with a substantial backlog of pending cases. The Ombudsman has estimated that on average an administrative appeal needs 3 to 5 years to reach the Council of State and costs around 2 000 dollars in lawyer's fees and other costs.[50] But the creation of the Ombudsman and a programme launched by the Ministry of Justice and the Ministry of Interior to computerise the judiciary system should quicken administrative justice.

Decentralisation is bringing regulatory decisions closer to the citizens, but regulatory quality controls should be strengthened in local governments.

Mechanisms for co-ordinating regulations between the regions and municipalities, the national government, and the European level will be crucial to establishing a quality regulatory environment.

In Greece as in other OECD countries, sub-national levels of government administration are inextricable elements of the regulatory framework. Policies and mechanisms for co-ordinating regulations between the regions and municipalities, the national government, and the European level have been integral in establishing a quality regulatory environment. Yet accountability and transparency have not yet been assured for regulatory decisions at regional and local levels, and more attention is needed here over the next few years.

Modernisation and restructuring of local governments have been a major reform effort in Greece since the late 1990s. The programme, known as *Ioannis Kapodistrias*, will have major impacts on the responsiveness of the public administration, and will significantly alter regulatory responsibilities among levels of government. Moving away from a highly centralised administration, Greece has today a three-tier system: 13 regions governed by a council and Secretary General appointed by the government, a "second level" of 54 prefectures (*nomos*), and a "first level" of 1 033 municipalities and communes. In parallel with administrative devolution, a 1994 law reformed the electoral process. Prefects (*nomarch*), previously appointed by the central government, are now directly elected.

Without such mechanisms, decentralisation of regulatory responsibilities risks reducing regulatory quality and increasing regulatory inflation.

Decentralisation of regulatory responsibilities also carries the risk of reducing regulatory quality and increasing regulatory inflation, at least in the short to medium term. In Greece, licences for industrial activities are often blocked at municipal levels, adding significantly to delays and business start up costs. Zoning permissions seem to be a particular problem. A problem is the capacity of civil servants. In Greece, redeployment of public servants from the centre to municipalities is lagging the transfer of policy responsibilities.[51] Improving the technical capacities of local government officials will require resources and time.

As devolution accelerates, lower levels of government will need to develop better regulatory quality skills. OECD country experience indicates that rapid devolution with weak co-ordination and accountability mechanisms can create significant regulatory problems and reduce the overall quality of domestic regulation. In Greece, this is particularly important as reforms have created a system where multiple levels are responsible for related policy areas. This raises the potential for duplication of services/controls, and inefficient delivery of services. Box 2.4 points out initiatives underway in Greece, such as by the Ministry of Development, to reduce the costs and delays of licensing at all levels of government.

Independent sectoral regulators are needed to promote market competition in newly privatised markets.

Economic structural reforms promoted as part of EU membership and accelerated through the drive to join EMU have required the establishment of new or the remodelling of existing sectoral regulators. These regulators are designed to provide regulatory oversight in liberalised sectors. The most notable are the Capital Markets Commission established in 1996, the Energy Regulatory Authority established in 1999, and the National Telecommunications and Postal Services Commission established in 1998.

Establishment of effective sectoral regulators has lagged behind deregulation and privatisation.

However, in most cases, the establishment in Greece of sectoral regulators has lagged behind the deregulation and privatisation process, they do not operate as truly independent regulatory authorities and resource constraints limit the scope of their mission.

Greece does not have a co-ordinated institutional framework for creating and operating these sectoral regulators. They tend to be established in an *ad hoc* manner, often due to an international obligation or commitment. This is particularly evident where the role of the regulatory authority is circumscribed and true regulatory oversight remains vested within the ministries. For example, the recently established Energy Regulatory Authority will not set tariffs for transmission or user charges, nor will it assess applications and grant authorisations for generation of supply licences.[52] Its role is limited to one of providing advice to the Ministry of Development that will ultimately make such decisions (see Chapter 5).

A key element in an adequate institutional architecture is ensuring an appropriate relationship between the Competition Committee and the sectoral regulators. In a number of sectors – including transport, telecommunications, broadcasting, petroleum, and electricity – regulations produce exclusion or exemption from competition laws. This has the potential to undermine free competition and confuses the market about the role of the sectoral regulator and the Competition Commission (see Chapter 3).

In contrast to the reluctance of ministries to cede power to sectoral regulators, the establishment of the Capital Market

Commission has been accepted as a highly successful step in building long-term confidence in a key economic sector.[53] Importantly, the independence of this Commission is based not only on a clear statute with well-defined functions but also on an adequate resource base independent from the government budget and a flexible staffing policy that allows the Commission to attract and keep competent staff. In this case, the Commission has been partially exempted from the most rigid recruiting rules centrally overviewed by ASEP and it is free to pay staff according to market prices rather than the official government salary scale.[54]

The successful operation of sectoral regulators and appropriate oversight of liberalised markets requires co-ordination between regulators, they must be granted sufficient independence from ministries and firms being regulating, and the resources and skills must be adequate for the sector being supervised.

Box 2.4. Battling the high cost of red tape in Greece

Compared to other OECD countries, Greek citizens and businesses face high costs from government red tape and formalities. Regulatory burdens of permits, approvals and licences are stifling Greek businesses and handicapping traditionally strong entrepreneurial energies, particularly in the large SME sector.[1]

An important area where excessive burdens have accumulated is business licensing, where approvals are granted by multiple ministries, municipalities, prefectures and regulatory agencies. A recent research project commissioned by the European Commission[2] concluded that in four cases investigated in Greece 2 to 8 licences were required, involving 3 to 9 different authorities. The time elapsed from the submission of the file to the granting of the authorisation varied from 4 months for the simplest case (renewal of mechanical equipment) to 33 months for a case including an approval for traffic connection. Using data provided in 2000 by the Greek government, the table below shows that obtaining a building licence involved up to six different agencies (ministries and local government) and required compliance with sections in 6 different

Procedure	No. of regulations involved (1996/2001)	No. of agencies involved (1996/2001)	Supporting documents (1996/2001)	Approximate time for approval (1996/2001)
Electricity connection	4L, 6D	3	5	15 days
Building licence	6L, 3D	Up to 6	17	1 month (minimum)
Ratification of environmental effects study	1L, 2D, 5MD, 1EUD	3	6	Ranges between 8 months – 2 years
Investment on Industrial Plant	10L, 3D, 2MD, 1 PD	5	14	50 days (minimum)
	/1L, 2 MD		/8 to 16	/43 days (average)
Quarry Licence	6L, 2D, 2EUD	11	6	
	/3L, 2D, 2EUD	/2	/5	1 year (minimum)
Fishery Licence	2L, 4D, 4MD, 4EUD	7	12	1 year (minimum)
	/2L,1D, 2MD, 4EUD	/2	/5	/60 days to 1 year

L= Legislation, D = Presidential Decree, MD = Ministerial Decision, C = Interpretative Circular, EUD = European Union Directive, BD = Board Decision, PD = Prefecture Decision.

Source: Ministry of the Interior, Public Administration, and Decentralisation, 2000, using data from 1996.

Battling the high cost of red tape in Greece (*cont.*)

pieces of legislation, and 3 Presidential Decrees. Recent reforms have reduced some of these costs. For instance, the government reported that by early 2001 only one agency was involved in issuing a building license, instead of 6, and that the license could be obtained in less than 20 days.

In employment regulations, permits are required to allow workers work overtime, government notification is required for new employees including part-time employment and approval from the Ministry of Labour is required to layoff workers (depending on the size of the firm[3]). Tax compliance certificates are required to obtain insurance and ongoing credit with banks. Furthermore, it can take up to one year and 45 individual approvals to establish a new business enterprise.

The incentives of local governments may be to increase red tape. In carrying out licensing, a local government is regulated by the Municipal and Communal Code.[4] The cost of a licence is set annually by the Law of Finance. However, municipalities keep the payment as revenue. To raise revenues, municipalities may have an incentive to create new licences with fees, to shorten renewal periods to increase the frequency with which licence fees are paid, and to use enforcement proceedings to collect penalty payments.

Excessive regulation of business activities through licenses and other controls add significant costs to business activities and discourage new ventures and business expansion. The Federation of Greek Industries (SEB) estimates that paperwork burdens increase production costs by more than 5% of operating costs. The National Confederation of Greek Trade (ESEE) estimates that a SME business spends at least 30 hours per month or an average of 12.5% of total work time complying with non-productive bureaucratic regulations and procedures.[5]

The government has launched initiatives to reduce administrative burdens on businesses and citizens:

– Law 2516 of 1997 simplified industrial licensing procedures by synchronising industrial development and environmental protection. It consolidated permits for establishment of industrial activities into a single licence, issued by the regional department of the General Secretariat for Industry (GSI) in each Prefecture. In case of non-respect of the deadlines, responsibility for issuing or refusing the licence is with the Ministry of Development, the silence of all other administrations equalling consent. Silence of the Ministry beyond 3 months can be taken to administrative courts. But the law did not produce the efficiency gains anticipated, because the lack of resources and co-ordination with other departments did not allow GSI services to meet prescribed deadlines and requirements. The judicial recourse provided for non-respect was not efficient relief, since delays in judicial procedures are generally longer than licensing procedures.

– To deal with these problems, the Ministry of Development codified all requirements and displayed them on the Internet with an interactive guide to help applicants in filling them out online; developed industrial zones with attractive infrastructure conditions, in which no zoning permits are needed;

established precise descriptions of all requirements introduced by other administrations to help GSI departments meet them; suppressed some unnecessary requirements; and trained regional GSI departments. As a result, formalities for establishing stock companies now take 4 to 8 days, down from 45 to 50 days. To operate, a business is entitled to an interim decision within 15 days from filing the application and can start operating while the licensing process is completed.

– A new public management programme called "Quality for the Citizen", approved by the Council of Ministers in 1998, and a new comprehensive programme for the reform of the public administration called Politiea, aim to reduce administrative burdens imposed on citizens. A simplification programme for administrative procedures and formalities with high costs for citizens has, for example, reduced by seven the number of documents required for obtaining a driving licence. Inter-ministerial working groups have redesigned more than 600 forms.[6]

– Information is provided within the local administration via electronic means over the Internet, and the ARIADNE programme will permit the Internet to be used to access and file all documents that citizens find necessary for government applications.

Battling the high cost of red tape in Greece (*cont.*)

– Beginning in 1994, the Ministry of Interior piloted one-stop-shops for citizens at the regional level for services of social security, agricultural development, and commerce. But implementation of the programme has been slow. It is intended that the programme be extended to all prefectures in 2001 with the devolution of competencies to regions and prefectures.

– Tax-related compliance burdens are expected to improve considerably with the completion of the Integrated Taxation Information System (TAXIS),[7] which rationalised the whole process through the use of modern communication systems. The system became fully operational as of May 2000.

– The Ministry of Interior has helped public entities, such as the electricity public monopoly (PPC) and national railways, to comply with the law requiring them to establish citizens' charters. This law requires the citizens charters to provide for specific compensation to citizens for deficient services.

---

1. 85% of Greece's enterprises employ between 1 and 4 persons.

2. Austrian Institute of Economic Research (WIFO) "Benchmarking Licensing, Permits and Authorisations for Industry, Emphasising SMEs", Background Document for the Industry Council of 18 May 2000

3. Retrenchments can occur at will for firms of below 20 employees, up to 5 between 20-50 employees, and a maximum of 2% for larger firms.

4. Presidential Decree 410/95 (Municipal and Communal Code).

5. National Confederation of Greek Trade (ESEE) (1999), "The increase of the functional cost of a commercial enterprise because of the necessary bureaucracy procedures", Athens.

6. This programme is distinct from the simplification programmes of the ministry of Development and the ministry of Finance who also have undertaken efforts to reduce licences and permits and improving the tax administration (see section 4.2).

7. The Integrated Taxation Information System (TAXIS) is one of the major computerisation programs of the Ministry of Finance in the framework of the Operational Project for the Modernisation of the Public Administration ("Kleisthenis" Project), co-financed by the European Communities. It aims at speeding-up procedures and reducing operational costs by "de-materialising" (through fax, Internet and mobile phones) the contacts between the citizen and the administration. This includes general and detailed fiscal information and assistance manuals, and the possibility to submit fiscal declarations or deliver compliance certificates. It is also designed to allow electronic payment of taxes in the future.

Chapter 3

THE ROLE OF COMPETITION POLICY
IN REGULATORY REFORM

Competition policy is central to regulatory reform, because, as regulatory reform stimulates structural change, vigorous enforcement of competition policy is needed to prevent private market abuses from reversing the benefits of reform. Competition principles and analysis provide a benchmark for assessing the quality of economic and social regulations, as well as motivate the application of the laws that protect competition.

Competition policy has not been strong in Greece...

In Greece, recognition of the key role of effective competition policy has been slow to emerge.

In Greece, recognition of the key role of effective competition policy has been slow to emerge. And yet, values in Greece have long encouraged an entrepreneurial culture. Industry has tended to be small scale, while services, also small-scale, have flourished. A high proportion of the working population has been self-employed. However, long-standing social values and expectations about the proper role of government present obstacles to a rule-based system of competition policy. In a business and policy culture that has been characterised by extensive state regulation, direct control of prices, and substantial state-owned enterprises, competition policy has not been a high priority.

Lack of attention to competition policy is consistent with the fact that Greek commitment to market competition has been uncertain.

- Despite the long-term policy of conforming to European norms, delays and derogations from EU liberalising directives are common.

- Traditions of planning and price controls are strong. "Gentlemen's agreements" that constrain free price competition have been tolerated, and even encouraged, to meet EMU inflation criteria, though a better approach to moderating price increases would be to promote competition in sheltered sectors.

- An example of the effort to postpone rather than encourage competition was the award to local firms, in December 1997, of a huge package of long-term utility procurement contracts totalling 3.5% of GDP – just before an EU directive would have required open competition for them (Greece had already obtained a one-year extension for compliance).

– Competition problems include the permits and licenses that control entry, which the Competition Committee has never examined.

– Many observers report that overt agreements among firms about their prices, operating hours, and services are common, despite the competition law's prohibitions.

...and hence the benefits of market liberalisation will be harder to achieve than necessary.

Competition policy in Greece can contribute to promoting structural adjustment, economic efficiency, and innovation in competitive markets only if staff resources are expanded and priorities shifted...

These examples suggest that Greece does not have the competition infrastructure needed to guide a successful liberalisation programme. Competition policy in Greece can make a serious contribution to promoting structural adjustment, economic efficiency, and innovation in competitive markets only if staff resources are expanded and priorities shifted. Additional resources should be devoted to issues that are more important than unnecessary merger reviews. In particular, attention should shift to horizontal agreements and to competition problems that are arising in the process of establishing competition in previously-monopolised sectors. Analysis and vigorous advocacy across the whole of the government should become higher priorities.

Major reforms of network infrastructure are proceeding (see Chapters 1, 5, and 6), but unless the Competition Committee's resource problems are resolved, it will not have the capacity to participate in designing these reforms, nor to follow market development to ensure that abuses do not harm consumers in the post-liberalisation phase.

Some expect that after Greece joins the euro zone, the "shock" of exposure to stronger competition may lead to demands for more effective competition policy and enforcement. Then, resources and staff would be increased to deal with "new" problems. But this sequence would be unfortunate and would increase the social transition costs. The problems that result from weak competition policy institutions are present now, and they will continue to undermine reforms until corrected.

In late 2000, Greece took positive steps to strengthen the competition agency, but EU reforms may require further steps.

...and legislation adopted in August 2000 takes positive steps to address these problems.

Legislation adopted in August 2000 takes positive steps to address these problems by authorising a doubling of staff, reducing the merger review burden, enabling the Competition Committee to undertake policy advocacy on its own initiative, and protecting the Committee's independence. However, more will be needed.

The European Commission is calling for shifting many enforcement responsibilities to national agencies, so the European Commission can concentrate on the largest transactions and most important restrictive agreements. The effect could be to increase national agencies' workloads, because those agencies will be increasingly responsible for the most difficult and resource-intensive cases, that is, those involving agreements which the parties try to keep secret. The Greek competition agency, already stretched with current resources, will need more resources to keep pace.

Formal competition policy has been in place since 1977, but it developed slowly...

Greece's first general competition law was adopted in 1977, as part of EU membership. Except for the goal of conforming to EU expectations, the law did not respond to any domestic demand or pressure, and was not based on pre-existing Greek laws or institutions. European models were transposed directly, in substance and procedure. Two years after the law was enacted, the first decision was issued. Shortly afterwards, the Competition Committee was shorn of its decision-making power, and became solely an advisory body.

In 1991, when the government changed again, the Competition Committee regained the power of decision. But the power was exercised cautiously at first. Over two years, the Competition Committee issued only 10 decisions. Merger notification and control were added to the law, but no decisions blocked mergers during that period. Reforms, in 1995, were intended to strengthen competition policy, but instead, they weakened it. The 1995 reforms compelled the Competition Committee to devote most of its resources to the low-priority task of merger review, while leaving it dependent for support on a ministry that did not share its policy goals.

...and even today competition principles are not well integrated into policy-making processes in the government.

The Competition Committee has played almost no role in the development of policy outside of its area or in the reform of regulatory regimes that may affect competition.

Competition policy has little impact on policy-making. Government-wide, the policy framework for the use of regulation in carrying out social and economic policy objectives has made too little use of competition principles. By law, the Competition Committee can offer opinions about the implications of other government actions on competition. But the law implied that the Competition Committee must be asked for its opinion, and its opinion has virtually never been requested. Hence, the Competition Committee has played almost no role in the development of policy outside of its area or in the reform of regulatory regimes that may affect competition.

Recent amendments to the competition act provide for greater co-operation with other regulators, and permit the Competition Committee to take a more independent advocacy role, if it chooses to do so.

Underlying many problems is a lack of resources and skills in the Competition Committee and its secretariat,...

The Competition Committee's staff complement is among the smallest in OECD countries.

Resource commitment measures seriousness and likely effectiveness. By that standard, Greece gives a low priority to effective competition policy. The Competition Committee's staff complement is the smallest among OECD countries, except perhaps for that of Ireland, a country that is only one-third the size of Greece. Other OECD countries with populations about the same as Greece have competition policy agencies that are from 50% larger (Austria, Belgium) to from four to six times larger (Czech Republic, Hungary, Sweden).

The staff problem is not just one of numbers, but also of approach and expertise. In particular, there is a need for more economic expertise, because the Competition Committee's decisions depend on analysis of market facts and conditions. On the Competition Committee itself, there is only one economist. In 2000, the Parliament's Transparency and Institutions Committee found that the Competition Committee had been unable to handle its responsibilities because of lack of resources, traceable ultimately to lack of financial independence, and because of insufficient staff and expertise.

Recent amendments, though, increase the Competition Committee's ability to recruit staff directly, without going through the process that was previously required.

Recent amendments increase the Competition Committee's ability to recruit staff directly, without going through the process that was previously required. The Competition Committee has lacked the flexibility, in hiring and compensation authority, to get the staff it needs. The Competition Committee estimates that its salaries would have to be raised 50% to attract the right people. Since 1995, the Competition Committee has requested exemption from general hiring rules so it could recruit directly and pay higher salaries than the basic levels. And the hiring process has been painfully slow. In 1997, the Competition Committee requested authority, through the public sector recruitment office to hire 7 expert staff. The positions were posted in 1998; applicants were interviewed in 1999; and hiring did not happen until 2000.

...which, in combination with low thresholds for merger notification that have wasted available resources,...

Recent moves to reduce emphasis on unimportant mergers will permit resources to be focussed on real competition problems.

Much of Greek law and regulation about mergers parallels EU merger regulations, but a key problem, which contributed to the mis-allocation of resources, is the threshold that triggers notification and review. Notification is required if the combined market share exceeds 35%, or if combined turnover exceeds 150 million euros (and at least two participants have turnover in Greece of more than 15 million euros each). These thresholds recently increased; before August 2000, they were 25% or 25 million euros. Including market share as a criterion for notification is a generally unsatisfactory approach which the law originally borrowed from EU models. Notification had also been required after a deal if the parties' combined market share was over 10% or if the merging firms' combined turnover exceeded 15 million euros; this "post-merger" notification requirement was dropped in the August 2000 amendments.

Merger decisions comprise nearly all of the decisions in the last few years. Only two mergers have been blocked (and one of those mergers was ultimately permitted, after a ministerial decision overrode the Competition Committee), and three were approved with conditions (OECD CLP, 1998). An increasing proportion of transactions are now subject to "pre-merger" control, rather than the post-transaction notification process which has just been eliminated. The large number still listed as "pending" suggests a problem with decision backlog, probably due to lack of staff resources. Yet, so far at least, Greece has not faced much of a problem with anti-competitive concentrations.

The delay that the review process imposes on transactions in Greece is perceived as a major problem. The risk of delay is countered somewhat by a provision permitting parties to show reasons why they must proceed to close the transaction before a decision can be issued; the Competition Committee can give them special, but conditional, permission to do so. This happens in about 15% of prior-notification cases. The Competition Committee recognises that Greece's present circumstances generally would support and even encourage mergers, which often involve major foreign investments or implement the program of privatisation. Thus a process that delays mergers also undermines progress toward a healthier economy.

Changes in the merger law and administration should make competition policy a more effective tool for reform. The Competition Committee recognises that the attention to mergers has had a distorting effect on its priorities. Dealing with the problem by exempting certain economic sectors from notification and review, as some have suggested, could be a mistake.

...has weakened enforcement against costly competition abuses.

This is needed because the Committee has undertaken little systematic enforcement or other activity in sectors that show significant competition problems.

The Committee has undertaken little systematic enforcement or other activity in sectors that show significant competition problems. The staff does not have adequate resources for reviewing complaints, doing ex officio investigations, or engaging in policy analysis and advocacy.

The merger workload has been overwhelming, and other parts of the law have been neglected. Table 3.1 implies that the Competition Committee has not imposed sanctions or orders against any restrictive agreement since 1995. There are 300 pending notifications and complaints about restrictive agreements and abuse of dominance, which the staff has virtually no resources to follow up. The Competition Committee and the Secretariat have had virtually no involvement in advocacy or in actions involving reforming sectors.

The rules for horizontal agreements are adequate, but have gone disused due to lack of resources.

Enforcing the prohibition against horizontal agreements should stimulate price competition.

The Competition Committee has been perceived as limiting its attention to approving mergers, rather than performing a wider role as competition watchdog. But anti-competitive mergers are not likely to be a major issue as Greece integrates better with the EU. On the contrary: businesses are small-scale, and there is substantial opportunity for consolidation to improve efficiency and international competitiveness in many sectors. Meanwhile, there have been no resources to deal with horizontal issues, which are likely to be significant in the wake of a tradition of formal and informal price control. Enforcing the prohibition against horizontal agreements should stimulate price competition.

The Competition Committee has been too dependent on a ministry that was not committed to market competition.

Recent amendments and appointments are good steps toward greater strength and independence for the Competition Committee.

Increasing the Competition Committee's strength and autonomy was a principal purpose of the 1995 amendments of the competition law (OECD CLP, 1998). Those goals were not fulfilled, though. Recent amendments and appointments are promising steps toward greater strength and independence. Currently, the Competition Committee is an "independent authority", and in its decision-making, the Competition Committee is reportedly more independent of political oversight and manipulation than is typical in the Greek public service.

There is little in the administrative or legal structure to protect and re-enforce that independence, though, and there are indirect controls on its effectiveness. Although administratively separate, the Competition Committee is supervised by the Minister of Development, and its budget is a special item in that Ministry's budget. In the past, the Ministry has consistently rejected the Competition Committee's requests for additional resources. The August 2000 amendments take a significant step to increase the Competition Committee's independence by providing a source of funds that will not depend on the Ministry, namely a levy of a small percentage (0.001) of the value of the capital of newly formed companies or increases in registered capital. However, the Competition

Table 3.1. Trends in competition policy actions in Greece

	Horizontal agreements	Vertical agreements	Abuse of dominance	Mergers
1999: matters opened	23		159	
Sanctions or orders sought			2	
Orders or sanctions imposed			2	
Total sanctions imposed, Drs				135 000 000
1998: matters opened	27		128	
Sanctions or orders sought			4	
Orders or sanctions imposed			4	
Total sanctions imposed, Drs				86 150 000
1997: matters opened	13		195	
Sanctions or orders sought			5	
Orders or sanctions imposed			5	
Total sanctions imposed, Drs				63 150 000
1996: matters opened	12		124	
Sanctions or orders sought			2	
Orders or sanctions imposed			2	
Total sanctions imposed, Drs				241 694 000

Source: OECD CLP (1998); OECD CLP (1997); Greece (2000).

Committee's "representative" structure, with several members appointed by outside groups including trade and industry bodies, may undermine its decision-making independence.

The oversight of the Competition Committee by the Ministry of Development has been a particularly dangerous element of the institutional design, as the Ministry has not supported market forces. In 1999, the Ministry endorsed "gentlemen's agreements" between the government and the sellers of consumer products to keep price increases down. The Ministry is responsible for administering many potentially anti-competitive constraints on entry, in the form of licensing requirements. And it has recently proposed rules to control prices for auto spare parts and set minimum prices for local truck transport of containers.

Consumer protection policy has no clear connection to competition policy goals, and application is left principally to private action.

The relationship between consumer policy and competition policy is informal. The General Secretariat for Consumer Protection is within the administrative structure of the Ministry of Development, the same ministry that oversees the Competition Committee. Thus, there is a natural channel for co-ordination among these policies. Since 1995, there has been a consumer representative on the Competition Committee (Greece, 2000).

Consumer protection laws and rules are mostly consistent with EU norms, but there are problems with the effectiveness of their enforcement,

Consumer protection laws and rules are mostly consistent with EU norms, but there are problems with the effectiveness of their enforcement, and in some cases with transposition of EU norms into local law. In insurance, for example, policies contain provisions such as unilateral rights to increase premiums that, according to consumer groups, do not conform to EU directives. The government's consumer protection office appears weak and under-funded, like the Competition Committee. A National Consumers Council attached to the Ministry of Development has essentially no staff support. It is rarely asked for its opinion about legislation affecting consumers. There was no consumer input into deliberations about recent proposals for regulations affecting competition in taxi services and service station hours.

Ensuring that consumers are adequately protected against abuses in the developing market economy is left to private groups. In the absence of effective public enforcement, a principal means of enforcing consumer protection principles is private, class-action litigation. Consumer organisations can, in principle, go to court on behalf of consumers to correct market abuses. And some have done so. There is, however, no provision for class actions for actual damages.

Box 3.1. Consumers are harmed by anti-competitive regulations

The ability of competition policy to provide a suitable framework for broad-based regulatory reform is partly determined by the extent and justification for general exemptions or special treatment for types of enterprises or actions. In Greece, there are few formal exemptions, but particular regulations that impair competition take precedence when they conflict with the more general provisions of the competition law.

The law applies to publicly owned enterprises, in principle. But it also permits exemption, by joint decision of the Ministers of National Economy and Development, for undertakings of "public utility" that are of "general importance to the national economy." The Competition Committee is to be consulted before the Ministerial decision. There is no explicit exemption or special treatment for small and medium sized businesses, such as a formal *de minimis* market share test for liability, either in the law or in enforcement guidelines. Agreements, the "exclusive aim of which is to insure, promote or strengthen exports," are also exempted from the competition law, unless the Ministers of National Economy and Development decide otherwise, after consulting with the Competition Committee.

Regulations and government decisions about many sectors have impaired free competition:

– Some of the most important transport areas where regulation has displaced competition policy oversight, trucking and ferry services, are discussed in Chapter 5.

– In air transport, development of competition has had to accommodate the interests of the publicly-controlled national airline, Olympic Airways.

– Poor taxicab service is one of the principal consumer complaints in Greece. One proposal to improve service was to authorise a "mini-bus" service, intermediate between taxis and regular-route local buses. The taxi industry has objected. The state of competition in local taxicab markets is unclear. The number of officially issued licenses is evidently limited, but there are many unauthorised, unlicensed taxis in operation too. The unlicensed taxis provide competition, but they probably escape consumer protection oversight.

– The National Broadcasting Commission is responsible for some competition-related issues in that sector. Legislation in 1995 was intended to reduce concentration in broadcast ownership and incorporate EU rules about advertising. But no licenses have been issued under the new rules, and stations are thus operating on provisional authorisations that are nearly a decade old.

– The retail petroleum industry has been reasonably competitive, but there have been constraints, such as rules that hamper imports, in intermediate distribution stages. And even in retail sales, in early 2000, gas station operators reached an agreement to limit their opening hours. Despite the risk that this step will limit competition and create inconvenience for consumers, it was evidently considered politically acceptable because of the large number of small private operators.

– The natural gas industry is now being developed, after the high pressure pipeline from Russia was completed in 1997. The system is set up to be a monopoly. Greece is not under EU obligation to provide for open access until 2006, because of an exemption in the EU directive for countries that only recently set up a gas system. The low-pressure distribution system will be established over the next 20 years by award of local monopoly concessions. Private sector participants will have only minority stakes. A majority will be held by subsidiaries of the national pipeline monopoly, which is mostly government-owned (85%). Hellenic Petroleum has the right to repurchase those government shares over time, so it could succeed to the gas monopoly.

– As of July, 1997, the accounting profession was to have been liberalised in the EU. Greece tried to reserve some protections for the previous state monopoly during the transition period, 1994-97. A November, 1997 Presidential Decree concerning audits set minimum fees and restricted the use of different types of personnel. It also prohibited audit firms from doing other kinds of work for a client. The regulations were defended as necessary to promote objectivity and quality. One effect, though, may be to impair the competitiveness of multinational accounting firms operating in Greece.

Consumers are harmed by anti-competitive regulations (*Cont.*)

– In general, professions in Greece demonstrate many of the anti-competitive aspects of self-regulation typically found elsewhere, in limitations on entry, regulated or recommended fees, and prohibitions against potentially efficient methods of providing services and against non-deceptive advertising. The Ministry of National Economy recently documented the negative impact of the regulatory barriers hampering professions on domestic competition and consumer welfare and is now promoting wide-scale liberalisation, in particular with respect to quantitative restrictions, price setting by the government or professional associations, and artificial creation of demand through administrative requirements.

Chapter 4

ENHANCING MARKET OPENNESS THROUGH REGULATORY REFORM

Market openness further increases the benefits of regulatory reform for consumers and national economic performance. Reducing regulatory barriers to trade and investment enables countries in a global economy to benefit more fully from comparative advantage and innovation. With the progressive dismantling of traditional barriers to trade, "behind the border" measures are more relevant to market access, and national regulations are exposed to unprecedented international scrutiny by trade and investment partners. Regulatory quality is no longer (if ever it was) a purely "domestic" affair.

Greece is pursuing market opening policies...

The current programme of regulatory reform across several sectors is likely to further enhance international market openness.

During most of the 1990s, the policy stance in Greece toward opening its economy to international markets was largely determined by the European Union. Today, however, market openness is widely accepted on its own merits as essential to sustainable growth. Greek economic policy recognises the adverse effects of a restrictive domestic environment, of state controls over the economy, and of extensive recourse to command and control regulations, on the competitiveness of domestic enterprises and the attractiveness of the country to foreign investors. The current programme of regulatory reform across several sectors is likely to further enhance international market openness.

...which are important for a small country dependent on trade, ...

Greece is a small, import-dependent economy. In 1997, imports of goods and services accounted for 25.5% and exports for 16.1% of GDP.[55] Chronic trade deficits are balanced by strong invisible receipts, mainly tourism and shipping. About 65% of Greek trade is with other EU states, while trade with Balkan countries, particularly Bulgaria and Albania, has developed strongly in recent years and represents today around 15%. Greece imports a large proportion of its energy, some food, virtually all transport equipment and most machinery and electrical goods. Its main exports are food (fresh and processed), raw cotton and tobacco, textiles (yarns, fabrics and ready-made clothing), chemicals, semi-processed mineral and metal products, cement and refined oil products.

...but Greece has a poor record in attracting foreign investment.

Foreign direct investment has played a relatively small role in the Greek economy.

Foreign direct investment has played a relatively small role in the Greek economy. Among potential investors, there has been limited interest in developing activities exclusively aimed at servicing the Greek market, mainly because of its small size. The main reason for establishing in Greece is to gain access to wider markets, such as the European Union and the Balkan and Eastern European area.[56]

The most important factors limiting the attractiveness of Greece for FDI were reported to be weak macroeconomic performance, shortfalls in infrastructure, and poor public administration.

The three most important factors limiting the attractiveness of Greece as a destination for FDI were reported in surveys (Hassid, 1997) to be weak macroeconomic performances, shortfalls in infrastructure (in particular, telecommunications and transport), and poor quality of public administration. The recent improvement in macroeconomic performance and infrastructure has likely played an important role in the increase of FDI inflows in the last three years. The stock of FDI amounted to US$4 billion (market prices) by end 1996, it had reached US$13.1 billion by end 1998. However, it is

---

Box 4.1.   The OECD efficient regulation principles for market openness

To ensure that regulations do not unnecessarily reduce market openness, "efficient regulation" principles should be built into domestic regulatory processes for social and economic regulations, and for administrative practices. These principles, described in *The OECD Report on Regulatory Reform* and developed in the OECD Trade Committee, have been identified by trade policy makers as key to market-oriented, trade and investment-friendly regulation. They reflect basic principles underpinning the multilateral trading system. This review does not judge the extent to which Greece has complied with international commitments, but assesses whether and how domestic regulations and procedures give effect to these principles.

—   *Transparency and openness of decision-making.* Foreign firms, individuals, and investors seeking access to a market must have adequate information on new or revised regulations so they can base decisions on accurate assessments of potential costs, risks, and market opportunities.

—   *Non-discrimination.* Non-discrimination means equality of competitive opportunities between like products and services irrespective of country of origin.

—   *Avoidance of unnecessary trade restrictiveness.* Governments should use regulations that are not more trade restrictive than necessary to fulfil legitimate objectives. For example, performance-based rather than design standards should be used as the basis of technical regulation, and taxes or tradable permits should be used in lieu of regulations, where appropriate.

—   *Use of internationally harmonised measures.* Compliance with different standards and regulations for like products can burden firms engaged in international trade with significant costs. When appropriate and feasible, internationally harmonised measures should be used as the basis of domestic regulations.

—   *Recognition of equivalence of other countries' regulatory measures.* When internationally harmonised measures are not possible, necessary or desirable, the negative trade effects of cross-country disparities in regulation and duplicative conformity assessment systems can be reduced by recognising the equivalence of trading partners' regulatory measures or the results of conformity assessment performed in other countries.

—   *Application of competition principles.* Market access can be reduced by regulatory action condoning anticompetitive conduct or by failure to correct anticompetitive private actions. Competition institutions should enable domestic and foreign firms affected by anti-competitive practices to present their positions.

impossible to identify the respective contribution of these and other factors to FDI growth.

Generous investment incentives also played a role in increasing FDI inflow. In 1997, the Hellenic Centre for Investment approved 43 FDI applications totalling US$486 million. Local content and export performance are taken into consideration by Greek authorities in evaluating applications for tax and investment incentives. Greece is divided into four investment zones, according to regional development and unemployment levels. Investments in the most disadvantaged regions can benefit from cash grants of 15% to 45% of the total sum invested or tax allowances of 40% to 100%. Sectoral incentives exist for high technology, environmental protection services, and leisure facilities, as well as for manufacturing and mining companies engaged in export, or in import substitution.

Greece has integrated several of the efficient regulation principles into domestic regulations, but falls short on transparency of the rulemaking process, avoidance of unnecessary trade restrictiveness and application of competition principles.

Over the last years, significant steps were taken domestically to enhance regulatory quality and promote a trade-friendly regulatory environment...

Greece has a mixed record in integrating the OECD's six efficient regulation principles for market openness (see Box 4.1) into its domestic regulations. Over the last years, significant steps were taken domestically to enhance regulatory quality and promote a trade-friendly regulatory environment. New procedures have been introduced to make regulatory information more widely available and to facilitate the access of individuals and businesses to administrative services. Administrative "one-stop-shops" have been created to simplify the issuance of licences and permits at the local level. Criteria used in public procurement procedures have been clarified.

...but transparency of the regulatory process, avoidance of unnecessary trade restrictiveness and application of competition principles raise concerns about market openness.

Due to these steps, non-discrimination, the use of internationally harmonised measures and the recognition of equivalence of foreign measures appear to be well integrated into the Greek regulatory framework, in part through disciplines set by the European Union. On the other hand, transparency of the rulemaking process, avoidance of unnecessary trade restrictiveness and application of competition principles still raise concerns relating to the market orientation of the Greek regulatory framework.

The discretionary character of public consultation has reduced market confidence among foreign parties...

To ensure international market openness, the process of creating, enforcing, reviewing and reforming regulations needs to be transparent and open to foreign firms and individuals seeking access to a market. Transparency offers market participants a clear picture of the rules by which the market operates, enabling production and investment decisions to be based on accurate assessments of potential costs, risks and market opportunities. It safeguards equality of competition for market participants and thus enhances the security and predictability of the market.

Regulatory transparency problems are particularly acute for foreign firms...

Several problems with regulatory transparency in Greece are discussed in Chapter 2. These problems are particularly acute for foreign firms, since they are "outsiders" and new market entrants, and are more likely to find the playing field tilted against them. From the viewpoint of market openness, significant efforts have been made by Greek authorities to improve the transparency of the regulatory framework. Creation of the Hellenic Centre for Investment and streamlining of public procurement procedures have been supplemented by increasing use of public consultation and the Internet. EU rules have promoted transparency, particularly in the area of product regulations and of public procurement.

However, more could be done to ensure that complete, accurate and timely information is offered to all market players. The most important formal consultation with affected parties when preparing or reviewing regulations takes place through the Economic and Social Council of Greece (OKE), which, as noted in Chapter 2, is organised along a tripartite model of representation. It is not itself a suitable consultation mechanism for foreign partners, due to its limited membership.

Other forms of consultation on draft regulations are informal. Each ministry establishes its informal networks to exchange views on prospective regulation. The main avenue for foreign parties to participate is through domestic associations and entities, although it is not uncommon for foreign enterprises to directly contact ministries when their views differ from those of domestic associations. Satisfaction of the parties involved in these informal consultative processes appears low. Constituencies complain about not being heard, not having sufficient time to react, or not being consulted at all. As recommended in Chapter 2, more transparent consultation practices, with timetables and participation criteria would build confidence and enhance the efficiency of consultation for domestic and foreign parties alike.

A few ministries have taken useful initiatives. A recent example was the presentation on the Ministry of Transport and Communications website of a strategy paper and draft law on telecommunications liberalisation. In December 1999, the Ministry invited public discussion on the project. This initiative elicited considerable interest from domestic and foreign market players, academic institutions, associations, and other government entities. The ministry found the consultation to be helpful. Following a major rethinking of the proposal, a new version of the law was publicised in June 2000, again calling for public comments.

...while the one-stop shop for foreign investors was not given the means to be effective.

...and efforts to make information more accessible to foreign investors have reduced the time required for some procedures.

The Hellenic Centre for Investment, or ELKE was established in 1997 to assist foreign investors with information as well as procedures. ELKE provides information to foreign investors about requirements for starting new investments in Greece, and assists those that plan to apply for the subsidy for new investments. The assistance is provided only to large foreign investors (with invests of about euro 9 million). Although its consulting and support services are available only to larger investments, its information services are available to all.

ELKE is not a true one-stop-shop, as the various procedures, such as licenses, are still dealt with by the ministries. ELKE has no authority to speed up their decisions. Moreover, while ELKE tries to track the various laws concerning foreign investment, even it finds it difficult to keep abreast of all ministerial decisions. The main value added for large investors concerns the application for capital subsidies. ELKE has cut by half the time required to obtain approval of such subsidies. Smaller investors usually employ consulting firms to assist them with the licenses and other procedures required for establishment. Given that ELKE services are provided free, while consulting firms charge fees, ELKE provides a subsidy to large foreign investors, and it is doubtful whether such investors need it.

Market openness is further reduced by regulatory complexity and inefficient administration.

Transparency of regulation is also reduced by ambiguous and contradictory regulatory provisions, which frequently create the need for interpretative statements by the Parliament (for Laws), or interpretative Ministerial circulars (for Decrees). According to the US government, *"Foreign companies consider the complexity of government regulations and procedures – and their inconsistent implementation by the Greek civil administration- to be the greatest impediment to operating in Greece."*[57] The call in Chapter 2 for simplification of domestic regulations and more consistent implementation would, if implemented, improve not only regulatory compliance in Greece, but would also greatly improve market openness and help to boost FDI. Steps have been taken to tackle this problem, for example, one-stop-shops for citizens at the regional level for services of social security, agricultural development, and commerce have reduced complexity and improved transparency.

Foreign enterprises in Greece also say that inefficient bureaucracy and contacts with central and local authorities are problems.

According to surveys conducted in 1997 among foreign enterprises in Greece, inefficient bureaucracy and contacts with central and local authorities are a significant problem for businesses operating in Greece.[58] Chapter 2 has noted the costs associated with business licensing at central and local levels, but also (Box 2.4) notes the efforts underway in Greece to reduce these costs. The Federation of Greek Industries believes that a couple of major greenfield investment projects in recent years may have been driven out of Greece because of excessive delays that prevented them from meeting their own time constraints. New telecommunications entrants have found dispute resolution procedures too long, and have reported delays in licensing for liberalised services. The main complaints are lack of operational flexibility in administration and considerable delays in handling matters, due to insufficient co-ordination between departments and between the centre and lower levels of administration. In addition, the absence of a long-term perspective and frequent changes in procedures and policies, particularly in the fiscal area,[59] are seen as limiting predictability and inhibiting strategic planning by firms.

Significant improvements have been realised in Greek customs procedures.

An area that is improving is customs procedures. As tariff levels have declined, costs imposed by customs procedures have attracted growing attention from businesses. Customs services in the Greek Ministry of Finance have taken measures to simplify customs procedures. With other EU customs authorities, the Greek authorities have implemented trade facilitation measures such as pre-arrival import declarations. Computerisation of the customs system was organised and financed in the framework of successive Community Support Framework Programs, and the average clearance time fell to 30 minutes from 5 to 6 hours. These measures have significantly improved transparency in customs regulations and operations, and accelerated customs clearance, without compromising regulatory objectives, such as revenue collection.

Public procurement is formally open, but in practice problems still arise.

For public procurement, EU publication requirements are widely observed by Greek governments...

Transparency in government procurement is essential to ensure that markets for public works, supplies and services are open to international competition. Greece has a mixed record here. EU publication requirements are widely observed by Greek governments. In 1998, tenders published in the Official Journal of the European Communities represented around 44.5% of total public procurement in Greece, against an average of 13% for all EU countries.

Box 4.2.   Transparency in the regulation of the Greek Capital Market

Transparency and accountability of the supervisory authority are essential to build confidence in the operation of the Stock Exchange. To develop investors' trust and ensure that regulation meets market needs, the Greek Capital Market Commission has established a series of information dissemination and consultation practices. These practices include:

- Extensive consultation with affected parties at an early stage of regulation by the Commission. The Commission issues a consultation paper with a preliminary version of the draft to concerned professional associations, such as the Federation of Greek Industries, the Union of Brokers, the Union of Institutional Investors, and the Hellenic Bankers Association. Constituencies are given 30 days to react, in practice commonly extended to 45 days. After receiving comments, usually extensive, the Commission organises a meeting between the associations and Commission staff to discuss the comments. This procedure was recently used to elaborate three Codes of Conduct for institutional investors, underwriters and brokerage firms and investment firms and for regulations on public offers.

- Publication of decisions on licenses and sanctions. These decisions, taken by the Board of Directors, are based on publicised criteria and are subject to judicial review by the administrative courts.

- An open policy on requests for information, comments or recommendations by foreign companies or institutions.

- Public information campaigns to educate inexperienced investors on the operation of the Stock Exchange.

In addition, the Commission is creating a Mediator for the Capital Market, responsible for arbitrating conflicts between investors and listed companies.

...and inadequate technical preparation of tenders seen in the past has been addressed through clearer technical standards and award criteria.

Openness of public procurement in Greece has, in the past, been undermined by the use of "...*loosely written specifications which are subject to varying interpretations.*"[60] Inadequate technical preparation of tenders is believed to have been the main reason for conflicting requirements, incomplete supporting studies and miscalculations of projected costs, which have led to regular reconsiderations of tenders. This has reduced transparency and even given rise to allegations of corruption. Obtaining relief through judicial proceedings was also hampered by the ambiguity of selection criteria and by delays of up to five years in appeals to superior courts. Greece has moved to improve this situation. Adequacy of specifications has been improved through increasing use of internationally harmonised technical standards, and by tightening procedures for drafting pre-selection and award criteria. A practical guide of all procedures, bodies, documents and remedies involved in tender and award procedures is now available online and aims to help in particular SMEs and new entrants in the Greek market. Enforcement of these improved procedures was enhanced by the introduction of strict deadlines for judicial relief, which can no longer exceed 30 days for interim measures and 5 months for the final order.

Greek public procurement markets are open to European suppliers in accord with EU rules, although implementation of the rules has been very slow, even relative to the deferred deadlines granted to Greece. For example, implementing legislation for third country access to procurement by utilities was due in Greece by mid-February 2000, but has not been introduced yet.

Measures to ensure non-discrimination should concentrate on the services sectors.

Overtly discriminatory regulation is exceptional in Greece, and is mainly limited to services.

Overtly discriminatory regulatory content is exceptional in Greece, and is mainly limited to the services area. However, the costs of such restrictions on market development may be high, given the importance of the services sector in the Greek economy.

Greece maintains some exceptions to national treatment, such as the need for non-EU residents to obtain authorisation for certain investments, and limitations on ownership in domestic airline companies, flag vessels and broadcasting companies. As do other OECD countries, Greece maintains exceptions to the non-discrimination principle in many professional services. In addition to EU-wide exemptions in the WTO services schedules, Greece discriminates against non-EU nationals such as legal practitioners, engineers, architects, doctors, dentists and midwives, nurses, and many other professions.

The absence of prior assessment of regulatory impact on the economy raises the risk of unduly trade-restrictive regulation.

Unnecessary trade restrictiveness of regulations, regulatory enforcement and administrative practice seem to be a major short-coming of the Greek regulatory framework. This is in part because the administration has neither the experience nor the tools to assess the potential impacts of regulation on business activity. In

79

Greece there are no provisions requiring or encouraging regulations or administrative practices to be trade and investment friendly. As a result, regulation tends to impose burdens that are disproportional to its aims and the risk of unforeseen barriers to trade and investment is high. The development of regulatory impact assessment tools recommended in Chapter 2 will be critical for devising a successful simplification policy that reduces negative trade impacts.

Greece ranks high on use of internationally harmonised standards...

Greek legislative practice emphasises harmonising domestic legislation with the country's international obligations under international treaties and agreements. Moreover, Greek policy aims at establishing a regulatory and standardisation system applicable in a market economy and accepted world-wide, so as to facilitate the access of Greek products to world markets. This policy has been shaped to a large extent by the commitments undertaken in the European Single Market. In addition, Greece has been very active in promoting international harmonisation in standards-setting outside the EU through technical assistance to neighbouring transition economies.

...and is advanced in recognition of equivalence of other countries' regulatory measures, but institutions for accreditation should be strengthened.

Recognising the equivalence of differing standards applicable in other markets, or of the results of conformity assessment performed elsewhere can greatly contribute in reducing regulatory costs. As in the area of standardisation, the major driving forces behind recognition of equivalence in Greece are the commitments undertaken in the framework of the EU. Although this obviously benefits EU manufacturers first, the positive impact for non-EU manufacturers should not be disregarded. Indeed, the opening of Greek markets on the basis of EU rules not only increases the transparency of the regulatory environment, but also offers third partners the multiplier effect of the intra-community mutual recognition. Greece has been among the few EU members to have complied with the monitoring requirements for mutual recognition and its record with respect to mutual recognition infringement cases is good (10 cases out of 228 in the period 1996/98).

Accreditation is a procedure whereby an authoritative body gives formal recognition that a body or person is competent to carry out specific tasks.[61] Accreditation mechanisms have been developed only recently in Greece. A National Accreditation Council (ESYD) was instituted in 1995, but was inactive until 1999. Accreditation activities were thus exclusively undertaken by foreign institutions until recently. The lack of accreditation mechanisms has proved a serious hindrance for certification activities, as the reliability of non-accredited laboratories was widely questioned by the private sector.[62] Strengthening of accreditation mechanisms is essential to improve business confidence.

To facilitate the access of Greek products to world markets, Greek policy aims to establish regulations and standards that are accepted world-wide.

Greece has been among the few EU members to have complied with the monitoring requirements for mutual recognition and its record with respect to mutual recognition infringement cases is good.

Chapter 5

REGULATORY REFORM IN ELECTRICITY, DOMESTIC FERRIES, AND TRUCKING

Regulatory and competition reforms are underway in Greece in the transport (road and ferry) and electricity sectors.

In its 1998 Economic Survey of Greece, the OECD reported that almost all Greek public enterprises had been poorly managed, and had often been used to implement multiple policy objectives unrelated to their primary objective of efficiently providing quality goods and services. As a result, public enterprises were usually inefficient, provided low service quality, and were a costly drain on the public purse. From 1996, however, the need for change to respond to the demands of market opening under EU directives, and the desire to meet the Maastricht public finance criteria, spurred concrete reforms. This chapter reviews regulatory and competition reforms in Greece in the transport (road and ferry) sector and electricity sector, both of which provide key inputs into large parts of the economy.

Regulatory reform in the electricity sector must account for a range of economic and social policy objectives.

In this complex area, the regulatory challenges are formidable: the regulatory framework must provide for the development of a competitive market that benefits consumers, but must also find efficient ways to meet environmental, safety, social and consumer protection objectives. The framework must support long term security and reliability of supply for electricity and deal with converging interests between electricity and gas regulation, and electricity and competition regulation. A sound regulatory regime will help attract sufficient investment to ensure that demand is satisfied and that competition is sustainable. These tasks require both targeted deregulation and careful construction of new and transparent regulatory regimes and institutions. Greece is doing both.

Greece has taken many of the steps needed to improve the performance of its electricity sector, but the package is not yet complete.

Greece must open at least 30% of its electricity demand to competition by 19 February 2001, and has created an Energy Regulatory Authority and System Operator.

The most immediate spur to reform of the Greek electricity sector is its obligations under the EU electricity directive. Under this directive, Greece must *inter alia* open at least 30% of its electricity demand to competition by 19 February 2001. Greece's 1999 law was adopted to comply with the directive. The 1999 law also creates the

For Greece to enjoy significant efficiency gains, however, it should take additional steps to promote effective competition.

Energy Regulatory Authority and System Operator, and formalises the relationship between the monopolist, PPC, and the Ministry of Development.

These are positive steps. As a package, however, they do not yet create an adequate regulatory environment for the market entry and vigorous competition needed to provide pressure for greater economic efficiency. Market forces will continue to be impeded by the sector's structure and the regulatory framework. For Greece to enjoy significant efficiency gains, it will need to take additional steps to promote the development of effective competition. Important steps include reducing barriers to entry for generators, splitting PPC into competing generating companies with distinct ownership, transferring regulatory responsibility to an effective regulatory authority that is independent of the industry and of the day-to-day political pressures of government, and improving the corporate governance of PPC.

Efficiency is promoted by competition. Endesa, in Spain, estimates it can cut operating costs by half between 1996 and 2006. (OECD 2000) ENEL, in Italy, is expected to be able to reduce the number of its employees by a quarter by 2004, largely through incentives and early retirement. (CNN 1999a) There is significant scope for reducing costs in PPC, partly by reducing investments in unprofitable activities and partly by reducing the number of employees. Efficiency gains should be passed on to consumers as lower prices, or to taxpayers as lower subsidies.

Electricity prices are at OECD averages, but these prices mask inefficiencies and distortions that reduce job creation and economic growth.

While industrial prices of electricity in Greece are low, and household prices are average, these price comparisons do not reflect PPC's relative efficiency: input prices are distorted.

Average industrial prices of electricity in Greece are low, and household prices are average, compared with other European IEA countries. But these price comparisons do not reflect PPC's relative efficiency: input prices are distorted and the company has significant non-commercial public service obligations, such as supplying some consumers below cost. Regulated electricity prices were used as an anti-inflation tool, hence the real (inflation-adjusted) price fell 24% in the decade to 1999. Average industrial prices are distorted because PPC supplies large quantities of electricity at about half price to aluminium and nickel firms, while commercial and small industrial customers pay prices well above their cost of supply (these subsidies are due to be phased out in 2006 and 2003, respectively). Revenues collected from households covered only about 60% of the costs in 1997, but 90% by 1999. Agricultural and other special categories of customers pay even less.

Transfer prices for fuels are not necessarily market prices, either. Besides lignite, other fuels are bought from other predominantly or wholly state-owned firms, although in some cases PPC pays market-based prices. Return on equity has been far below normal. DEI has a high debt to equity ratio for a company without recent acquisitions – its gearing was 185% at the end of 1999. In sum, PPC has used financial resources that might have been put to better use elsewhere, and has charged higher prices to those parts of the economy that are normally responsible for the greatest job creation.

The integrated structure of the Greek electricity sector is the largest barrier to market competition.

The electricity sector in Greece is comprised almost completely of a single state-owned corporation.

The electricity sector in Greece is comprised almost completely of a single state-owned corporation, PPC, and as one of the most concentrated sectors in the OECD (Figure 5.1). PPC faces no competition from abroad. PPC is vertically integrated in all aspects of the electricity sector, from lignite mining to selling power. Only trivial amounts of power are supplied by others or imported. The 1999 law largely retains this structure. PPC remains vertically integrated, retains exclusive ownership of transmission and distribution, and retains ownership over its generation and supply facilities.

Figure 5.1.   **One and two firm concentration ratios in selected countries and regions, 1998[1]**

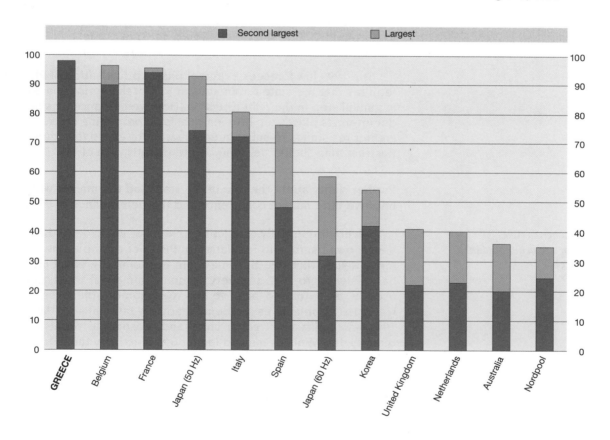

1.   Data refers to 1999 for Greece and Ireland.

Source: OECD, IEA, Electrabel annual report (Electrabel + SPE), EdF and Charbonnage de France annual reports, Edison April 1999 presentation to shareholders, Spanish and Korean Ministry of Industry and Energy, Ofgem (NatPower and PowerGen in England and Wales 97/98), NEMMCO, Macquarie and Delta annual reports (SE market only), Nordpool annual report and Vattenfall, Statkraft.

Greek authorities have made several choices, such as not creating immediate competition by splitting generation, whose effect is to discourage entry and ensure that the sector remains a monopoly.

Under the new regime, PPC must produce separate accounts for generation, transmission and distribution and, for non-electricity activities, consolidated accounts. Its legal monopoly in generation and supply of liberalised customers is eliminated. But Greek authorities have made several policy choices, such as not creating immediate competition by splitting generation, whose combined effect is to discourage entry and ensure that the sector remains a stable monopoly.

To meet its goals of efficiency and energy security, the fastest and easiest route for Greece to follow would be to make structural splits in PPC's generation by selling the two gas-fired plants along with their long-term gas supply contracts, to two separate companies. Other countries have created competing generating companies both before and after privatisation. This has been done in the United Kingdom (England and Wales), New Zealand, Australia (three largest states), some states of the United States, and Argentina, and is planned in Italy and South Korea. Some might object to splitting up PPC's generating capacity, claiming that the resulting firms would be "too small." However, small generating companies persist, or are being deliberately created, elsewhere. It would be feasible to spin off several competing generating companies from PPC. This step alone would not create effective competition in Greece, but it would be the necessary first step.

The 1999 law foresees eventual partial privatisation of PPC, but requires that the state retain at least 51% of the voting shares. This is a small step in the right direction. However, reliance on shareholder interests places too little emphasis on promoting efficiency and greater resistance to subsequent creation of effective competition. Restructuring should be done before privatisation of PPC.

Further clarity about the role of the state and the market will improve both market confidence and the performance of PPC...

Inconsistent objectives for the sector are being gradually rationalised.

Several potentially conflicting objectives coincide in the governance, ownership, and regulation of PPC. For example, the government wishes that PPC become more economically efficient, but it has assigned to PPC a variety of non-commercial tasks, and has used it as a tool to achieve macroeconomic objectives. These inconsistent objectives are being gradually rationalised. Under the 1999 law, tariffs must cover costs and reasonable profits; consequently, the Minister may no longer use electricity tariffs to control inflation.

...such as designing the corporate governance of PPC to encourage commercial incentives for efficiency.

... and the corporate governance of PPC is improving.

Part of building a stable regulatory framework, in the Greek case, is improving the corporate governance of PPC. The Ministry, as owner, retains a deep control over decisions that would normally be made by corporate managers, such as review of investment plans. Listing on the Athens Stock Exchange will force some changes in this relationship, but following more stringent principles of corporate governance would make this relationship more arms' length. This, too, would reassure potential entrants that they would be treated by the Ministry in a way similar to the treatment of PPC.

More attention is needed to access issues to open the markets to new entrants.

Access to transmission and distribution, and access to fuel could be further bottlenecks to market entry.

Access to transmission and distribution, and access to fuel could be further bottlenecks to market entry. PPC owns 49% of the Transmission System Operator, itself staffed by personnel seconded or transferred from PPC. Access conditions – set out in the Grid and Distribution Codes – will be drawn up by the System Operator or PPC itself as Distribution Operator. Self-regulation of transmission and distribution access prices, albeit monitored by the ERA, and virtual self-regulation of other access terms, imply that an entrant would not be offered access to essential facilities at efficient prices and terms. In other countries, access to transmission, especially, has been a source of discrimination if not carefully regulated. Resolving the inevitable disputes will need to be done efficiently in Greece, since delayed access benefits the incumbent, and the new law contains mediation provisions that could help.

Access to fuel, particularly gas, constitutes a further barrier to entry, since gas is sold on negotiated terms by a monopolist until 2003, and there is not yet a framework for access to lignite.

- Most new generating plants use natural gas. Greek Public Gas Corporation (DEPA) is the vertically integrated monopolist in the Greek gas sector. DEPA is owned by the state, except for a blocking share owned by Hellenic Petroleum, itself mostly state owned. DEPA has the exclusive right to import, transport and supply large customers – such as power plants – with gas. The Greek gas sector will not be liberalised before 2003, three years before Greece's derogation from the EU gas directive ends.

- Lignite is, at present, the most important fuel for electricity generation in Greece. While the Greek state owns the lignite deposits, PPC exploits the deposits under license. The state does not collect royalties (although a 0.4% levy goes to local authorities), so PPC's cost of lignite is much lower than the cost of lignite for other European utilities.

Low prices to large customers also discourage entry. In Greece, the existing contracts with the aluminium and nickel companies will provide for prices below the cost of supply for the next several years. Matching those prices would be unprofitable for an entrant. By reducing the size of the potentially profitable liberalised market, entry is less attractive.

Resources and regulatory powers must be placed in a regulatory body, independent of Ministry and the regulated companies.

Greater reliance on independent regulation can reduce regulatory barriers, promote entry and investment, and accelerate the development of competition in the Greek electricity sector.

Greater reliance on independent regulation can reduce regulatory barriers, promote entry and investment, and accelerate the development of competition in the Greek electricity sector. Many OECD countries have independent regulators. Specific arrangements differ in each country, but the main features of independent regulation are complete independence from the regulated companies, a legal mandate that provides for separation of the regulatory body from political control, a degree of organisational autonomy, and well defined obligations for transparency (*e.g.*, publishing decisions) and accountability (*e.g.*, appealable decisions, public scrutiny of expenditures). There are three sources of concern about the Greek regulatory framework:

- First, the Minister of Development, rather than the ERA, makes regulatory decisions. The Minister controls authorisations, sets tariffs, and can impose tariff and other conditions on all authorisation holders under the rubric of "public service obligations." Ministers may also make trade-offs that discourage investment: in Greece, there would be concern that the Minister might continue the practice of using electricity prices to influence inflation.

- Second, PPC itself retains substantial influence over regulation. The the System Operator and the Distribution Network Operator have regulatory powers associated with granting access and operating their respective grids. PPC will own 49% of the System Operator and PPC is assigned the role of the Distribution Network Operator. Each of these is a route for PPC influence.

- Third, the Ministry needs to develop an independent ability to make energy policy. The practice of transferring and seconding PPC personnel is indicative of this need. In Greece, state-owned energy companies provide an important source of information, expertise and advice in relation to energy policy matters on an *ad hoc* basis if not formally (IEA, pp. 28, 30). This practice discourages the development of independent expertise within ERA and the Ministry. Greece needs to develop the expertise of its agencies, and broaden the consultation process, in order to develop the credibility of its regulatory regime.

Once the ERA is functioning, final regulatory authority for generating and supply authorisation, tariffs, and access to transmission and distribution need to be transferred to ERA. Both the Ministry and ERA need to develop expertise to regulate and to make policy.

The domestic ferry sector is crucial in Greece and historically has been highly regulated.

Domestic ferries are vital to the economic life of Greece's islands and, through their role in tourism, the health of the national economy. There are about 150 ports in Greece, and about a thousand ferry links are made a day. Demand for ferry services grew rapidly through the 1990s, and further growth is expected.

Reform to the regulation of the domestic ferry sector is urgently needed...

Reform to the regulation of the sector is urgently needed, as recognised by market participants and by the responsible ministry, which has launched a programme of reform. In late 2000, the government developed a draft law to liberalise the domestic ferry sector, aiming at free and fair competition and protection of public interest, that should be the basis for further reform. The ministry's earlier move toward an integrated approach to the sector, focusing on passenger transport needs and the interactions with port infrastructure, is another positive development. The Greek ferry sector is, as the ministry has recognised, a network. Like other transport networks, an optimal shape may involve hubs and spokes, and like those other networks, it may involve feeder lines and main lines.

...and would encourage lower prices and better services, while permitting more attention to efficiency and safety.

Further reforming the regulatory framework would benefit consumers by encouraging lower prices and better services, while permitting more attention to efficiency and safety. Competition would provide incentives for innovation, which would result in lower costs and prices, and in new services. Public policy objectives related to service to designated islands and to safety can be met in ways that do not unnecessarily impede competition. The main innovation in this sector is faster ferries. New ships are much faster than the ships they replace, and often have larger capacity. However, to date, with the exception of hydrofoils and some catamarans that cannot carry vehicles, there are few high-speed ferries in the Greek domestic market. That this is primarily due to a rigid regulatory structure can be seen in the faster innovation in the Adriatic Sea (Box 5.1).

Regulatory institutions need to be modernised so that producers do not have undue influence.

Greek regulatory institutions are more appropriate to a system of self-regulation than a regime of transparent, accountable regulation focused on the needs of passengers and ensuring equitable treatment of all market players.

Greek regulatory institutions have been more appropriate to a system of self-regulation than to a regime of transparent, accountable regulation focused on the needs of passengers and ensuring equitable treatment of all market players. The domestic ferry sector is at present highly regulated by the Ministry for Merchant Marine (MMM), which regulates market entry, licensing, pricing, route scheduling, manning, public service obligations, tendering for unprofitable routes, enforcement, and inspection of ferries for safety. An advisory body, the Coastal Transport Advisory Committee (CTAC),[63] makes non-binding recommendations about licenses and prices which the Minister has always followed. Six of 12 members of CTAC were, before September 2000, split among four representatives of shipping, one of the Piraeus Chamber of Commerce and Industry, and the National Tourist Organisation (to represent consumers). In September 2000, membership in the CTAC was expanded to include more consumer groups, both commercial and island residents.

In these arrangements, the Ministry becomes deeply involved in commercial decisions, rather than policy results, and industry participants seem to have influence over the economic regulation enforced by the Ministry. Under the existing system, new investors, whether Greek or foreign, have a basis for concern that potential competitors might influence crucial business decisions. This concern could discourage entry.

Increased representation of consumer interests on the CTAC, whether tourist, island resident or non-marine transport companies, will help offset the influence of producer interests. More use of public hearings in the decision-making process would also increase transparency. As important would be for each Ministerial decision to be accompanied by a public, reasoned explanation of the objective criteria applied, and the policy objective driving the decision.

Box 5.1.   Regulation matters: Adriatic ferries versus Aegean ferries

There is substantial international ferry traffic between Greece and Italy. Ferries in the Aegean domestic routes and the Adriatic international routes are governed by different regulatory frameworks. The international routes of the Adriatic are under European Commission competence and have been subject to liberalisation of entry, pricing, and frequency since 1993. International traffic between Greece and Italy does not come under the Greek domestic cabotage, institutional and legal umbrella, except that part that links Greek ports, *e.g.*, among Patras, Igoumenitsa and Corfu. Also, international routes are subject to enforcement of European Union competition laws by the Commission.

In contrast to the Aegean, entry is free on the Adriatic routes: The quality of service has risen, the number of passengers has grown, and prices are lower, per kilometer, than in the Aegean. Passengers on Adriatic routes have benefited from liberalised entry.

Faster ferries were introduced first in the liberalised Adriatic market, while in the Aegean, the introduction of faster ferries has been delayed by the ministry's licensing decisions. As a result, companies use their newer and faster ships on the longer, liberalised Adriatic routes and slower, older ships on the Aegean. The introduction of faster ferries significantly affects markets and market structure. For example, the two 27-knot ships that entered the Patras-Bari via Igoumenitsa route in the Adriatic won about two-thirds of the market in less than a year, increased the size of the market by 5 to 36% (depending on whether trucks, private vehicles, or passengers are measured) and shifted traffic toward Bari from other southern Italian ports.

The Adriatic has had free pricing for several years. Fares in the Adriatic are much lower, per unit distance, than fares in the Aegean. Two very popular routes are Piraeus-Herakleion, Crete, a distance of 175 nautical miles, and Patras-Ancona, Italy, a distance of 510 nautical miles. As the table shows, the price per unit distance is much lower for the Adriatic route.

	Piraeus-Herakleion		Patras-Ancona	
	Fare (GRD)	GRD/nautical mile	Fare (GRD)	GRD/nautical mile
Passengers	63 000	360	145 600	285
Car	33 700	193	31 200	61
Truck	156 750	896	140 000-170 000	275-333

Assumptions: Passengers: two persons in a double outside cabin; Truck: 16.5 meters (price includes tax, which is normally rebated).

Economic regulation should be eased, so that the companies make choices about commercial operations in response to consumer wishes and developments in the marketplace.

Entry should be liberalised by changing the economic licensing system from authorisation to notification.

Entry should be liberalised in the domestic market by changing the economic licensing system from authorisation to notification (safety-related licensing is not addressed in this report). Licenses should cease to be route-based, so that companies can design their own networks on the basis of commercial criteria. Fares and frequencies should be decided on a commercial basis by individual companies, so that capacity can be better utilised throughout the year. The competition thus engendered would provide incentives for fleet modernisation, just as competition across the Adriatic does today.

Currently, licenses, specific to each vessel, are granted for specified itineraries at specified, invariant frequencies, on the basis of criteria that are not always transparent. The CTAC considers other views on the feasibility of requests, including those in direct competition with the company requesting the license. The evaluation does not include a review of the economic or competition impacts. There had been a tendency to maintain the *status quo*, enabling incumbent companies to remain unchallenged, though very recently the CTAC has approved almost all of the requests for licenses, taking under consideration safety issues.

The European Commission characterised the legal and regulatory framework for domestic ferries as "rigid...particularly as regards the grant of operating licenses and the fixing of fares...." (EC, par. 105) Full application of the EC directive on cabotage[64] should begin in November 2002, pending adoption of the draft law currently being developed by the Greek government. This may mean that entry restrictions or regulation of frequency and fares will be lifted, which is preferable, but it may mean that the existing regulatory framework would be applied equally to Greek and other EU flagged ships. Restrictions on route entry harm consumers by reducing competition and pressure for lower prices and better services.

As producers make more commercial decisions, the Ministry should ensure that the regulatory framework is transparent, accountable, and pro-competition.

Transparency and accountability of regulation require more attention,...

Transparency and accountability of regulation would be increased by publishing explanations of regulatory decisions, both in terms of the objective criteria used and the way in which the decision promotes public policy objectives. This would assure both consumers and market participants of the reliability, effectiveness, and neutrality of the new regulatory framework.

Several regulatory reforms would increase efficiency and reduce the costs of ferry service, such as a focus on service to islands rather than to routes....

...along with a possible conceptual shift to serving islands rather than routes.

The MMM should not pre-judge the route over which each island would be most economically served, that is, which island would be the local hub. The commercial decision about where to locate a hub would normally take many features into account, such as location and availability of labour, and port facilities, that influence the cost and reliability of the hub. A shift to focus incentives for service on islands for which there is low traffic demand would have positive effects. Development of hub-and-spoke service to "public service" islands would enable them to be served at lower cost. The (profitable) destination islands could be served at greater speed – time would not be spent at intermediate stops, and it may be economic to use faster ships – and thus lower total cost to those passengers.

...extending competitive tendering for unprofitable routes...

By extending tendering to all low-demand islands, the Ministry would reduce the cost of service.

Service to islands with low demand is subsidised. Service to islands as part of a licensed itinerary is cross-subsidised by passengers on other routes, and service to those on "unprofitable route" is subsidised by the state and, perhaps, other passengers. The annual state subsidy is 2.5 billion drachma. A more flexible framework for providing these services would lower their cost. The most efficient way to identify the least-cost provider is to competitively tender (for a subsidy) the obligation to serve a low-demand island. The Ministry already uses such a method for "unprofitable routes." By extending the tendering process to all low-demand islands, the Ministry would reduce the cost of service. This would reduce the total amount of subsidy needed. In addition, unbundling winter and summer service makes possible additional cost-saving through allowing flexibility of vessel and route network during winter, in order to better match demand conditions.

...and freeing up fares over competitive routes.

By freeing fares and making them subject to the prohibition against collusion, the Ministry could greatly increase the efficiency with which vessels are used.

The Ministry regulates fares and freight rates of all services (except for A class rates) and companies in the domestic sector, but the institutional framework provides substantial scope for collusion. In its decision on price-fixing from the late 1980s to 1997 by seven ferry companies on routes between Italy and Greece, [EC, par. 97, 153-154] the European Commission found a practice of fixing domestic ferry fares in Greece. In the consultation process of the MMM, all domestic operators submitted a common proposal. By freeing fares over potentially competitive routes, and thus making them subject to the competition law prohibition against collusion, the Ministry could greatly increase the efficiency with which vessels are used. Liberalisation of prices on potentially competitive routes would aid the economy as a whole.

With reform, service can be maintained to all designated islands, but at lower cost...

Reform would expand the public tendering system to ensure service to all islands...

One of the main policy objectives for this sector is ensuring service to all the designated Greek islands. The recommended reform would expand the public tendering system to ensure service to all islands that would be left unserved, under-served, or served only at high price under free commercial decision-making. Service to some islands would continue to require subsidy, and the subsidy of service to additional islands in winter would be made explicit. By holding a public tender, competition in bidding ensures that the subsidy is no higher than necessary to provide the service, and it ensures that the service is provided at lowest cost. Funding for these subsidies would come either from general funds, or from a fee, acting like a tax, on all ticket sales, so that, as now, other passengers support these vital services.

... while employment can be increased by more competition.

Crews must be maintained year round, even when a ship is idle, insulating labour from the seasonal fluctuation of demand for ferry services. On-board hotel service composition, including number of cooks and stewards, is specified as a function of ship size. The Ministry has explained that some of its crewing requirements are aimed at increasing employment, while others relate to safety. The effect on employment may well be the opposite of that intended, since the rule on year round employment discourages seasonal expansions in capacity – with associated employment – by raising the cost of expansion.

...and have a long-term positive effect on employment.

Reforms would likely have a long-term positive effect on employment. More demand for ferry services means more demand for seamen as well as more employment in destinations. More shipbuilding means more employment in shipyards, including perhaps those in Greece. To the extent that hub-and-spoke networks develop, the increase in inter-island traffic would mean more employment on the islands. If year-round employment requirement were eased, this would introduce greater seasonal variation in employment, but expand the average. This report has not addressed safety regulation, which is of primary concern to consumers, regulators, and ship owners alike.

Box 5.2.   Creating a new regulatory framework for domestic ferries

In mid-2000, the Greek government took the first steps to reform of the domestic ferry sector by expanding participation in the Coastal Transport Advisory Committee and by convening law-drafting committees. The draft law under discussion in early 2001 aims to create non-discriminatory conditions for competition and to otherwise protect the public interest. Public interest objectives include securing the safety and quality of service, and safeguarding the country's territorial integrity and the economic and social cohesion of the island parts of Greece. The Minister for Merchant Marine will be able to impose public service obligations, such as ports served, capacity to provide transport service, freight rates, and manning. For those routes where entry does not occur in a free market, a Europe-wide tender for a contract to provide service will be issued. An independent Regulatory Authority for Domestic Maritime Transport will be established to monitor the sector, impose fines, and submit its opinion to the Minister on issues falling within its competence. Transparent assessment procedures and proposal selection will be introduced. Licensing procedures will be abolished, and controls limited to ship safety, capacity and reliability of the ship owner and quality of service. These steps are in line with many of the OECD's recommendations on reform of the sector.

In a more competitive ferry industry, the role of the regulating ministry would shift to protecting competition and safety.

The reforms recommended in this report would fundamentally change the relationship between the MMM and the domestic ferry companies. The Ministry and its advisory committee, CTAC, would withdraw from regulating routes entry, prices, and other dimensions of competition. The MMM would ensure service to low-demand islands. The Ministry would retain its monitoring role, and take on greater responsibility to prevent collusion and, carefully defined so as to distinguish it from tough competition, predation. The CTAC would have greater consumer representation, but economic liberalisation and greater use of broader consultation methods would diminish its role.

The Greek regulatory regime for trucking is unsustainable.

Greece's current regulatory framework for trucking services is unsustainable...

Regulation of the Greek trucking sector is consistent with regulation of other sectors. A heavy reliance on traditional, command-and-control methods leads to restrictions on entry, and regulated prices. These constraints unnecessarily raise costs. Indeed, Greece's current regulatory framework for trucking services is unsustainable, because liberalised foreign truckers are competing against Greek truckers who are hampered by national restrictions on entry, innovation, and pricing.

Deregulation, in other countries, of third-party haulage, has resulted in lower prices, and improved service and flexibility. The trend in Europe is to shift away from own-account to third party provision of trucking services. Outsourcing trucking allows companies to have access to an entire network and pay only for usage. This lowers barriers to entry into markets for which transport is an input, which increases competition in those markets. Development of a flexible, reliable trucking or logistics sector has positive effects throughout an economy. Outsourcing trucking services, however, cannot occur among Greek-registered trucks since the number of permits for third party transport is fixed. Instead, the number of trucks registered for own-account transport is growing. This suggests inefficiency. Another indicator of efficiency is the number of empty back-hauls. Truckers for third-parties tend to have fewer empty back-hauls than own-account truckers.

...and entry should be freed. A new initiative is underway to reform the sector.

If the objective of the regulation is to protect the third party truckers, then it is failing. Under EU rules, other European truckers can, provided they have an authorisation to operate internationally from any Member State, unrestrictedly enter the Greek national market. Competitors will continue to put pressure on Greek third-party truckers' prices and costs. If the purpose of the regulation is to increase safety levels and reduce environmental effects, then the regulation is misdirected. A better approach is one Greece is already taking: better enforcement of safety and environmental standards by direct regulation and inspection. In March 2001, a formal joint committee was set up by a ministerial decision, published in the Official Gazette. This committee consists of representatives of ministries, hauliers, unions, and transport experts, and aims to map out a reform of the entire sector.

Chapter 6

REGULATORY REFORM IN
THE TELECOMMUNICATIONS INDUSTRY

The telecommunications industry is extraordinarily dynamic. Rapid evolution of technologies has shaken up industries and regulatory regimes long based on older technologies and market theories. Twenty-seven OECD countries have unrestricted market access to all forms of telecommunications, including voice telephony, infrastructure investment and investment by foreign enterprises, compared to only a handful a few years ago. The industry's boundaries are blurring and merging with other industries such as broadcasting and information services.

Regulatory regimes must simultaneously promote competition and protect other social policies in dynamic markets.

Strong competition policies and efficiency-promoting regulatory regimes are crucial to the development of the industry.

Strong competition policies and efficiency-promoting regulatory regimes that work well in dynamic and global markets are crucial to the performance and future development of the industry. The central regulatory task is to enable the development of competition in local markets, while protecting other public interests such as reliability, universal service and consumer interests. Entry must be actively promoted in markets where formerly regulated monopolists remain dominant, and consideration must be given to convergence of separate regulatory frameworks applicable to telecommunications and broadcasting infrastructures and services.

Greece reformed its telecommunications sector later than most OECD countries, and competition is relatively undeveloped...

Greece's market liberalisation is occurring several years after most EU countries fully opened their markets, and it is unlikely that new entrants will be able to compete before mid-2001 at the earliest.

Greece's market liberalisation is occurring several years after most EU countries fully opened their markets (on 1 January 1998) and established new regulatory frameworks. This late start could have provided Greece with a unique opportunity to draw on the experience of these countries to apply best practices of regulatory reform. Unfortunately, this opportunity has not been used. By the third quarter of 2000, key pieces of legislation and regulation had yet to be implemented, including the new draft law and the licensing framework. For example, the commitment to competition should have been followed up by early licensing of new entrants so that on 1 January 2001 they would be prepared to enter the market. The late licensing that occurred in December 2000 means that it is unlikely that new entrants will be able to compete before mid-2001 at the earliest. This will retard the potential benefits to consumers from market liberalisation.

Delay in the regulatory regime has, in turn, penalised Greece's market actors relative to major companies in other OECD countries. The incumbent state monopoly (OTE) has made considerable gains in efficiency and improving quality of service over the last several years, but requires significant changes in corporate culture, laying stress on customer needs and marketing, to become competitive. Progress is likely here, since privatisation of OTE is expected to continue and the government is seeking a foreign strategic partner for OTE.

The new communications law of December 2000 is a significant step forward, but positive signs have been marred by key decisions inconsistent with a move to market.

There are recent indications of a greater commitment to reform in Greece, notably in the new telecommunications law adopted by parliament in December 2000. The new law is a significant step forward, relative to earlier drafts. The decision to reduce the government's share in OTE is also an important reform. Yet these positive signs have been marred by key decisions inconsistent with a move to market competition. A decision to grant OTE a FWA licence without a requirement that it participate in the auction, perhaps an attempt to add value to a company for which the government is seeking a strategic partner, is discriminatory and may enhance OTE's dominant position in the market. Actions of this kind are inconsistent with a commitment to market forces and undermine the credibility of reform. Greater emphasis on ensuring consistent decisions and on creating a strategic vision for the development of competition in the telecommunication service sector would be of great benefit to Greece.

With the right reforms, Greece could quickly build a transparent and neutral regulatory framework based on sound economic principles.

The regulatory regime in Greece displays potential strengths, depending on how the new law is implemented by the regulator (EETT) and the extent to which the government takes an arm's length position towards the incumbent, OTE, and its new strategic partner. The recent law, although it has weaknesses, provides a good basis in which a stronger EETT can begin to implement the necessary details of regulations. Another strength is that Greece already has high penetration rates for fixed telephony and a competitive mobile sector with good levels of penetration.

If implemented consistently, the current regulatory framework can position Greece for effective competition...

These strengths in the regulatory framework can position Greece for effective competition now that the voice telephony market is open for competition since January 2001. A concerted effort to change behaviour through leadership and necessary institutional and structural change would quickly transform the Greek telecommunication scene into a leader and provide strong support in bringing the Greek economy into the information age.

...which can lead to new growth and employment opportunities for the Greek economy.

In the longer-term, the most important impact of pro-competitive regulatory reform will be to accelerate broadband development and provide the foundations for electronic commerce and the information society. These developments can lead to important new growth (and employment) opportunities for the Greek economy. The government has placed high priority in its policy agenda on the Information Society. If adequate measures are not in place to enhance public access to broadband communication infrastructures and allow Greece to participate in the emerging Information Society, these goals will not be attained.

An urgent issue is that important requirements of the EC derogation are still unmet.

The Greek decision to maintain the full derogation for EU liberalisation directives is a lost opportunity.

The Greek decision to maintain the full derogation, unlike some other EU countries, indicated a lack of commitment, during 1996-1999, to create a competitive telecommunications market. The derogation provided to Greece is another lost opportunity. The main objective of the derogation, to rebalance OTE's prices, was not achieved, which indicates an insufficient effort to prepare for market liberalisation. A number of other deadlines set by the derogation had either not fully been met by the third quarter of 2000 or had been considerably delayed. This applied in particular to the requirement to award licenses before 31 December 2000, which materialised in late December, and to the requirement to issue a new operating licence for OTE providing for the abolition of its exclusive rights. These delays have had serious implications for the rapid development of competition in the Greek market.

Due to delays in implementing the regulatory framework, essential regulatory safeguards are still missing.

Of concern is the lack of safeguards to promote competition, and a clear timetable. These include:

A particular concern is the lack of necessary safeguards to promote competition in the marketplace, and a clear-cut timetable to implement these policies. These policies include:

...Cost-based interconnection prices...

– *Cost-based interconnection prices.* Publication of interconnection charges applicable to public voice services has not yet taken place. Interconnection charges need to be cost-based with accounting separation introduced.

...Price rebalancing...

– *Price rebalancing.* The terms of the EU's derogation stated that OTE's fixed telephony prices should be aligned to costs no later than 1/1/2001. The derogation granted to Greece was to allow OTE time to rebalance its tariffs before market liberalisation. Such rebalancing had not been completed before full market liberalisation, as required. Local telephony continues to be subsidised by revenue generated from long distance and international services.

...Price caps...

– *Price caps.* No price cap regulation is applied to OTE. The most transparent and effective way to regulate prices is through a price cap formula. The EETT should consider imposing a price cap.

... Methodology to calculate the cost of universal service...   ·

– *Methodology to calculate the cost of universal service.* Universal service obligations are defined in the new law; however, a method of funding and delivering them in a cost-effective,

Box 6.1.   Greece is strengthening the independent regulatory authority, which is key to competition

Experience has shown that a key to creation of competitive conditions is establishment of an independent telecommunication regulatory body, separate from the telecommunication operators and from line ministries which maintain responsibility for policy-making, and separate from the incumbent. Independence rests on clarification of responsibilities of the different bodies with a role in the sector. In the past, Greek law has been inadequate in this area because it gave insufficient powers to EETT and reduced its role to an advisory body. Without the ability to make and implement binding decisions in important areas such as provision of licences, abolishment of individual licenses, and entry on the basis of general licensing, EETT has been in a weak position. The new law adopted in 2000 should improve matters considerably.

EETT should have the authority and capacity to exercise its powers to the full: in terms of budget and staff, in relation to licensing, interconnection, price controls, universal service, numbering, the taking of binding decisions, and the implementation of other regulatory safeguards. The European Commission noted in 1999 that the boundaries between EETT's powers and those of the ministry had not always been clearly defined. Market participants have raised similar concerns. They attributed this phenomenon to (a) the large number of provisions (mainly secondary legislation) that have created confusion for market participants, and (b) to insufficient human resources in EETT and lack of expertise.

The new 2000 law reinforces EETT by transferring powers to it from the ministry, as mandated by the EC regulatory provisions regarding national regulatory authorities (NRAs), in relation to licensing, supervision of interconnection, universal service, the implementation of cost-accounting systems, numbering, and frequencies. The independence provided to the regulator in the context of the new law has still to be tested.

A second problem is that EETT and the General Secretariat of Communications (GST) suffer from understaffing, which has resulted in slow decisions in dispute resolutions and licensing. A lack of skills is partly due to rigidities in recruiting under the centralised civil service system. The skills that the EETT's staff requires to regulate effectively in a competitive environment may change over time due to the globalisation of telecommunication markets. Hence, EETT should be allowed to design its own recruitment policy, and training programmes, as well as have some freedom in setting salary scales outside of civil service constraints.

Under the new law, EETT's authorised staffing level will increase from 70 to 180 employees, of which 120 should be highly qualified scientists and engineers. For an initial period of four years EETT will also be allowed to employ from other public organisations for a maximum period of two years. The Law defines the categories of personnel EETT should have, their professional qualification, and the number of employees in each category, but also includes a provision that allows EETT the right to change these categories and the number of personnel, and allows it to deviate from the salary rates of civil servants.

In addition, the independence of EETT is jeopardised through its resource dependency. This is evident not only in the provisions of the Law imposing limits on EETT in terms of human resources but also in not allowing EETT to retain and administer any unspent funds. This will not change under the new law.

The Competition Authority is not as actively involved in the regulation of anti-competitive conduct in the Greek telecommunication market. There is no formal link between EETT and the Competition Authority, but there is well-established informal co-operation between the two agencies. The role of the Competition Authority is expected to change with the new Competition Law adopted by Parliament in August 2000, which states that the Competition Authority should have sole responsibility over the enforcement of competition principles in all incidents reported to it by the independent authorities.

As discussed in Chapter 2, regulators should create open and effective consultative procedures. EETT has begun to take a more open approach in decision-making by initiating public consultation processes on matters such as unbundling the local loop, allocation of fixed-wireless access licences, etc. A recent positive development expected to open the way to new entrants in the market for wireless services was EETT's decision in June 2000 to launch two public consultations: one for the allocation of a fourth mobile operating licence, and the second for the licensing of operators offering fixed-wireless access (FWA) in the local loop market.

technologically neutral, way needs to be established. The new law also relates the concept of universal service to the development of an Information Society without, however, imposing any additional burden on telecommunication operators to subsidise educational, health, and other social policy objectives. This decision conforms to best policy practices and should be applauded. It is the Government's intention to fund the development of an Information Society directly through the structural funds allocated to the country from the 3rd Community Support Framework Programme.

...Number portability...

– N*umber portability* refers to the ability of customers to keep their numbers when they change their location, service provider, or type of service. The absence of number portability can put a new entrant at a disadvantageous position since "switching costs" are a strong disincentive for customers to switch from the incumbent to a new entrant. Taking full advantage of the EU transition period offered,[66] the new law allows for number portability to be introduced at the latest by 1 January 2003, two years after the market is liberalised. This is too late. The government should empower EETT to oblige operators, and in particular OTE, to introduce number portability as soon as technically possible.

...Carrier Selection and pre-selection...

– *Carrier Selection and pre-selection*. Greek officials argue that, in line with national and EU legislation, carrier selection will be introduced no later than December 2002. However, no plans have yet been made for carrier pre-selection. Carrier pre-selection should be in place as soon as markets are opened to competition.

...Spectrum allocation...

– *Spectrum allocation*: A Ministerial decision based on Law 2246 specifies the procedure to be followed by an applicant for the provision of services that require the use of frequency spectrum. This remains to a large extent inactive due to the fact that neither the Ministry nor EETT have taken any decisions regarding the most suitable method for the allocation of available frequency spectrum.

...Quality of service...

– Q*uality of service*. OTE's license prescribes specific quality of service targets to be achieved in urban areas by the end of 2003, and states that OTE should improve the quality of its telephony services each year between 1996 and 2003 and reach certain development objectives. Specific quality requirements for the provision of leased line services are defined elsewhere. EETT monitors, but does not publish the results of its quality monitoring. EETT should publish quality of service data and could also examine the possibility of publishing quality of service data for mobile operators.

... Licensing for third generation mobile services.

– *Licensing for third generation mobile services*. No specific plans have yet been made regarding the introduction of the UMTS system. According to Greek officials, the granting of UMTS licenses is anticipated by June 2001. Given that FWA licences have been allocated by auction the same procedure should be used for UMTS. EETT needs to ensure that all licences are allocated on the basis of the same objective and transparent procedures.

Regulation of entry and licensing is unnecessarily burdensome, and discourages market entry.

Licensing procedures have been extremely lengthy and bureaucratic.

The majority of new players in the market have expressed dissatisfaction with Greek licensing procedures in the past. In particular, they have complained that licensing procedures have been extremely lengthy and bureaucratic. In one case, it was reported that a company received the first individual license to deploy a fibre optics alternative network 15 months after it had submitted an application.[67] In 1998, the same company filed an application for a license to offer international facility-based services and intended to buy capacity for this purpose, but the Ministry revoked its application due to a lack of secondary legislation.

There are several categories of general licenses according to the type of services. For example, voice telephony services needs separate licenses for local, long-distance, and voice over IP services. In each case, the prospective licensee needs to file a separate application for each type of service it wishes to offer. The development and exploitation of alternative networks, including radio, mobile, and satellite networks are subject to individual licenses.

Part of the problem relates to the difficulties encountered by new entrants over access to rights of ways. An interviewee reported that for a company to lay a fibre optic cable in the sea it needed 40 different licenses from public authorities. The case of satellite services is worse. The first company to obtain a license to build and operate a satellite network was granted the license in December 1999, almost three and a half years after it first filed an application in summer 1996.

With the involvement of EETT in establishing procedures for 'one-stop-shopping' these conditions should change for the better.

With adoption of the new Telecommunications Law and the involvement of EETT in establishing procedures for 'one-stop-shopping' these conditions should change. A positive step was made with a recent law that provides EETT with regulatory powers over the award of both general and individual licences and the relevant criteria for their award. Further improvement in the length of the licensing process is envisaged. The new law determines that a general license should be granted within 15 days of application and an individual license within 6 weeks. Although these new timeframes represent a considerable improvement, further streamlining in the classification system is necessary, for example, by abolishing the requirement for individual licenses for fixed infrastructure and services.

Some market players have also complained that the Ministry systematically delayed the award of licenses for the provision of services that require use of frequency spectrum. In particular, it has been reported that only OTE and the three mobile operators enjoy the right to use radio frequencies to provide services beyond those for which they were initially granted frequencies, whereas other companies have repeatedly asked for the right to use microwave frequencies without any success. In 1999 the Ministry in collaboration with EETT made a positive step by setting up a Committee to manage the frequency spectrum.

Interconnection and regulation of interconnection prices.

The Ministry expects that LRAIC methodology will be applied to interconnection costs.

Interconnection charges in Greece have not been based on costs, nor on an commonly agreed objective methodology. The methodology proposed by regulators and the EC is the long-run average incremental cost (LRAIC), based on forward looking costs and a sufficient return on investment for the incumbent. The LRAIC methodology will be applied at the end of 2001, and OTE says that it is in the final stage of adopting and implementing a comprehensive cost accounting system which will enable it to determine the costs of interconnection conforming to the EC requirements.

However, OTE is unlikely to make known well in advance the terms and conditions of access to its network.

The regulator should determine a general framework for interconnection and prices before full market liberalisation. It is necessary for OTE to make known well in advance the terms and conditions of access to its network. However, OTE is unlikely to do this on time and it appears that the regulator with its limited resources cannot put any pressure on OTE to conform to this requirement. Given the importance of developing electronic commerce and Internet applications the EETT should also give consideration to

Figure 6.1.   **Comparison of EU peak interconnection rates based on a call duration of 3 minutes**

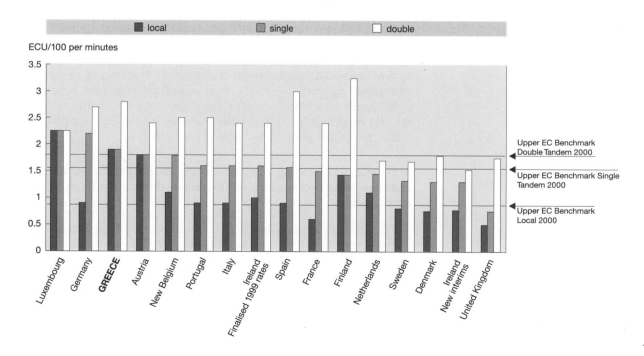

developing a flat rate Internet access call origination product which would facilitate the offer of unmetered Internet connections. The requirement imposed on BT in the UK has led to important changes in the UK Internet market and allowed for cheaper access and the development of an "always-on" environment.

As of March 2000 OTE's interconnection rates (peak time) exceeded by a considerable margin EU benchmarks for local, single transit and double transit interconnection (see Figure 1). For local and single transit interconnection Greece was the highest in Europe and the third highest for double transit. Since then some improvements have occurred, and today local Greece is the third most expensive in the EU, the second most expensive for single transit and the fifth most expensive for double transit.

Greece is taking positive action to open access to the local loop, but a lack of alternate infrastructure will slow competition.

Current initiatives to unbundle the local loop will help enhance competition in the local loop...

An important initiative has been taken to unbundle the local loop. OTE is required to provide unbundled access to its local loop to other operators on reasonable terms, including any ADSL enhanced segments. To maintain incentives on new entrants to deploy their own infrastructure rather than depend indefinitely on the incumbent's, the requirement on OTE to provide unbundled elements of its network is restricted to a specific period (four years). Such policies will help enhance competition in the local loop if they are supplemented by regulatory oversight ensuring collocation, reasonable prices for unbundled local loops, and effective arbitration.

...and this is particularly important since Greece is extremely weak in terms of alternative infrastructures.

Unlike many OECD countries Greece is extremely weak in terms of the availability of alternative infrastructures. A particular weakness is that a cable television infrastructure does not exist, nor are there any plans to significantly improve the situation. In most OECD countries cable is viewed as providing an important means of access to high-speed infrastructure to support electronic commerce and multimedia applications, and provide the means to compete effectively against the PSTN. It is important that new broadband and narrow band technologies be allowed to enter the market as rapidly as possible, in particular wireless in the local loop technologies and third generation mobile technologies.

In parallel with adding new pro-competition regulations, the arduous task of continual streamlining of the regulatory regime must go on.

Greece is currently in the process of establishing a new regulatory framework for the sector. However, at the same time, officials responsible for the sector should question whether all regulations are necessary or whether the costs of establishing new regulations outweigh the benefits envisaged. In areas such as licensing, streamlining could be rapidly implemented. This could best be achieved through a system of class licensing and eliminating the onerous requirements presently imposed.

Chapter 7

CONCLUSIONS AND POLICY OPTIONS
FOR REGULATORY REFORM

Today, Greece is moving further and faster than at any time in the post-war period.

Under the spur of intensifying European competition and seizing the opportunity of a stable political and macroeconomic environment, Greece has launched itself on the road to market liberalisation. This road, trod later in Greece than in most European countries, is necessary to fuel the sustainable economic growth that will create jobs and drive convergence with other European countries. Now that the vicious economic cycle of the previous twenty years, from 1974 to 1994, has been broken, Greece is moving further and faster on microeconomic reforms than at any time in the post-war period. Sustained and consistent reforms over the next few years will do much to bring Greek regulatory practices up to OECD good practices and build valuable credibility in the market for Greek reforms.

Most Greeks will benefit from regulatory reform, but the resistance of many protected groups to needed change is hard to overcome.

Comprehensive regulatory reform in Greece can help manage a smoother transition to a dynamic market economy.

Greek experience has shown that sustaining reform will not be easy. Unwinding the accumulated inefficiencies and rigidities of many decades will benefit most Greeks, but incur the opposition of many protected groups. The transition period will be painful for some of those groups. A comprehensive regulatory reform strategy – in which competition policy, market openness, and governance reforms are integrated to build high quality regulatory regimes – will go a long way in smoothing the bumps of the transition, spreading the costs and benefits of reform across society, and yielding concrete benefits more quickly. That is, comprehensive regulatory reform should be seen in Greece as a way to more effectively manage the transition to a dynamic market economy.

Greece has been the slowest country in Europe to comply with EU liberalisation directives, which is equivalent to self-handicapping in a footrace.

A major barrier to successful regulatory reform in Greece is that domestic policymaking seems to frequently place a higher priority on protecting established interests than on meeting consumer needs and supporting economic vitality. Greece has usually been the slowest country in Europe to comply with EU liberalisation directives, repeatedly negotiating derogations that put it years behind its EU competitors. This is equivalent to self-handicapping in a footrace. Poor regulatory practices through the whole of the economy are slowing structural adjustment and job creation, discouraging market entry and foreign investment, encouraging the growth of the informal sector, and reducing public sector effectiveness. The key structural problems in Greece continue to be inefficient regulatory regimes in key sectors, poor performance of public enterprises particularly state-controlled banks, ineffective competition policy, public administration performance, a relatively rigid labour market, and the social security and pension system.

Despite the pervasiveness of regulations and controls that could stifle competition, some aspects of the Greek economy appear to be thriving. The explanation is probably a combination of a strong entrepreneurial culture, combined with extensive de facto deregulation due to extensive regulatory non-compliance, particularly in the informal sector.

The benefits of further regulatory reform for Greece are likely to be substantial, higher than for most OECD countries.

Since Greece is one of the most regulated countries in the OECD, economic benefits of regulatory reform may be as high as 9-11% of GDP.

The likely improvements in efficiency and output from further reform have been well documented. Estimates for Greece of the overall economic benefits of regulatory reform suggest that they are likely to be substantial, as much as 9-11% of GDP if reforms are sustained over a several years. The benefits will be higher for Greece than for most OECD countries because Greece is one of the most regulated countries in the OECD, as indicated in Figure 1.1, and Greece also has higher numbers of small enterprises who are disproportionately harmed by inefficient regulation. Economic growth induced by regulatory reform is especially beneficial because it is non-inflationary, based on productivity improvements throughout the economy.

Already, in Greece, implementation of reforms generates concrete benefits...

Structural reforms can remove institutional biases that, by inhibiting competition and misallocating resources, result in higher prices and low levels of efficiency. Reforms can lower costs, encourage greater efficiency and stimulate business dynamism and entrepreneurial activity. The benefits of sectoral reform are amplified when competition is vigorous in upstream and downstream sectors, in service as well as manufacturing sectors. Already, in Greece, implementation of reforms in different sectors is beginning to generate benefits in some areas:

...by boosting consumer demand and welfare through lower prices, better service quality, and greater choice...

– *Boosting consumer demand and welfare through lower prices, better service quality, and a greater variety of goods and services.* Deregulating domestic air service has led to lower fares in Greece. Opening the sale of securities to new entry stimulated extraordinary price competition. Liberalisation of international ferry travel in the Adriatic is largely responsible for faster ferries and lower prices relative to domestic ferry travel in the Aegean. There is early evidence that market liberalisation and competition in telecommunications are bringing significant benefits to Greece by lowering national and international long distance prices; stimulating investment and innovation in mobile services; and improving quality of service.

...reducing the domestic cost structure of exporting sectors to improve their competitiveness...

– *Reducing the domestic cost structure of exporting sectors to improve their competitiveness* in regional and global markets, while reducing the risk of trade tensions due to possible regulatory barriers. Integration into regional and global markets further boosts the benefits of reform. Regulatory reform is urgently needed for the adaptation of the Greek economy to the conditions of a global economy. Prosperity in Europe today, and more so under the euro, depends on flexibility and nimbleness in adjusting to new opportunities and constraints. This is particularly the case for small countries such as Greece. Foreign investment will be a critical driver of economic growth and innovation, and Greece will pay a mounting cost for regulations that unnecessarily discourage foreign investors because they are inefficient, trade-restrictive, or non-transparent.

– *Improving the flexibility of the supply-side of the economy* by stimulating investment, by increasing the efficiency of the allocation of capital, and by lowering barriers to the creation of new firms, products and services.

...increasing the potential employment by creating new job opportunities...

– *Helping to increase employment by creating new job opportunities.* Greek reforms have not been sufficient to boost employment. Initiatives to reduce government formalities and licensing should help boost business startups and expansion throughout the economy, with positive effects on jobs. In the telecommunications sector, employment has declined steadily and is unlikely to show a net increase until the third quarter of 2001 as new entrants develop customer bases. In this sector, from a longer-term perspective, pro-competitive regulatory reform will accelerate broadband development and provide the foundations for electronic commerce and the information society, leading to important new growth (and employment) opportunities for the Greek economy. Ferry reform would also likely have a long-term positive effect on employment. More demand for ferry services means more demand for seamen as well as more employment in destinations. More shipbuilding means more employment in shipyards.

...maintaining and increasing high levels of regulatory protections for citizens and the environment.

– *Maintaining and increasing high levels of regulatory protections* in areas such as health and safety, the environment, and consumer interests by introducing more flexible and efficient regulatory and non-regulatory instruments, such as market approaches. Enforcement and compliance deficiencies have undermined regulatory protections in Greece. Key elements for improving regulatory protections include controls on inconsistent application of the law by public servants, and clear rules and regulations governing business inspection and the authorisation processes. Recent initiatives such as the Code of Administrative Procedure and the Civil Service Code will improve regulatory performance. Recent progress in the use of market-based alternatives to regulation in the area of environmental protection will also boost protection in Greece, and could be a pilot for other policy sectors.

More effective competition policy is essential.

Partly because competition policy and institutions are weak, Greece has made relatively little progress in eliminating anti-competitive regulations.

One of the sharpest tools to cut away thickets of bad regulation is effective competition policy. In Greece, competition policy and institutions have played little role in the process of reforming economic regulations to stimulate competition. Partly as a result, Greece has made relatively little progress, compared to its EU neighbours, in reforming economic regulations that restrict competition.

The new competition law adopted in 2000 shows a new commitment to solving these problems.

Changing priorities and strengthening the competition authorities, as reflected in the new competition law adopted in 2000, is a major step towards solving these problems. The 1995 changes in the law had forced the Competition Committee to spend nearly all of its time and resources on mergers, many trivial, and on applications for relief against alleged abuses of economic dependence, most unrelated to competition policy. On the other hand, harmful restrictive agreements are common, but the Competition Committee could do virtually nothing about them because it lacked funds, facilities, and personnel. Despite its nominal independence, the Competition Committee was too dependent for its budget on the Ministry of Development, which was characterised by a different and inconsistent philosophy dating from the period of price control.

Enduring governance issues are at the heart of the regulatory challenges facing Greece.

Governance issues are at the core of most regulatory problems in Greece.

It is hard to escape the conclusion that governance issues are at the core of most regulatory problems in Greece. Governance problems in the public administration include a lack of necessary skills and incentives for efficiency, institutional rigidities, poor co-ordination, legalistic traditions and a high level of risk avoidance, overly-centralised administration, an environment of non-compliance, and cultural mistrust of market solutions. Clientelism and capture of the policy process by interest groups have, in the past, displaced policy-making in the general public interest. Together, these problems create complex and inefficient regulatory regimes that increase costs and market uncertainties, while reducing the effectiveness of public policy. A large part of the economy – the informal sector – has grown up in part to escape government regulation completely.

Greek regulators still tend to replace the market with state decisions.

Mutual suspicion between the state and the market hampers the performance of both. This is in part a legacy of Greece's post-war decades in which, as Chapter 1 notes, market forces were muted, distorted, or contravened entirely through regulation. Greek regulators still tend to replace the market with state decisions. Current fears of "destructive competition" in the ferry sector, and intentions to ensure "balance in the market" in trucking services illustrate a deep-seated distrust of market forces, andthe inclination to favour the interests of incumbent producers rather than consumers, innovators, and new market entrants.

A recurring problem in Greek market liberalisation is incoherence in implementation of policy decisions. In the crucial telecommunications markets, regulatory reforms are so incomplete or delayed that the market cannot develop. Anti-market decisions, such as awarding the incumbent firm a FWA licence outside of the auction, have eroded market confidence and government credibility, both essential to underpin the investment and market entry that will build the Information Society. Another costly attempt to avoid competition was the 1997 award to local firms of long-term utility procurement contracts – totalling 3.5% of GDP – just before an EU directive would have required open competition for them. This pre-emptive action raised utility costs to the entire economy. In electricity, Greek authorities made several policy choices whose effect is to ensure that the sector remains a stable monopoly, such as not creating immediate competition by splitting generation.

Implementation of sensible reform policies is hampered by a lack of understanding of the market and by policy institutions that are highly vulnerable to vested interests.

These and other examples suggest that implementation of sensible reform policies is hampered by a lack of understanding of the market and by policy institutions that are highly vulnerable to vested interests. Greater emphasis on ensuring consistent implementation decisions, on reducing the capture of policies by special interests, and on creating a strategic vision for the development of competition would provide a more stable and credible policy environment in Greece. As recommended below, a clear reform strategy is needed to avoid piecemeal approaches, conflicting measures and equivocal remedies.

Initiatives of the Greek government over the past decade are, step-by-step, shaping a capacity for better regulatory quality.

Initiatives of the Greek government over the past decade are, step-by-step, shaping a capacity for better regulatory quality. De-politicisation and meritorious promotion of public officials will build public confidence. The multi-year programme to devolve administrative and political powers to local governments will bring the centralised state closer to the citizens and small businesses. Efforts to communicate better and more often with the citizens or public service customers will increase trust and responsiveness. As reflected in the recommendations below, further necessary reforms include better framework laws for the civil service, new regulatory institutions at the centre of government and in the line ministries, more accountable and results-oriented administration, and implementation of disciplines for regulatory quality, such as transparency and regulatory impact analysis tools.

POLICY OPTIONS FOR REGULATORY REFORM

The areas reviewed in this report show that Greece suffers from costly and inefficient regulatory practices. This section identifies actions that, based on international consensus on good regulatory practices and on concrete experiences in OECD countries, are likely to be beneficial to improving regulation in Greece. The summary recommendations presented here are discussed in more detail in the background reports to Chapters 2-6, published in this volume. They are based on the recommendations and policy framework in the OECD Report on Regulatory Reform.

Speed up and improve the implementation of regulatory reform by enhancing accountability in the central government for regulatory quality, and by promoting tools for regulatory quality throughout the public administration.

Regulatory reform can be faster and more effective...

- *To consolidate the various reform initiatives already underway in Greece, adopt at the political level a broad policy statement on regulatory management that establishes clear objectives, accountability principles, and frameworks for implementation.*

...with a government-wide policy on the objectives and tools reform...

The Greek public administration suffers from a mistrust of markets and a vulnerability to special interests that reduces the coherence and implementation of reform. To improve consistency and credibility in regulatory reform programmes, the government should adopt a government-wide regulatory reform policy. The policy should be based on explicit market principles of good economic, social, and administrative regulation such as those in the 1997 OECD *Report to Ministers*. This over-arching framework would:

- Stimulate and direct the efforts of all ministries, building on the efforts on regulatory reform of ministries such as the Ministry of Interior and the Ministry of the National Economy;

- Provide a clearer basis to assess performance and results, and assist in correcting problems more quickly;

- Improve overall coherence and greater accountability of ministries for the quality of their regulations;

- Reduce the risk of capture by special interests by reducing the capacity for decisions contrary to principles of good regulation. Given the web of entrenched interests and traditions of ministerial independence in Greece, personal involvement and direction from the highest political levels will aid greatly regulatory reform.

...backed up by a ministerial-level committee...

- *Establish a ministerial-level Regulatory Reform Committee, with an expert secretariat, to make key regulatory reform decisions and to co-ordinate regulatory reform across government.*

A ministerial-level committee should be created to promote consistent implementation of regulatory reform, to make key regulatory reform decisions, and to co-ordinate reform across government. The committee would also resolve controversies between policies and prepare an annual report to the Parliament assessing progress by the ministries. Participants on the committee could include the Prime Minister's Office and Ministries of, the National Economy, the Interior, Public Administration and Decentralisation, Development and Justice. A representative of the competition authority should be included on the committee. This political body could be modelled on the Netherlands' Ministerial Committee in charge of the influential MDW ('Functioning of Markets, Deregulation and Legislative Quality') programme.

...supported by an expert unit on regulatory reform. ·

- *As a secretariat to the ministerial-level committee, establish an oversight unit with (i) authority to make recommendations to the Regulatory Reform Committee, (ii) adequate capacities to collect information and co-ordinate the reform programme throughout the public administra-*

tion, and (iii) resources and analytical expertise to provide an independent opinion on regulatory matters.

Greece will need an expert institution to provide day-to-day oversight of the ministries and to provide the necessary support to the ministerial committee. Its mandate, political accountability, and operation should be focused on implementation of tools such as regulatory impact analysis and public consultation. The United Kingdom and Italy have created units for good regulation that Greece may want to consider as models, and Mexico has just established an independent Better Regulation Commission that offers a different approach.

Whatever model is used, the unit will need a well-resourced secretariat with cross-governmental authority. It should have sufficient financial resources to collect and assess information and buy the expertise of private experts and scholars. Its mission, powers and legal status in the government's legislative and regulatory process should be formalised. The unit will need authority to advocate and design thematic and sectoral programmes of reform, co-ordinated across relevant policy areas. The unit could develop performance targets, timelines, and evaluation requirements, review regulatory proposals from ministries against quality principles, and advise the centre of government on the quality of regulatory and reform proposals from regulatory ministries.

A step by step programme for regulatory impact analysis is key.

– *Improve the quality of new regulations by implementing across the administration a step-by-step programme for regulatory impact assessment, based on OECD best practice recommendations, for all new and revised regulations. The analysis should begin with feasible steps such as costing of direct impacts (other than budgetary) and provide a qualitative assessment of benefits, and move progressively over a multi-year period to more rigorous quantitative form of analysis as skills are built in the administration. The assessments should be made public so as to enhance transparency as well as provide external discipline to improve the quality and content of the assessments.*

Impact assessment and the use of innovation or regulatory alternatives is poor in Greece relative to other OECD countries, reducing the government's capacity to develop the high quality regulatory framework needed for the current needs of citizens and the market. Most OECD countries now use RIA and the direction of change is universally toward refining, strengthening and extending the use of RIA disciplines. However, in Greece, RIA is in its infancy. Lack of information on impacts of regulatory proposals means that Greece's laws are vulnerable to influence from special interests and less transparent to outside parties.

OECD's best practice principles should be the basis for the Greek RIA programme. The quality of RIAs should be overseen by the expert unit recommended above. A comprehensive trainin programme should be introduced to support capacities for impact assessment. Adequate funding for the programme should be planned (for the production by ministries and review by a central unit).

Use of benefit-cost analysis is the long-term goal, but steps for less demanding forms of analysis consistent with current administrative skills could be implemented immediately. These include incorporating in the justification report required by Article 74 of the Constitution the ten quality dimensions of the 1995 OECD regulatory quality checklist. The OECD checklist could be made mandatory for subordinate legislation, Presidential Decrees and ministerial decisions. Transparency and accountability would be increased if the checklist responses were published on the Internet.

In the medium term (*e.g.* 12 months), the government could create a RIA structured around the benefit-cost principle. A RIA report would be prepared by ministries and agencies and reviewed by a technical and independent unit assessing the quality, content, scope, and adequacy of the analysis. A consistent practice to assess trade and investment effects of proposed regulations should be developed so that RIA can address impacts of proposed regulations on trade and investment. The Cabinet should refuse to discuss proposals that are not accompanied by a RIA, and subordinate regulations should not be signed by the responsible minister if a RIA has not been reviewed by the independent body. RIA should be targeted to only the most important regulations to avoid wasting time and resources on less significant measures. RIA should also be used as the vehicle for a systematic consideration of regulatory alternatives for new regulatory proposals. Preparation of an annual report to Parliament on trends in the use of RIA could increase incentives for its use within the ministries.

Better regulatory and non-regulatory instruments will improve policy results.

- *Promote the systematic consideration of regulatory alternatives for new regulatory proposals, including subordinate legislation.*

A significant omission from the current regulatory quality programme is the failure to promote the use of market based alternatives to regulation when government intervention is justified. The OECD *Report to Ministers on Regulatory Reform*[68] documented movement toward a range of alternative instruments in OECD countries and pointed to evidence on gains in policy effectiveness. By explicitly requiring the consideration of alternatives as mandatory for regulatory proposals including subordinate regulation, Greece can over time move toward a more flexible and efficient regulatory structure that uses markets to achieve public policy goals. The RIA should include a section devoted to the alternatives considered, explaining why those alternatives were not accepted. An initial phase of training and awareness will allow the public sector to gain greater familiarity with alternative policy tools before a formal requirement is imposed across all of government.

Regulatory transparency should be strengthened by…

Improve regulatory transparency through more systematic use of public consultation, continued clarification of procurement criteria, communication to affected members of the public, and codification.

…systematic public consultation…

- *Strengthen the public consultation process to include all subordinate regulations, and adopt uniform notice and comment procedures.*

Prospective regulation should be made available to concerned constituencies for information and comments through formal channels. A mandatory public consultation requirement, based on objective criteria, would substantially improve regulatory quality and transparency. An effective means to improve transparency and accountability would be to adopt a government-wide 'notice and comment' process for all regulations to complement other consultation mechanisms and safeguard against capture by special interests. Recent examples of "notice-and-comment" procedures used by the Ministry of Transport and Communications could serve as a model for expanding and formalising this tool across the administration. Additionally, the government could require the disclosure of regulatory impact analysis as part of the notice and comment process. All responses and comments should be available to the public.

To improve the efficiency of consultation, it is essential to promote the confidence of the private sector and the citizens in general in the consultation mechanisms. Confidence-building measures mainly consist of clear rules of the game and transparent outcomes. Consultation timetables and participation criteria should be clearly identified.

...improving the practice of public procurement...

– *Ensure that new controls to improve the clarity of public procurement procedures are well-enforced in practice.*

Ongoing efforts to improve the clarity of pre-selection and award criteria for public procurement are welcome, and should be effectively enforced. The recent improvement of opportunities of affected parties to obtain effective judicial relief through speedy and low-cost appeal procedures is an important step.

...and improving communication.

– *Make information on applicable regulations more easily accessible.*

Informal and occasional initiatives to display information on the Internet should be formalised and applied in a systematic manner across the administration. Efforts should be made to display elements of interest to foreign partners in English. Information desks and call centres should also be more widely used across the administration. Local gateways allowing access to information at the prefectural and municipal level should be further developed. Authorities initiating new regulation should have the responsibility to consistently bring local or central information desks, such as the ELKE, up-to-date with regulatory requirements.

Codification can reduce uncertainty.

– *To reduce legal uncertainty, initiate a programme of codification.*

Greece should aim initially to prepare an inventory of all laws, including subordinate regulations. This should allow for the development of a single authoritative source for all regulations that is easily understood and accessible to the citizens and business alike. Furthermore, it would significantly enhance transparency for users in terms of the content and form of permissible regulatory actions thus helping improve compliance levels.

Administrative barriers such should be attached through several strategies.

Intensify efforts to reduce administrative barriers to businesses by establishing a central registry of administrative procedures and licences, considering the "silence is consent" rule, and initiating a comprehensive review to determine how to reduce burdens.

Administrative burdens, and in particular business licences and permits are among the most important barriers to Greek entrepreneurs and to market entry. By fostering non-compliance and promoting grey regulation they nourish unfair competition with the legal economy and maintain barriers to market access. Abolition of this type of regulation can bring swift economic gains, reduce the size of the informal economy, and build a constituency among SMEs for further reform.

Greek authorities have engaged in a series of projects to rationalise administrative procedures affecting citizens in general and businesses in particular. Some of them, like the TAXIS project, are now operational, while others, like the simplification of industrial licensing procedures, are still in the process of being set up. The Greek government will have to monitor the operation of these projects in close consultation with affected parties, in order to check their efficiency, single out failures and gaps and identify further needed improvements. Other tools can be considered. For instance, in the area of licensing procedures, deadlines should be introduced for regulatory action, after which silence is considered consent. The prefectural "one-stop-shops" should be assessed with respect to the concrete impact of their actions on business activity.

To obtain results rapidly, a mandatory and complete registry of all formalities should first be organised, with positive legal security. If a formality is not registered in the inventory, then it should not be enforced. As a second step, the formalities in the inventory should be reviewed systematically against consistent criteria, and if possible eliminated or replaced by less burdensome instruments. To accelerate benefits to SMEs, priority in the selection of forms should be based on business opinions. Examples which Greece could consider include the French Centre d'Évaluation et de Registre des Formalités (CERFA), the Mexican Registro Federal de Tramites,[69] the American Paperwork Reduction Act process, and the Spanish Comision de Simplificacion.

Review of old regulations will help modernise domestic policies.

To combat regulatory inflation and update older regulations, review and evaluate existing regulations and paperwork.

Regulatory inflation is undermining the integrity of the Greek regulatory system. Although this is a very large task, efforts should be made to develop a rolling, systematic process of codification and evaluation of existing laws and other regulations. A sector by sector review, with more economically-important sectors reviewed first, would be one way to organise such a programme. The review should incorporate regulatory impact assessments. In such reviews, the 1995 OECD regulatory quality checklist could be used as a reference to check the continued necessity and appropriateness of regulations. To support the review, the Parliament or government could directly or though an independent commission review the main areas of legislation. The review process undertaken in Australia as part of its National Competition Policy is illustrative. Under that policy, all legislation was reviewed and anti-competitive restrictions were required to be removed unless it could be demonstrated that those restrictions were in the public interest and that there was no other way to achieve public policy objectives.[70] The Australian review will take 5 years to complete and, to ensure ongoing quality, will be repeated every 10 years.

Coordination with local governments will preserve regulatory quality as decentralisation proceeds.

Encourage greater co-ordination between local government and the central administration by i) defining clearly relevant regulatory competencies for each level of government, ii) providing resources, people, and financing for delivery of services that those competencies dictate, and iii) assisting in the development of management capacities for quality regulation at all levels of administration.

The decentralisation process undertaken since the mid-1990s has enhanced local government capacities and competencies. As decentralisation proceeds, other countries' experiences show that intensive efforts are needed to safeguard regulatory quality at sub-national levels. Overlapping responsibilities between levels of government require co-ordination and co-operation to avoid regulatory layering and new burdens and costs on business and citizens. Strong accountability and transparency measures, such as the notice and comment mechanism, would reduce the risk that local governments will be captured by special interests. Adoption by local governments of regulatory quality principles would be useful, as would processes and mechanisms to resolve issues arising from regulatory conflicts or overlap. This will help ensure greater policy coherence. Monitoring (or even benchmarking) from the national administration would help to avoid reversals, while encouraging progress at the sub-national level.

A focus on quality of public sector outcomes is needed

Improve mechanisms within the administration to produce quality outcomes for the citizens through further reform of the civil service.

The culture of the Greek public administration is gradually moving away from legalism and formalism to focus on results. This will have direct and positive impacts on all phases of regulatory quality, including regulatory development, enforcement and compliance. Elements of further reform could include performance-based management focussed on policy results, pay incentives for public servants, greater flexibility within the public administration, and enhanced co-ordination and co-operation between ministries. Improving the output of the public administration requires a flexible recruitment system in which skills match policy needs, particularly for economic policy analysis. Incentives should be aligned with written and public objectives. Flexibility should be introduced to encourage public servants to move within and between ministries. Training and skills development should be enhanced. Of particular importance will be the adequate enforcement and encouragement of public servants to comply with the new Code of Administrative Procedure Act and the Civil Service Code.

Competition policy should be strengthened by...

Following the new competition law of August 2000, take further steps to strengthen the capacities, expand the role, and target the priorities of the Competition Committee.

...expanding resources...

– *Expand staff resources at the Competition Committee, at least to levels already authorised by statute, and authorise recruitment and compensation comparable to what has been authorised for other, high-profile agencies.*

Some bodies, such as the Capital Markets Committee, have authority to hire outside of the usual process and to pay up to 50% more than the standard pay scale in order to attract people with the qualifications they need. If competition policy is to have a significant role in reform, its institutions should have equivalent treatment. Recent amendments to the law give the Competition Committee power to hire independently, and double the authorised staff level.

...bolstering independence...

– *Provide for independence of financial support, so that the formally independent Competition Committee is not subject to oversight by a ministry with inconsistent priorities.*

To ensure that competition policy institutions can operate independently, their sources of funds must not be tied to such a narrow and changeable base. One way would be for the budget to be separately authorised by Parliament. Another, which was adopted by recent legislation, would be to establish an independent source of funding, such as fees for applications or small charges on capital market transactions and registrations. The appearance of being tied to industry interests should also be overcome, by eliminating the power of business and industry associations to designate members of the Competition Committee

...targeting merger reviews...

– *De-emphasise merger review by setting higher merger thresholds or otherwise changing the decision rules.*

This will permit the Competition Committee to concentrate only on the small number of mergers that may actually have anti-competitive effects and will no longer delay other transactions for too long, or use too many of its resources processing them. Greater resources for the competition institutions would be wasted, if they continued to be spent on detailed reviews of mergers that are highly unlikely to present problems for competition. The law was recently amended to increase the thresholds. Another step would be to fundamentally change the decision process so that most mergers can be treated quickly under a more summary process, like that which applies to the "notification" category.

...emphasizing horizontal abuses...

– *Shift attention to horizontal agreements.*

Additional resources in competition policy should be assigned to the endemic problem of excessive co-operation among Greek businesses. Clear enforcement of the statutory prohibition will help Greek businesses prepare for the vigorous competition of the wider European market.

...wider advocacy powers...

– *Empower the Competition Committee to advocate competition principles throughout the public sector.*

Normally, where there is a long tradition of state ownership and government control over market institutions, a high priority should be given to advocacy. A change in the law has made it clear that the Competition Committee can offer opinions on its own initiative, without waiting for a request from some other entity. In addition, though, the Competition Committee's prestige and credibility must be restored, through more effective enforcement, before policy advice and advocacy can be credible. A prime subject of attention could be the potentially anti-competitive effect of the extensive licensing requirements that are used to control entry into many businesses, administered principally by the Ministry of Development. For this advocacy to be effective, the Competition Committee must achieve full independence from ministerial influence.

...participation in de-monopolisation policies...

 – *Assign the Competition Committee a role in the process of introducing competition into previously monopolised network industries.*

Such a role could increase its prestige as well as help ensure that the process promotes competitive outcomes. The relevant sectoral institutions, which are just being set up, appear to have had little contact with the Competition Committee so far. Both the Competition Committee and these sectoral institutions would profit from more extensive and formal interaction. The Competition Committee should be involved in the process of creating institutional responsibilities and relationships needed to achieve the appropriate division of labour.

...expanding responsibilities for promoting competition...

 – *Broaden the base of responsibility for supporting competition.*

Making other ministries as well as sectoral regulators responsible for eliminating constraints on competition within their own jurisdictions would extend the scope of competition policy and emphasise its broad, horizontal importance. The Competition Committee should play a central role. These other bodies should be held responsible for co-ordinating with the Competition Committee to promote expeditious enforcement.

...and ensuring that market openness issues are considered.

 – *Promote the application of competition principles from an international perspective.*

Market openness will be improved by...

Promote market openness by reducing discrimination in domestic regulation and encouraging the use of international standards and quality certification.

...reducing regulatory discrimination...

 – *Reduce discriminatory elements in the regulatory framework for services.*

Constraints on entry into regulated service markets, and in particular limitations on foreign service providers, should be assessed and eliminated unless they can be clearly justified as the best way to obtain legitimate public policy goals. The current review of the regulatory framework for professional services is a good opportunity to reconsider discriminatory elements.

...and wider use of international standards.

 – *Continue to encourage the use of international standards as a basis for national standardisation activities and to promote international harmonisation at European, regional and international levels.*

The use of internationally harmonised standards facilitates the access of new and innovative foreign products to the domestic market for the benefit of Greek consumers and enhances the market opportunities of Greek firms and products world-wide. Assisting neighbouring countries to move towards harmonised standardisation systems will help consolidate efficient and transparent markets in the wider Balkan and Black Sea area, where many Greek businesses actively seek to expand activities. The increased reliance on market-driven specifications will offer domestic firms the necessary flexibility to pursue the most efficient business strategies and promote innovation.

Quality control and certification should gain more prominence in the business culture if the Greek market is to benefit fully from international standards. Information campaigns by the government and major professional associations to promote the concept of quality control should be pursued. Domestic firms, and especially SMEs, should be encouraged and assisted in using certification. ELOT should continue its efforts to reinforce its quality control and certification mechanisms. As part of a wider endeavour to build market confidence in the operation of harmonisation and mutual recognition systems, the Greek government should step up efforts to activate domestic accreditation mechanisms. The National Accreditation Council should intensify operations and should establish a reputation of reliability.

Privatisation must proceed rapidly.

Complete privatisation of structurally competitive services and industries.

Chapter 1 noted that public enterprises account for 6% of employment and 27% of investment, yet almost all public enterprises are poorly managed and inefficient. Structurally competitive services and industries for which privatisation should be completed include tourist facilities, travel agencies, airline catering, airlines, and petroleum product distribution. In this process, it must be clear that competition policy institutions have the ability, and the responsibility, to ensure that these transactions do not perpetuate market power in private hands but instead result in workably competitive markets.

Structural and regulatory reforms are needed to boost efficiency in electricity...

In the electricity sector, develop effective competition in generation and supply,...

– *Separate the ownership of the networks from ownership of generation and supply. Where this is not feasible, create an Independent System Operator with a governance structure to ensure efficient and non-discriminatory access.*

Effective competition requires an adequate number of competitors and efficient, non-discriminatory access to essential networks. Separate ownership of the networks from the potentially competitive activities of generation and supply reduces incentives for discrimination, whereas separate operation of the system from generation reduces the ability to discriminate. An Independent System Operator, with a governance structure that ensures the reflection of consumers and generators' interests, is more likely to operate the system in an efficient and non-discriminatory manner.

— *Access to transmission and distribution grids should be subject to regulation by an independent regulator.*

Even where ownership, or operation, of the networks is separated from that of generation, there remain incentives to price access above efficient levels. Independent regulation can ensure that the access terms are efficient.

— *Ensure efficient and non-discriminatory access to international transmission links. Reduce barriers to foreign supply, including specifically by requiring PPC to make available reserve capacity at regulated, cost-reflected prices*

The structure and small size of the Greek electricity market imply that foreign competitors will be important in reducing market power.

— *Take steps to reduce barriers to domestic entry, notably regulate access to the grids so that access is granted on terms that are efficient and non-discriminatory. Also, provide an expedited procedure to resolve access disputes.*

Domestic entry would increase the number of independent competitors. There are a number of features of the regulatory regime that discourage entry. Among these are the limited enforcement regime for access.

— *Create competing generating companies, without common ownership, designed to create effective competition.*

Splitting generation into competing companies, sold separately, would create a healthier competitive environment. It would also reduce the need to rely on competitors from outside the European Union.

— *Ensure that the application of competition law to the electricity sector prevents abuse of dominance or anti-competitive agreements, mergers, and long-term contracts that risk frustrating the development of competition.*

...develop regulatory institutions that promote investment, efficiency, and competition,...

— *Transfer to the Energy Regulatory Authority final regulatory authority for generating and supply authorisation, tariffs, and access to transmission and distribution. Endow the ERA with human and other resources that enable it to independently and effectively regulate the sector. Ensure that the budget, personnel and other internal decisions, of ERA are independent of the Ministry. Ensure that the ERA decision-making process is transparent, such as through public consultation processes, and that it is accountable.*

Greece needs to establish a non-discriminatory, stable regulatory framework. The first step is to establish the institutions of this framework. Among the requirements is for the regulator to be independent of day-to-day political pressures, and independent of the regulated companies.

– *Ensure that the Ministry of Development acquires or develops the technical expertise, independent of any company, to make electricity policy.*

...improve the corporate governance of PPC to a fully commercial basis,...

The government should transform the relationship between itself and PPC to a more commercial basis. The government should expect to receive dividends at the same rate as a private shareholder and should not be responsible for guaranteeing any new debt of PPC. The management and board of directors of PPC require sufficient autonomy so that they can make investment and other decisions on commercial criteria. Finally, after PPC is partially privatised, to enhance the board's decision-making process, the government should make appointments to the board of directors that would represent the interest of the minority shareholders.

...and evaluate the state of the electricity sector, after some time, with a view to further reform.

Reform of the electricity sector is an on-going process, with experience prompting demand for further reform or fine-tuning. The government should review the sector in the short term (*e.g.* two to three years) to judge whether effective competition is developing and electricity companies are increasing efficiency. Comparisons with other countries would be particularly valuable.

...and regulatory safeguards are needed in telecommunications to create a Greek information society.

The newest telecommunications law made much progress, but essential regulatory safeguards should be established to lay the foundation for the Greek information society by ensuring full competition in the market.

– *Organise EETT as an independent communications sector regulator and thus clearly differentiate between MTC's policy responsibilities from regulatory responsibilities.*

Creation of an independent regulatory body is of prime importance in Greece to ensure transparent and non-discriminatory regulations aimed at maximisation of consumer welfare through a market-oriented regime. The allocation of a number of important responsibilities to the independent regulator, as foreseen in the new law, should improve the effectiveness of regulation and help eliminate any potential conflict between the regulator and Ministry. An urgent effort needs to be made to rapidly increase the number of EETT's staff and improve its level of expertise.

– *Implement a price cap system for OTE's PSTN prices. Ensure an efficient system of prior approval of prices for prices outside of a price cap basket.*

The regulation of prices through government authorisation is not appropriate for current competitive circumstances particularly since so far it has been driven by political considerations rather than the pro-competitive need for price flexibility. There has been insufficient competitive pressure in a number of market segments on OTE to increase efficiency and improve pricing structures. The independent regulatory body should implement price cap regulation rapidly. For prices outside the price cap basket a system of prior approval needs to be put in place which is efficient and rapid. OTE should also be required to implement 'per second' pricing for voice services.

> – *Implement an interconnection pricing framework using long-run average incremental cost (LRAIC) as the appropriate cost basis for pricing. and ensure that an agreed interconnection offer is available to support full market liberalisation.*

> – *Ensure that prices are rebalanced as rapidly as possible providing a transparent target to the incumbent to achieve this goal.*

Assuring interconnection to the incumbent's public switched telephone network is a key competitive safeguard. Such safeguards are particularly important where the incumbent carrier, like OTE, is vertically integrated into local, long distance and other services and therefore has strong incentives to hinder equal access. Progress in establishing an effective interconnection regime is important to assuring that the benefits generated from competitive market structures are fully realised. The current methodology used to determine interconnection charges forces new entrants to pay high interconnection charges. Efficient pricing needs to be based on forward-looking LRAIC costs, including a reasonable profit margin. An interconnection offer should have already been made available for new entrants. It is important that such an agreed offer is available before full market opening otherwise this will lead to delays. Consideration should also be given to introducing an interconnection offer to allow for unmetered interconnection services. Development of competition and local loop unbundling require that prices are rebalanced. OTE and the regulator need to agree on a target date to achieve rapid rebalancing.

> – *Implement number portability and full pre-selection as rapidly as possible and ensure that numbering allocation policies for both wireline and mobile carriers are competitively neutral.*

Local loop competition will not be able to develop effectively unless number portability and pre-selection allows customers to reduce the "transaction costs" of changing service provider and choosing the cheapest provider. The further delay that has been given to OTE to implement these requirements effectively strengthens its market power and slows down competition. OTE has had a sufficient lead-time to prepare for competition so that no further delays are necessary. This is important in the fixed telecommunication service market but should also be implemented for the mobile market.

> – *Develop an adequate methodology to cost universal service.*

The government needs to establish a transparent universal service funding mechanism that is competitively and technologically neutral. Current universal service obligations on OTE will be maintained until the end of 2001.

> – Use auctions to allocate licences in the mobile sector and also to allocate licences for the 3rd generation mobile services. Ensure that the incumbent is required to participate for a fixed wireless access licence on the same terms and conditions as other potential licensees.

Auctions allow for more transparency and increasing regulatory efficiency in spectrum allocation. The auction system chosen for wireless in the local loop licences should be maintained for all wireless licences. The incumbent should not be provided a FWA licence on an unfair and discriminatory basis, but should be subject to the same requirements as other potential new market entrants.

> – Reduce barriers to entry by introducing a system of general authorisations rather than individual licences. Conditions which need to be attached to licences can be through a general licensing framework.

In order to simplify and streamline regulations Greece could immediately adopt a class licensing system that relies on simple authorisation for market entry. This would accelerate market entry and reduce bureaucratic barriers to market entry. It would also be an important step in implementing best-practice regulatory models.

> – Review regulations in all areas of telecommunications regularly and systematically with a view to streamlining and where appropriate abandoning them.

The government already reviews regulations, but these reviews need to be conducted more systematically and in depth to ascertain whether the regulations are still in the public interest, benefit users, and whether such regulation should be abandoned or modified. "Forbearance" procedures (or "sunset clauses") should be incorporated to ensure that regulations no longer necessary are eliminated and the industry should be given the right to request reviews of laws and regulation's to increase efficiency and reduce market barriers. EETT should be required in its Annual Report to examining the potential for streamlining regulations.

> – Ensure independent operation of the incumbent.

Although subject to asymmetric regulation, it is important that the incumbent be allowed to act independently in the market without undue interference from the government, its major shareholder. The ongoing procedure to obtain a strategic partner for the incumbent is encouraging and the aim should be to achieve rapid full privatisation of the incumbent. In the meantime the government should not attempt to maintain control over its operation other than through transparent laws and regulations.

MANAGING REGULATORY REFORM

Maintaining and strengthening the support of key groups in society is vital for the future of reform.

Maintaining and strengthening the support of key groups in society is vital for the future of reform. Yet many SMEs do not perceive differences in their operating environments as a result of efforts to reduce administrative burdens.

A vigorous public debate will be needed if regulatory reform is to be seen as a strategy for achieving domestic social and economic objectives, rather than as painful crisis management that can be abandoned once recovery is underway.

The sustainability of regulatory reform in Greece will depend on the balance of programme goals, and on the achievement of tangible results. Managing this change to ensure that consumers, small business and others are equipped to protect their interests in a more open and competitive marketplace is essential if unnecessary costs are to be avoided and support for reform is to be maintained. A vigorous public debate will be needed if regulatory reform is to be seen as a strategy for achieving important domestic social and economic objectives, rather than as grudging accommodation of external pressures that is preferably delayed as long as possible.

NOTES

1. Minister of Development, Press Conference on 11th May 2000. Reproduced in the website of the Ministry at www.ypan.gr. Unofficial translation by the Secretariat.

2. European Union Single Market Scoreboard, November 1999.

3. Carey J. and Carey A. (1968), *The Web of Modern Greek Politics*, New York and London: Colombia University Press, p. 85, as cited in Stergiou Kaloudis, George (2000), *Modern Greek Democracy: The End of Long Journey?*, University Press of America, p. 14.

4. OECD (2000), *Economic survey of Greece 2000*.

5. Labour Institute of GSEE-ADEDY (1999).

6. Nikiforos Diamandouros "Greek Politics and Society in the 1990s" in *The Greek Paradox*. *Promise vs. Performance*, The MIT Press, 1997. The author identifies three structural weaknesses explaining in part the underperformance of the economy from 1974 to 1995: the discriminatory political system in post-war Greece, which introduced political non-meritocratic and clientelistic criteria for state employment, causing deficiencies in civil service skills and the impossibility of effective quality control; the particularistic logic of distribution of social and economic benefits in society, reducing the accountability of the State and producing perceptions of inequity; and the resulting fragmentation of productive structures, which made them dependent on State protection for their continued growth and survival.

7. Katseli (1990).

8. The share of public sector expenditures in GDP increased from 38.8% in 1973 to 48.5% in 1981. Ministry of National Economy (1998).Total transfers of the general government (including transfers to individuals), as a per cent of GDP, surpassed 13% by 1979.

9. Alogoskoufis (1996).

10. Alogoskoufis (1996).

11. The investment incentive law of 1982 provided subsidies, and favoured labour-intensive industries, as well as investments in areas outside Athens. However, the effectiveness of the law was low, as it resulted in investment largely in traditional industries, and in many cases the companies thus subsidised failed.

12. United Nations, Economic Commission for Europe (1998).

13. Sarris, *et. al.* (1999).

14. Currently, a committee is investigating the options for deep tax reform and will report in early 2002.

15. Kanellopoulos, Tsatiris, and Mitrakos (1999).

16. Balfousias (1998).

17. Angeletos and Kollintzas (2000).

18. Zografakis and Sarris (1997). The model simulates recursively a sequence of annual equilibria for the economy, and has been calibrated on a 1988 complete benchmark data set, including sectoral detail. The simulations assumed that full liberalisation occurred in the first period and that the regulatory framework remains unchanged for 10 years. The economy-wide employment effects of the decline in prices of the relevant sectors appear to be slightly negative, with total employment, compared to the no reform scenario, declining gradually to a maximum of around 0.4% of the total labour force by the tenth year of the simulation. This decline results primarily from the decreased employment in the liberalising sectors, as a consequence of overmanning, and is probably an overestimate, as the model does not take into account the potential entry of new firms in these sectors

19. For a relevant model of unproductive public labour see Gelb et. al. (1991), while for a theoretical model of the negative impact of corruption and growth see Angeletos and Kollintzas (1999).

20. Zografakis and Sarris (1997).

21. Prime Minister's programme declaration to Parliament on 22 April 2000.

22. In 1998 the OECD measured the number of public sector employees in Greece, not including state owned enterprises, as representing approximately 10% of the total work force. This is not high relative to France (25%), Finland (24%), Portugal (18%), or Spain (15%) and it is below OECD average of 17%. OECD (1998) The Public Employment Service: Greece, Ireland, Portugal, Paris, Table 1.4.

23. One factor that has impinged on the flexibility of the public sector is the high rate of growth of the number of employees in the past decade. Public sector employment grew from 106 000 in 1961, 116 000 in 1963, 134 000 in 1974, 157 000 in 1977, 200 000 in 1981, 234 000 in 1985, 237 000 in 1990, to 290 000 in 1999. (Government of Greece, Ministry of the Interior, Public Administration, and Decentralisation, data supplied in April 2000). With the introduction of a new recruiting policy, the Greek government also tried to reduce the size of the public sector work force. In 1998, the government introduced a policy of "1 for 5" that means that for every five positions that become vacant due to retirement or departure, only one position is replaced. ASEP is supposed to enforce this policy. However, due to numerous exemptions, this initiative has had little impact.

24. Spraos (1998), "Quality in Public Administration: Recommendations for Changes", Commissioned for the examination of the long-term economic policy, Financed by the National Bank of Greece.

25. Refer to Law 2190/1994.

26. OECD (1996), *Report on Public Sector Pay*, Paris.

27. OECD (1997), *The OECD Report on Regulatory Reform: Synthesis*, Paris, p. 37.

28. Spraos (1998), idem.

29. Deighton-Smith, Rex (1997), "*Regulatory Impact Analysis: Best Practice in OECD Countries*" in OECD (1997), *Regulatory Impact Analyses: Best Practice in OECD Countries*, Paris, p. 221.

30. The Council of State was created in 1929 and modelled on the French Conseil d'État, though its members are magistrates and not civil servants. It is also the supreme administrative appeal court.

31. It should be noted though, that the choice of instrument is not always open between Presidential Decree and ministerial decision.

32. See also Spanou, Calliope (1996), "On the Regulatory Capacity of the Hellenic State: a Tentative Approach Based on a Case Study" in *International Review of Administrative Science*, Vol. 62.

33. Spraos (1998), *Quality in Public Administration: Recommendations for Changes*, financed by the National Bank of Greece

34. The ESC involvement in the legislative process was formalised by Law 2232/1994

35. The Council is made up of 9 associations, 8 social bodies, and 2 scientists, and it meets 4-5 times a year. The Council was created under Law 2251/94.

36. For more information, see www.parliament.gr and www.et.gr.

37. OECD (1999), "Background Report on Government Capacities to Produce High Quality Regulations" in *Regulatory Reform in Mexico*, Paris.

38. A Ministerial Decision by the Minister of Public Administration established in November 2000 a Regulatory Reform Committee. The Committee consists of the Vice- President of the Council of State, public law professors, special scientists and high-level bureaucrats in public administration (Ministries of National Economy, Justice, Development, Labour, Public Works, Telecommunications, the Competition Committee, Capital Market Commission etc.).The Committee's work has been supported by international experts.

39. The *Spraos Report* recommended to the Prime Minister in 1998 that RIA as recommended by the OECD should be implemented, Spraos (1998).

40. See article 74 of the Constitution.

41. Views expressed by the Ministry of Development, the Ministry of Finance, the Ministry of the National Economy, and the Ministry of the Interior, Public Administration, and Decentralisation.

42. For further guidance see Broder, I and Morral, J (1997), "Collecting and Using Data for Regulatory Decision-Making" in OECD (1997), *Regulatory Impact Analysis: Best Practices in OECD Countries*, Paris.

43. Spanou, Calliope (1996), p. 219.

44. US Department of Commerce, Country Commercial Guide, Greece Fiscal Year 2000, Chapter Investment Climate, http://www.usatrade.gov/website/CCG.nsf/byuid/.

45. Response to the OECD Regulatory Reform questionnaire (March 2000).

46. Information provided by the Ombudsman.

47. IOBE, The Greek Economy, 2/99, No. 22 November 1999, pp24-26 and US Department of Commerce, idem, p. 6. Greece ranks 36th in the Transparency International Index for Corruption Perceptions index. For further information see http://www.transparency.org/documents/cpi/index.html.

48. See OECD (2000), *Regulatory Compliance Report*, Paris.

49. This is provided for by the Code of Administrative Procedure and in Law 2690/1999 which sets rules of administrative action and the conditions for the communication and carrying out those actions.

50. Ombudsman, personal interview.

51. Formal competencies were transferred from the State both to regions and local authorities by Law 2647/98.

52. See Law 2773/1999.

53. IMF Staff Report on Greece for the 1999 Article IV Consultation Supplementary Information pp 200-201 and the Economist Intelligence Unit (1999-2000) Country Profile Greece, pp. 32-34.

54. See Law 2651/1998 and Law 2744/1999.

55. Figures in this and the following paragraph come from the OECD Main Economic Indicators of July 2000, and the National Statistical Service of Greece.

56. According to the World Markets Research Centre "it is as a base for expansion into the Balkans that the country will lay claim to further foreign direct investment." http://www.worldmarketsonline.com. The interests of investors have changed considerably to adjust to the geopolitical and economic development of the region. In 1992, surveys indicated that 42% of investors viewed Greece as an entry point to EU markets and another 23% aimed primarily at the Balkans and Eastern Europe. In 1997, however, these percentages were 3% and 80%, respectively (Hassid, 1997).

57. Country Commercial Guides. Greece FY 2000 "Investment Climate". See also the World Markets Research Center Country Assessment for 1999.

58. See Hassid, Joseph, *Strategies for the Attraction of Foreign Direct Investment in Greece*, Study commissioned by the Ministry of Development to the University of Piraeus, July 1997 and Foreign Enterprises in Greece, Survey conducted for the American Chamber of Commerce in Greece, September 1997. On the problems related to the fiscal legislation and to labour and social security legislation, see Chapter 1 on the Regulatory Reform in Greece, covering macro-economic issues.

59. *"The complexity and excessive amount of regulation … are due to the frequent changes of the fiscal regulation, its innumerable cross-references and exceptions and the absence of popularisation informative material for the taxpayer."* Spraos (1997), A More Efficient Management of Public Revenues, Commission for the Review of Long-term Economic Policy, Athens.

60. USTR 1999 National Trade Estimate Report on Foreign Trade Barriers – European Union.

61. ISO/IEC Guide 2, EN45020.

62. See Nikos Kastrinos and Fernando Romero (1997), "Policies for Competitiveness in Less-favored Regions of Europe: a Comparison of Greece and Portugal" in *Science and Public Policy*, 24(2), June.

63. The composition of the Coastal Transport Advisory Committee is: the Secretary General of the Ministry of Merchant Marine (Chairman), the Director of the Domestic Sea Transport Directorate of the MMM, the General Director of Merchant Ships Control General Directorate of MMM, a shipping expert appointed by the Minister, and one representative each from the following organisations: Ministry of the Aegean Sea, Ministry of Transport and Communications, Greek National Tourist Organisation, Hellenic Chamber of Shipping, Piraeus Chamber of Commerce and Industry, and three ship-owners (one from short coastal shipping, one from Mediterranean cargo shipping, and one from passenger coastal shipping).

64. Council Regulation No. 3577 of 7 December 1992 applying the principle of freedom to provide services to maritime transport within Member States (maritime cabotage) OJ L 364 of 12.12.92, p. 7.

65. The Greek government's primary concern, in 1995, with respect to the Italian-Greek routes was the viability of the route and the avoidance of any possible "price war" which could possibly hinder the smooth promotion of export and import trade or the transport of vehicles and passengers, (EC para. 103).

66. Article1, para 2 of Directive 98/61/EC with regard to operator number portability and carrier pre-selection allows for a maximum period of two years for the implementation of number portability in those countries which have been granted an additional transition period for full liberalisation of voice telephony services.

67. According to company officials they had submitted an application in February 1999 and were awarded a license in May 2000.

68. Jacobs, Scott *et al.* (1997), pp. 220-222.

69. See OECD (1999), "Background Report on Government Capacities to Produce High Quality Regulation" in *The* OECD *Report on Regulatory Reform: Regulatory Reform in Mexico,* Paris.

70. For further information see, Hilmer, F, Raynor, M., and Taperell, G. (1993), The Independent Committee of Inquiry, *National Competition Policy,* AGPS, Canberra, Australia.
Or http://www.ncc.gov.au/nationalcompet/Legislation%20Review/Legislation%20Review.htm.

BIBLIOGRAPHY

Cited

A. In English

Angeletos G-M. and Kollintzas, T. (2000),
"Rent Seeking/Corruption and Growth: A Simple Model", Centre for Economic Policy Research, Discussion Paper No. 2464, May.

Center for Economic Research and Environmental Strategy (CERES) (1996),
"Trade, Labour and Capital Flows: The Less-Developed Regions", report prepared for the European Commission, DG V, Athens.

Gelb, A., Knight, J.B. and Sabot, R.H. (1991),
"Public Sector Employment, Rent Seeking, and Economic Growth", *Economic Journal*, V.ol. 101, September.

Kanellopoulos, K., Tsatiris, G., and Mitrakos, T. (1999),
Structural Change and Banking Employment, Hellenic Bank Association, December.

Katseli, L.T. (1990),
"Economic integration in the enlarged European Community: structural adjustment of the Greek economy", in C. Bliss and J. Braga de Macedo (editors), *Unity with diversity in the European economy: the Community's Southern frontier*, Cambridge, Cambridge University Press.

Lianos, T., Sarris, A.H., and Katseli, L. (1996),
"Illegal Immigration and Local Labour Markets: The Case of Northern Greece", *International Migration*, vol. XXXIV, No. 3, September.

Ministry of National Economy (1999),
"The 1999 Update of the Hellenic Convergence Program: 1999-2002", December.

Nicoletti, G. Scarpetta, S, and Boylaud O. (1999),
"Summary indicators of product market regulation with an extension to employment protection legislation", OECD Economics Department, Working Paper 226.

OECD (1993, 1995-96, 1997, 1998, 2000),
Economic Surveys of Greece: 1993, 1995-96, 1997, 1998, 2000, Paris.

Sarris, A., and Markova, E. (2000),
"The Decision to Legalise by Bulgarian Immigrants in Greece", mimeographed, Department of Economics, University of Athens, April.

Sarris, A.H., Papadimitriou, P. and Mavrogiannis, A. (1999),
"Country case study: Greece", in M. Brulhart, and R.C. Hine, (editors), *Intra-Industry Trade and Adjustment: The European Experience*, MacMillan Press.

Sarris, A. and S. Zografakis (1999),
"A Computable General Equilibrium Assessment of the Impact of Illegal Immigration on the Greek Economy", *Journal of Population Economics*, Vol. 12, No. 1.

B. In Greek

Alogoskoufis, G. (1996),
"The two faces of Janus: Institutions, Economic Development and Balance of Payments in Greece", Meletes Oikonomikis Politikis, IMOP, June.

Balfousias, T. T., (1998),
"Management Cost of the Greek Taxation System", Center for Planning and Economic Research (KEPE), Athens, September.

Demekas, D. G., and Z. G. Kontolemis (1998),
"Unemployment in Greece: Review of problems", Institute of Economic and Industrial Research (IOVE), Economic Subjects, No. 7, January.

Institute of Labor of the General Confederation of Labor (GSEE) and Confederation of Public Employees (ADEDY), (1999),
The Greek Economy and Employment, Annual Report, 1999, Report No. 1, Athens, August.

Institute of Labor of the General Confederation of Labor (GSEE) and Confederation of Public Employees (ADEDY), (2000),
The Greek Economy and Employment, Annual Report, 2000. Report No. 2, Athens, August.

Ministry of National Economy, (1999a),
Community Support Framework, Third Evaluation Report, Section A. Athens, July.

Ministry of National Economy, (1999b),
"Current Developments and Prospects for the Greek and International Economy, Semi-annual Report", Issue No. 31, Athens, December.

Sarris, A. (co-ordinator) (1995),
"A Social Accounting Matrix for Greece for 1980", University of Athens, Department of Economics, research report for project "Construction of multisectoral general equilibrium model for Greece" financed by the General Secretariat for Research and Technology (GGET).

Zografakis, S. and A. Sarris (1997),
"A Dynamic General Equilibrium Model of the Greek Economy", final report prepared under research programme EPET2 of the General Secretariat of Research and Technology, Ministry of Development, University of Athens, Department of Economics, Athens, December.

United Nations, Economic Commission for Europe (1998),
Economic Survey of Europe, New York and Geneva.

2. Not cited but utilised

In English

International Monetary Fund (1999),
Greece: Staff Report for the 1999 Article IV Consultation, IMF Staff Report No. 99/131, November.

Koedijk, K., and Kremers, J. (1996),
"Market Opening, Regulation and Growth in Europe", Economic Policy, No. 23, October.

Leandros, N. and R. Loufir (1998),
The Future of Pensions in Greece, Institute of Economic and Industrial Research (IOVE), June.

Mylonas, P. and I. Joumard (1999),
"Greek Public Enterprises: Challenges for Reform", OECD Economics Department Working Paper No. 214, Paris.

In Greek

American Hellenic Chamber of Commerce (1997),
Foreign Firms in Greece, Athens, September.

Bank of Greece (Various Years),
Annual Report of the Governor.

Bank of Greece (2000),
Monetary Policy 1999-2000, Athens, February.

Committee for the Examination of Long Term Economic Policy (1997),
Economy and Pensions, National Bank of Greece.

Committee for the Examination of Long Term Economic Policy (1997),
Price Deflation and Incomes Policy 1998-99. National Bank of Greece.

Committee for the Examination of Long Term Economic Policy (1997),
   More Efficient Management of Public Revenues, National Bank of Greece.

Committee for the Examination of Long Term Economic Policy (1998),
   Quality in Public Administration, National Bank of Greece.

Ioakeimoglou, E. (1998), The EMU,
   Salaries, and Unemployment, Institute of Labor of the General Confederation of Labor (GSEE) and Confederation of Public Employees (ADEDY), Study No. 9, October.

Ioakeimoglou, E. (1999),
   Salaries, Competitiveness, and Unemployment, Institute of Labor of the General Confederation of Labor (GSEE) and Confederation of Public Employees (ADEDY), Study No. 10, May.

Institute of Economic and Industrial Research (IOVE) (2000),
   Quarterly Report 1/00, Number 24, March.

Kintis, A. (editor) (1997),
   The Present and the Future of the Greek Economy, Volumes A,B,C, Athens University of Economics and Business.

Kollintzas, T. (2000),
   The Inertia of the Status Quo, Kritiki, April.

Economic Policy Studies (Meletes Oikonomikis Politikis), Institute of the Study of Economic Policy (IMOP), Various Issues.

Mertzanis, H. (1999),
   "Growth and Regulation of the Capital Markets in Greece", *Emerging Markets Quarterly*, winter.

Ministry of Development (1997),
   "Report on Competitiveness and Industrial Strategy in Greece", Athens, October.

Ministry of Development and University of Piraeus (1997),
   Strategy for Attracting Foreign Direct Investment to Greece, Athens, July.

Ministry of Labor and Social Security (1999),
   Social Budget for the Year 1999. Athens.

Ministry of National Economy (1998),
   "The Greek Economy 1960-1997", General Directorate of Economic Policy, Macroeconomic Analysis Section, Athens.

Ministry of National Economy, Development Plan for Greece 2000-2006.

Patsouratis, V. A. (1995),
   Obstacles to the Improvement of Competitiveness of the Greek Industry, Institute of Economic and Industrial Research (IOVE), Special Studies No. 24, Athens.

Provopoulos, G. and V. Rapanos (editors) (1997),
   Functions of the Public Sector: Problems and Prospects, Institute of Economic and Industrial Research (IOVE), Athens.

Republic of Greece, State Budget 1998, 1999, 2000, Ministry of Finance.

Part II

BACKGROUND REPORTS

BACKGROUND REPORT ON GOVERNMENT CAPACITY TO ASSURE HIGH QUALITY REGULATION*

* This report was principally prepared by **Cesar Córdova-Novion**, Principal Administrator for Regulatory Management and Reform, with the participation of **Martin Stokie**, Consultant, Department of Treasure and Finance, Melbourne, Australia, on secondment to the OECD and **Scott H. Jacobs**, then-Head of Programme on Regulatory Reform, in the Public Management Service. It has benefited from extensive comments provided by colleagues throughout the OECD Secretariat, by the Government of Greece, by Member countries as part of the peer review process, and by the Trade Union Advisory Committee and the Business Industry Advisory Committee. This report was peer reviewed in July 2000 in the OECD's Working Party on Regulatory Management and Reform of the Public Management Committee.

TABLE OF CONTENTS

List of Boxes

List of Tables

1. REGULATORY REFORM IN A NATIONAL CONTEXT

1.1. Administrative and legal environment in Greece

Regulatory reform emerged in Greece as part of a larger set of reforms to domestic policies and institutions carried out mainly in response to changing external pressures. In particular, regulatory reform has developed over the last two decades as a result of European Union membership, though Greece has moved more slowly than other EU members to take advantage of the opportunities offered by the single market. Since the mid-1990s, the pace of reform has accelerated with the drive to qualify for membership in the euro area. In parallel, the government has launched a series of positive reforms to modernise its public administration, which will have substantial benefits in improving the efficiency and effectiveness of governance in Greece.

External pressures have moved faster than domestic responses, though, and a gap has opene between new social and economic demands and opportunities, and the capacities of the Greek public sector to perform roles compatible with those new needs. Important modernisation and structural reforms have been accomplished, but there has not been a corresponding reform of the public administration and its capacities to develop and implement high quality regulatory regimes that are compatible with a more open and dynamic economy. Regulatory regimes in Greece tend to be interventionist, costly, rigid, and focussed on details rather than results. The absence within the Greek public administration of a government-wide regulatory reform strategy, regulatory impact assessments, a public notice and comment process, independent and transparent sectoral regulators, and use of regulatory alternatives is in contrast to practices recommended by the OECD and adopted by many OECD countries (see Box 1).[1]

Box 1.   **Good practices for improving the capacities of national administrations
to assure high quality regulation**

The OECD Report on Regulatory Reform, which was welcomed by ministers in May 1997, includes a co-ordinated set of strategies for improving regulatory quality, many of which were based on the 1995 Recommendation of the OECD Council on Improving the Quality of Government Regulation. These form the basis of the analysis undertaken in this report, and are reproduced below.

A. BUILDING A REGULATORY MANAGEMENT SYSTEM

  1. Adopt regulatory reform policy at the highest political levels.

  2. Establish explicit standards for regulatory quality and principles of regulatory decision-making.

  3. Build regulatory management capacities.

B. IMPROVING THE QUALITY OF NEW REGULATIONS

  1. Assess regulatory impacts.

  2. Consult systematically with affected interests.

  3. Use alternatives to regulation.

  4. Improve regulatory co-ordination.

C. UPGRADING THE QUALITY OF EXISTING REGULATIONS
  (*In addition to the strategies listed above*)

  1. Review and update existing regulations.

  2. Reduce red tape and government formalities.

However, a new view is emerging in Greece on regulatory reform and the need to "reinvent" the relationship between the public administration, the market, and civil society. This was most recently stated in April 2000, when the Prime Minister stated to Parliament that his government intends to introduce policies to create a service mentality in the public service, complete decentralisation, and reduce administrative burdens hindering investment.

In reaching these goals, Greece must confront entrenched obstacles and traditions in its existing administrative and legal practices at national and subnational levels. Three key challenges face the reform of public administration and its use of regulatory instruments. The first challenge arises from current practices for public sector employment, management, and accountability:

–   The productivity and the efficiency of the public sector should be improved. The Greek public service is not large compared to those of other European countries[3] (though it is growing quickly[4]), but administrative practices favour legalism and formalism instead of management based on results and market-orientation. Skills tend to be focused on procedure and conformance rather than substantive policy analysis. For example, the competition commission has little economics expertise. At the telecommunications regulatory agency, most senior administrators lack the background necessary for regulatory oversight of complex markets. Centralised and standardised procedures for hiring and movement of personnel, created legitimately to increase professionalism and competition and to reduce clientelism in public sector employment, have been effective, but have introduced rigidities that have slowed the introduction of new competencies and the adoption of new regulatory techniques.

–   Close links between the top levels of the public administration and the political parties have contributed to hierarchical structures that concentrate decision-making powers at the highest levels, slow response times, reduce flexibility, create bottlenecks, and reduce accountability of lower level administrators.

–   Working for the government brings advantages (such as life-time employment enshrined in Article 103 of the Constitution), but the attractiveness of the public sector as an employer is declining. Salaries are lower than in the private sector for high quality managers and regulators. Pay increases are not based on performance related criteria, and poor performance is not sanctioned. Incentives are not aligned to encourage good practices and discourage bad.[5]

The second challenge concerns policy coherence, co-ordination, and implementation in the Greek public administration. Institutions for these functions are weak, and are replaced by continuous political oversight and intervention. Co-ordination and reform initiatives, for example, often depend on personalities rather than institutions, thus weakening continuity between changes in governments.[6] In part because of the *ad hoc* and political nature of policy-making, policy implementation can be uncertain and policy effectiveness reduced. Recent examples illustrate the challenges. In 1999 the National Food Safety Council (EFET) was established to be responsible for all food safety issues in Greece, and should help improve the quality of regulations in this sector. It is still not fully operational, in part due to bureaucratic delays and resistance from ministries in transferring staff to the new agency. In the case of three EU water quality directives, implementation was not undertaken in tandem with a review of the division of labour among relevant ministries. This resulted in *ad hoc* adjustments in the field and a duplication of enforcement by each service.[7] The certification and quality control functions of the Greek Standards Office took ten years to become effective due to the time needed to develop metrology and accreditation structures.

A potential issue for regulatory implementation is the existence of excessive regulatory discretion, which was raised in relation to broad interpretative powers provided to regulators in some laws and subordinate regulations. Recently the Social and Economic Council (OKE) found excessive discretion when reviewing an important draft law on Incentives for Private Investment.[8] There are few external controls on subordinate legislation and administrative procedures regulating inspections or formalities, such as licences and permits.[9] Such uncontrolled discretion may create opportunities for unethical behaviour, in particular at the delivery or service end of public administration, *e.g.* licence application, government approvals, and tax related matters.[10] In an over-regulated or rigid environment, though, discretion can provide "flexibility" that compensates for regulatory failures. For example, in Greece, local government interpretation of laws and inspection measures can reduce business costs and provide "breathing space" for compliance by SMEs. This "flexibility" is nevertheless based on personal connections and knowledge, which is unavailable to outsiders to the region, town or city. Since rigid implementation of poor regulations would greatly increase unnecessary regulatory costs in Greece, controls on discretion should proceed in parallel with improvements to regulatory flexibility and cost-efficiency.

A third general challenge facing the Greek public service is a culture of distrust toward market mechanisms in general and the business sector in particular.[11] Regulators tend to prefer command-and-control approaches over results-oriented and market mechanisms. In part, this has been nurtured by a formalistic approach to law focusing on legal content and in part it is due to past politicisation of the civil service.

One of the results of these practices and tendences in the Greek public administration is a general trend of regulatory inflation.[12] Box 2 shows that the flow of new primary laws has increased over the last decade. This phenomenon – known in Greece as *polynomie* – is partly the result of the adoption of EU laws and directives, but it is also due to inadequate regulatory quality controls on the flow of new regulations and ineffective review mechanisms on the accumulation of national laws.

Box 2. Regulatory inflation in Greece

The Greek administrative legal system is adapted from the French system. In broad terms, the domestic legal system is composed of many instruments: laws (sometimes organised in codes for important matters); Presidential Decrees; Ministerial Decisions; circulars; and local government by-laws. EU instruments and other international obligations add another layer to the legal system.

Regulatory inflation can be seen in the upward trend in the number of new laws made over the last decade. Further, according to estimates of the Ministry of the Interior, Public Administration, and Decentralisation (MIPAD), the number of pages of legislation in the early 1990s was eight times the number in the mid 1970s. As in other countries, new laws rarely repeal previous laws, and hence the existing stock continuously increases. MIPAD believes that each new law produces on average six new Presidential Decrees and 63 Ministerial Decisions. That is, between 1987 and 1998, there was an average of 450 new Presidential Decrees and over 5 200 new Ministerial Decisions every year.

Number of new laws enacted annually

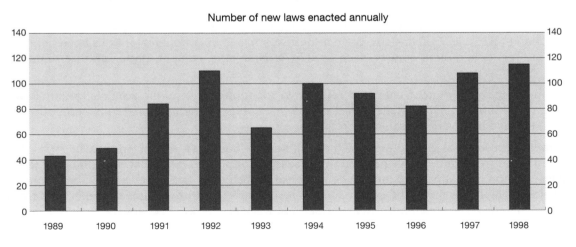

Source: Ministry of the Interior (2000), Public Administration, and Decentralisation, April.

This has important consequences for transparency. A recent report indicated that regulatory transparency has been reduced due to "… overlapping laws and confusion in their application. Foreign companies consider the complexity of government regulations and procedures – and their inconsistent implementation by the Greek civil administration – to be the greatest impediment to operating in Greece".[13] This situation is aggravated by contradictions and overlaps between regulations, particularly between different levels of government (see Section 2.3).

The issue of real concern, though, is less the number of regulations and more the quality of those regulations. There is little concrete evidence or evaluation of the efficiency, benefits, and costs of Greek regulatory regimes (see Section 4), which itself suggests that opportunities exist for improvement. Laws tend to be statements of problems with little prior assessments of compliance costs. The growing flow of new regulations may produce significant benefits, but also increases compliance costs on society (government, citizens, and national and foreign businesses), and opportunity costs by impeding innovation and growth. If the new regulations are poorly designed and implemented, they reduce social welfare and waste investment by not achieving policy goals. This underlines the importance of ensuring that adequate quality control mechanisms are in place inside the public administration to ensure that new laws and other regulations actually contribute to Greek social and economic progress.

Resolving these challenges will require a clear, government-wide policy and implementation strategy for regulatory quality, sustained by determined political will. A range of new programmes and initiatives is required to improve the efficiency of the public administration. Changing formal and informal regulatory approaches will require the adoption of a regulatory quality programme based on good practices found in other OECD countries. Awareness among stakeholders and the broad public of the importance, benefits, and costs of such a programme will be a powerful ally in overcoming obstacles from vested interests inside the public administration, as well as interests outside of the administration, such as lobbies or "connected" businesses.

1.2. Recent reform initiatives to improve public administration capacities

Although many economic and governance reforms undertaken in Greece are intended to increase transparency and accountability in the use of the regulatory instruments, an articulated policy to improve regulatory quality has not been formulated at either the political or administrative level. Yet a great many regulatory reforms are underway. As part of its structural reforms, mainly in implementing the European single market programme and preparing for accession to the euro area, Greece has introduced significant financial and structural reforms, including privatisation and liberalisation of government owned enterprises. Liberalisation reforms have affected utilities such as transport, energy, and communications, as well as non-utility sectors such as duty free shops, travel agencies, and lotteries. Market liberalisation has also been undertaken in sectors where major firms have been under direct or indirect government control, such as shipyards, mining, cement, paper, and petroleum (see Chapter 1).

In parallel, the government launched reforms to modernise the public administration (Table 1). These reforms will have an important impact on the functioning of the administration and indirectly on improving the quality of Greek regulatory regimes.

Upgrading the neutral competence of the civil service has been a high priority. In 1994, Greece introduced a new recruitment and promotion process for public servants that was aimed at reducing clientelism and politicisation, and increasing technical capacities.[14] The policy established centralised mechanisms to manage all public sector human resources. The three main elements are: rigorous controls on all new posts; the creation of an independent agency (ASEP) in charge of recruiting staff; and the development of transparent procedures for promotion.

To co-ordinate recruitment and promotions across ministries, a high-level committee known as the Tripartite Committee decides monthly on the distribution of new vacancies for the whole government. The committee consists of representatives from the Ministry of Interior, Public Administration and

Decentralisation (MIPAD), the Ministry of Finance and the Secretary General of the Prime Minister Office. The committee's decisions are communicated to an independent and centralised recruiting agency.

The recruiting agency, ASEP, operates as an independent agency in charge of organising recruitment in the public service. To assure independence, its governance body is appointed by Parliament. Its main role is to prepare and administer the recruitment based on written exams and to audit the recruitment of other bodies of central and local government.

Few bodies are exempted from the recruitment procedure. To grant greater flexibility to parts of the government competing more directly with the private sector for specialised skills, the Capital Market Commission, the Committee for the Protection of Private Citizen Data, the Central Bank, the Ombudsman, and State-owned enterprises have been exempted. (Oddly, the competition policy authority is not exempted, though perhaps should be, as should sectoral regulators who require market-valued skills.) However, exempted bodies must follow rules set by ASEP, such as having public interviews when recruiting, and they are audited periodically by ASEP.[15] The only two full exceptions are the Committee for the Organisation of the Olympic Games, which can recruit from the private sector directly, and the heads of private hospitals, who are also recruited directly from the private sector.

ASEP was a clear success in de-politicising the recruitment process, which was formerly tainted by clientelism and favouritism in a highly politicised environment. The ASEP experience showed that centralised co-ordination, high professional standards, and consistent application of policy can increase trust and confidence in the public service in the public and in political spheres. From the viewpoint of the previous situation in Greece, ASEP was a necessary and positive reform. But ASEP had unanticipated side-effects inconsistent with the needs of a modern and more flexible public sector. Notably, the

Table 1. Selected reform legislation relating to regulatory reform in Greece

Law	1662/1986	Granted more independence to the local level.
Law	1558/1986	Specifies the competencies of each ministry.
Law	1892/1990	Introduced liberalisation and competition policy.
Law	1943/1991	Strengthened independence and transparency in the civil service.
Law	2026/1992	Restructured the bureaucracy to reinforce the role of Ministries.
Law	2190/1994	Required public sector recruitment to be based on competition.
Law	2218/1994 & 2232/1994	Decentralised government competencies to the sub-national level.
Law	2232/1994	Established the Economic and Social Committee.
Laws	2229/1994 & 2234/1994	Designed to harmonise Greek policy making with EU processes.
Law	2251/1994	Created the National Consumers Association Council.
Law	2477/1994	Established the Ombudsman.
Law	2333/1995	Created the National Public Administration Commission.
Law	2414/1996	Changed the laws governing public enterprises provide management independence.
Law	2914/1996	Required the development of Citizens Charters for public services.
Law	2414/1996	Provided for the modernisation of Public Enterprises and Organisations.
Law	2539/97	Established the Quality Programme for the Citizen.
Law	2503/1997	Established new administrative structure for local government (Ioannis Kapodistria).
Law	2672/1998	Allowed for electronic signatures for filing of forms.
Law	2668/1998	Reformed the Postal Service.
Law	2647/1998	Decentralised 139 competencies from central Government to into 13 regions.
Law	2738/1999	Collective Negotiations in Public Administration.
Law	2773/1999	Established the Electricity Regulatory Authority.
Law	2690/99	Introduced the Administrative Procedure Code.
Law	2683/99	Introduced the Civil Servants Code.

centralised recruiting system increased rigidities and made it more difficult to recruit skilled staff in a timely manner for specialised positions, for example, for staffing sectoral regulators. In late 2000, positive reforms to ASEP were made. Procedures for recruiting skilled staff were speeded up by Law 2839/2000, which transferred some aspects of recruiting procedures to the public organisations concerned, while leaving final control of results to ASEP.

With the introduction of the new recruiting policy, the Greek government also tried to reduce the size of the public sector work force.[16] In 1998, the government introduced a policy of "1 for 5" that means that for every five positions that become vacant due to retirement or departure, only one position is replaced. ASEP is supposed to enforce this policy. However, due to numerous exemptions, this initiative has had little impact.[17]

The second high-impact governance reform undertaken in the late 1990's concerns the modernisation and restructuring of local governments. Under a 1994 law, all government responsibilities that do not have a national character should be devolved, but the actual transfer of powers has been realised only in the past two years (1998-1999). This programme, known as Ioannis Kapodistrias, will have longstanding impacts on the quality of the public administration, and will significantly alter the responsibilities of the central government in terms of rule making (see Section 2.3). Through the transfer of personnel, the programme will also have impacts on the quality of services and accountability of the various levels of administration. No study has yet analysed the full impact of the decentralisation of services, yet some changes are now perceptible in terms of tasks and activities of administrators. For example, the central administration is now concentrating on planning and policy direction rather than executing tasks, as it did previously.

In parallel to administrative devolution, a 1994 law reformed the electoral process. The prefect (nomarch), previously appointed by the central government, is now elected together with a prefectural council. Taken together, these reforms could substantially change the governance of Greece toward a more responsive and needs-oriented administration.

The programme has not yet been completed and the readjustment and redeployment of public servants from the centre to municipalities is lagging the transfer of policy responsibilities.[18] Also, impro-

---

Box 3.   **Main features of the Ioannis Kapodistrias Programme**[1]

The Problem: Too many small local authorities that lacked adequate political representation, that had insufficient capacity to provide desired services to the community, and that had limited participation in the procedures of local and regional development.

Previous attempts to solve the problem involved voluntary mergers stated in the Laws 1416/84 and 1622/86, and in the Regional Councils Law 2218/94. While partly successful, these programmes failed to produce significant improvements in local government.

1. *Kapodistria Programme* introduced a new legal framework for local government via Laws 2539/1997. These laws defined the powers of local authorities, new geographical boundaries that merged local authorities and improved economies of scale, new financing arrangements to allow for the delivery of services (such as water supply, sewage, roads, etc), adequate staffing for those services (to be drawn predominately from ministries), and specific monitoring and enforcement mechanisms

The programme has resulted in the restructuring of 5 775 local jurisdictions which existed prior to 1997 into 1 033 municipalities and communities. The first elections of mayors was held in 1998 under the new system. Also, 139 competencies were transferred to 13 regions, and significant powers were transferred to local government (see Table 2).

---

1.   See http://www.ypes.gr/kapodristria/english/kapo/programme.htm.

ving the technical capacities of local government officials will require resources and time. The Greek Agency for Local Development (EETA) with the assistance of EU funds has been organising training programmes for more than 2500 local officials.

With the Law 2503/97 the administration and organisation of the Region, as a decentralised unit of the country's administration was established. With the Law 2647/98, responsibilities were transferred to the Regions, the Prefectural Local Governments and the Municipalities in separate.

As a third pillar of the modernisation and structural change of the public administration, MIPAD is managing a new public management programme called "Quality for the Citizen". This initiative, part of a "Quality Principle" approved by the Council of Ministers in 1998, is a multifaceted programme designed to improve the services provided by the administration to the citizen.[19]

The programme, run by a unit of 30 persons in MIPAD, aims to improve the quality of administration and to reduce administrative burdens imposed on citizens. Significant initiatives include:

a) Publication of a range of materials to inform citizens of the services provided by the Ministry. This includes the development and publication every two years of a citizens' guide (an 800 page book on administrative issues relevant to the citizen[20]), and the editing of a weekly newspaper that includes job vacancies in the public service.

b) A simplification programme focusing on improving selected administrative procedures and formalities with high costs for citizens. For example, MIPAD has improved frequently-used formalities such as reducing by seven the number of documents required for obtaining a driving licence. Through this programme, inter-ministerial working groups have redesigned more than 300 forms.[21]

c) Creation of a Citizens' Bureau in every prefecture and in every municipality to deliver services, information and administration forms. As well, information is provided within the local administration via electronic means over the Internet, such as the Ariadne programme (see Box 4). Information Kiosks have been provided in 39 Prefectures. A recent law on electronic signatures will build on these mechanisms to permit online filing of forms and authorisations.[22]

d) Started in 1994, MIPAD piloted one-stop-shops for citizens at the regional level for services of social security, agricultural development, and commerce. But implementation of the programme has been slow. Currently, only 3 of the 54 prefectures are involved, and the programmes cover only a part of the service and administrative areas in each prefecture. It is intended that the programme be extended to all prefectures in 2000/01 with the devolution of competencies to regions and prefectures.

e) MIPAD has helped public entities, such as the electricity public monopoly (DEH) and national railways, to comply with the law requiring them to establish citizens' charters. It is interesting to note that this law requires the citizens charters to provide for specific compensation to citizens for deficient services. Since December 1999, nearly 60 cases of delays have been examined by MIPAD, and over GRD 120 000 paid in compensation.[23] To date, citizen's charters have been established for the Ministry of Transport and Communications and for all the authorities and agencies which are supervised by that Ministry, the Regions of East Macedonia of Kalamata.

f) In February 1998, the Ministry started a help-line call centre for citizens all over Greece to apply for certificates to be sent to their home, such as birth certificates, apply for passports, or obtain more information. Since then the call centre has received over 40 000 calls per month.[24] In a survey conducted by MIPAD over 88% of users were satisfied with the services and almost all users indicated that they would use the service again.

In late 2000, these initiatives were reorganised and strengthen into a more comprehensive programme called "Politeia", which aims to improve the quality of services. Among its main aims are the recruitment of trained personnel who support reforms, development of new technologies and adoption of modern techniques of administrative control to improve transparency and eliminate corruption, adoption of modern financial management for the public service based on benefit-cost analysis and comparative measurement of service and employee effectiveness, and reduction of administrative procedures which impose burdens on business and citizens.

The fourth recent governance initiative relevant to regulatory quality is in response to the need to increase the accountability, transparency, and responsiveness of the public service. In 1999, the Greece adopted a new Code of Administrative Procedure and a new Civil Service Code.[25] The new Code of Administrative Procedure regulates administrative procedures in terms of time limits and deadlines for acting on citizens' cases. It also obliges the public servant to explain delays, specifies the procedures for accessing administrative documents, defines rules governing contracts between the administration and the private sector, and establishes requirements on how to access administrative appeal mechanisms.

The new Civil Service Code further details the recruitment procedures associated with ASEP, requires work plans and training requirements to be specified annually for public servants with MIPAD to act as the co-ordinating body, and establishes anti-corruption mechanisms. The anti-corruption measures include obligatory declaration of civil servants' assets on a regular basis, require documentation for purchase of fixed assets or goods of significant value by the civil servant or by a member of the family, establish a capacity to investigate sources of income of the civil servant if assets have been modified in a disproportionate way in relation to salary or general financial situation, and provide for prosecution and disciplinary action.

These codes are positive steps to improve the public administration and to curb inappropriate use of public power. Together with the fight against politicisation of the public service, appropriate enforcement of these codes should significantly increase transparency and public confidence by reducing practices of petty corruption and abuses. Of concern though, is that previous efforts to reduce corruption have had great difficulty in being implemented. Resources and staff will be needed to adequately promote the letter and spirit of the codes, and provide efficient and rapid appeal and redress mechanisms through the administrative courts systems or through the new institutions such as the Ombudsman. A critical aspect for their success will be a change in the culture of the bureaucracy toward a more open and accountable style of decision-making, and in the willingness of the judiciary to critically review administrative actions.

Box 4. The ARIADNE programme [1]

At the beginning, the Programme was intended to resolve a problem faced by people living on islands in the Aegean Sea. Previously, obtaining and lodging government forms could take two or more days as citizens had to travel to the island where the prefecture was located.

The idea was to use the Internet for access and filing of administrative forms required for the issue of every certificate or permit. The programme involves the redesign of more than 300 application forms and the placing of the new forms on the Internet. By the end of 2000, the programme will include all documents that citizens all over Greece may find necessary for government applications.

The pilot application of the programme is now operating in 96 municipalities on the Islands in the Aegean Sea, providing access to computer terminals for all citizens who are not connected to the Internet. During the first two months of operation In 1999, more than 10 000 people were served.

Convenience for the islands has stirred interest in providing similar access to those living on the mainland. The "Ariadne" programme Is now being extended to other areas of Greece, beginning from the Prefectural Local Government of Magnesia and Messinia.

---

1. For further information see www.ypai.aegean.gr.

2. DRIVERS OF REGULATORY REFORM: NATIONAL POLICIES AND INSTITUTIONS

2.1. Regulatory reform policies and core principles

The 1997 OECD *Report on Regulatory Reform* recommends that countries adopt at the political level broad programmes of regulatory reform that establish clear objectives and frameworks for implementation.[26] The 1995 OECD *Council Recommendation on Improving the Quality of Government Regulation* contains a set of best practice principles against which reform policies can be measured.[27] The efforts in Greece discussed in the previous Section are steps toward convergence with good regulatory practices. If well-implemented, they will improve, for example, transparency and accountability in the application of regulations.

Yet they do not represent a coherent or complete programme of regulatory quality improvement, and in themselves are not a sufficient programme of regulatory reform to contribute significantly to economic performance or to regulatory efficiency. An explicit policy on quality of regulation, with the institutions to carry it out, would boost the benefits of reform for Greece. The absence in Greece of a government-wide policy promoting regulatory quality for social, administrative, and economic regulations is in contrast to many other OECD countries, such as the Netherlands, the United States, Mexico, Hungary, Korea, and Italy. Recent initiatives in Greece indicate that formulation of such a policy may have already begun in practice.

A noteworthy action by the Prime Minister was the commissioning in 1998 of a series of reports on, among other things, the Quality of the Public Administration.[28] This report, known as the Spraos Report, recognises that problems exist within the Greek regulatory framework relating to quantity, cost of regulation, quality, and democratic legitimacy. The Spraos Report recommended the adoption of the 1995 OECD *Council Recommendation on Improving the Quality of Government Regulation*. The Report advocated the establishment of an agency to co-ordinate regulatory reform across government, with authority to express opinions on the quality of new regulations, such as legislation, Presidential Decrees, and Ministerial Decisions. Further, the report recommended that this agency should prepare a report to be tabled before Parliament on issues relating to regulatory quality. It is encouraging to note that in late 2000 the government has started implementing some of the Report's recommendations.

Box 5. Principles of good regulation

OECD country experience shows that quality standards and an effective regulatory management institution are interdependent. Central oversight is more effective if objective quality standards for regulation are specified to regulate quality. But quality standards and principles are often not enough to improve regulatory habits and counter incentives. An expert government-wide institution should be accountable for overseeing compliance. A concrete and market-oriented set of quality standards should be based in the OECD principles accepted by ministers in 1997, which read:

Establish principles of "good regulation" to guide reform, drawing on the 1995 OECD Recommendation on Improving the Quality of Government Regulation. Good regulation should: (i) be needed to serve clearly identified policy goals and effective in achieving those goals; (ii) have a sound legal basis; (iii) produce benefits that justify costs, considering the distribution of effects across society; (iv) minimise costs and market distortions; (v) promote innovation through market incentives and goal-based approaches; (vi) be clear, simple, and practical for users; (vii) be consistent with other regulations and policies; and (viii) be compatible as far as possible with competition, trade and investment-facilitating principles at domestic and international levels (OECD *Report to Ministers on Regulatory Reform*, 1997).

Concrete implementation of the core principles espoused by the OECD can be found in the recent regulatory reform review conducted by the Ministry of the National Economy. This pilot programme, begun in July 1999, systematically reviewed all regulations made over the last five years within the ministry. The 1995 OECD *Council Recommendation on Improving the Quality of Government Regulation* was used as a guiding principle to assess the quality of the regulations (Box 5). The six month assessment involved the establishment of a regulatory reform group, composed of senior officers from different divisions within the ministry, who prepared the first inventory of all regulations including legislation, Presidential and Ministerial Decisions.[29]

The review is an attempt to systematically assess regulatory quality within the Ministry of the National Economy, and could be a good starting point for other ministries. The lessons learned suggest that its design could be improved. The review lacks, for example, an independent and rigorous assessment of the impacts of regulations, the key information needed to test regulatory quality, and instead begins with qualitative statements about what the laws require. In fact, the review concluded that all legislation, Presidential Decrees, and Ministerial Decisions within the Ministry are effective and necessary. This includes the 54 ministerial orders that govern the financial sector (these make up more than half the ministerial orders for the Ministry) and the 23 ministerial orders that govern capital markets. The only negative conclusion was that for the establishment of ELKE, the one-stop-shop investment promotion agency (Section 4.2), more could have been done to ensure its success. Without independent input, self-assessment rarely yields highly critical conclusions and provides grounds for the argument that regulatory reform should be co-ordinated by a central agency or at arms-length of the ministries being reviewed.

As a fundamental element of a new regulatory reform policy, the Greek government should develop more explicit and measurable government-wide criteria, such as those in Box 5, for making decisions as to whether and how to regulate, and support those principles with written guidance to ministries. This would help ensure that reform principles are applied equally to new and old regulations, by all ministries. The OECD recommends as a key principle that regulations should "produce benefits that justify costs, considering the distribution of effects across society." This principle is referred to in various countries as the "proportionality" principle or, in a more rigorous and quantitative form, as the benefit-cost test. This test is the preferred method for considering regulatory impacts because it aims to produce public policy that meets the criterion of being "socially optimal" (*i.e.*, maximising welfare). Greece will need to strengthen, step-by-step, capacities for regulatory impact analysis to apply the benefit-cost test.[30]

2.2. Mechanisms to promote regulatory reform within the public administration

Mechanisms for managing and tracking reform inside the administration are needed to keep reform on schedule and to avoid a recurrence of over-regulation. It is often difficult for ministries to reform themselves, given countervailing pressures, and maintaining consistency and systematic approaches across the entire administration is necessary if reform is to be broad-based. This requires the allocation of specific responsibilities and powers to agencies at the centre of government. As in many OECD countries, Greece emphasises the responsibility of individual ministries for reform performance within their areas of responsibility. This is formalised through Law 1558/1986, which specifies the respective responsibility and competencies of each ministry. Co-ordination of reform in Greece is carried out by inter-ministerial commissions and a few independent bodies that rely on legal controls and peer pressure. As yet, no dedicated body in the Greek administration is charged with monitoring and promoting a programme of regulatory reform and quality improvements.

The procedure for preparing legislation and subordinate regulation is usually initiated through bilateral discussions between the ministry proposing the new law and the Prime Minister's Office. While the Constitution specifies the general process for making legislation, specific procedures are not specified in law but rather rely on a Prime Minister's circular (No. Y866/21-11-1996.) and various administrative procedures. The Office of Legislative Work of the General Secretariat of Council of Ministers examines all the phases in the procedure for preparing legislation and specifically.

- Checks for the prerequisites in draft laws and Presidential Decrees;
- Prepares, in conjunction with the responsible minister, draft legislation;
- Checks the attestation of the proofs of the Official Gazette before publishing;
- Forwards Draft Presidential Decrees to the Council of State;
- Provides advice to the Prime Minister on issues of legality of government functions.

Development of new legislation follows in general terms the procedure depicted in Box 6. The initial decision to proceed with draft legislation is made by the Prime Minister and the competent minister. The law drafts are prepared either from the competent services or from special law-drafting committees or working groups that are constituted *ad hoc* for this reason. Intra-governmental consultation is undertaken with other ministries and the Ministry of Finance. At the discretion of the minister, consultation with affected outside parties can be organised at this stage. The draft is sent to the Prime Minister's Office. From this moment, the Office of Legislative Work takes responsibility for the draft. As stated in the formation Law of the Economic and Social Committee (2232/1994), the Minister who drafts the law is required to ask for consultation from the Economic and Social Committee for draft laws that are of economic or social nature (Section 3.1.2). In some cases, all or important sections of the proposed bill are published in newspapers or relevant professional journals. The Central Law Drafting Committee provides legal control to the drafts, then the drafts are sent back to the Ministries for checking and finally the Office of Legislative Work sends the drafts to the Parliament for debate and passage. In the case of amendments to existing laws, the process tends to be quicker and less structured. For ministerial decisions, inter-ministerial and public consultation is left to the discretion of the ministry and is often less than what occurs for primary legislation. However, they are controlled by a special commission of the Prime Minister's Office for their legality and by the Ministry of Finance for their budgetary impacts.

A few other institutions provide quality control or guidance. The *Council of State* has been a strong promoter and key participant in past codification processes. For instance, many of its counsellors have participated to the responsible Committee of MIPAD for reviewing and preparing the new Code of Administrative Procedures of 1999. The *Ombudsman*, whose mission is to investigate citizen's complaints against Public Sector Services, has the power to identify major problematic areas and to recommend specific legal and procedural reforms addressed to the competent ministries, prefecture or local authorities. The latter is achieved mainly through a comprehensive annual report, submitted to the President of Parliament, the PM and the Minister of the Interior, Public Administration and Decentralisation. So far, the *Ombudsman*, established in 1998, has produced two annual reports and a series of shorter reports, and it has witnessed the first positive governmental responses (legal amendments and changes to administrative practices)."[31] Most recently, he has made his first recommendations on reform options to curb petty corruption.

Throughout this process, the legality of the proposed legislation is considered many times. After the responsible minister instructs the ministry to prepare draft legislation, issues such as constitutionality, consistency with other laws including EU directives and legal quality issues are assessed by the Central Law Drafting Committee, the Office of Legislative Work, and the Standing Parliamentary Committee. By contrast, the economic impacts of proposals are not formally evaluated. The Ministry of Finance provides a budget impact assessment for bills and amendments of laws (see Section 3.3), but this covers only a small fraction of the total costs of most regulations, and is not a sufficient assessment of regulatory costs. Specific authorisation is needed when creating a new post in the administration.

For Presidential Decrees, the independent Council of State is charged with responsibility for controlling the legality and the quality of drafting.[32] It also provides advice on substantive and administrative issues. In many ways, it plays a similar role to the Central Law Preparing Committee. In carrying out its functions, some observers indicate that its high technical standards have won a reputation as a tough guardian of legality. Indeed, in a kind of strategic "institution-shopping," some ministers have opted to prepare a legislative amendment or ministerial decision to avoid the rigorous scrutiny of the Council of State.[33]

For ministerial decisions, the responsible ministry prepares and publishes the measure. For ministerial decisions, no external review or assessment for either legal quality or economic impact is performed.

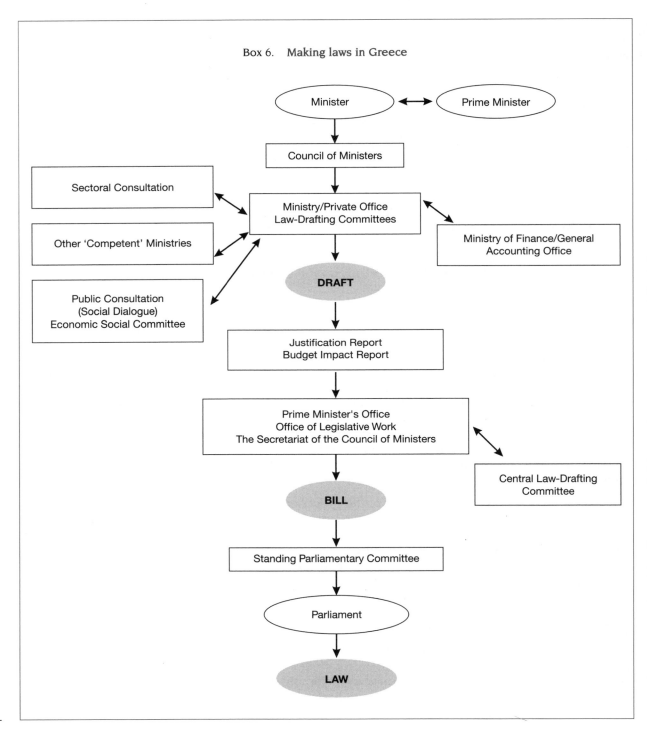

Box 6.   Making laws in Greece

In addition to the bodies already mentioned and directly involved in rule making, other institutions, ministries and agencies intervene on an *ad hoc* basis in managing and proposing regulatory reforms. Located within the Prime Minister's Office is the *Economic Office*. This is a main economic policymaking body and main advocate and co-ordinator of bills and Presidential Decrees. It is charged with the promotion of social dialogue on important matters of socio-economic policy such as employment issues, tax, regional development, consumer protection, and competition. In addition, it co-ordinates inter-ministerial consultation and plays a significant role in ensuring overall consistency of the Government's regulatory proposals.

2.3. Co-ordination between levels of government

Multi-layered regulatory systems are a subject of concern with respect to the efficiency of national economies and the effectiveness of government action. In Greece, sub-national and supranational levels of government administration are inextricable elements of the regulatory framework, and developments at one level affect others. The policies and mechanisms for co-ordinating regulations between the regions and municipalities, the national government, and the European level have been integral in establishing a quality regulatory environment in Greece. In general, accountability and transparency have not yet been adequately assured for regulatory decisions taken at regional and local levels, and more attention is needed here over the next few years.

Until the early 1990s, Greece had a highly centralised structure relying on deconcentrated government offices at the prefecture level (*nomos*). As indicated above, through a series of major reforms undertaken in the past decade, the subnational level has been restructured and empowered. Today, Greece has a three-tier system: 13 deconcentrated regions governed by a council and Secretary General appointed by the government for four years, a decentralised "second level" of 54 prefectures (nomos) with each region containing two to five prefectures, and a decentralised "first level" of 1 033 municipalities and communes. The presidents of the first and second levels have been elected since 1998.[34]

The current reforms intended that all government responsibilities with a sub-national character be devolved. The current distribution of powers between levels of governments is illustrated in Table 2. The municipalities and communities have overall responsibility for the administration of local matters and promote social, finance, cultural and spiritual interests of their citizens.[35] Second level local authorities have responsibility for administrative matters at the prefecture level and for any functions conferred on them by law or Presidential Decree.

The Council of State is responsible for the judicial control of the legality of the regions' decisions and regulatory powers. *The General Secretary of the Region* exercises the legality control over the acts of the organs of municipalities and communities. All the acts of municipal and communal councils are submitted to the General Secretary of the Region and if he considers them to be illegal he sends them within 15 days to a special *Control Committee*. However, this control focuses only on the legality of the measure, not its necessity or impact. No consultation is required for the preparation of these by-laws, although the Regional Council may organise a public meeting. On the other hand, many communes have occasionally used 'notice and comment' systems. Disputes between communes and nomos are settled by the Regional Council and the Secretary General of the region. In the case of disagreement, an appeal can be lodged with the administrative judicial system.

In terms of ex post controls, administrative tribunals, followed by appeals to the Council of State, control the acts and decisions of local governments. However, it may take some time before the devolution of powers and electoral reforms are met by corresponding changes in the relationships between appointed administrators and elected officials. For instance, the Ombudsman cited an example of a newly elected mayor who was reluctant to accept a Council of State resolution on one of his decisions, citing as justification the self-regulating nature of the new communes.

In carrying out functions of licensing, a local government is regulated by the Municipal and Communal Code.[37] This code establishes a maximum 30 day limit for acting on a licence. The cost of a licence is set annually by the Law of Finance. However, municipalities keep the payment as revenue. In an effort to

Table 2. **Division of main regulatory powers across levels of government in Greece**

Policy area	State	Prefectures	2nd level local authorities	1st level local authorities
Security, police	*	*		*(1)
Justice	*	*		
Fire fighting	*	*	*	*
Civil protection	*	*	*	*
Pre-school education	*	*	*(2)	*(3)
Primary and secondary education	*	*	*(2)	*(4)
Vocational and technical education	*	*	*(2)	*(4)
Higher education	*	*		
Adult education	*	*	*	*
Hospitals	*	*		
Individual health departments	*	*	*	*
Family and Youth Services	*	*	*	*
Rest homes	*	*	*	*
Social insurance	*	*	*	
Housing	*	*		
Town planning	*	*	*	*
Water treatment	*	*		*
Household sewage and waste				*
Cemeteries				*
Slaughter houses				*
Environmental protection	*	*	*	*
Theatres, concerts	*	*	*	*
Museums, art galleries, libraries	*	*	*	*
Parks, open spaces	*	*	*	*
Sport and leisure	*	*		*
Religious worship	*	*		
Highways	*	*	*	*
Urban road transport	*	*	*	*
Urban transport, railways	*	*	*(5)	
Ports	*	*	*(6)	*(6)
Airports	*	*		
Gas	*	*		*
Water (irrigation)			*	*
Farming, Fishing	*	*	*	*
Electricity	*	*		*
Commerce	*	*	*	*
Tourism	*	*	*	*
Forestry	*	*		
Licences for other services			*(7)	*(8)

(1) Municipal police
(2) Construction of schools – auxiliary staff
(3) Nurseries and kindergartens
(4) Repair and maintenance of schools
(6) By Presidential Degree the management of the ports can be transferred to prefectural or local Port – funds
(7) License for enterprise function
(8) License for creation & function of certain enterprises

Source: Information provided by Greece, March 2000.

raise revenues, municipalities may have an incentive to create new licences with accompanying fees, to shorten the renewal periods and hence increase the frequency with which licence fees are paid, or to strictly monitor and enforce the licence conditions (which may be onerous) to impose penalty payments.

Two representative bodies are in charge of co-ordination and consultation between the national government and lower-levels of government: the Central Union of Municipalities and Communes (KEDKE) and the Central Union of Prefects. Mayors and prefects directly elect the members of these bodies, which are equipped with small secretariats in Athens. These bodies are the main channels for discussion of central government draft proposals or any other issues.

As devolution accelerates and materialises, lower levels of government will need to develop new competencies. OECD country experience indicates that rapid devolution with weak co-ordination and accountability mechanisms can create significant regulatory management problems and reduce the overall quality of regulation. In Greece, this is particularly important as reforms have created a system where multiple levels are responsible for related policy areas. Overlap of responsibilities can been seen in Table 2, where each of the levels of Government has overlapping responsibilities in almost all policy areas. This raises the potential for duplication of services/controls, and inefficient delivery of those services. Furthermore, licences for industrial activities are often blocked at municipal levels, adding significantly to delays and business start up costs.

Transposition of European Union directives has had a very positive influence on the market orientation of Greece's regulatory system. In many cases, this effort has brought impetus and commitment for reform within Greece. Transposition of EU law has allowed Greece to implement laws that would otherwise have been extremely difficult, such as in liberalisation of telecommunications, and electricity. However, implementing the *acquis communautaire* has been difficult in terms of content and speed of transpositions, and Greece has appeared reluctant to take advantage of the opportunities offered by the European single market. In some areas, Greece has sought derogations that delayed important reforms and the benefits for Greek consumers and workers that they would have brought. In the latest EU Scoreboard, Greece has the highest deficit of directives yet to be transposed.[38]

For the preparation and negotiation of new directives, the responsibility is delegated to competent ministries supervised when necessary by the Ministry of Foreign Affairs and/or the Ministry of National Economy". These two ministries have alternated as the centre of European policy co-ordination, while their relations have sometimes been tense.[39] In principle, the line ministries are responsible for organising public consultation on draft directives and co-ordinating with the Greek delegation in Brussels. In practice, public consultation has been limited.

Since Greece's accession to the EU in 1981, the Parliament has delegated to the government the task of transposing EU Directives (Law 1338/83). This law provides discretion to enact through a fast track procedure the EU obligations through amendments of new texts of laws, Presidential Decrees or Ministerial Decisions. In practice, the choice of instrument used to transpose an EU directive depends on long-standing tradition or the discretion of the ministry's legal services.[40] Very often, ministries use Presidential Decrees or Ministerial Decisions, as they speed up the adoption process. During the transposition process, quality control and consistency across the government is provided via the Law 1338/83, which requires the Ministry of the National Economy to sign off on all EU measures. This co-ordination has been particularly important for Greece, and deserves some credit for the progress made in reaching the criteria for joining EMU.

3. ADMINISTRATIVE CAPACITIES FOR MAKING NEW REGULATION OF HIGH QUALITY

3.1. Administrative transparency and predictability

Transparency of the regulatory system is essential to establishing a stable and accessible regulatory environment that promotes competition, trade, and investment, and helps ensure against undue influences by special interests. It reinforces the legitimacy and fairness of regulatory processes yet as a multi-faceted concept it is not always easy to establish in practice. Transparency involves a wide range of practices, including standardised processes for making and changing regulations; consultation with interested parties; plain language in drafting; publication, codification, and other ways of making rules easy to find and understand; and implementation and appeal processes that are predictable and consistent.

In Greece, a growing number of reforms are promoting more transparent, open, and consultative procedures for making regulations. At the same time, long-standing practices continue to hinder openness and participation by the public in Greek regulatory development. On the whole, compared to other OECD countries, Greece is lagging behind in improving regulatory transparency.

3.1.1. *Transparency of procedures: administrative procedure laws*

Transparent and consistent processes for making and implementing regulation are fundamental to confidence in the rulemaking process and to opportunities of stakeholders to participate in decisions important to them. The rulemaking process is less structured in Greece than in many OECD countries. Greece does not have a specific law or regulation setting out rule-making practices, apart from the general provisions in the Constitution, as discussed in Section 2.2. Relevant practices arise from various sources, and important elements of rule-making procedures are left to informal administrative traditions and the discretion of ministries.

Most regulatory development and quality control activities are wholly internal to ministries. Even within the public administration, inter-ministerial communication on draft legislation is limited to "competent" ministries. A ministry not specifically defined by law as "competent" will discover a proposed bill only when it is discussed by the Council of Ministers. This limits the scope for ministries to have meaningful input into the development of laws and compounds the fragmented or "silo" effect of policy.

Box 7.   **Transparency of regulatory systems in selected OECD countries**[1]

Based on self-assessment, this broad synthetic indicator is a relative measure of the openness of the regulation-making and regulatory review system. It ranks more highly national regulatory systems that provide for unrestricted public access to consultation processes, access to regulation through electronic and other publication requirements, access to regulatory impact analysis, and participation in reviews of existing regulation. It also ranks more highly those programmes with easy access to licence information, which tends to favour unitary over federal states. Greece scores below the EU, the OECD, and G7 averages. This is due to the fact that Greece does not publish its forward plans for regulation, public consultation does not occur for all regulatory proposals, and impact assessment is not required.

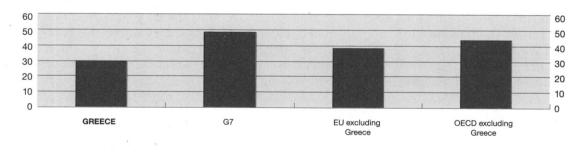

1. The indicators used here are part of a dataset under construction as a contribution to the OECD Secretariat's horizontal work programme on regulatory reform. They are based in part on a survey of all OECD countries carried out in March-April 1998.

Source: Public Management Service, OECD 1999.

This is compounded by the fact that amendments to existing legislation are not subject even to the minimal processes for primary laws. Supporting documentation is not required, except on budgetary impacts. No external institution reviews the content of amendments or their consistency with other laws. "Social dialogue" is seldom undertaken. In this regard, the Speaker of the House recently made considerable efforts to reduce the number of amendments before Parliament.[41]

As in most OECD countries, subordinate regulations must be authorised by a higher-level law or regulation, but administrative processes for developing subordinate regulations mostly lack any check of economic impacts or policy results.

3.1.2. *Transparency as dialogue with affected groups: use of public consultation*

From ancient times, the Greeks have set the global benchmark for vigorous public debate and discussion on policy issues. Rule making today continues to create considerable public interest. However, except for a few limited mechanisms (see below), public consultation is not formalised. Mechanisms for consultation are left to the discretion of individual ministers or senior officials. The lack of a systematic and transparent public consultation mechanism reduces the quality of Greek regulation in several ways:

- It increases the vulnerability of the public sector to capture or undue influence by particular interests.

- It can also cause regulatory mistakes, due to inadequate information about nature of the problem and the real-world impacts of decisions.

- It reduces government credibility and the legitimacy of government action. In some cases, the lack of adequate consultation mechanisms has meant that, when they are made public, regulatory issues rapidly turn into protest and negative media reactions.

- Lack of adequate consultation is a missed opportunity to obtain crucial information on compliance and impacts. This may be compounded by a tradition of corporatist culture prone to capture, which makes reformers weary of consultation.

In practice, the informal public consultation processes actually used depend on the ministry and the inclination of the minister in charge. Many advisory committees exist, often created by sectoral laws. For instance, since 1994 the Ministry of Development consults consumer associations on issues related to consumer welfare via the National Consumer Association Council.[42] To date the Association has been called upon twice to express its opinion on laws that effect consumers. On the other hand, some minis-

---

Box 8.   Consultation in Greece in the reforms of the postal service

During the three-year period from 1997-1999 a number of regulatory changes were made to enhance the capacity and efficiency of the Hellenic Postal Organisation (ELTA). The application of Law 2414/96 (on the modernisation of Public Enterprises and Organisations) and Law 2668/98 (on the organisation of the sector providing postal services) brought the regulatory framework for the operation of the postal market in line with EU regulations.

Throughout this reform process, consultation with the public service unions was integral part. Consultation involved the publication of studies on the proposed changes as well as supporting documentation produced and distributed for comment. According to the Greek Trade Union Confederation (GSEE) this process, including forward notification and early participation should be considered as a model for other sectoral reforms in Greece.

Sources: Hellenic Post, OECD Economic Survey – Greece (1998), and information provided by Greek Trade Union Confederation (GSEE).

tries, such as the Ministry of Development, organise *ad hoc* meetings to discuss drafts with interested parties. In such cases, the ministry itself chooses the participants. A consultation mechanism on the reform of the administration was recently established in Law 2839/2000: the National Council for Administrative Reform. This Council discusses administrative reform proposals and is comprised of representatives of social and financial institutions, labour unions, scientific institutions, and the Parliament.

Public consultation is particularly limited for subordinate regulation, such as ministerial decisions, interpretative circulars and Presidential Decrees. They are seldom discussed outside the ministry or the Council of State (in the case of Presidential Decrees). Furthermore, in the preparation of EU directives, consultation is rarely undertaken, limiting Greece's ability to put forward a comprehensive view when negotiating.

The only formal consultative mechanism is the tripartite Economic and Social Committee (ESC).[43] It was formed in 1994 to represent interest groups in Greece: employers and businessmen as one group; employees and civil servants as another; and citizens, local authorities, independent professions as the third. The separate views of each of these three groups are given equal treatment and are all distinct from State power. The role of the ESC is to promote "social dialogue" through the formation of common positions on issues concerning society as a whole.

Box 9.   **Best practices in consultation: "notice and comment" in the United States**

The 1946 Administrative Procedure Act (APA) established a legal right for citizens to participate in rule-making activities of the federal government on the principle of open access to all. It sets out the basic rule-making process to be followed by all agencies of the US Government. The path from proposed to final rule affords ample opportunity for participation by affected parties. At a minimum, the APA requires that in issuing a substantive rule (as distinguished from a procedural rule or statement of policy), an agency must:

i) Publish a notice of proposed rulemaking in the Federal Register. This notice must set forth the text or the substance of the proposed rule, the legal authority for the rulemaking proceeding, and applicable times and places for public participation. Published proposals also routinely include information on appropriate contacts within regulatory agencies.

ii) Provide all interested persons – nationals and non-nationals alike – an opportunity to participate in the rulemaking by providing written data, views, or arguments on a proposed rule. This public comment process serves a number of purposes, including giving interested persons an opportunity to provide the agency with information that will enhance the agency's knowledge of the subject matter of the rulemaking. The public comment process also provides interested persons with the opportunity to challenge the factual assumptions on which the agency is proceeding, and to show in what respect such assumptions may be in error.

iii) Publish a notice of final rulemaking at least thirty days before the effective date of the rule. This notice must include a statement of the basis and purpose of the rule and respond to all substantive comments received. Exceptions to the thirty-day rule are provided for in the APA if the rule makes an exemption or relieves a restriction, or if the agency concerned makes and publishes a finding that an earlier effective date is required "for good cause". In general, however, exceptions to the APA are limited and must be justified.

The American system of notice and comment has resulted in an extremely open and accessible regulatory process at the federal level that is consistent with international good practices for transparency. The theory of this process is that it is open to all citizens, rather than being based on representative groups. This distinguishes the method from those used in more corporatist models of consultation, and also from informal methods that leave regulators considerable discretion in who to consult. Its effect is to increase the quality and legitimacy of policy by ensuring that special interests do not have undue influence.

The ESC expresses a reasoned opinion on important issues related to labour relations, social security, taxation measures, and matters of socio-economic policy in general. The procedure involves the competent ministry requesting the opinion of the Committee. The committee issues its view within 30 days. The ESC reviews all "important" regulations, but the criteria for an important law are unclear, and the Council has no enforcement powers. As a result ministers choose when they want to consult the ESC and if they wish to accept its opinion. For example, changes to the telecommunication law were not discussed by ESC.

Notwithstanding this, the ESC is seen as an important improvement in the consultative approach to the development of legislation. Today, it has become a well-accepted forum by the unions and the employers for important regulatory discussions.

In terms of forward planning of regulations, Greece co-ordinates its legislative production through the Secretariat of the Council of Ministers. This secretariat prepares a list every three months (according to the No. Y866/21-11-1996) of proposed laws as well as a concise report on the planning and progress of the legislative production of ministries, including Presidential Decrees and ministerial decisions.[44] However, this report is not made public and thus public awareness of future regulatory proposals is limited to political announcements, EU decisions prior to introduction in Greece, and advertisement of draft legislation in newspapers prior to consideration by parliament. There is no forward planning for other forms of regulation.

Greece has lagged other OECD countries in creating public consultation mechanisms. This weakens the accountability of the ministries, and reduces their ability to assess impacts, reactions, and compliance issues for new regulations. A government-wide policy on the use of consultation in making and amending regulations is key to improving regulatory quality. A wide variety of forms of consultation (including notice and comment, circulation for comment, information consultation, advisory groups and public hearings) can be developed, together with guidance and methodological help for successful application. Notice and comment processes are the most open form of consultation, and should be implemented as a complement to other forms of consultation (see Box 9). It will be important to ensure that ministries carry out any new procedures systematically and consistently, that draft regulations are published early enough to allow meaningful public review, and that ministries actually respond to public comments, even if to explain why comments were not accepted.

3.1.3. *Transparency in implementation of regulation: communication*

Transparency requires that the administration effectively communicates the existence and content of all regulations to the public, and that enforcement policies be clear and equitable. In Greece, once passed by Parliament (in the case of legislation) or signed by the President after approval by the Council of Ministers (in the case of Presidential Decrees), new regulations are published in the Official Gazette. This material is also available electronically through the National Printing House.[45]

In addition, Greek laws, codified 40 different sections can be found in the "Permanent Code of Legislation", which contains their update. The code consists of 105 volumes and is published in the magazine "Pandektis" which is sent to subscribers. The index is to be computerised by early 2001. Moreover, the government (MIPAD and the Ministry of Justice) with the help of the Council of State has embarked on a continuing effort to prepare codes of the decisions of courts covering specific policy areas.

De facto transparency can be reduced when a legal and regulatory framework faces instability through constant revision and amendments. In such a case, understanding the current state of law is beyond most citizens and most businesses. Greece seems to be confronting such a situation. For instance, a growing consulting industry has emerged to provide advice on government requirements as well as to provide physical services such as queuing for certificates and filing of applications.[46]

A second problem that reduces regulatory communication in Greece is the lack of formal requirements to publish ministerial decisions and circulars in the Official Gazette. It can be difficult for business and citizens to identify the full requirements of the law. For example, ELKE, the one-stop-shop for foreign investors, has made considerable efforts to compile a complete database with all licences and permits needed to start a business in Greece. But despite the considerable investment in continuous research on the forthcoming parliamentary agenda (to know what laws are likely to be passed), despite reviewing every issue of the Official Gazette, professional journals, and other legal documents, they have not been able to assure that their list is complete and accurate. A few years ago, Mexico confronted a similar problem and resolved it through a programme that created a central registry of formalities. This registry has positive security, that is no licence, permit or other formality is allowed unless on the registry and no licence can be placed on the registry unless approved by an independent assessor who ensures a minimum quality criteria. The register is now available through the Internet.[47]

Finally, it should be noted that through the numerous legal review processes the quality of legislation is improved, but understanding and accessibility to the average Greek is hindered by the fact that plain language drafting is not required as part of those review processes.

3.1.4. *Compliance, application and enforcement of regulations*

Greece faces important challenges in terms of application and compliance of laws and regulations due in part to a lack of communication and co-ordination between ministries. A scarcity of funds to enforce regulations and delays in establishing enforcement institutions compounds the problem,[48] as does a lack of consideration, at the development stage of a regulation, of the ability of citizens and entrepreneurs to comply. An increasingly complex legislative system seems to focus more on the creation of new laws than on the performance of existing laws.

A study on the implementation of EU directives on water quality illustrates these challenges. The study concluded that "taking a broader perspective, the [compliance and implementation problems] tend[ed] to discredit rules and regulations, to encourage de facto situations and to undermine the development of a civic culture or respect for law and order".[49] Additionally, anecdotal evidence related to the large informal sector suggests a serious challenge to regulatory compliance in Greece. Key elements for improving the situation include strict controls on inconsistent application of the law by public servants, and clear rules and regulations governing business inspection and the authorisation processes (licences and permits).[50] Recent initiatives such as the Code of Administrative Procedure, and the Civil Service Code are welcome steps, and will need to be strictly enforced.

Weaknesses in regulatory enforcement processes, due in part to budgetary constraints and co-ordination difficulties among different parts of the administration, also undermine compliance. Difficulties can also be related to the political process. For instance, owners of a building without an official building permit sometimes use personal contacts to get connected to public services (telephone, water, electricity, etc.). After a certain time, the owner organises a support group in the neighbourhood to lobby a local politician to legalise the building. This example provides a strong demonstration effect that compliance is unnecessary and that laws can be navigated around rather than complied with.

Administrative justice is provided by administrative courts and by the Council of State as the Supreme Court.[51] The system is accepted as fair and effective. However, as in many OECD countries, the administration of justice in Greece is slow and expensive, with a substantial backlog of pending cases. For instance, the Ombudsman has estimated that on average an administrative appeal needs 3 to 5 years to reach the Council of State and costs around 2 000 dollars in lawyer's fees and other costs.[52] But the creation of the Ombudsman and a programme launched by the Ministry of Justice and the MIPAD to computerise the judiciary system should quicken administrative justice.

3.2. Choice of policy instruments: regulation and alternatives

A core administrative capacity for good regulation is the ability to choose the most efficient and effective policy tool, whether regulatory or non-regulatory, while respecting the principles of transparency and accountability. The range of policy tools and their uses is expanding in OECD countries as experimentation occurs, learning is diffused, and understanding of the markets increases. At the same time, administrators often face risks in using relatively untried tools, bureaucracies are highly conservative, and there are typically strong disincentives for public servants to be innovative. Reform authorities must take a lead role that is supportive of innovation and policy learning, if alternatives to traditional regulation are to make serious headway into the policy system.

For Greece, the use of command and control regulations is heavily predominant, and there are few examples of the use of innovative policy instruments. Even compared to the low rates of use in other OECD countries, Greece seems relatively un-innovative. A tradition of using legalistic and administrative procedures as the main regulatory instrument hinders the consideration of alternatives, as does the lack of a specific policy and awareness of alternative mechanisms. Furthermore, low levels of compliance with traditional regulation makes the bureaucracy sceptical about the prospects of new techniques.

Recent progress in the use of alternatives in the area of environmental protection may be a pilot for other sectors.[53] The main type of alternative instrument used is economic instruments.[57] A number of economic instruments are in used in Greece (see Table 3). Municipal water and sewerage charges are mostly based on volumetric rates, but sometimes are levied per square metre of surface area of the buildings connected to the networks and are earmarked for financing the water supply and sewerage networks operated by municipalities.

Table 3.   Economic instruments used in Greece

Instrument	Rate/calculation method	Observations
Industrial water supply charges	One-off charge for connecting to public water supply: GRD 1 400 – 30 000 Pricing in Athens (per month): GRD 230/m³ for up to 1 000 m³ GRD 270/m³ for over 1 000 m³	In Thessaloniki, craft industries pay about one-third of charge.
Irrigation water charges	Annual charge of GRD 30 000 – 70 000/ha for surface irrigation canals Volumetric rates recently introduced for newly built piped networks	Payable to local land improvement boards by farmers receiving water from community irrigation projects (40% of total); farmers supplied by private projects not subject to the charges fees cover administration, operation and maintenance costs.
Municipal water supply charges	Fixed charge GRD 480/month for network maintenance Pricing in Athens (per month) 0-5 m³ : GRD 100 5-20m³ : GRD 155 20-27 m³ : GRD 427 27-35 in³ : GRD 600 >35ni³ : GRD 750 Pricing in smaller cities varies considerably, for instance: In Orestiada :GRD 88/rn3 In Kerkyra :GRD 543/m3	An upper bound on water charges is applied for families with 3 or more children.
Municipal waste disposal charge	Dumping charge, EUR 6-15 per tonne.	Payable to local government associations running landfills.
Municipal waste water treatment charge	Progressive volumetric rate applied in Athens – equal to about 40% of water supply charge.	Revenue is earmarked to finance collective treatment infrastructure.
Industrial waste water treatment charge	One-off charge for connecting to public sewerage system: GRD 1 000 – 285 000 Flat rate of GRD 50 per cubic metre.	Applies to industries in areas equipped with waste water treatment plants only.
Fines for violating air emission limits	Cars: GRD 5 000 – 10 000 Stationary combustion sources: GRD 1 million.	Revenue channelled to Green Fund.

153

Economic instruments used in Greece (*Cont.*)

Instrument	Rate/calculation method	Observations
Special tax on PPC	0.4% of revenue of PPC's lignite-fired power plants	Part of proceeds used to fund environmental protection activities in regions surrounding lignite-fired power plants.
Excise tax on vehicle fuels	Leaded gasoline: GRD 127/litre Unleaded gasoline: GRD 111/litre Diesel/gas oil: GRD 77/litre LPG (propellant): GRD 32/litre Kerosene (propellant): GRD 77/litre	GRD 5/litre is channelled to Green Fund; half earmarked for air pollution control measures. Reduced excise tax on used oil may apply in some regions.
Income tax exemption for purchase of natural gas appliances	75% of expenses incurred for purchase and installation of appliances.	Funded under Energy Operational Programme.
VAT on motor vehicles	18% on all motor vehicle fuel. 8% on fuel used for public passenger transport. 6% on fuels used for travel within and between certain islands by air and sea.	
VAT on energy products	18% for energy products 0% for natural gas not used as propellant (economic incentive).	The funds collects by applying this taxation go to the general budget of Greece.
Special consumer tax on imported cars	Calculated as a function of the engine capacity of the car and its sales price.	Tax was reduced by 60% for lightweight vehicles during a scrapping program introduced by the I Ministry of Environment in the early 1990s.
Road vehicle circulation fee	GRD 15 000-50 000 per vehicle per year.	Applies to private cars, motorcycles. trucks, other vehicles that use public roads. Funds collects go to the general budget and are allocated for the maintenance of the public road network.
Tax on quarry products	2-5% of product value	Payable by quarry owners to the respective municipality to be used for environmental protection ends.
Performance bond for quarry operators	GRD 250 000-300 000 per 1 000 m^2 of quarry	Bond serves as a guarantee to ensure that site restoration will be carried out after the end of operations.
Fines for causing marine pollution	400 fines imposed in 1997 yielded GRD 388 million	Revenue channelled to Blue Fund.
Entrance fees to national parks	GRD 200 – 1 200 per visitor	Revenue generally used for park maintenance.

Source: OECD (2000), *Environmental Performance Reviews – Greece* (based on data available up to September 1999; EU.

Over recent years, Greece has made use of voluntary instruments concerning environmental issues. An example of voluntary environmental action in this context, on the part of industry, is provided by the creation In 1992 of the Hellenic Recovery and Recycling Association (HERRA) at the initiative of the aluminium industry, before any legislation, on the subject had appeared. HERRA operates recycling programmes in co-operation with schools and municipalities. Nevertheless, Greek Government has used voluntary agreements with economic sectoral groups to a lesser extent.[55]

As part of EU membership, Greece is also implementing various programmes on Eco-Management and Audit Scheme (EMAS) as well as Eco-labelling.

Concerning EMAS, the Greek Chamber of Commerce and Industry and the Hellenic Organisation of Small and Medium sized Enterprises provide guidance to their members on implementing

EMAS, advising them for example, to organise seminars. The Hellenic Ministry for the Environment, Physical Planning and Public Works has begun to encourage EMAS implementation in state-owned industry through the implementation of various pilot projects and intends to promote it to Small and Medium sized private Enterprises in the near future. Moreover, the General Secretariat of Industry, under the Ministry of Development, recently launched a pilot programme for the implementation of ISO 14001 and EMAS in private companies, with a total budget of GRD 900 million; 104 companies have already been approved for ISO 14001 or EMAS implementation under this initiative.

Moreover and in the context of voluntary instruments, there are various on-going Eco-labelling programmes in Greece and others which are currently being put in place, including:

- The Eco-label Awa d Scheme implemented In Greece through the Supreme Board for Awarding Ecological Labels (ASAOS), on which industry organisations, unions, NGOs and consumer groups are represented. It should be noted that Greece is the leading country for the bedmattresses product group and a pilot project of tourist services. In this respect, the General Secretariat of Industry, has recently launched a pilot programme to encourage eco-labelling of products in private companies, with a total budget of GRD 50 million, under which ten companies have already been approved,

- Energy efficiency labelling for household appliances, particularly refrigerators and freezers.

3.3. Understanding regulatory effects: the use of Regulatory Impact Analysis (RIA)

The 1995 OECD *Recommendation on Improving the Quality of Government Regulation* emphasised the role of RIA in systematically ensuring that the most efficient and effective policy options were chosen. The 1997 OECD *Report to Ministers on Regulatory Reform* recommended that governments integrate RIA into the development, review, and reform of regulations. A list of RIA best practices is discussed in detail in *Regulatory Impact Analysis: Best Practices in OECD Countries*, and provides a framework for the following description and assessment of RIA practice in Greece.[56]

Greece is drawing closer to adoption of a formal requirement to undertake regulatory impact analysis, due to the work of an interministerial committee created by the Public Administration Ministry in 2001 that is considering the OECD's recommendations, including those on RIA.[57] However, there is as yet no requirement to undertake RIA, and its lack has been a major gap in Greece's regulatory quality controls.[58] Policy officials do not base decisions on a clear assessment of the costs and benefits of proposed government actions, such as impacts on economic activity. But in moving to a market-led growth strategy fully integrated with Europe, such impact assessments are critical in ensuring that government actions are consistent with market-oriented principles of quality regulation.

For some time, business groups and academics within Greece have campaigned for RIA. In 1990, the Federation of Greek Industries (SEV) sent a proposal to the government to introduce a formal impact assessment process for all new regulations, and followed that proposal in 1991 with a further clarification.[59] Most recently, the *Spraos Report* recommended to the Prime Minister in 1998 that RIA as recommended by the OECD should be implemented.[60]

Since 1990, according to the Joint Ministerial Decision 69269/5387/90 which defines the various classes of projects subject to EIA, Greece has required the conduction and submission of EIA statements for public and private projects and investments. In this context, they provide full assessment of environmental issues relating to regulatory proposals and they are submitted to the Greek Ministry of the Environment, Physical Planning and Public Works for review and approval. Their impact on developments within Greece has been considerable. For example, in 1994, the Council of State ruled in favour of Greek environmental NGOs on the Acheloos River diversion project that aims to irrigate 380 000 ha in the Thessalia plains, supply water to the towns of Larissa, Trikala and Volos and allow 5 hydroelectric stations to be built. The Council of State with its ruling ordered the works to be discontinued because no conclusive complete EIA has been done for the entire project. The major claim was relating to a high risk for marine water intrusion in the Mesolonghi wetlands at the Acheloos Delta. A complete EIA which proposes a series of measures to prevent harmful impacts on the environment, has since been carried out.

–   All draft legislation is required to be accompanied by a Justification Report.[61] This report is a qualitative description of the intents and objective of the proposed measure. It is prepared by the ministries at the end of the legislative process and often contains one or two paragraphs describing in qualitative terms the benefits of the proposal. Its intent is to provide sufficient justification for the proposed bill. A justification report is not required for subordinate legislation, Presidential Decrees, and ministerial decisions.

–   Laws and regulations with impacts on the public budget need to be authorised by the Ministry of Finance. This procedure is strictly applied, and seems to be quite effective (see Box 10).

–   A proposing agency has to prepare a further report when requesting the recruitment of new personnel. A Tripartite Committee, in the Prime Minister's office, submits this document for written approval (see Section 2.2).

–   Since 1990, Greece has required environmental impact assessments (EIA) for public investments (see Joint Ministerial Decision (69269/5387/90) which defines the various classes of projects subject to EIA). They provide full assessments of environment issues relating to regulatory proposals and they are sent to the Greek Ministry of the Environment (YPEHODE) for review and approval. They have had real impacts on developments within Greece. For example, in 1994, the Council of State ruled in favour of Greek environmental NGOs on the diversion of the Acheloos Rivers and ordered that work be discontinued because no conclusive, complete EIA had been undertaken for entire project. The major claim related to a high risk of marine water

---

Box 10.   A step toward RIA: the budgetary impact report

Budgetary impact assessment within Greece provides an important precedent for establishing full regulatory impact analysis. Budgetary impact assessment is closely related to RIA, though the latter is a more comprehensive economy-wide assessment rather than a strict focus on fiscal costs to government.

Mandated by the Greek Constitution, all legislative proposals, including amendments, must be accompanied by a budgetary impact assessment.[1] This assessment reviews the future impact on the budget of the legislative proposal. It is prepared by a specific office in the Ministry of Finance, Directorate Number 21, and it is signed the Ministry of Finance. Without a Budgetary Impact Assessment, Parliament cannot discuss or vote on a proposed bill.

To prepare the budgetary impact assessment, ministries proposing new legislation need to send to the Ministry of Finance relevant information under a specific format. If this information is erroneous or inadequate, the Ministry of Finance has the authority to reject the format or require supplementary information. For example, a proposal in 1994 that would have changed the recruiting process for junior civil servants was required to be amended once the budgetary impact became fully known.[2]

Budgetary impact assessments tend to be extremely detailed with some containing hundreds of pages of spreadsheet data. The content is focused solely on the expenditure estimates and the material contained is sufficient to allow Greece's annual budget to be prepared and for Parliament to make informed decisions about future financial commitments.

1.   See Article 75 of the Constitution.
2.   Ministry of the Interior, Public Administration, and Decentralisation.

intrusion in the Missolonghi wetlands of the Acheloos delta. A complete EIA has since been carried out; it proposes measures to prevent harmful impacts on the environment.

Given that Greece's use of RIA is in its infancy, the following discusses best practice within the OECD and highlights how Greece's capacity can be enhanced, in the short and medium term, to meet OECD standards.

Maximise political commitment to RIA. Use of RIA to support reform should be endorsed at the highest levels of government. In the case of Greece, an explicit policy by the highest levels of government could be the next step, as there is already some recognition that RIA has considerable merit and should be undertaken across the administration. Perhaps, given the Greek legal culture this could be ratified by law and include subordinate regulation. Moreover, the Parliament, such as in Italy, could become a promoter of this decision-making tool.

Allocate responsibilities for RIA programme elements carefully. To ensure "ownership" by regulators, while at the same time establishing quality control and consistency, responsibilities for RIA should be shared between regulators and a central quality control unit. RIA should be prepared by the ministries proposed new regulations for two main reasons. First, RIA is a tool to improve the responsibility and accountability of those proposing regulations and second because an appropriate RIA needs the best information concerning the regulation. However, a central element of a RIA mechanism is the need to have an independent and objective assessment. As such, a technical unit should be established at the highest and at the closest level to the centre of government with the technical capacities to conduct the reviews, and with the clout and credibility to enforce the RIA discipline. To further increase account-ability, RIA should be signed-off by ministers or by high level officials.

Train the regulators. Regulators must have the skills to prepare high quality economic assessments, including an understanding of the role of impact assessment in assuring regulatory quality, and an understanding of methodological requirements and data collection strategies. All complex decision-making tools, such as producing adequate RIA demand a learning process. Greece's learning curve will be steeper for the proponent ministries due to the lack of economic evaluation training. It is thus vital that the Greek RIA programme considers from the outset a prolonged investment in training, guidance and a central help desk. Specific courses should be organised. Care should be taken to assure that RIA requirements are planned in an evolutionary way, making them more precise and stringent as the capacities of the ministries improve.

Use a consistent but flexible analytical method. Except when evaluating budgetary impacts, the current impact assessment in Greece are limited to qualitative impacts. However, a RIA programme in Greece should be based from the beginning on quantitative assessment and methodologies, which assure consistency and objectivity. A practical strategy with which to start can be to concentrate, like the UK, on compliance costs of businesses. As capacities to prepare and evaluate the RIA increase, the longer term goal could shift to establish a full benefit-cost analysis.

Target RIA efforts. RIA is a difficult process that is often opposed vehemently by ministries not used to external review or time and resource constraints. The preparation of an adequate RIA is resource intensive task for drafter of regulations. Experience shows that central oversight units can be swamped by a large numbers of RIA concerning trivial or low impact regulations. As such, it is thus vital from the outset for Greece to target RIAs for those proposals that are expected to have the largest impact on society. Alternatively, a two-step RIA mechanism could be devised requiring a simple RIA for all meas-ures and a complete RIA for specific proposals when the central evaluator or the proponent ministry deems that the compliance costs will be above a certain range.

Develop and implement data collection strategies. The usefulness of a RIA depends on the quality of the data used to evaluate the impact. An impact assessment confined to qualitative analysis would provide fewer incentives for regulators to be accountable of their proposals. Since data issues are among the most consistently problematic aspects in conducting quantitative assessments, the development of strategies and guidance for ministries is essential if a successful programme of quan-titative RIA is to be developed. An interesting practice that Greece could launch consists in adapting the Danish system of panel tests where randomly selected firms evaluate the potential costs of a proposed regulation.[63]

Integrate RIA *with the policy making process, beginning as early as possible.* Integrating RIA with the policy making process is meant to ensure that the disciplines of weighing costs and benefits, identifying and considering alternatives and choosing policy in accordance with its ability to meet objectives are a routine part of policy development. In some countries where RIA has not been integrated into policymaking, impact assessment has become merely an ex post justification of decisions or meaningless paperwork. Integration is a long-term process, which often implies significant cultural changes within regulatory ministries. For Greece, this could involve setting up a system similar to the Hungarian "two-step approach", where a pre-RIA focusing on the policy content is prepared before the drafting of the text starts. Then a second RIA is prepared progressively together with the drafting of the text and is annexed to it when the measure is discussed in the Council of Ministers, the Council of State or Parliament. A further step would be to publish such a list as a forward regulatory planning mechanism.

Involve the public extensively. Public involvement in RIA has several significant benefits. The public, and especially those affected by regulations, can provide the data necessary to complete RIA. Consultation can also provide important checks on the feasibility of proposals, on the range of alternatives considered, and on the degree of acceptance of the proposed regulation by affected parties. A powerful way that Greece could use to formalise public consultation and at the same time improve rapidly the quality of RIAs – and foster accountability across regulators – is to require the publication of a RIA through a 'notice and comment' mechanism. Indeed, a 'name and shame' mechanism is often the strongest incentive and/or sanction a public servant may have.

3.4. The changing institutional basis for regulation

Economic structural reforms promoted as part of EU membership and accelerated through the drive to join EMU have required the establishment of new or the remodelling of existing sectoral regulators. These regulators are designed to provide regulatory oversight in liberalised sectors. The most notable are the Capital Markets Commission established in 1996, the Energy Regulatory Authority established in 1999, and the National Telecommunications and Postal Services Commission established in 1998.

However, in most cases, the establishment in Greece of sectoral regulators has lagged behind the deregulation and privatisation process, they do not operate as truly independent regulatory authorities and resource constraints limit the scope of their mission. For example, the European Commission has issued a number of infringement procedures in regards to financial services and delay in implementing EU Directives that would enhance regulatory supervisory powers.[64]

Greece does not have an co-ordinated institutional framework for creating and operating these sectoral regulators. They tend to be established in an *ad hoc* manner, often due to an international obligation or commitment. This is particularly evident where the role of the regulatory authority is circumscribed and true regulatory oversight remains vested within the ministries. For example, the recently established Energy Regulatory Authority will not set tariffs for transmission or user charges, nor will it assess applications and grant authorisations for generation of supply licences.[65] Its role is limited to one of providing advice to the Ministry of Development that will ultimately make such decisions (see background report to Chapter 5).

A key element in an adequate institutional architecture is ensuring an appropriate relationship between the Competition Commission and the sectoral regulators. There are a number of sectors, including transport, telecommunications, broadcasting, petroleum, and electricity, that enjoy explicit exclusion or exemption from competition laws. This has the potential to undermine free competition and confuses the market about the role of the sectoral regulator and the Competition Commission (see background report to Chapter 3).

In contrast to the reluctance from ministries to cede power to sectoral regulators, the establishment of the Capital Market Commission has been accepted as a highly successful step in building long-term confidence in a key economic sector.[66] Importantly, the independence of this Commission is based not only on a clear statute with well-defined functions but also on an adequate resource base independent from the government budget and a flexible staffing policy that allows the Commission to attract and keep competent staff. In this case, the Commission has been partially exempted from the most rigid recruiting rules centrally overviewed by ASEP and it is free to pay staff according to market prices rather than the official government salary scale.[67]

The successful operation of sectoral regulators and appropriate oversight of liberalised markets requires co-ordination between regulators, they must be granted sufficient independence from ministries and firms being regulating, and the resources and skills must be adequate for the sector being supervised.

4. DYNAMIC CHANGE: KEEPING REGULATIONS UP-TO-DATE

4.1. Revisions of existing regulations, laws and subordinated regulations

Over the years most OECD countries have accumulated a large stock of regulation and administrative formalities. If not checked or reviewed these can lead to a highly burdensome regulatory system. The OECD *Report on Regulatory Reform* recommends that governments systematically review regulations to ensure that they continue to meet their intended objectives efficiently and effectively.

Since 1974, when Greece re-established democratic processes, there has been, except for a few specific areas such as transport and pensions, little systematic review of the legislative system. The review of legislation has mostly been left to individual ministries, who have responsibility for updating and adapting their laws, including adopting EU directives. The main instrument for this purpose is the codification of laws, which is painfully long and has a focus on clarity rather than on adapting the laws to modern circumstances. Tools like sunsetting or mandatory periodic reviews are absent from the Greek legal tradition. As a result, Greece's regulatory system is rigid and regulatory costs are unnecessarily high and increasing over time, with compliance lower than desired and confidence in the regulatory structure is undermined.

An important area where excessive burdens have accumulated over time is the licensing of businesses where approvals are granted by multiple ministries, municipalities, prefectures as well as some

Table 4. Recent changes concerning administrative burdens in Greece

Procedure	No. of regulations involved (1996/2001)	No. of agencies involved 1996/2001	Supporting documents (1996/2001)	Approximate time for approval (1996/2001)
Electricity connection	4L, 6D	3	5	15 days
Building licence	6L, 3D	Up to 6	17	1 month (minimum)
Ratification of environmental effects study	1L, 2D, 5MD, 1EUD	3	6	Ranges between 8 months – 2 years
Investment on industrial plant	10L, 3D, 2MD, 1 PD/ 1L, 2MD	5	14/8 to 16	50 days (minimum)/43 days (average)
Quarry licence	6L, 2D, 2EUD/3L, 2D, 2EUD	11/2	6/5	1 year (minimum)
Fishery licence	2L, 4D, 4MD, 4EUD/2L, 1D, 2MD, 4EUD	7/2	12/5	1 year (minimum) /60 days to 1 year

L= Legislation, D = Presidential Decree, MD = Ministerial Decision, C = interpretative Circular, EUD = European Union Directive, BD = Board Decision, PD = Prefecture Decision

Source: Ministry of the Interior, Public Administration, and Decentralisation, 2000, using data from 1996 and early 2001.

regulatory agencies. For example, until very recently obtaining a building licence involved up to six different agencies (ministries and local government) and required compliance with 6 different pieces of legislation, and 3 Presidential Decrees. Recent reforms reduced some of these costs. For instance, the government reported that by early 2001 only one agency was involved in issuing a building license, instead of 6, and that the license could be obtained in less than 20 days (see Table 4).

Excessive regulation of business activities via licensing or a complex legal system with overlapping controls add real costs to business activities and potentially stymie new ventures or expanding businesses. In this regard, the Federation of Greek Industries (SEB) estimates that paperwork burdens increase production costs by more than 5% of operating costs. The National Confederation of Greek Trade (ESEE) estimates that a SME business spends at least 30 hours per month or an average of 12.5% of total work time complying with non-productive bureaucratic regulations and procedures.[68] In terms of employment policies, permits are required to allow workers work overtime, government notification is required for new employees including part-time employment and approval from the Ministry of Labour is require to layoff workers (depending on the size of the firm[69]). The 1998 employment law, however, introduced some flexibility into working hours. As a general rule, tax compliance certificates are required to obtain insurance and ongoing credit with banks. Furthermore, it can take up to one year and 45 individual approvals to establish a new business enterprise. In sum, the regulatory burden, permits, approvals and licences are stifling Greek businesses and it is handicapping a traditionally strong entrepreneurial spirit, in particular SMEs.[70]

Facing these challenges, the government has undertaken a number of initiatives to reduce the administrative burden on both business and citizens. Box 11, for instance shows that Greece has been active in trying simplification mechanisms. One such initiative was the establishment in 1996 of the one-stop-shop for foreign investors, the Hellenic Centre of Investment ELKE. Through ELKE's intercession the processing time for applications for investment assistance has been reduced from a 6-month average to three months. Further ELKE has created a database of licence and permit requirements that informs potential investors about government obligations.[71]

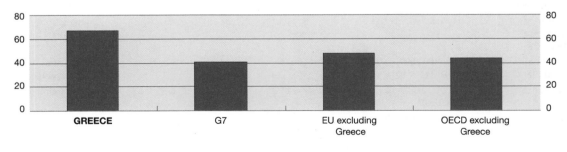

Box 11. Simplifying business licences and permits

The OECD created an indicator to measure the efforts of OECD countries in simplifying licence and permit processes. This indicator weights more highly those programmes where countries use the "silence is consent" rule to speed up decisions, where one-stop shops have been set up, where there is a complete inventory of permits and licences; and where there is a specific programme, co-ordinated with lower levels of government, to review and reduce burdens of permits and licences. Greece ranks high on these scores relative to other G7, EU and OECD countries. This is due more so to the number of programmes to review and reduce the number of licences and permits rather than an overall trend of reduced burdens.

Source: Public Management Service, OECD, 1999.

Nevertheless, ELKE, along with other initiatives, is struggling to produce tangible results for companies. Moreover ELKE is designed for big companies out of reach of national SMEs.[72] This has created a bias in favour of foreign or big firms and discriminates against domestic investment. Important services and tools ELKE has developed such as the licenses database or advocacy services with different ministries are not accessible to small and medium sized firms. Plus, ELKE only provides information and advice, they do not have the authority to issue licences.

5. CONCLUSIONS AND RECOMMENDATIONS FOR ACTION

5.1 General assessment of current strengths and weaknesses

Since the re-establishment of democratic institutions in 1974, Greece has experienced substantial social, political, and economic changes. Coupled with the influence of European Union membership and the drive to join the European Monetary Union, Greece has taken many steps to modernise its economic infrastructure, and is in the process of converging with most OECD countries. The pace of change toward market-oriented policies and transparent and accountable institutions has accelerated in recent years through economic reforms, including deregulation, privatisation, and liberalisation. Government institutions, culture, and capacities to produce high quality regulations have, however, lagged behind and this gap reduces the potential benefits such reforms could bring to the Greek consumers, entrepreneurs and citizens using public services.

A challenge already accepted by political leadership is modernisation of the public service. From a governance perspective, reform of the Greek system seems to be hindered by a lack of trust in the public administration of the capacities of businesses and society. This has resulted in over-regulation of the private sphere, and is matched by over-regulation of the civil service by politicians. This two-edged polynomia has stifled creativity and dynamism throughout the public administration and society. Regulatory reform should be perceived as a strategy to cut the Gordian knot of distrust and restore effective relations and confidence among the state, the market, and civil society.

Efforts and initiatives over the past decade indicate that a strategy for regulatory quality is emerging, step by step. The de-politicisation and establishment of meritorious promotion of public officials will raise the status and prestige of the civil service inside and outside the administration, and thus public confidence. The sustained effort to devolve powers to local governments, linked to direct elections, will bring the administration closer to the citizens and small businesses. A profusion of new public management initiatives coupled with efforts to communicate better and more often with the citizens or public service customers will increase expectations of responsiveness. Initiatives by some ministries to reassess their regulations, such as the Ministry of the National Economy, show awareness of the limits of the current regulatory structure and the need for continuing regulatory review.

However, these initiatives, while essential, are not yet sufficiently coherent and targeted at regulatory practices to reinvent the administration's regulatory relations with the market and society. For instance, clear results in streamlining bureaucratic procedures such as licensing have not yet been produced. Public sector incentives are not aligned to encourage good practices in producing new regulations, excessive discretion weakens the regulatory framework, and an emphasis on legal training and a neglect of economic skills hinders the administration of the new market based regulatory system. Impact assessment and the use of innovation or regulatory alternatives is poor relative to other OECD countries, limiting the government's capacity to develop the high quality regulatory framework needed for the current needs of citizens and economic development.

The low quality of existing regulations, created through decades of regulatory inflation, discourages citizens, encourages non-compliance and the grey market, penalises those who comply in good faith, reduces business competitiveness, and creates disincentives for trade and investment. Unless resolute action is taken to review and rationalise the stock of current regulations, efforts to improve new practices will be ineffective.

Decentralisation has been a positive reform to enhance local government capacities and competencies. But the process must be completed with the transfer and acquisition of staff and resources. Overlapping responsibilities between levels of government require co-ordination and co-operation without which, regulatory layering will add excessive burdens and costs on business and citizens. Stronger accountability and transparency measures would also avoid capture by local interests of the benefits that this effort can bring to the whole community.

5.2. Policy options for consideration

The policy recommendations below identify actions that, based on good regulatory practices and on concrete experiences in OECD countries, are likely to be beneficial to improving the quality of regulations in Greece. Most of the recommendations form a comprehensive approach that can be combined in the short-term in a reform package. Implementation of these reforms, however, such as building new institutions, may take considerable time and sustained attention.

– *To consolidate the various reform initiatives already underway in Greece, adopt at the political level a broad policy on regulatory management that establishes clear objectives, accountability principles, and frameworks for implementation.*

To organise and drive reform on the capacity to produce high quality regulations, the government should adopt an government-wide regulatory reform policy based on explicit principles of good economic, social, and administrative regulation such as those in the 1997 OECD Report to Ministers. In particular, the principle that regulatory costs should be justified by benefits should be adopted. This would stimulate and guide the efforts of all ministries, and build on the efforts on regulatory reform of ministries such as MIPAD and the Ministry of the National Economy. It would provide a basis for the performance of those efforts to be assessed, and the efforts themselves to be corrected to improve results. It would improve greater accountability within ministries for their regulatory systems and the results. Given the web of entrenched interests and traditions of ministerial independence in Greece, personal involvement and direction from the highest political levels will aid greatly regulatory reform.

– *Establish a ministerial-level Regulatory Reform Committee, with an expert secretariat, to make key regulatory reform decisions and to co-ordinate regulatory reform across government.*

A ministerial-level committee should be created to promote implementation of the regulatory reform policy, to make key regulatory reform decisions, and to co-ordinate regulatory reform across government. Bodies representing competition principles should be included on the committee. The committee would also resolve controversies between policies and prepare an annual report to the Parliament. Participants on the committee could include the Prime Minister Office and the Ministries of, the National Economy, the Interior, Public Administration and Decentralisation, Development and Justice. This political body could be modelled on the Netherlands' Ministerial Committee in charge of the influential MDW ('Functioning of Markets, Deregulation and Legislative Quality') programme.

– *As a secretariat to the ministerial-level committee, establish an oversight unit with (i) authority to make recommendations to the Regulatory Reform Committee, (ii) adequate capacities to collect information and co-ordinate the reform programme throughout the public administration, and (iii) enough resources and analytical expertise to provide an independent opinion on regulatory matters.*

Greece will need a technical institution or agency in charge of assuring the quality of the regulation and to provide the necessary support to the ministerial committee. Its mandate, political accountability, and operation should be focused on objective controls such as regulatory quality and regulatory impact analysis similar to those of the unit in place in the UK or Italy. It should also monitor and promote the necessary economic and public management skills needed to complement work on legal quality within the ministries.

The unit should deliver expert advice and co-ordinate. First, the unit would need a well-resourced secretariat with cross-governmental views and an attractive staffing policy. It should have sufficient financial resources to collect and assess information and buy the expertise of private experts and scholars. Its mission, powers and legal status in the government's legislative and regulatory process should be formalised to reduce opposition. The unit would need authority to advocate and design thematic and sectoral programmes of reforms, co-ordinated across relevant policy areas. The unit could develop performance targets, timelines, and evaluation requirements, review regulatory proposals from ministries against quality principles, and advise the centre of government on the quality of regulatory and reform proposals from regulatory ministries.

- *Improve the quality of new regulations by implementing across the administration a step-by-step programme for regulatory impact assessment, based on OECD best practice recommendations, for all new and revised regulations. The analysis should begin with feasible steps such as costing of direct impacts (other than budgetary) and provide a qualitative assessment of benefits, and move progressively over a multi-year period to more rigorous quantitative form of analysis as skills are built in the administration. The assessments should be made public so as to enhance transparency as well as provide external discipline to improve the quality and content of the assessments.*

Most OECD Member countries now use RIA and the direction of change is universally toward refining, strengthening and extending the use of RIA disciplines. However, in Greece, RIA is in its infancy. Yet experience in many countries shows that RIA can be a powerful tool to boost regulatory quality. Lack of information on impacts of regulatory proposals means that Greece's laws are vulnerable to influence from special interests and less transparent to outside parties.

OECD's best practice principles should be the basis for the Greek RIA programme. Quality control of RIA's should be overseen by the technical unit recommended above. A comprehensive training programme should be introduced to support capacities for impact assessment. Adequate budgetary funding for the programme should also be planned (for the production by ministries and review by a central unit) to reduce the risk that RIA will become just one more paperwork hurdle in the administrative procedures.

While it is acknowledged that benefit-cost analysis is the long-term goal, constructive steps consistent with current administrative skills could be implemented immediately. These could include incorporating in the justification report required by Article 74 of the Constitution the ten quality dimensions of the 1995 OECD checklist. The checklist could be made mandatory for subordinate legislation, Presidential Decrees and Ministerial Decisions. Transparency and accountability would be increased if the checklist responses were published on the Internet.

In the medium term (*e.g.* 12 months), the government could have in place a traditional RIA structured around an *ex ante* quantitative analysis of impacts, that is, a RIA report prepared by ministries and agencies and reviewed by a technical and independent unit assessing the quality, content, scope, and adequacy of the analysis. The Cabinet should refuse to discuss proposals that are not accompanied by a RIA, and subordinate regulations should not be signed by the responsible minister without a RIA that had been reviewed by the independent body. RIA should be targeted on only the most important regulations to avoid wasting time and resources on less significant measures. RIA should also be used as the vehicle for asystematic consideration of regulatory alternatives for new regulatory proposals. Preparation of an annual report to Parliament on trends in the use of RIA could increase incentives for its use within the ministries.

- *Promote the systematic consideration of regulatory alternatives for new regulatory proposals, including subordinate legislation, so that the use of alternatives flows beyond the area of environmental protection to all regulatory controls.*

Another significant omission from the current regulatory quality programme is the failure to promote the use of market based alternatives to regulation when government intervention is justified. The OECD *Report to Ministers on Regulatory Reform*[73] documented movement toward a range of alternative instruments in OECD countries and pointed to evidence on gains in policy effectiveness. By explicitly requiring the consideration of alternatives as mandatory for regulatory proposals including subordina-

163

te regulation, Greece can over time move toward a more flexible and efficient regulatory structure that uses markets to achieve public policy goals.

Evidence should be provided that alternatives have been given due consideration. This could be achieved by gradually building into a RIA programme a section devoted to the alternatives considered and why those alternatives were not accepted. An initial phase of training and awareness will allow the public sector to gain greater familiarity with alternative policy tools before a formal requirement is imposed across all of government.

- *Improve transparency by strengthening the public consultation process to include all subordinate regulations, and adopt uniform notice and comment procedures.*

Currently, public consultation of legal and regulatory proposals is done informally. Formal consultation is based on a corporatist approach. Consultation is not carried out for legislative amendments or subordinate regulations. Low levels of consultation reduce regulatory quality, and leave Greek regulators vulnerable to organised interest groups, which often represent "insiders". A mandatory public consultation requirement, based on objective criteria, would substantially improve quality and transparency. An effective means to improve transparency and accountability would be to adopt an across-the-board 'notice and comment' process for all regulations, to complement other consultation mechanisms and work as a safeguard against capture by special interest groups. Additionally, the government could develop clear guidelines and parameters for consultation methods and require disclosing RIA with draft texts as part of the notice and comment process. Ministries proposing new regulations should be required to prepare written and public replies to the comments and all responses and comments should be available to the public.

- *Establish a central registry of administrative procedures and business licences and permits, and initiate a comprehensive review to determine how to reduce burdens.*

Administrative burdens, and in particular business licences and permits are among the most important barrier to Greek entrepreneurs and to market entry. By fostering non-compliance and promoting grey regulation they nourish unfair competition with the legal economy and maintain barriers to market access. Rapid and resolute abolition of this type of regulation can bring swift economic gains and build a constituency among SMEs for further reform. To obtain such results rapidly, a mandatory registry of all forms should first be organised, with positive legal security. If a form is not registered in the inventory, then it should not be enforced. As a second step, the forms of the inventory should be reviewed and reformatted, and if possible eliminated or replaced by less burdensome instruments. To accelerate benefits to SMEs, priority in the selection of forms should be based on business opinions. Examples which Greece could adapt include France with the Centre d'Évaluation et de Registre des Formalités (CERFA), Mexico with its Registro Federal de Tramites[74] and Spain with its Comision de Simplificacion.[75]

- *On a rolling and priority basis, review and evaluate the stock of existing regulations and paperwork, including launching a programme of codification to reduce legal uncertainty.*

Regulatory inflation is undermining the integrity of the Greek regulatory system. Although this is a very large task, efforts should be made to develop a rolling, systematic process of codification and evaluation of existing laws and other regulations. This may require application government-wide of the pilot programme within the Ministry of the National Economy, revised to include more rigorous reviews. It would probably be based on a sector by sector review, with more economically-important sectors reviewed first. The review should incorporate regulatory impact assessments. For such reviews, the 1995 OECD regulatory quality checklist could be used as a reference to check the continued necessity and appropriateness of Greece's regulations. To support the review, the Parliament or government could directly or via an independent commission review the main areas of legislation and produce a programme of reform. The review process undertaken in Australia as part of its National Competition Policy is illustrative. Under that policy, all legislation was reviewed and anti-competitive restrictions were required to be removed unless it could be demonstrated that those restrictions were in the public interest and that there was no other way to achieve public policy objectives.[76]

A full review of Greek regulations is a daunting task and would take many years. The Australian review will take 5 years to complete and, to ensure ongoing quality, will be repeated every 10 years. Greece should aim initially to prepare an inventory of all laws, including subordinate regulations and then review that inventory as part of a more rigorous process. This would allow for the skill and experience development that subsequently would be utilised in the reviews.

Implementation of this recommendation should allow for the development of a single authoritative source for all regulations that is easily understood, accessible, and agreeable to the citizens and business alike. Furthermore, it would significantly enhance transparency for users in terms of the content and form of permissible regulatory actions thus helping improve compliance levels.

— *Encourage greater co-ordination between local government and the central administration by defining more clearly relevant regulatory competencies for each level of government, by providing the necessary resources, people, and financing for delivery of services that those competencies dictate, and by assisting in the development of management capacities for quality regulation at all levels of administration.*

The decentralisation process undertaken since the mid-1990s is impressive. However, managing regulations at different levels creates potential concerns of coherence, overlap, and inconsistency. Other countries' experiences show that safeguarding gains made at the national level through regulatory reform will require intensive efforts to promote regulatory quality at sub-national levels. Adoption by local governments of regulatory quality principles should form the basis for formal co-operation measures. Consideration should be given to establishing processes and mechanisms to resolve issues arising from regulatory conflicts or overlap. This will be critical to help ensure greater policy coherence, as is currently the case with the licensing system. A complementary, but critical strategy should also be to develop transparency and accountability measures. In that sense, the notice and comment mechanism together with a close monitoring (or even benchmarking) from the centre administration should help to avoid reversals, while encouraging experimentation at the sub-national level. Such monitoring could also be carried out by the technical unit.

— *Improve the mechanisms within the administration to produce quality outcomes for the citizens, through further reform of the civil service. Elements to be considered could be performance based management, pay incentives for public servants based on merit and achievements, greater flexibility within the public administration for movement of resources and competencies, and effort to enhance co-ordination and co-operation between ministries.*

Improving the public administration requires a flexible system that matches the existing skills based within the public service to current policy directions and where necessary the acquisition of new skills and staff, particularly for the area of economic analysis. Until today the Greek approach has been one of central command of key functions such as recruiting and promotion. Such measures have been beneficial in the short and medium term as the goals and procedures are accepted across the administration. But after a certain state, the rigidity of the system may produce diminishing returns. A bolder approach based on transparency and accountability of high officials is needed. In particular, incentives need to be aligned with written and public objectives. Flexibility must be introduced to encourage public servants to move within and between ministries. Training and skills development must be enhanced. Of particular importance will be the adequate enforcement and encouragement for public servants to comply with the requirements of the new Code of Administrative Procedure Act and the Civil Service Code. Without widespread knowledge of these requirements, without consistent application across the whole of the public administration, and without visible commitment by senior bureaucrats and government then the codes will be of limited value.

165

NOTES

1. Prime Minister's programme declaration to Parliament on 22 April 2000.

2. Spraos (1998), "Quality in Public Administration: Recommendations for Changes", Commissioned for the examination of the long-term economic policy, Financed by the National Bank of Greece.

3. In 1998 the OECD measured the number of public sector employees in Greece, not including state owned enterprises, as representing approximately 10% of the total work force. This is not high relative to France (25%), Finland (24%), Portugal (18%), or Spain (15%) and it is below OECD average of 17%. OECD (1998) The Public Employment Service: Greece, Ireland, Portugal, Paris, Table 1.4.

4. One factor that has impinged on the flexibility of the public sector is related to its high rate of growth in number of employees over the past decade. The number of public sector employment has grown from 106 000 in 1961, 116 000 in 1963, 134 000 in 1974, 157 000 in 1977, 200 000 in 1981, 234 000 in 1985, 237 000 in 1990, to 290 000 in 1999. Government of Greece, Ministry of the Interior, Public Administration, and Decentralisation, data supplied in April 2000.

5. OECD (1996) Report on Public Sector Pay.

6. See Spanou, Calliope (1998) "European Integration in Administrative Terms: a Framework for Analysis and the Greek Case" in *Journal of European Public Policy* 5:3, September. p. 475.

7. See Spanou, Calliope (1996), "On the Regulatory Capacity of the Hellenic State: a Tentative Approach Based on a Case Study" in International Review of Administrative Science, Vol. 62.

8. OKE, Report on the Draft Law on Incentives for Private Investment (February 1998)

9. Information provided by the Ombudsman.

10. IOBE, The Greek Economy, 2/99, No. 22 November 1999, pp. 24-26 and US Department of Commerce, idem, p. 6. Greece ranks 36th in the Transparency International Index for Corruption Perceptions index. For further information see http://www.transparency.org/documents/cpi/index.html

11. See for instance Greek approach to technical standard settings in Kastrinos, Nikos and Fernando Romero (1997) idem.

12. OECD (1997a).

13. US Department of Commerce, Country Commercial Guide, Greece Fiscal Year 2000, Chapter Investment Climate, http://www.usatrade.gov/website/CCG.nsf/byuid/.

14. Refer to Law 2190/1994.

15. It is worthwhile noting that "flexibility" to undertake employment actions on its own behalf proved quite costly for the Ombudsman as their 450 interviews effectively became public hearings.

16. Although, it could be argued though that this has been more the result of a desire to meet the Maasticht criteria for joining EMU than about ensuring an efficient appropriately staffed public service.

17. Mainly because the health, education, and national security sectors are exempted from the rule and they account for more than half of all public employment.

18. Formal competencies were transferred from the State both to regions and local authorities by Law 2647/98.

19. Information provided as part of the responses to the Regulatory Reform Questionnaire (March 2000).

20. The citizens guide includes telephone numbers and other reference material. It is now available on the Internet.

21. This programme is distinct from the simplification programmes of the ministry of Development and the ministry of Finance who also have undertaken efforts to reduce licences and permits and improving the tax administration (see Section 4.2).

22. Law 2672/98 entered into force in March 1999.

23. Since the introduction of Law 2690/1999, individual ministries now determine the adequacy of compensation claims. From December 1999, 58 cases were examined by MIPAD and 3 were found sufficient to require compensation. Prior to Law 2690/1999 there was only one committee for all the public service to review compensation claims. In the period 1/3/1998 to 5/12/1999 that committee examined 182 cases with 21 being found sufficient to warrant compensation and a total of 800 000dr was paid.

24. During 1999, 448 834 calls were received of which 205 807 calls concerned requests for application forms or information.

25. See Law 2690/1999 and Law 2683/1999.

26. OECD (1997b), p. 37.

27. OECD (1995), *Recommendation of the Council of the OECD on Improving the Quality of Government Regulation*, Paris.

28. Spraos (1998), idem.

29. Ministry of the National Economy (2000), "Team work for the Study of Regulation". The review examined 17 pieces of legislation, 12 Presidential Decrees, and 100 Ministerial Orders.

30. Deighton-Smith, Rex (1997c), p. 221.

31. The Ombudsman is selected by the Council of Ministers following a recommendation by the Parliamentary Standing Committee on Institutions and Transparency. The Ombudsman is appointed for a five-year non-renewable period and is supported by four Deputy Ombudsmen and a staff of 30 senior investigators (all of whom hold post graduate degrees) and 40 seconded civil servants with the same qualifications.

32. The Council of State was created in 1929 created and modelled on the French Conseil d'État, though its members are magistrates and not civil servants. It is also the supreme administrative appeal court.

33. It should be noted though, that the choice of instrument is not always open between Presidential Decree and Ministerial Decision.

34. For the purpose of the discussion, the distinction between deconcentration and decentralisation refers to the level of autonomy of the executive/legislative power (i.e. the former is appointed by the central government, the latter is directly elected).

35. Article 24 of the Municipal and Communal Code.

36. Government of Greece, response to OECD regulatory reform questionnaire.

37. See Presidential Decree 410/95 (Municipal and Communal Code).

38. European Union Single Market Scoreboard, November 1999.

39. Spaniou, Calliope (1998), idem, p. 475.

40. Issues relating to taxation, fundamental rights and external relations can only be introduced via legislation.

41. Government of Greece, Information provided to the OECD, April 2000.

42. The Council is made up of 9 associations, 8 social bodies, and 2 scientists, and it meets 4-5 times a year. The Council was created under Law 2251/94.

43. The ESC involvement in the legislative process was formalised by Law 2232/1994.

44. Government of Greece, response to Regulatory Reform Questionnaire.

45. For more information, see www.parliament.gr and www.et.gr.

46. Information provided by EuroAuditing during interview with the OECD, March 2000.

47. OECD (1999), "Background Report on Government Capacities to Produce High Quality Regulations" in *Regulatory Reform in Mexico*, Paris.

48. Response to the OECD Regulatory Reform questionnaire (March 2000).

49. Spanou, Calliope (1996), idem, p. 219.

50. See OECD (2000), *Regulatory Compliance Report*.

51. This is provided for by the Code of Administrative Procedure and in Law 2690/1999 which sets rules of administrative action and the conditions for the communication and carrying out those actions.

52. Ombudsman, personal interview.

53. See OECD (2000), *Environmental Performance Reviews*, Paris.

54. In fact, the *Environmental Protection Law* 1650/16-10-1986 includes provisions regarding the polluter pays principle in Articles 28, 29, 30 on "Sanctions and Civil Liability" where It provides for sanctions of any unauthorized action and violation that result in environmental pollution, levying of waste and wastewater user charges and compensation for any damages or environmental degradation.

55. OECD(2000), *Environmental Performance Reviews* (Greece), Paris, based on data available up to September 1999.

56. OECD (1997c), Paris.

57. A Ministerial Decision by the Minister of Public Administration established in November 2000 a Regulatory Reform Committee. The Committee consists of the Vice- President of the Council of State, public law professors, special scientists and high-level bureaucrats in public administration (Ministries of National Economy, Justice, Development, Labour, Public Works, Telecommunications, the Competition Committee, Capital Market Commission etc.).The Committee's work has been supported by international experts.

58. The *Spraos Report* recommended to the Prime Minister in 1998 that RIA as recommended by the OECD should be implemented, Spraos (1998).

59. SEV (1/10/90), "Propositions for Administrative Simplification".

60. Spraos (1998) idem.

61. See Article 74 of the Constitution.

62. Views expressed by the Ministry of Development, the Ministry of Finance, the Ministry of the National Economy, and the Ministry of the Interior, Public Administration, and Decentralisation.

63. For further guidance see Broder, I and Morral, J "Collecting and Using Data for Regulatory Decision-Making" in OECD (1997c).

64. See European Commission Infringement Procedures involving Greece (1999).

65. See Law 2773/1999.

66. IMF Staff Report on Greece for the 1999 Article IV Consultation Supplementary Information pp 200-201 and the Economist Intelligence Unit (1999-2000) Country Profile Greece, pp. 32-34.

67. See Law 2651/1998 and Law 2744/1999.

68. National Confederation of Greek Trade (ESEE) (1999), "The increase of the functional cost of a commercial enterprise because of the necessary bureaucracy procedures", Athens.

69. Retrenchments can occur at will for firms of below 20 employees, up to 5 between 20-50 employees, and a maximum of 2% for larger firms.

70. 85% of Greece's enterprises employ between 1 and 4 persons.

71. Interestingly, ELKE has the authority to advocate a change of regulations to ministries but as yet this power has seldom been used and when used the result has been disappointing.

72. ELKE reviews and provide assistance for projects valued over 3 billion drachmas ($10 million) or 1.5 billion drachmas ($5 million) if there is foreign participation.

73. Jacobs, Scott *et al.* (1997c), pp. 220-222.

74. See OECD (1999), "Background Report on Government Capacities to Produce High Quality Regulations" in OECD *Reviews of Regulatory Reform*, *Regulatory Reform in Mexico*, Paris.

75. See OECD (2000), "Background Report on Government Capacities to Produce High Quality Regulations" in OECD *Reviews of Regulatory Reform*, Regulatory Reform in Spain, Paris.

76. For further information see, Hilmer, F, Raynor, M., and Taperell, G. (1993), The Independent Committee of Inquiry, *National Competition Policy*, AGPS, Canberra, Australia. Or
http://www.ncc.gov.au/nationalcompet/Legislation%20Review/Legislation%20Review.htm.

BIBLIOGRAPHY

Broder, I and Morral, J (1997),
"Collecting and Using Data for Regulatory Decision-Making" in OECD (1997) *Regulatory Impact Analysis: Best Practices in OECD Countries*, Paris

Deighton-Smith, Rex (1997),
"Regulatory Impact Analysis: Best Practice in OECD Countries", in *Regulatory Impact Analyses: Best Practice in OECD Countries*, Paris

Economist Intelligence Unit (1999-2000),
Country Profile Greece, pp. 32-34.

European Commission, *Infringement Procedures involving Greece*, http://europa.eu.int/comm/dg15/en/update/inf/index.htm.

Government of Greece (2000),
responses to Regulatory Reform Questionnaire, March.

Hilmer, F, Raynor, M., and Taperell, G. (The Independent Committee of Inquiry) 1993,
National Competition Policy, AGPS, Canberra, Australia.

http://www.et.gr

http://www.ncc.gov.au/nationalcompet/Legislation%20Review/Legislation%20Review.htm

http://www.parliament.gr

www.ypai.aegean.gr

http://www.ypes.gr/kapodristria/english/kapo/programme.htm

International Monetary Fund (1999),
IMF *Staff Report on Greece*, Article IV Consultation Supplementary Information pp 200-201

IOBE (1999),
The Greek Economy, 2/99, No. 22 November, pp. 24-26.

Jacobs, Scott *et al.* (1997),
Regulatory Quality and Public Sector Reform, in OECD (1997), *The OECD Report on Regulatory Reform Volume* II: *Thematic Studies*, Paris, pp. 220-222.

Kastrinos, Nikos and Fernando Romero (1997),
"Policies for Competitiveness in Less-favoured Regions of Europe: a Comparison of Greece and Portugal" in *Science and Public Policy*, 24(2), June, pp. 189-195.

Ministry of the National Economy (2000),
Team work for the Study of Regulation, Greece.

National Confederation of Greek Trade (ESEE) (1999),
The increase of the functional cost of a commercial enterprise because of the necessary bureaucracy procedures, Athens.

OECD (1995),
Recommendation of the Council of the OECD on Improving the Quality of Government Regulation, OCDE/GD(95)95, Paris.

OECD (1996),
Report on Public Sector Pay, Paris.

OECD (1997a),
The OECD Report on Regulatory Reform: Volume I, Sectoral Studies, Paris.

169

OECD (1997b),
> The OECD Report on Regulatory Reform: Synthesis, Paris.

OECD (1997b),
> Regulatory Impact Analysis: Best Practices in OECD Countries, Paris.

OECD (1998),
> The Public Employment Service: Greece, Ireland, Portugal, Paris.

OECD (1999),
> "Background Report on Government Capacities to Produce High Quality Regulations" in Regulatory Reform in Mexico, Paris.

OECD (2000),
> "Background Report on Government Capacities to Produce High Quality Regulations" in Report on Regulatory Reform in Spain, Paris.

OECD (2000),
> Environmental Performance Reviews: Greece, Paris.

OECD (2000),
> Regulatory Compliance Report.

OKE (1998),
> Report on the Draft Law on Incentives for Private Investment.

Spanou, Calliope (1996),
> "On the Regulatory Capacity of the Hellenic State: a Tentative Approach Based on a Case Study" in International Review of Administrative Science, Vol. 62.

Spanou, Calliope (1998),
> "European Integration in Administrative Terms: a Framework for Analysis and the Greek Case" in Journal of European Public Policy 5:3, September.

Spraos (1998),
> Quality in Public Administration: Recommendations for Changes, financed by the National Bank of Greece.

Social and Economic Committee, Greece (OKE) (1998),
> Report on the Draft Law on Incentives for Private Investment.

Transparency International (2000),
> Index for Corruption Perceptions, http://www.transparency.org.

US Department of Commerce, Country Commercial Guide, Greece Fiscal Year 2000, Chapter Investment Climate, http://www.usatrade.gov/website/CCG.nsf/byuid/.

BACKGROUND REPORT ON
THE ROLE OF COMPETITION POLICY
IN REGULATORY REFORM*

* This report was principally prepared by **Michael Wise** in the Directorate for Financial and Fiscal Affairs of the OECD. It has benefited from extensive comments provided by colleagues throughout the OECD Secretariat, by the Government of Greece, and by Member countries as part of the peer review process. This report was peer reviewed in June 2000 in the OECD's Competition Law and Policy Committee.

TABLE OF CONTENTS

List of Boxes

List of Tables

Executive Summary

Background Report on The Role of Competition Policy in Regulatory Reform

Is competition policy sufficiently integrated into the general policy framework for regulation? Competition policy is central to regulatory reform, because (as background report to Chapter 2 shows) its principles and analysis provide a benchmark for assessing the quality of economic and social regulations, as well as motivate the application of the laws that protect competition. Moreover, as regulatory reform stimulates structural change, vigorous enforcement of competition policy is needed to prevent private market abuses from reversing the benefits of reform. A complement to competition enforcement is competition advocacy, the promotion of competitive, market principles in policy and regulatory processes. This report addresses two basic questions: First, is Greece's conception of competition policy, which depends on its own history and culture, adequate to support pro-competitive reform? Second, do national institutions have the right tools to effectively promote competition policy? That is, are the competition laws and enforcement structures sufficient to prevent or correct collusion, monopoly, and unfair practices, now and after reform? And can its competition law and policy institutions encourage reform? The answers to these questions are assessed in terms of their implications for the strategies and sequencing of regulatory reform.

One of Greece's long-term priorities has been establishing more complete economic integration with Europe, first through EU membership and most recently through joining the euro zone. Recognition of the key role of competition policy, both in the larger sense of policies supporting and promoting competition and markets and in the narrower sense of laws and institutions applying rules about competitive behaviour, has been slower to emerge. Despite the long-term general policy of conforming to European norms, delays and derogations from EU liberalising directives are common. The memory and habit of planning and price control are recent. "Gentlemen's agreements" that constrain free price competition have been tolerated and even encouraged, in order to meet EMU inflation criteria. A better approach to moderating price increases would be to promote competition in sheltered sectors and in historically state-dominated sectors.

The institutions of competition policy, an independent decision-making Competition Committee supported by a Secretariat that is responsible to it rather than to a ministry, are relatively new. They lack resources and political support. Although personnel has been increased by three positions (about 15%), the Secretariat staff is still a small fraction of the size of the competition agencies of similar sized OECD countries. The Competition Committee's representative structure is more suited to compromise among interests than to consistent application of policy. Nearly all of the Competition Committee's time and resources has been devoted to reviewing merger applications, even though anti-competitive mergers are not likely to be a major issue as Greece integrates better with the EU. On the contrary: businesses are small-scale, and there is substantial opportunity for consolidation to improve efficiency and international competitiveness in many sectors. Meanwhile, there have been no resources to deal with horizontal issues, which are likely to be significant in the wake of a tradition of formal and informal price control.

Competition policy has had little impact on policy-making generally. The Competition Committee has not used its authority to offer policy advice about regulations and government decisions that impair competition. The Competition Committee does not have the capacity to deal with competition problems raised by policies and decisions by other bodies that seek to protect inefficient state-owned enterprises, and it has undertaken little systematic enforcement or other activity about sectors that show significant competition problems. The Competition Committee has not been consulted about reforms in network infrastructure sectors or about other aspects of policy. It is nominally independent in its decision-making function, but it has been made too dependent on the Ministry of Development, which has not shared its policy goals, for budget and other support.

Competition policy can make a serious contribution to promoting efficiency and innovation in competitive markets only if staff resources are expanded. Additional resources must be devoted to issues other than unnecessary merger reviews. In particular, attention should shift to horizontal agreements and to the competition problems that are arising in the process of establishing competition in historically monopolised sectors. Analysis and advocacy should thus become higher priorities. Legislation adopted in August, 2000 addresses these problems, by authorising double the staff, reducing the merger review burden, enabling the Competition Committee to undertake policy advocacy on its own initiative, and protecting the Committee's independence.

175

Box 1.   Competition policy's roles in regulatory reform

In addition to the threshold, general issue, whether regulatory policy is consistent with the conception and purpose of competition policy, there are four particular ways in which competition policy and regulatory problems interact:

Regulation can contradict competition policy. Regulations may have encouraged, or even required, conduct or conditions that would otherwise be in violation of the competition law. For example, regulations may have permitted price co-ordination, prevented advertising or other avenues of competition, or required territorial market division. Other examples include laws banning sales below costs, which purport to promote competition but are often interpreted in anti-competitive ways, and the very broad category of regulations that restrict competition more than is necessary to achieve the regulatory goals. When such regulations are changed or removed, firms affected must change their habits and expectations.

Regulation can replace competition policy. Especially where monopoly has appeared inevitable, regulation may try to control market power directly, by setting prices and controlling entry and access. Changes in technology and other institutions may lead to reconsideration of the basic premise in support of regulation, that competition policy and institutions would be inadequate to the task of preventing monopoly and the exercise of market power.

Regulation can reproduce competition policy. Rules and regulators may have tried to prevent co-ordination or abuse in an industry, just as competition policy does. For example, regulations may set standards of fair competition or tendering rules to ensure competitive bidding. Different regulators may apply different standards, though, and changes in regulatory institutions may reveal that seemingly duplicate policies may have led to different practical outcomes.

Regulation can use competition policy methods. Instruments to achieve regulatory objectives can be designed to take advantage of market incentives and competitive dynamics. Co-ordination may be necessary, to ensure that these instruments work as intended in the context of competition law requirements.

1.   COMPETITION POLICY FOUNDATIONS

Although Greece's competition law was adopted to conform to EU standards, it is not being used to support related, larger-scale reforms. Greece's approach to competition policy has been derivative. The principal direction that emerges clearly is a general intention to follow EU models. The goals of EU membership, and of the single market and monetary union, could have been anchors for substantive reform. But the general goals have been embraced more strongly than the many particular, concrete policy changes needed to conform to EU norms. Government-wide, the policy framework for the use of regulation in carrying out social and economic policy objectives has made too little use of competition principles. The lack of a clear conception of competition policy and its objectives has made competition policy ineffective as a general framework for market-oriented regulatory reform.

1.1. Formal competition policy has been in place since 1977, but its roots are still shallow

Values and habits in Greece have long encouraged a strong entrepreneurial culture. Industry has tended to be small scale (with notable exceptions, such as cement and primary metals), while services, which also tend to be small-scale, have flourished. An unusually high proportion of the working population has been self-employed. Thanks in part to conditions that encourage initiative, there has been substantial material progress since the 1950s; however, the style of governance, institutional infrastructure, and policy frameworks have been slow to adapt and modernise (Clogg, 1992).

Long-standing social values and expectations about the proper role of government present some obstacles to establishing a rule-based system of competition policy. These values and attitudes may even date from the centuries before independence, when the rule of law was weak and people sought protection in family and clientelist relationships. Since the 19th century, Greek reformers have installed new institutions, such as criminal and civil codes, based on borrowed models, to displace existing laws, institutional relationships, and cultural traditions (Clogg, 1992). The practice of incorporating borrowed, external models still characterises some contemporary reforms, notably competition policy itself. In a business and policy culture that has long been characterised by extensive state regulation, direct control of prices, and substantial state-owned enterprises, competition policy has not been a high priority. The basic method of regulatory intervention for many years was direct price and market control.

Greece adopted a competition law as part of the program of preparing for membership in the European Community. Greece's first general competition law was adopted in 1977 (Law 703/1977 on the Control of Monopolies and Oligopolies and the Protection of Free Competition). Except for the general goal of conforming to EU expectations, the law did not respond to any domestic policy issue or impetus, and it was not based on pre-existing Greek laws or institutions. Rather, European models were transposed directly, in substance and procedure.

Two years after the law was enacted, the first decision was issued. When the government changed in the early 1980s, the Competition Committee's powers were reduced – along with those of other independent bodies – because the new government wanted to bring policies more closely under its control. The Competition Committee became an advisory body, and actual decisions were taken by the Minister, based on the Competition Committee's recommendations. The Minister usually followed those recommendations, although he also usually reduced the recommended fines. Most of the enforcement concern was about abuse of dominance, but the Competition Committee also handled some matters involving horizontal agreements. A few mergers were also reviewed, under the provisions about abuse of dominance, despite the lack of explicit merger authority in the law at that time. Much of the Competition Committee's work was dedicated to increasing awareness of the law, and not just among the public and the business community. In that period, the purpose of competition policy was not always clearly understood elsewhere in the government; for example, ministries sometimes asked the Competition Committee to intervene to control prices and profits.

In 1991, when the government changed again, the Competition Committee regained the power of decision. But the power was exercised cautiously at first. Over a two year period, the Competition Committee issued only 10 decisions. Merger notification and control were added to the law, but no decisions blocked mergers during that period. The Competition Committee was given the power to initiate enforcement action, in addition to deciding about applications and notifications (OECD CLP, 1998). Other changes that year included providing for block exemptions, issued by the Minister of Commerce, and adding the concept of "economic dependence" to the section of the law dealing with abuse of dominance.

Amendments adopted in 1995 were intended to strengthen the enforcement structure further. One step that was intended to make enforcement more independent was to put the Secretariat under the Competition Committee's direct control. Up until then, the Competition Committee was supported by the Directorate for Market Research and Competition of the Ministry of Commerce. The competition policy aspects of merger control were made more important, by establishing a two-stage process for review and approval. The Competition Committee was given the power to order interim relief and the power to issue opinions about other policy matters. The power to issue negative clearances was reinstated. Competition Committee membership and organisation were also revised (OECD CLP, 1998).

The Competition Committee may have been justified in asserting that the old regulatory approach, of heavy reliance on direct controls, was being replaced by the principles of protection of free competition and consumer protection (OECD CLP 1997b). But the Minister responsible for these reforms (Costas Simitis, who later became Prime Minister) left office, and his successors did not give competition policy the same priority. Indeed, most of the staff from the Ministry refused to join the new inde-

177

pendent body, and even went on strike protesting the proposals to strengthen competition policy and make it independent. The 1995 reforms did not strengthen competition policy; instead, in important ways they weakened it. The 1995 law compelled the Competition Committee to devote most of its resources to the low-priority task of merger review, while leaving it dependent for support on a Ministry that has not shared its policy goals. Although the professionals who work in and with the Competition Committee have a clear understanding of the economic and other benefits of market competition, the institutional infrastructure of competition policy has been neglected.

1.2. Reform has made little use of competition policy or principles

The goals for competition policy in Greece must be inferred from the circumstances. There is no explicit statement of policy or purpose in the competition law itself. In connection with adoption of the original legislation in 1977, the government stated two purposes: to protect free market competition for the benefit of the economy in general and of consumers in particular, and to harmonise Greek law with EC legislation, anticipating accession to the Common Market (OECD CLP, 1998). The 1995 amendments were intended to strengthen the enforcement of the law, so that the historic methods of state intervention in the economy, namely price control, could be replaced by reliance on free market competition (OECD CLP, 1998).

These plain statements, and the evident lack of further elaboration in decisions or other pronouncements, suggest that Greece has not been concerned about some of the potential conflicts among goals that are often encountered elsewhere. Invocation of policy goals has not played a major part in interpreting and elaborating the law, although the stated goals have no doubt guided its administration. For example, the inclusion of consumer benefit as one of the explicit purposes in 1977 may have helped the Competition Committee resist misuse of the prohibition against abuse of economic dependence.

Liberalisation and privatisation brought changes in the 1990s. Competition policy did not contribute much, though, to these changes. The progress of reform does not show a general embrace of the principles of competition, but rather slow accommodation in particular situations, in response to external pressures. Over period of these changes, the prestige and effectiveness of the competition authorities declined, while competition was introduced in regulated settings only to the degree required by externally imposed constraints. An example of the effort to postpone, rather than encourage, competition was the award to local firms, in December 1997, of a huge package of long-term utility procurement contracts – totalling 3.5% of GDP – just before an EU directive would have required open competition for them. (Greece had already obtained a one-year extension for compliance) (OECD, 1998, p. 108). The fact that Greece has consistently sought more time to comply with EU market-opening and liberalising directives shows the relative importance assigned to competition compared to the nurturing of domestic constituency interests.

A November 1997 "pact of confidence" among the government and social partners acknowledged the need for a number of structural reforms, particularly about labour markets but also about product markets. Recognising the importance of competition in development, one objective of the pact was to strengthen the role of the competition committee (OECD, 1998, pp. 72-73). At that time, the Competition Committee was perceived as limiting its attention to approving mergers, rather than performing a wider role as competition watchdog. Those perceptions remained accurate as of 2000.

Public enterprises have been a principal focus of concern about the extent and vigour of market competition. Public enterprises have been misused as vehicles for policy objectives (such as job creation) unrelated to the objective of providing goods and services most efficiently (OECD, 1998). Yet restructuring moved slowly, and competition policy concerns have played no part in the process. The public enterprise sector has been dominated by about 10 firms, mostly monopolists providing key inputs such as transport, energy, and communications. But it also has included several dozen other firms, a few of them in industrial sectors. In addition, until recently several important industrial firms, most of them not financially healthy, were de facto state-controlled, being under the control either of the Industrial Restructuring Organisation (IRO) or of state-owned banks. Sectors where major firms have been under direct or indirect government control included (and in some cases, still include) shipyards, mining, textiles, metal working, cement, paper, and petroleum (OECD, 1998). Among the non-utility enterprises in public hands were duty free shops, real estate, airline catering and travel agency, horse racing, and football pools and lotteries (IOBE, 1999a). Privatisation is under-way, in stages, of the National Tourist Organisation, which owns or controls many small and medium sized hotels and other tourist facilities (IOBE, 1999c). Direct controls of manufacturing firms have been eliminated, except for four defence firms, and two of those have been set for partial privatisation in 2000. The IRO is to be liquidated after the firm remaining on its books is disposed of (Greece, 1999, p. 4). Because that firm is in a cyclical industry, timing a profitable sale is difficult. But indirect holdings may remain, as the Bank for Industrial Development still had major interests in large, troubled industrial firms in 1999.

A major national policy goal is joining the euro zone, and thus attention is concentrated on the macroeconomic performance measures that determine qualifications. Thus there may be a temptation to intervene in markets to control prices, notably for petroleum products, to help meet the inflation standards (EIU, 1999, p. 19). The government reportedly sought "gentlemen's agreements" from large producers to keep price increases in 1999 below 3% (EIU, 1999, p. 21). And the government is concer-ned that inflation in private services and some retail sectors has been particularly intractable, indica-ting some combination of demand pressure and inadequate competition (IMF, 1999, p. 7). There is no sign that competition policy was considered relevant to these concerns, even though competition is the only sustainable approach to tempering price increases in a market economy.

1.3. Key issues in competition policy today

The situation of competition policy in Greece is critical. The Competition Committee lacks influen-ce, support, and resources. The members are not paid much and their expenses are not reimbursed, so attendance at meetings is inconsistent. Vacancies on the Competition Committee have sometimes remained open for as long as a year. Economic expertise is limited: there is only one economist on the Competition Committee and only one Ph.D economist on the staff. The staff does not have adequate resources for reviewing complaints, doing ex officio investigations, or engaging in policy analysis and advocacy. Greece was the only EU member that did not respond in the EU's process of revising its poli-cies about vertical restraints.

The Competition Committee has been subject to influence by a ministry that has disagreed with its policy direction. In 1999, the Ministry of Development, which supervises the Competition Committee's budget and appointments, endorsed "gentlemen's agreements" between the government and the sel-lers of consumer products to keep price increases down. The Ministry is responsible for administering many potentially anti-competitive constraints on entry, in the form of licensing requirements. And it has recently proposed rules to control prices for auto spare parts and set minimum prices for local truck transport of containers. The Ministry's response to the Competition Committee's request for more staff was unsatisfactory: rather than increase its staff complement or budget, the Ministry agreed only to authorise detailing other Ministry staff to assist the Competition Committee part-time. In that status, it would be difficult for the Competition Committee to use the help effectively. Moreover, there are other reasons to be concerned that the staff detailed from the Ministry would not be helpful; it was their refu-sal to join the new Competition Committee Secretariat that had crippled it in 1995.

Major reforms of network infrastructure are proceeding slowly (see Chapter 1 and background reports to Chapters 5 and 6). Programs of privatisation and liberalisation of energy, telecommunica-tions, and transport have slowly opened national markets and traditional monopolies to active compe-tition. These tentative steps toward reform are being undertaken with little or no consultation with the Competition Committee or its staff. Unless the Competition Committee's resource problems are resol-ved, it is doubtful that it would have the capability of participating in designing and implementing these reforms. Market-opening reforms should be a reason to strengthen competition institutions, to deal with the kinds of problems that appear in an increasingly liberalised economy.

Competition problems that deserve attention include the systems of permits and licenses that control entry, which the Competition Committee has never examined. Many observers report that overt agreements among firms about their prices, operating hours, and services are common, despite the competition law's prohibitions. Even industry trade groups believe that the Competition Committee should be reinforced in resources to deal with important problems and to demonstrate to the business community that competition policy is to be taken seriously. A sign that priorities are changing is the adoption in August 2000 of several amendments to the Competition Act.[1] Among other things, these amendments could substantially increase the Competition Committee's resources and enable it to shift its resources to horizontal restraints and advocacy.

2. SUBSTANTIVE ISSUES: CONTENT OF THE COMPETITION LAW

The basic content of the substantive law about agreements and dominance tracks standard EU principles. The merger rules also track EU regulations, but a market share test still applies to notifications and the merger rules require spending too many resources for merger reviews. The substantive legal criteria and available sanctions should be adequate to deal with competition problems that may have been required or encouraged by regulation, or that will appear as regulatory structures change.

2.1. Horizontal agreements: The rules are adequate, but they have gone disused for lack of resources

The first section of the law is the prohibition of restrictive agreements, both horizontal and vertical. (Art. 1). Both the basic prohibition and the criteria for exemptions are transposed from the EU legislation (see Box 3). Individual exemptions are granted by the Competition Committee, and block exemptions can be issued by the Minister of Development, with the concurrence of the Competition Committee (Art. 7(2)).

A famous early case, from 1981, highlighted the relationship between the prohibition of horizontal agreements and the impact of other regulations. The Athens newspapers colluded to triple the rates for printing formal notices that were required by law. They enforced their collusion through a pooling scheme that discouraged cheating. The newspapers tried, unsuccessfully, to defend themselves from liability by claiming that they were not commercial "undertakings" but rather were performing political and cultural functions (Christoforou, 1990). Other enforcement actions include an order against a public announcement by the bakers association calling for a uniform price increase. And during the same period (1993-94), research by the Ministry staff into the car repair industry uncovered a price agreement, which the Competition Committee ordered the firms to terminate (OECD CLP, 1997).

The criteria for granting exemptions permit agreements for pro-competitive joint actions. An example is the decision permitting a production joint venture between two competing suppliers of bottled gas, Petrolina and EKO; the parties would supply raw materials independently and their branded products would continue to compete downstream, with prices set by the parents separately (OECD CLP, 1997c). So far, the power to issue block exemptions has not been exercised. The Minister may also issue decisions, again with the concurrence of the Competition Committee, defining agreements or categories of agreements that are not considered to fall within the prohibition (Art. 7(3)).

2.2. Vertical agreements

Restrictive agreements between parties in different stages of supply and distribution may maintain or establish relationships that impair competition where regulations of related conduct are changing. As the EU proceeds with changing its substantive rules about vertical agreements (in the standards for granting exemptions), Greece will no doubt follow.

A 1997 decision imposing conditions on a "franchise" arrangement concerning cosmetics and luxury items demonstrates the Competition Committee's thinking: the Competition Committee disapproved of clauses that controlled franchisee advertising, that described the covered products generally

Box 2. The competition policy toolkit

General competition laws usually address the problems of monopoly power in three formal settings: relationships and agreements among otherwise independent firms, actions by a single firm, and structural combinations of independent firms. The first category, **agreements**, is often subdivided for analytic purposes into two groups: "horizontal" agreements among firms that do the same things, and "vertical" agreements among firms at different stages of production or distribution. The second category is termed "**monopolisation**" in some laws, and "**abuse of dominant position**" in others; the legal systems that use different labels have developed somewhat different approaches to the problem of single-firm economic power. The third category, often called "**mergers**" or "**concentrations**," usually includes other kinds of structural combination, such as share or asset acquisitions, joint ventures, cross-shareholdings and interlocking directorates.

Agreements may permit the group of firms acting together to achieve some of the attributes of monopoly, of raising prices, limiting output, and preventing entry or innovation. The most troublesome **horizontal** agreements are those that prevent rivalry about the fundamental dynamics of market competition, price and output. Most contemporary competition laws treat naked agreements to fix prices, limit output, rig bids, or divide markets very harshly. To enforce such agreements, competitors may also agree on tactics to prevent new competition or to discipline firms that do not go along; thus, the laws also try to prevent and punish boycotts. Horizontal co-operation on other issues, such as product standards, research, and quality, may also affect competition, but whether the effect is positive or negative can depend on market conditions. Thus, most laws deal with these other kinds of agreement by assessing a larger range of possible benefits and harms, or by trying to design more detailed rules to identify and exempt beneficial conduct.

Vertical agreements try to control aspects of distribution. The reasons for concern are the same – that the agreements might lead to increased prices, lower quantity (or poorer quality), or prevention of entry and innovation. Because the competitive effects of vertical agreements can be more complex than those of horizontal agreements, the legal treatment of different kinds of vertical agreements varies even more than for horizontal agreements. One basic type of agreement is resale price maintenance: vertical agreements can control minimum, or maximum, prices. In some settings, the result can be to curb market abuses by distributors. In others, though, it can be to duplicate or enforce a horizontal cartel. Agreements granting exclusive dealing rights or territories can encourage greater effort to sell the supplier's product, or they can protect distributors from competition or prevent entry by other suppliers. Depending on the circumstances, agreements about product combinations, such as requiring distributors to carry full lines or tying different products together, can either facilitate or discourage introduction of new products. Franchising often involves a complex of vertical agreements with potential competitive significance: a franchise agreement may contain provisions about competition within geographic territories, about exclusive dealing for supplies, and about rights to intellectual property such as trademarks.

Abuse of dominance or **monopolisation** are categories that are concerned principally with the conduct and circumstances of individual firms. A true monopoly, which faces no competition or threat of competition, will charge higher prices and produce less or lower quality output; it may also be less likely to introduce more efficient methods or innovative products. Laws against monopolisation are typically aimed at exclusionary tactics by which firms might try to obtain or protect monopoly positions. Laws against abuse of dominance address the same issues, and may also try to address the actual exercise of market power. For example under some abuse of dominance systems, charging unreasonably high prices can be a violation of the law.

Merger control tries to prevent the creation, through acquisitions or other structural combinations, of undertakings that will have the incentive and ability to exercise market power. In some cases, the test of legality is derived from the laws about dominance or restraints; in others, there is a separate test phrased in terms of likely effect on competition generally. The analytic process applied typically calls for characterising the products that compete, the firms that might offer competition, and the relative shares and strategic importance of those firms with respect to the product markets. An important factor is the likelihood of new entry and the existence of effective barriers to new entry. Most systems apply some form of market share test, either to guide further investigation or as a presumption about legality. Mergers in unusually concentrated markets, or that create firms with unusually high market shares, are thought more likely to affect competition. And most systems specify procedures for pre-notification to enforcement authorities in advance of larger, more important transactions, and special processes for expedited investigation, so problems can be identified and resolved before the restructuring is actually undertaken.

rather than specifically, that prevented the franchisee from buying from other franchisees or authorised distributors, that prohibited acquiring interests in competing firms (regardless of whether the holding influenced policy concerning the franchise operations), and that imposed a six-year non-compete obligation after the end of the franchise contract. Hondos Center (OECD CLP, 1998). An exemption decision indicates a degree of suspicion about exclusive dealing: even though Aramco had been permitted (by the EU) to acquire control over Hellenic Motor Oil, the long-term exclusive supply contract between the parent and the subsidiary (for crude oil) was cut back from 25 years to 15 years (OECD CLP, 1997c).

Suggesting maximum resale prices may be permitted. At least, the Competition Committee gave the Minister of Commerce a favourable official opinion, in response to the Minister's request, concerning the Minister's decision to permit bottlers to print prices on consumer packages of bottled water and similar refreshments. The concern was to prevent "gouging" at resorts, stadiums, and tourist attractions, by permitting the packager to indicate what was hoped would become a maximum price (OECD CLP, 1998).

Box 3. The EU competition law toolkit

The law of Greece follows closely the basic elements of competition law that have developed under the Treaty of Rome (now the Treaty of Amsterdam):

Agreements: Article 81 (formerly Article 85) prohibits agreements that have the effect or intent of preventing, restricting, or distorting competition. The term "agreement" is understood broadly, so that the prohibition extends to concerted actions and other arrangements that fall short of formal contracts enforceable at civil law. Some prohibited agreements are identified explicitly: direct or indirect fixing of prices or trading conditions, limitation or control of production, markets, investment, or technical development; sharing of markets or suppliers, discrimination that places trading parties at a competitive disadvantage, and tying or imposing non-germane conditions under contracts. And decisions have further clarified the scope of Article 81's coverage. Joint purchasing has been permitted (in some market conditions) because of resulting efficiencies, but joint selling usually has been forbidden because it amounts to a cartel. All forms of agreements to divide markets and control prices, including profit pooling and mark-up agreements and private "fair trade practice" rules, are rejected. Exchange of price information is permitted only after time has passed, and only if the exchange does not permit identification of particular enterprises. Exclusionary devices like aggregate rebate cartels are disallowed, even if they make some allowance for dealings with third parties.

Exemptions: An agreement that would otherwise be prohibited may nonetheless be permitted, if it improves production or distribution or promotes technical or economic progress and allows consumers a fair share of the benefit, imposes only such restrictions as are indispensable to attaining the beneficial objectives, and does not permit the elimination of competition for a substantial part of the products in question. In the past, such exemptions might be granted in response to particular case-by-case applications; however, the EU is changing the enforcement regulation so that the exemption criteria would apply directly, without the need for application and specific approval. In addition, there are generally applicable "block" exemptions, which specify conditions or criteria for permitted agreements, including clauses that either may or may not appear in agreements (the "white lists" and "black lists"). Some of the most important exemptions apply to types of vertical relationships, including exclusive distribution, exclusive purchasing, and franchising.

Abuse of dominance: Article 82 (formerly Article 86) prohibits the abuse of a dominant position, and lists some acts that would be considered abuse of dominance: imposing unfair purchase or selling prices or trading conditions (either directly or indirectly), limiting production, markets, or technological development in ways that harm consumers, discrimination that places trading parties at a competitive disadvantage, and imposing non-germane contract conditions. In the presence of dominance, many types of conduct that disadvantage other parties in the market might be considered abuse. Dominance is often presumed at market shares over 50%, and may be found at lower levels depending on other factors. The prohibition can extend to abuse by several firms acting together, even if no single firm had such a high market share itself.

The content of the law about restrictive agreements, being essentially consistent with that of the EU, is generally adequate as a tool to support reform. But application of the law has been seriously compromised by the Competition Committee's resource problems. This effect is perhaps less critical for vertical restraints than for horizontal ones, both because vertical agreements tend to be notified to enforcement agencies, so fewer resources are needed to investigate them, and because vertical agreements tend to be less anti-competitive, so there is less reason for concern if they are relegated to a lower priority.

2.3. Abuse of dominance

The basic prohibition of abuse of dominance is copied from the EU model, Art. 82 of the Treaty of Amsterdam (Art. 2). This provision could in principle be used to prevent or remedy market power, including that arising from reform-related restructuring of historically monopolised industries.

The prohibition against abuse of dominance has rarely been applied to network industries or others that may be subject to restructuring and reform. In 1997, a bus line complained about the railway's low fares on a competing route, but the Competition Committee decided that the railway did not have a dominant position. In the absence of experience applying the law, it is difficult to say how effective it would be in practice to control against abuses such as denial of access or monopolistic pricing strategies.

In the same section of the law, there was a separate prohibition against the abuse of a relationship of economic dependence (Art. 2a). This prohibition, modelled on German law, was added in 1991. An enterprise is in a relationship of "economic dependence" when, as a buyer from or supplier to another firm, it has no equivalent alternative suppliers or outlets. Abuse may consist of imposition of arbitrary trading conditions, exercise of "discretionary" behaviour, or sudden and unjustified termination of long term established commercial relationships. The Competition Committee could issue orders for interim, that is, immediate, relief in these cases.

Complaints about abuse of economic dependence are usually disputes about contract termination, which may have little to do with public-interest competition policy. The Competition Committee tried to apply the rule without becoming an arbiter of private contract controversies. For example, it refused to order interim relief, that is, to force a supplier to fill an order, where the customer had only made one previous order – and had sent most of it back – and had not complied with the suppliers' usual conditions about terms of payment and condition of sales premises. Yet the decision seemed to turn on the supplier's low market share, under 10% (in the cosmetics market) and thus the absence of dominance, as much as on the failure of these contract issues to disclose any abuse of economic dependence. E. Mastoris-Sosifar Hellas SA (OECD CLP, 1998). For other complaints about contract termination, decisions have often turned on the fact that the alleged offender actually had a tiny market share, so the "victim" had other sources to turn to (OECD CLP, 1996).

This provision has not been as important in Greece as its counterpart has been in other jurisdictions that have similar rules (Tzouganatos, 1998). As could be expected, small business representatives strongly support devoting resources to its enforcement, though. Since July 1995, the Competition Committee has dealt with 35 cases. The Competition Committee seemed to be trying to decide them on the basis of an implicit de minimis test, that there can be no problem if the relevant market share is below 10%. But even applying that standard means the Competition Committee must do enough analysis to identify the market and the share. And the demand to consider petitions for interim relief on a short deadline would distract enforcement attention from other issues. The August 2000 amendments to the Competition Law eliminated the ban on abuse of economic dependence, because these complaints about essentially private controversies were taking too much of the Competition Committee's time.

2.4. Mergers: substantive rules are adequate, but administration has distorted priorities greatly

Concentrations are regulated by a separate provision of the statute (Art. 4). Much of the law and regulation about mergers parallels the EU Merger Regulation. The Competition Committee is to prohibit mergers that "may significantly impede competition in the national market or in a substantial, with respect to the characteristics of the products or services, part of it and particularly by creating or strengthening a dominant position." (Art. 4c). The coverage is defined according to the same concepts used in the EU merger regulation. The law makes explicit that a "concentration" covered by this section is not to be separately considered under other parts of the law; that is, "a concentration between undertakings, as such, shall not fall into the scope of the prohibitions of Article 1(1) and Article 2 of the present Act." (Art. 4.1). Conversely, this language means that an otherwise illegal restrictive agreement does not necessarily become legal simply by taking the form of a corporate combination (Christoforou, 1990).

A market definition standard is implied in the language setting out the market share test for notification: "products or services which are regarded as identical because of their properties, their prices and their intended use." Factors to be considered include "the structure of all the relevant markets concerned, the actual or potential competition from undertakings located either within or outside Greece, the existence of any legal or other barriers to entry, the market position of the undertakings concerned and their financial and economic power, the alternatives available to suppliers and users by the undertakings concerned as well as by actually or potentially competitive undertakings, their access to suppliers or markets, the supply and demand trends for the relevant goods or services, the interests of the intermediate and ultimate consumers and their contribution in the development of technical and economic progress provided that it is to consumers' advantage and does not form an obstacle to competition." (Art. 4c(2)). An otherwise prohibited merger can be allowed if it is "regarded as being indispensable for the public interest, especially where it contributes to the modernisation and rationalization of production and economy, the attraction of investments, the strengthening of competitiveness in the European and International market and the creation of new employment positions." (Art. 4c(3)).

Notification before a deal can be consummated is required if the combined market share exceeds 35% in a national market or a substantial part of it (with "substantiality" determined by reference to characteristics of the products or services at issue), or the combined turnover exceeds 150 million Euros (and at least two participants have turnover in Greece of more than 15 million Euros each). These thresholds were recently increased; before August 2000, they were 25% or 25 million Euros. Including market share as a criterion for notification is a generally unsatisfactory approach (Art. 4a), which the law originally borrowed from EU models. The Competition Committee has considered removing the market share criterion from the notification thresholds, but it recently decided to retain it for another 2 or 3 years. Notification had also been required after a deal took place if the parties' combined market share was over 10% or if the merging firms' combined turnover exceeded 15 million Euros; this "post-merger" notification requirement was dropped by the August 2000 amendments.

Merger control is a two-stage process. In the first stage, the Competition Committee decides whether the merger may significantly restrict competition. If so, it issues a decision prohibiting the concentration within two months from the date it is notified to the Competition Committee. In the second stage, the Ministers of National Economy and Development can nonetheless permit the merger if it has economic advantages in the public interest. This decision must be fully explained and published and is subject to judicial control (OECD CLP, 1998). But the grounds for a Ministerial decision to override the Competition Committee are not specific: "advantages of general economic nature that counterbalance the resulting restriction of competition." Some authority to decide about transactions that do not meet the pre-consummation notification threshold has been delegated to the President of the Competition Committee. The President of the Competition Committee is to issue a decision within a month concerning mergers that fall below the pre-merger reporting thresholds (Greece, 2000).

One of the only mergers that the Competition Committee has disapproved would have combined two Greek baking companies and led to a domestic market share of between 75% and 83% (depending on whether the product market included unpacked as well as packaged products). The Competition Committee also imposed a fine because the parties did not await the Competition Committee's decision before they closed the transaction. By contrast, the Competition Committee approved an acquisition that combined two major Greek cement companies. Despite the high resulting market share in

Greece (between 48% and 53%), the Competition Committee found the resulting structure was not a significant impediment to competition. Some of the reasons appear sound: lack of barriers to entry into the market through imports, and the presence of two domestic competitors and two significant importing firms. Some of the other reasons are less convincing. That demand is price-inelastic would normally argue for being more, rather than less, concerned about high concentration, for example. Here again, the parties were nonetheless fined for failure to notify on time and for putting the agreement into effect without awaiting the Competition Committee's decision (OECD CLP, 1997c). The cement industry was the focus of the most recent test of Greece's merger policy, as a UK firm proposed to acquire the merged Greek firm, while a consortium of Greek construction firms submitted a competing offer.[2] The Competition Committee's investigation, which was initially set to end 31 March, was extended with the consent of the parties; the Committee's decision approving the acquisition was issued in May.[3]

Merger decisions comprise about half of all of the Competition Committee's decisions, and nearly all of the decisions in the last few years. Only two mergers have been blocked (and one of those mergers was nonetheless permitted, after a Ministerial decision overriding the Competition Committee), and three were approved subject to conditions (OECD CLP, 1998). An increasing proportion of transactions are now subject to "pre-merger" control, rather than post-transaction notification. The large number of matters still listed as "pending" suggests that there is a problem with decision backlog, probably explained by lack of staff resources. Since 1995, the Commission has handled 183 merger cases, fully reviewing each application. Yet this work has disclosed that, so far at least, Greece has not faced much of a problem with anti-competitive concentrations. The Competition Committee has spent so much time because the statutory thresholds for notification and decision were very low and review is mandatory. The threshold had been even lower; it was raised in 1999, with the result of eliminating 11% of the merger cases that required full decisions. Further increases in August 2000, along with ending post-merger notification, should eliminate many more.

Problems in the administration of the merger law may be limiting its relevance to assessing competition issues in sectors subject to reform or in efforts to promote reform. A recent amendment to the privatisation law creates an exemption from the notification and review process for privatisation transactions involving bankrupt firms. The specific object of this special exemption is evidently a state-owned paper plant, which IRO was trying to sell.

The delay that the review process imposes on transactions in Greece is perceived as a major problem. The Competition Committee estimates that the average time required to process a merger from notification to decision is from two to two and a half months, but private parties who deal with the

Table 1.   Merger filings and decisions

	Notified transactions	
	Post-merger (Art. 4a)	re-merger (Art. 4b)
1995 (May-December)	30	17
1996	74	15
1997	71	45
1998	76	52
1999	82	77
2000 (January)	11	6
Total	338	212
Decisions	12	144
Closed	141	23
Pending	185	45

Source: Greece, 2000.

Competition Committee believe it is somewhat longer. But the Competition Committee notes that companies do not always provide the information needed promptly, without further inquiry and effort by the Competition Committee. The risk of delay is countered somewhat by a provision permitting parties to show reasons why they must proceed to close the transaction before a decision can be issued; the Competition Committee can give them special, but conditional, permission to do so. This happens in about 15% of prior-notification cases. Though it avoids some of the costs of holding up the transaction, the parties are still in a position of uncertainty until the Competition Committee issues its final decision, and the process requires the Competition Committee to consider the transaction twice. The Competition Committee recognises that Greece's present circumstances generally would support and even encourage mergers, which often involve major foreign investments or implement the program of privatisation. Thus a process that delays them would undermine achievement of reform goals.

Changes in the merger law and administration should make competition policy a more effective tool for reform. The time periods and deadlines are too long for approving mergers that have no competitive effects. Amendments to the legislation may shorten them (Greece, 2000). The Competition Committee recognises that the attention to mergers has had a distorting effect on its priorities. The Competition Committee should develop, either in practice or by change in the law, an abbreviated procedure for dealing with the transactions that are obviously non-problematic. Now, the Competition Committee cannot make such a distinction, and it must follow the entire process for transactions that meet the statutory thresholds. But dealing with the problem by exempting certain economic sectors from notification and review, as some have suggested, could be a mistake. So far, Greece has evidently chosen not to shift all merger control to *ex post* review and regulation of any resulting dominant positions. This is good, because remedies after the fact are likely to be costly, ineffective, or both.

2.5. Unfair competition: The privately-applied rules could impair competition, if they were strongly enforced

The law of unfair competition can protect markets and the competitive process, or it can protect competitors in ways that make markets work less well. Greece has had legislation to control unfair competition since 1914. The law on unfair competition is enforced principally by private lawsuits for damages or other relief, brought by competitors and trade associations. As a result, activities such as false advertising, deception, passing off, and trademark disputes are handled by the civil courts, not by the Competition Committee (Greece, 2000). Wilful deception may also, in theory, be subject to criminal penalties, although the fine is trivial (Drs 3 000) and imprisonment is unlikely (Law 146/1914, Art. 4). Offering discounted prices without authorisation (that is, without a formal liquidation or outside of the end-of-season discount period) is also subject to criminal penalties. Offering discounts on some goods in order to attract customers who might then buy other products is especially condemned as "against moral principles and business ethics" (Law 146/1914, Art. 7.12). Such rules, found in many jurisdictions, that prevent firms from attracting customers by calling attention to low prices, can seriously inhibit retail-level competition. The Competition Committee has not undertaken to determine whether the actual application of these laws has been consistent with competition policy principles and goals, of ensuring free competition for the benefit of the economy and of consumers.

2.6. Consumer protection: Policy has no clear connection to competition policy goals, and application is left principally to private action

The relationship between consumer policy and competition policy is informal and implicit, at best. The General Secretariat for Consumer Protection is within the administrative structure of the Ministry of Development, the same ministry that oversees the budget and legislation for the Competition Committee (and is housed in the same building). Thus, there is a natural channel for co-ordination among these policies. Since 1995, there has been a consumer representative on the Competition Committee (Greece, 2000). Before that time, that is, before there were organised consumer groups under Greek law, there was a labour representative on the Competition Committee, who also was considered to represent consumer interests.

Consumer protection laws and rules are for the most part formally consistent with EU norms, but there are problems with the effectiveness of their enforcement, and in some cases, with the transposition of EU norms into local law. In insurance, for example, the terms of policies contain provisions such as unilateral rights to increase premiums that, according to consumer groups, do not conform to pertinent EU directives. The government's own consumer protection office appears weak and underfunded, like the Competition Committee. The consumer protection Department in the Ministry of Development lacks status, resources, and experienced staff. Its total staff, which once numbered about 35, is now below 20. There are administrative fines, ranging up to Drs 25 million, which can be doubled for repeated violation, and licenses could be revoked in cases of repeated violation. These rules and sanctions are not often applied, though. There is a National Consumers Council, which is not strictly a consumer group, because it includes producer interests as well. It is attached to the Ministry of Development, but has essentially no staff support – one individual performs its secretariat functions. It meets only a few times per year and is only rarely asked for its opinion about legislation affecting consumers. It could be a vehicle for consultation about policies, but it is not always used or respected. Indeed, in the course of a consultation about consumer problems in credit contracts a few years ago, the Ministry of Development excluded the Council representative and limited the consultation to the government and the banks themselves. There was no consumer input into deliberations about recent proposals for regulations affecting competition in taxi services and service station hours.

Ensuring that consumers are adequately protected against abuses in the developing market economy is left to private groups. In the absence of effective public enforcement, a principal means of enforcing consumer protection principles is private, class-action litigation. Consumer organisations can, in principle, go to court on behalf of consumers to correct market abuses. And some have done so. More than a dozen cases have been brought about such issues as telemarketing, abusive contract term (against banks and insurance companies), and mobile phone services, and about advertisements addressed to children. These actions takes time and resources. The parties that bring these suits on behalf of consumers risk not being compensated for their efforts, for the court may order the parties to bear their own costs, if the issue is not clear. These suits can recover "moral" damages, in theory, and in fact they have resulted in awards of Drs 385 million for "moral distress". But this money, if paid (and so far, none of these judgements has actually been collected), is to be deposited in a fund to be distributed by the ministry for social purposes; it is not used to reimburse the litigants' expenses nor to reimburse consumers for their injuries. There is no provision for class actions for actual damages.

The NGO consumer groups that undertake these efforts get very little support from the Greek government. Most depend on EU support, membership fees, and other sources. Consumer groups are not strong enough to counter pressures by business and other interest groups for rules and laws limiting competition. Consumer groups fear that the government downplays consumer protection rules because it feels they are perceived as an obstacle to foreign investment, and that the government is content for Greece to have a reputation of being a lower-cost place to do business, to the extent enforcement of these rules is lax.

3. INSTITUTIONAL ISSUES: ENFORCEMENT STRUCTURES AND PRACTICES

Reform of economic regulation can be less beneficial, or even harmful, if the competition authority cannot act vigorously to prevent abuses in developing markets. Institutional reforms are needed to ensure against this. The Competition Committee, which is solely responsible for applying the general competition law, is legally autonomous but practically weak. Its representative membership structure implies that it is considered to be a body for balancing interests, rather than applying policy. It has insufficient staff and resources to do more than review routine applications.

The Competition Committee has nine statutory positions. Of these, only three are appointed by the government. Appointments to the other six are within the power of other institutions, including four from interest groups. Each member has a deputy, so that there are 18 persons who may be involved in Competition Committee decisions. The Competition Committee may take action in divisions of four members; that power has been little used, though, and the Competition Committee acts as a body. The required membership, and the bodies that have the power to designate members, are:

–   A member (or former member) of the Council of State;

–   A judge (or former judge) (designated by the Supreme Court);

–   Federation of Greek Industries;

–   National Confederation of Greek Trade;

–   General Confederation of Small & Medium Sized Businesses, Craftsmen & Traders of Greece;

–   National Consumers' Council;

–   Professor of competition law (designated by the Minister of Development);

–   Professor, experienced in competition matters (designated by the Minister of Development); and

–   "A person of recognised status with experience in the competition field" (designated by the Minister of Development).

Members serve terms of three years, which can be renewed. The Minister of Development appoints the President of the Competition Committee from among the members. The August 2000 amendments to the law provide that the Minister must get the opinion of Parliament for this appointment; this change is intended to give the President more legitimacy and independence from the government. The President is considered "a state functionary being exclusively employed." The President has a casting vote in the event of ties, and is responsible for ensuring the execution of Competition Committee decisions, directing the Competition Committee's Secretariat, and representing the Competition Committee in international forums (a power that can be delegated to the Director). Only the President of the Competition Committee is occupied with Competition Committee business full-time. Judges and other public officials appointed to the Competition Committee may be relieved of their other public obligations while serving.

The Competition Committee is supported by a Secretariat, headed by a Director appointed by the Minister of Development after consultation with the Competition Committee. The Director serves for a 5 year term, which may be renewed. Up to 80 staff positions are authorised by statute; the August 2000 amendments increased that number from the previous level of 40. That number could be increased by presidential decree (Art. 8c(2)). But the actual staffing levels have been far short of these levels. At first (that is, in 1995), the Secretariat had a staff of only 8 persons, and half of those resigned in 1996. The average staff level under the previous regime, before the 1995 amendments established a separate Secretariat, was 30 (OECD CLP, 1998).

The Competition Committee and its membership and powers have changed substantially several times. At first, in 1977, the Committee for Protection of Competition had decision-making power. Its seven members were not representatives of other bodies, except the chair, who was a member of the Council of State, and the Head of the Service for the Protection of Competition, which was the Competition Committee's staff in the Ministry of Commerce. In 1982, a joint ministerial decision replaced this body with the Competition Committee and transferred decision making authority to the Minister of Commerce. The new Competition Committee's role was now advisory, and its membership was changed so that it represented interest groups: the Ministry of Finance, the Bank of Greece, the Federation of Greek Industries, the association of small and medium sized enterprises, the Trade Union of Athens, and the General Confederation of Workers. That system lasted until the 1991 amendments, which established a structure similar to the current one: two judges (a president of the Administrative Court of First Instance, acting as chairman, and a judge of Civil Court of First Instance), a professor of commercial law or economics, an expert in the competition field, and representatives from the Bank of Greece, the Association of Greek Industries, and the Union of Greek Trade Associations (OECD CLP, 1998). At the outset, cases were prepared by the Service for the Protection of Competition in the

Ministry of Commerce; this office was renamed twice, as the Directorate for the Protection of Competition and later the Directorate for Market Research and Competition, but with the same functions (OECD CLP, 1998). The Secretariat was separated from the Ministry and attached to the independent Competition Committee in 1995.

Increasing the Competition Committee's strength and autonomy was a principal purpose of the 1995 amendments of the competition law (OECD CLP, 1998). Those goals were not fulfilled, but recent amendments and appointments are promising steps toward greater strength and independence. The Competition Committee is an "independent authority", but in the Greek context, that status appears to be a weakness, not a strength. By law, the members are not to be subject to direction by others, but are to decide matters solely according to the competition act and their consciences. In its decision-making, the Competition Committee is reportedly more independent of political oversight and manipulation than is typical in the Greek public service, and some long-time observers believe there is little outside pressure to control the Competition Committee's decisions. There is little in the administrative or legal structure to protect and re-enforce that independence, though, and there are indirect controls on its effectiveness. Although administratively separate, the Competition Committee is supervised by the Minister of Development, and its budget is a special item in that Ministry's budget (Arts. 8(1), 8(2)). In the past, the Ministry has, as a practical matter, consistently rejected the Competition Committee's requests for additional resources. Competition Committee members serve virtually as volunteers, as their remuneration and reimbursement for expenses are not significant. Only the President receives significant compensation, and that compensation is not very great. And there have been a few instances of more direct efforts to influence the membership of the Competition Committee and its enforcement priorities, such as the pursuit of actions against temporary price increases that accompanied devaluation, to support other goals. It is a demonstration of the weakness of "independent" bodies in Greece that such demands have been agreed to. The August 2000 amendments take a significant step to increase the Competition Committee's independence, by providing a source of funds that will not depend on the Ministry, namely a levy of a small percentage (0.001) of the value of the capital of newly formed companies or increases in registered capital.

The membership and structure of the Competition Committee do not overlap or intersect with other policymaking bodies. Its formal independence from the Ministry and the government has the effect of cutting it off from the process of considering policy matters. Its relationships with sectoral regulatory bodies and other government agencies are mostly through informal communication. By law, the Competition Committee can offer opinions about the implications of other government actions on competition. But because the law implied that the Competition Committee must be specifically asked for its opinion, and its opinion has virtually never been requested, the Competition Committee has played almost no role in the development of policy outside of its own area or in the reform of other regulatory regimes that may affect competition. The recent amendment provide for greater co-operation with other regulators, and permit the Competition Committee to take a more independent advocacy role.

3.1. Law enforcement tools are not well tested

Applicants, complainants, and respondents may be heard in person or by attorneys, at the Competition Committee's periodic meetings. Because of the "prohibition" nature of the law, the Competition Committee's principal law enforcement functions are imposing fines and reaching decisions on mergers and on applications for individual exemption or negative clearance (Art. 8a(2)(a)-(e)). The Competition Committee's power to require information appears very broad. It can require undertakings and natural and legal persons to respond to questions (Art. 25). In applying the statute's prohibitions, the Competition Committee and the Director have powers to examined documents and premises and take testimony (Art. 26). The Competition Committee does not report any defects in the law that impair its ability to obtain information and reach decisions; rather, the problem is lack of resources to undertake investigations that are needed against firms that do not volunteer their information.

189

Sanctions, which can be imposed directly by the Competition Committee, range from an order to cease infringing conduct though fines for infringements and penalty payments for repeated violations. The Competition Committee may threaten fines as well as impose them. The amount of a fine is flexible, determined by the duration and gravity of the violation; the ceiling is 15% of the infringing firms' annual gross receipts. Penalties for failure to comply with a Competition Committee decision and order can range up to Drs 2 million per day of continued failure. Non-compliance with merger notification requirements can result in a fine between Drs 1 million and 5 million (provided that the amount falls between 5% and 7% of the firms' aggregate turnover) (Articles 4a and 4b). Completing a merger before a decision is issued results in a fine of at least Drs 10 million, but not exceeding 15% of the firms' aggregate turnover; failure to comply with an order concerning a merger results in a fine of up to 15% of the firms' aggregate turnover and a penalty payment of up to Drs 3 million for each day of continued non-compliance (Greece, 2000). The Competition Committee may also order interim "provisional measures" where there is an "urgent need" to prevent "an imminent and incurable damage to the complainant or to the public interest." (Art. 9(4)). Complainants have most often sought such orders in cases alleging abuse of economic dependence.

Criminal sanctions against individuals are potentially available, but they have never been imposed. They include fines of Drs 1 million to Drs 5 million, and double those amounts for repeated violations. For impeding an investigation, refusing to supply information, or supplying false information, the law sets harsh penalties: imprisonment for a minimum (not a maximum) of three months and a fine of between Drs 1 million and Drs 3 million. The penal sanctions could apply to entrepreneurs, general partners, administrators of limited liability or co-operative enterprises, and the directors of joint stock companies who voted in favour of conduct that is found to be in violation of the law.

The Competition Committee is required to respond to complaints within six months (Art. 24). There is no deadline for responding to notifications, that is, to requests for exemption or negative clearance. But the applicant does not bear the risk of the Competition Committee's failure to decide on time. If the parties make a timely notification, any decision would have prospective effect only; their arrangement is considered provisionally valid until the Competition Committee acts (OECD CLP, 1998). Decisions, along with reasoning, are published in the official gazette. In addition, the Competition Committee can order an infringing party to bear the costs of publishing the decision in the national or local press. (If the Competition Committee's decision is reversed on appeal, then the Competition Committee has to bear the costs of publishing that decision in the same media) (Art. 13a).

Some expert observers have noted that the Competition Committee's procedures are not very transparent. It has not issued guidelines or made other efforts to explain the content of competition law and the obligations under it to the business public. Rather, competition policy appears to be carried on in a closed community among the Competition Committee and the lawyers who specialise in the subject.

Disappointed parties, including respondents, complainants, the Minister of Development, and indeed "any third party having a legitimate interest" can appeal Competition Committee decisions (and Ministerial decisions about mergers). Previously, those appeals were taken to the Athens Administrative Court (Art. 14). The process appears swift, at least in theory: the law says a hearing must be held in three months. The competition law provided for the possibility of establishing a special division of this court to deal with cases arising under the competition law. (If issues under the competition law arise in another legal proceeding, the court may decide about the validity of agreements or the existence and abuse of dominance or economic dependence, but it may not disregard a determination of individual exemption by the Competition Committee (Art. 18)). The recently adopted Code of Administrative Procedure has had the unfortunate effect of making the review of competition matters more complex, uncertain, and time-consuming. The Code eliminated most special panels for direct review of official decisions. Thus, parties challenging Competition Committee decisions had to go to the lowest level courts, from which they faced the prospect of two further levels of appeal. The August 2000 amendments corrected this anomaly, so challenges are heard by a second-level court, with only one further appeal possible, by writ of error to the Council of State.

3.2. Other means of applying general competition principles

The prohibition in the competition law, declaring offending agreements to be null and void, would support a right of independent private action for damages or other relief under the civil code. In addition, a party who believes it has been harmed by anti-competitive action can obtain independent, judicial consideration of its claims. If the Competition Committee rejects the complaint, it must explain its decision, and the disappointed complainant can appeal that decision to the courts (Greece, 2000).

The Competition Committee is designated by the statute as the competent national authority to take actions directly under the EU competition law (Art. 13b(3)). The EU is considering a fundamental change in its method of enforcing the prohibition against restrictive agreements. One key proposal would have the effect of eliminating the requirement that a potentially restrictive agreement must be notified in advance. If this aspect of EU practice changes, Greece may have to revise its law to remain consistent. And the European Commission is calling for shifting many enforcement responsibilities to national agencies, so the EU Directorate can concentrate on the largest transactions and the most widespread restrictive agreements. Changing the rules so that agreements need not be filed in advance would reduce the burden of processing routine filings. But net effect of the changes could be to increase national agencies' workloads, because those agencies will be increasingly responsible (under both EU and national law) for the most difficult and resource-intensive cases, that is, those involving agreements which the parties try to keep secret. If notification continues to be required in Greece, the substantive requirements would likely be on the basis of the new EU guidelines about vertical restraints. And in the meantime, it will be important to educate Greek courts about the EU's changes, because those courts may be called on to apply EU law directly.

3.3. International trade issues in competition policy and enforcement

Greece makes an expansive claim of extraterritorial jurisdiction, over all restrictions of competition that have effects or may have effects within the country, including combinations or agreements among firms that have no establishments in Greece and including abuses of dominance or economic dependence that are "manifested" within Greece (Art. 32). The 1995 amendments extended this jurisdictional claim to mergers with effects in Greece. But the claim of extraterritorial authority has actually been exerted only once in a non-merger setting[4] (Greece, 2000). Trans-national effects and concerns appear mostly in merger matters. Many notified transactions are among foreign firms, whose turnover in Greece is sufficient to require them to file there. To improve inter-jurisdictional co-ordination of merger oversight, the forms now call for firms notifying mergers to indicate whether they are filing in Greece, rather than the EU, solely because of the "two thirds" rule (under which national authorities may take responsibility for mergers that otherwise meet the EU filing requirements, but that involve parties that do two-thirds or more of their business in a single Member state), and to identify any other jurisdictions where the parties are filing notifications (OECD CLP, 1998).

The Competition Committee is authorised to co-operate with international and European competition agencies (Art. 13b(1)). In particular, the statute authorises use of Greek processes and institution in aid of EU competition law enforcement efforts (Art. 13b(2). The Competition Committee has not played any role in efforts to remove regulatory obstacles to competition from foreign producers (other than an opinion, described below, supporting a regulation that allegedly restricted market access, on the grounds that it served a legitimate consumer-protection purpose). In general, though, there is no indication of discrimination against foreign firms, which are in the same position with respect to their rights and protections as Greek firms are. The law may lack measures to apply if a firm uses market power in Greece to impair competition elsewhere, thus leaving parties to their remedies in the other jurisdiction. The issue does not appear to have arisen yet, however.

3.4. Agency resources, actions, and implied priorities

Resource commitment measures seriousness and likely effectiveness. By that standard, Greece gives a low priority to effective competition policy. The Competition Committee's staff complement is the smallest among OECD Member countries, except perhaps for that of Ireland, a country that is only one-third the size of Greece. Other OECD countries with populations about the same as Greece have competition policy agencies that are from 50% larger (Austria, Belgium) to from four to six times larger (Czech Republic, Hungary, Sweden). The total number of Competition Committee members and alternates (18) is almost as great as the number of staff supporting them (now 25, up from 22 two years ago). Observers who work with the Competition Committee consider the Secretariat's management to be very good and very co-operative. But below that level, the staff lacks expertise and experience, and there are not very many of them.

After the 1995 law was adopted, what had been a staff of 40 nearly disappeared, as fewer than 10 of the previous staff from the Ministry wanted to join the newly-separate Secretariat. The remaining staff – and half of those who did come to the new agency quit shortly afterwards – worked 7 days a week, 16 hours a day, to make up for the defections. The staff has been increased somewhat since, but it still falls far short of the statutory authorisation of 80 staff positions (40, before August 2000). The Competition Committee has been continuously asking for additional staff and financial autonomy, but the responses from the Ministry were meagre and, as a practical matter, useless. The 1999 revision to the law, Law 2741/99, provided that the Competition Committee could receive staff support from the other departments and agencies in the Ministry of Development. But most other parts of this Ministry are concerned with regulation, not with competition. Indeed, it was the staff of this Ministry that refused to join the Competition Committee's Secretariat. Their part-time involvement, not fully subject to the oversight and management of the permanent Competition Committee staff, could actually impair, rather than assist, sound competition policy.

Table 2. Trends in competition policy resources

	Person-years	Budget (Drs MM)
2000	25	122
1999	25	88
1998	22	134
1997	22	114
1996	8	99

Source: OECD CLP, 1998; Greece, 2000.

Table 3. Trends in competition policy actions

	Horizontal agreements	Vertical agreements	Abuse of dominance	Mergers
1999: matters opened	23			159
Sanctions or orders sought				2
Orders or sanctions imposed				2
Total sanctions imposed, Drs				135 000 000
1998: matters opened	27			128
Sanctions or orders sought				4
Orders or sanctions imposed				4
Total sanctions imposed, Drs				86 150 000
1997: matters opened	13			195
Sanctions or orders sought				5
Orders or sanctions imposed				5
Total sanctions imposed, Drs				63 150 000
1996: matters opened	12			124
Sanctions or orders sought				2
Orders or sanctions imposed				2
Total sanctions imposed, Drs				241 694 000

Source: OECD CLP, 1998, OECD CLP, 1997; Greece, 2000.

The staff problem is not just one of numbers, but also of approach and expertise. Increasing staff to the level authorised by statute is necessary, but it is also important for the staff to have the necessary skills. In particular, there is a need for more economic expertise, because the Competition Committee's decisions, and hence the Secretariat's recommendations, depend strongly on analysis of market facts and conditions. On the Competition Committee itself, there is only one economist, so if it ever sat in sections, one section would have no economist. About half of the Secretariat staff are economists, but only one has a PhD degree.

The Competition Committee has lacked the flexibility, in hiring and compensation authority, to get the staff it needs. It takes too long to hire, and the Competition Committee cannot pay enough. The Competition Committee estimates that its salaries would have to be raised 50% to attract the right people. Since 1995, the Competition Committee has requested some exemption from the general hiring rules so it could recruit directly and pay higher salaries than the basic levels, but that authority has not been granted. In 1997, the Competition Committee requested authority, through the public sector recruitment office under the provisions of Law 21/90, to hire 7 special expert staff. The positions were not posted until 1998; applicants were not interviewed until 1999; and hiring may not happen until after the election in 2000. Only 18 applications were submitted, most of them from persons who are not qualified. And despite the Competition Committee's need for economists, all the applicants were lawyers. Yet the Competition Committee cannot be too discriminating, for if it rejects applicants, it would have to wait another three years to go through the process again. The recent amendments increase the Competition Committee's ability to recruit staff directly, without going through the process that was previously required.

Deadline requirements and legal obligations forced the Competition Committee to focus this limited staff on mergers. The Competition Committee must reach a reasoned decision about each of the pre-notified "section 4b" mergers. For the "section 4a" mergers, the decision was delegated to the President of the Competition Committee, and since there was no real deadline for action on them, these could be treated more routinely, as matters of simple notification. But the overwhelming majority of the Competition Committee's actions have been merger decisions, and virtually all of these decisions approved the mergers as notified.

The other parts of the law have been neglected. The data imply that the Competition Committee has not actually imposed sanctions or orders against any restrictive agreement since 1995. There are 300 pending notifications and complaints about restrictive agreements and abuse of dominance, which the staff has virtually no resources to follow up. A handful of ex officio cases are under consideration, involving products and services such as pacemakers, dialysis, milk, petroleum, and shipping. And the Secretariat staff would like to look more closely at patterns of co-ordinated industry-wide price increases. But the merger workload has been overwhelming. Even concerning mergers, the pressure of meeting decision deadlines prevented the staff from studying the Section 4a "notification" mergers thoroughly, both to correct any that might be anti-competitive and to establish a "database" of information and experience in market analysis which could help in reaching decisions in all merger cases more quickly and confidently. The Competition Committee and the Secretariat have had virtually no involvement in advocacy or in actions involving sectors which are objects of reform efforts.

4. LIMITS OF COMPETITION POLICY: EXEMPTIONS AND SPECIAL REGULATORY REGIMES

4.1. Economy-wide exemptions or special treatments

The ability of competition policy to provide a suitable framework for broad-based regulatory reform is partly determined by the extent and justification for general exemptions or special treatment for types of enterprises or actions. In Greece, there are few formal exemptions, either broad-based or sector-specific. For example, there is no general provision in the competition law that subordinates it to other laws or regulatory actions. In practice, particular regulations that impair competition take precedence when they conflict with the more general provisions of the competition law.

The law applies to publicly owned enterprises, in principle. But it also permits exemption, by joint decision of the Ministers of National Economy and Development, for undertakings of "public utility" that are of "general importance to the national economy." Art. 5(1). The Competition Committee is to be consulted before the Ministerial decision. Exemptions can be granted both to particular firms and to "categories" of firms as well. On two occasions, the Competition Committee has considered whether the law would apply to allegedly anti-competitive actions by public firms. These involved the explosive and ammunition industry (1984) and the aerospace and arms industry (1980), where notified agreements received an exemption of 6 years. No other applications for exemption invoking this article have been issued since then (Greece, 2000).

There is no explicit exemption or special treatment for small and medium sized businesses, such as a formal de minimis market share test for liability, either in the law or in enforcement guidelines. In practice, though, the Competition Committee does apply a similar concept on a case by case basis (Greece, 2000).

Agreements the "exclusive aim of which is to insure, promote or strengthen exports" are exempted from the competition law, unless the Ministers of National Economy and Development decide otherwise, after consulting with the Competition Committee (Art. 6). These decisions, if any, would apply to categories of agreements.

4.2. Sector-specific exclusions, rules and exemptions

Although few sectors have explicit exclusions or exemptions from the law's coverage, regulations and government decisions about many sectors have impaired free competition there.

4.2.1. Agriculture, Forestry, and Fisheries

The Competition Act applies in principle to firms and associations in producing, processing, or trading in agricultural, livestock, forestry and fishery products. But a provision like the one that is applied to public enterprises permits exemptions for particular firms or for categories of firms, issued by joint decision of the Ministers of Economy, Development, and Agriculture. The Competition Committee must be consulted about these exemptions, but it has no decision authority. Evidently, the ministers' decision must be unanimous. The law sets no substantive criteria for this class of exemption (unless they are implied by the first part of this section, "general importance to the national economy") (Art. 5(2)).

4.2.2. Transport

The Competition Act applies in principle to transport firms and associations. Pursuant to a provision of the law like the ones that apply to agriculture and to public enterprises, joint decisions of Ministers can exempt firms or categories of firms. These exemptions require the assent of the ministers of National Economy and Development in all cases, along with that of the Minister of Transport and Communications for land and air transport and of the Minister of Merchant Marine for maritime transport. The substantive criterion for the exemptions is simply that they must be "necessitated by transport policy." (Art. 5(3)). Some of the most important transport areas where regulation has displaced competition policy oversight, trucking and ferry services, are discussed in another chapter of this review.

In air transport, development of competition has had to accommodate the interests of the publicly-controlled national airline, Olympic Airways. Competition in international service has reduced the market share of Olympic over the last 20 years. The share of foreign scheduled airlines has also declined, because charter service is relatively important, accounting for over 60% of total passengers. When some of the domestic market was opened to competition (from other Greek carriers) in 1992, several small carriers gained an aggregate market share of 25-30% and forced down prices on major routes such as Athens-Thessaloniki. Olympic's remaining monopoly, on scheduled service to the islands, ended in 1998, but the EU has granted Greece an extension until 2003 before non-Greek firms can offer that service. Some of the new entrants in Greece are in financial difficulty, in part because of intense competition. Olympic has additional reasons for its poor performance: labour policies that result in high costs, the costs of its obligation to fulfil other non-remunerative functions (such as linking the islands, daily press service, and free tickets for favoured groups – including unpaid arrears from political parties), and poor management and strategy. Olympic's profitability depended on revenues from its monopoly of airport ground handling. After EU objections to that monopoly position, a second passenger handling firm was introduced at Athens in 1999. The government has taken steps to replace and improve management, but change has proved difficult to accomplish (OECD, 1998). Further intervention has been needed to retain the strategic partner that was brought in to improve management; one such step was to end the requirement that Parliament approve Olympic's business plan.

A current controversy involves taxicab service. Poor taxicab service is one of the principal consumer complaints in Greece. One proposal to improve service was to authorise a "mini-bus" service, intermediate between taxis and regular-route local buses. The taxi industry has generally objected. The state of competition in local taxicab markets is unclear. The number of officially issued licenses is evidently limited, but there are many unauthorised, unlicensed taxis in operation too. The unlicensed taxis provide competition, but they probably escape consumer protection oversight.

4.2.3. Telecommunications

The National Telecommunications and Postal Services Commission is responsible for safeguarding competition in the industries under its jurisdiction, applying special rules in the telecoms legislation (Greece, 1999, p. 10). The sectoral regulator thus displaces the Competition Committee concerning competition issues in this sector, except for mergers, which remain under the Competition Committee's control (Greece, 2000). The division of responsibility is not completely clear; although it appears that the Competition Committee could impose fines for violations sections 1 or 2 of the Competition Act, it might not have the power to order any other relief. The sectoral body has taken some action, fining the national telecoms firm, OTE, Drs 80 million in October 1998 for non-competitive practices (OECD, 1998). The Commission does not have very many staff to handle these cases. There is no formal link between the Commission and the Competition Committee, although there is a well-established informal relationship. Despite the lack of precision and the potential for overlap, no practical problems about jurisdictional uncertainty have arisen yet. The Competition Committee has received some complaints about OTE, and the Commission has proposed getting together with the Competition Committee to work out how to handle such matters. But the Commission may prefer to do it through rules and decisions under the telecoms law.

Meanwhile, as detailed more in background report to Chapter 6, competition in telecoms is coming more slowly in Greece than in most of the rest of the EU. By derogation from the EU directive, Greece does not have to open its voice telephony market until the end of 2000 (EIU, 1999, p. 14). OTE is protecting its monopoly by filing complaints about firms that are using "call-back" to avoid it. The telecoms regulator has not finally decided these cases, a year after they were filed, and it may not decide them on the merits until after liberalisation in 2001.

4.2.4. Broadcasting and other media

The National Broadcasting Commission is responsible for some competition-related issues in that sector (Greece, 1999, p. 10). Mergers in the press and electronic media are subject to the oversight control of this Commission, which is exercised through the Commission's power to determine who may hold registered shares (Greece, 2000). Legislation in 1995 was intended to reduce concentration in broadcast ownership and incorporate EU rules about advertising. But no licenses have been issued under the new rules, and stations are thus operating on provisional authorisations that are nearly a decade old (EIU, 1999, p. 15).

4.2.5. Petroleum

Petroleum prices were liberalised in the early 1990s, in theory, and the retail market appears reasonably competitive now. But prices are still subject to some de facto administrative control. The government may impose upper limits on retail prices, locally or nationally, "to stem speculative surges" in price, usually in "crisis" periods, that are not justified by increases in costs (Greece, 1999, p. 4). One means of intervention is by government action capping the effective prices of products sold by the publicly owned refineries (IOBE, 1999c). Exploration and extraction rights belong to the state, which has assigned them to state-owned Hellenic Petroleum for further disposition through bidding. Some exploration and drilling permits have been granted. The petroleum industry is functionally dis-integrated. Refineries cannot distribute products directly in the inland market (although a refiner can own a wholesaler), and wholesalers cannot operate retail stations (although a wholesaler can own a retail station). Refining is essentially a duopoly of Hellenic Petroleum, with a share of about 60%, and Hellenic Motor Oil-Aramco, with about 20%; a third firm, Petrola, has limited capabilities but has announced plans to expand. (Greece, 1999, p. 14) (OECD, 1998). Hellenic Petroleum, as a state-owned firm (which has been partially privatised), has the competitive advantage of being able to rely on public funds, reducing its debt burden compared to its competitors, and another competitive advantage as the sole supplier to some large domestic consumers.

Imports offer little competition. Greek implementation of the EU's security stocking rules, Directive 68/414/EEC, does not permit traders to count stocks in other EU countries. Rather than undertake the insurmountable task of setting up storage facilities in Greece – licenses cannot be obtained – importers must transact through the incumbent firms to take advantage of their storage capacities. The EU has challenged this law as a constraint on the free movement of goods (EIU, 1999, p. 15). Because Greek law also requires that deliveries to retailers be carried on lorries owned by the marketers or by public transport companies, retailers cannot handle their own deliveries, thus increasing their costs and making deliveries less certain, and in effect they cannot import independently.

Despite the non-competitive structure of refining and distribution, there appears to be substantial retail-level competition. Most retailers are independent dealerships that do not have ties to the major oil companies. But in early 2000 the gas station operators reached an agreement to limit their opening hours. Despite the risk that this step will limit competition and create inconvenience for consumers, it was evidently considered politically acceptable because of the large number of small private operators.

4.2.6. Electric power

Derogation from the EU liberalisation deadlines means Greece will not start opening up its generation market until February 2001. The national monopoly, DEH, has been used as a device for promoting other policies, such as employment and regional parity (prices are uniform across the country despite higher costs in supplying islands that are not on the grid, for example). Prices in Greece (adjusted for purchasing power parity) are relatively high. Prices have been manipulated to combat inflation or to assist industrial sectors: DEH is required to sell power at half-price to aluminium and publicly-controlled nickel firms (the aluminium plant alone consumes one-fourth of industrial power in Greece). More detailed discussion of the competition issues raised by reforms in this sector is in background report to Chapter 5 of this review.

4.2.7. Natural gas

The natural gas industry is now being developed, after the high pressure pipeline from Russia was completed in 1997. The system is set up to be a monopoly. Greece is not under EU obligation to provide for open access until 2006, because of an exemption in the EU directive for countries that only recently set up a gas system. The low-pressure distribution system will be established over the next 20 years by award of local monopoly concessions. Private sector participants will have only minority stakes. A majority will be held by subsidiaries of the national pipeline monopoly, which is mostly government-owned (85%). Hellenic Petroleum has the right to repurchase those government shares over time, so it could succeed to the gas monopoly.

The pricing system may distort competition in downstream markets. The formula reference price for most customers, which is the basis for negotiation with industrial users, is based on the costs of competitive fuels (plus a margin) and yields a price that is in line with what appears in other countries. But major customers, including the electric power monopoly DEH, pay a price set on a different, cost-plus basis under long-term take-or-pay contracts. That price seems high, but for the electric company it may be effectively lower, because DEH has a profit-sharing arrangement with the gas company. The net result is unclear, but competition in electric generation could be impaired if other firms trying to enter cannot operate on the same cost footing. Moreover, the principal firms in three sectors are interlocked in ways that may encourage each to help the others resist competition: DEPA and Hellenic Petroleum are main suppliers of fuel to DEH, DEH and DEPA have a profit-sharing agreement (so DEPA has an interest in preserving DEH's monopoly position), DEPA's prices are set by reference to Hellenic Petroleum's ex-refinery prices, and Hellenic Petroleum has a long-term interest in buying back DEPA (OECD, 1998).

4.2.8. Accounting and other professional services

As of July, 1997, the accounting profession was to have been liberalised in the EU. Greece tried to reserve some protections for the previous state monopoly during the transition period, 1994-97. A November, 1997 presidential decree concerning audits set minimum fees, restricted the use of different types of personnel, and prohibited audit firms from doing other kinds of work for a client. The regulations were defended as necessary to promote objectivity and quality. One effect, though, may be to impair the competitiveness of multinational accounting firms operating in Greece. In general, professions in Greece demonstrate many of the anti-competitive aspects of self-regulation typically found elsewhere, in limitations on entry, regulated or recommended fees, and prohibitions against potentially efficient methods of providing services and against non-deceptive advertising.

4.2.9. Banking

One sector-specific competition rule applies in financial services. For mergers between banks, a different market share threshold is used in the regulation that determines which transactions must be notified to the Competition Committee.

4.2.10. Distribution

In the 1990s, large wholesale and retail chains began to move into Greece in competition with the hundreds of thousands of traditionally small family concerns. Most foreign branded products, especially electrical goods and automobiles, are imported under exclusive distributorships. Consumer goods franchises, particularly in food and clothing, are growing rapidly (EIU, 1999, p. 28). As is common in many countries, local governments in Greece appear to use powers over licensing, taxes, and operating hours to protect incumbent smaller retailers against the threat of competition from larger stores, discounters, and other new outlets. Despite this opposition, though, many large European retail firms have entered successfully while the number of small retail shops has dropped 50% since the late 1970s. The national government has no apparent plans to reduce the local governments' powers. The supermarkets' association complains that not enough is being done to protect Greek companies, as the multinationals find ways to enter yet local governments seem to prevent larger Greek firms from doing so.[5]

5. COMPETITION ADVOCACY FOR REGULATORY REFORM

It is difficult to identify any body that is promoting competitive, market methods and outcomes in the policy-making and regulatory processes in Greece. The Competition Committee does not participate in these processes. The new sectoral bodies are, in effect, charged with the task of introdu-

197

cing competition in their assigned sectors. And the Ministry of National Economy has made studies of competition policy issues. But it is not clear that any other body has a mandate or responsibility for promoting competition.

The Competition Committee has authority to issue opinions about competition matters in response to requests from identified bodies. The range of potential requesters is wide: the Parliament or its committees, the Ministries of National Economy and Development, and "associations of trade and industry and industrial or commercial unions." (Art. 8d). But only two such opinions have been requested and issued since June 1995 (OECD CLP, 1998). The Competition Committee could not offer an official opinion about ministerial decisions affecting competition unless it was officially asked, and it is rarely asked. The Competition Committee could communicate views unofficially even in the absence of a request, but it rarely did so. The Competition Committee recognises that the advocacy power has not been used to the extent that had been contemplated when the law was amended in 1995 to authorise this role (Greece, 2000). The August 2000 amendments include one to authorise the Competition Committee to issue opinions about policy issues on its own initiative.

Observers are unaware that the Competition Committee has issued any opinions, formal or informal, about the competitive impact of regulatory or legislative proposals. Once the Competition Committee was asked for an opinion about a rule requiring that labels for consumer packages of bottled water and soft drinks set out a recommended price. Importers complained that this rule restricted market access, because it would be costly to pre-print the price in Greek. The Competition Committee's opinion supported the proposed rule, arguing that pre-printed prices would not impair free movement of goods, but instead would protect consumers, especially tourists at hot, isolated archaeological sites, against seller opportunism. The end result was to require a posted price list at the point of sale. Because no one has asked for its opinion, the Competition Committee has not offered views about issues such as the system of uniform book prices or recent proposals about taxi regulation and service station hours.

A principal vehicle for advice about policy issues could be the annual report that the Competition Committee must submit each April to the Ministers of National Economy and Development and to the president of Parliament. In this annual report, the Competition Committee does not need an official request to justify discussing competition policies more broadly. But this outlet has not been used to comment on regulatory policy topics. And in any event, no such report was submitted in 1999. The Competition Committee's only recent, special report to Parliament was about its own resource difficulties. In November 1999, the Competition Committee met with the Parliament's Transparency and Institutions Committee to discuss the Competition Committee's work. That committee, in a report issued 10 March 2000, found that Competition Committee had been unable to handle its responsibilities because of lack of resources, traceable ultimately to lack of financial independence, and because of insufficient staff and expertise. The Parliamentary committee recommended bolstering the Competition Committee's independence by eliminating the Ministers'; power to overrule its merger decisions and by granting it financial autonomy, and providing for more specialised staff and staff training.

6. CONCLUSIONS AND POLICY OPTIONS

6.1. General assessment of current strengths and weaknesses

Competition policy and institutions have played little role in the process of reforming economic regulations to stimulate competition. In general, Greece has made relatively little progress, compared to most of its EU neighbours, in reforming aspects of economic regulations that restrict freedom of competition. Competition policy has not driven change. In implementing further reforms called for by the European community, Greece has not employed its own competition policy tools – even though those tools were themselves created in response to perceived EU requirements. Rather, each industry and issue has been approached as though it were sui generis. This approach reflects the pattern of domestic policymaking, in which a principal consideration seems to have been the protection of established interests.

One of the most experienced and authoritative experts on competition policy in Greece believes that the Competition Committee is "underfunctioning" even though, in his judgement, its members and the top managers of the Secretariat have been performing heroically. The 1995 changes in the law have forced the Competition Committee to spend nearly all of its time and resources on mergers, most of which have no competitive significance, and on applications for provisional relief against alleged abuses of economic dependence, most of which are unrelated to competition policy issues. Restrictive agreements are common, but the Competition Committee could do virtually nothing about them because it lacks funds, facilities, and personnel. Despite its nominal decision-making independence, the Competition Committee has been bound too much to the central administration, being dependent for its budget on the Ministry of Development, which was characterised by a different and inconsistent philosophy dating from the period of price control.

Despite the weakness of the competition policy institutions and the pervasiveness of regulations and controls that could stifle competition, some aspects of the Greek economy nonetheless appear to be thriving. The explanation is probably a combination of an individualistic, entrepreneurial culture and tradition with extensive de facto deregulation, as businesses and others ignore or evade regulations that impair their operations too much or that cost too much to comply with.

Reforms encouraged or required by outside pressures have worked. A notable example is financial services. Competition appears to be developing in this sector, and most of the biggest banks are now private, although the largest one is still state-owned. Reform of the financial and securities sectors could provide both an example and a foundation for further reform. But this concrete illustration of evident success of greater private initiative and competition has not been used as a model for reform elsewhere, at least not yet.

6.2. The dynamic view: the pace and direction of change

The impetus for change in competition policies still comes principally from outside Greece. To that extent, the prospects for further reform are not strong. Directives from the EU, and indeed the overall direction of change in EU economic policies, present Greece with motivations for change. Another "external" impetus for change is foreign firms, who would like to enter the Greek market if its regulatory structures were modernised. Much of the content of regulation comes from EU directives. In implementing these, Greece typically does the minimum necessary, and typically takes the maximum amount of time available – and sometimes more, as it has requested derogations from the deadlines of most if not all of the major liberalisation directives, when Greece has foreseen trouble with implementation.

The *status quo* has been defended by a network of alliances among political interests, public sector unions, bureaucracies and procurement officers, and private sector suppliers to the government and publicly-controlled firms. This system for avoiding conflicts with groups that might lose out in the transition to more competitive markets may have delayed achieving benefits to the Greek economy as a whole. But this system is not as strong now as it was perhaps ten years ago. Meanwhile a younger generation, educated abroad, is bringing new ideas into the system as advisors, lobbyists, and entrepreneurs. Greek entrepreneurs are pushing aggressively for new opportunities to invest and enter markets.

Structural reforms in Greece can be classified into three phases. First came education about the potential benefits of liberalisation, which lasted until early 1998. That was followed by deeper and faster implementation in a few sectors, beginning with banking; that phase was still in process in early 2000. In the next phase, these market principles would be introduced into the utility sectors. There seems to be a consensus among policy-makers that competition principles will inevitably be incorporated in the regulatory system, but there also seems to be a consensus that it will take a long time and will have to be done industry by industry.

This conception of phased reform, although it contemplates increasing reliance on competition principles, assigns no role to strong and independent competition policy institutions. Such institutions would probably call for more rapid and widespread reform.

6.3. Potential benefits and costs of further regulatory reform

A principal objective of reform, and of having a competition policy, has been to adopt the institutions of the EU in order to cement Greece's economic and other links to Europe. Of course, a reason for adopting the policies of the EU is to achieve economic benefits. The likely improvements in efficiency and output from further reform have been well documented. The 1998 OECD *Economic Survey of Greece* estimated the effects of major structural reforms, using the model and methodology of the 1997 OECD Report on Regulatory Reform. First, the effect of further reform on prices was estimated, based on benchmarking from other countries' experiences, taking into account the current situation in Greece. Major savings in labour costs would result if labour costs in these sectors were at the average level for manufacturing, and falling intermediate input prices, dependent on energy, would have significant wider effects. Some prices would fall, notably telecom and petroleum, but others would increase in order to come closer to the costs of fulfilling public service obligations. The need for infrastructure investment would increase capital costs, but innovation, in telecoms and electric power, would reduce costs and prices too. Most of the static price reduction effect appears to result from reforms in the sectors where a principal element of reform is greater competition, namely petroleum, electric power, and especially telecoms. When the economy's response to those price changes is considered, the model predicts an increase in output of 1.5% (which could be larger, because important sectors such as telecoms are still maturing), and a decline in employment of 0.5% (which could be smaller, if the maturing sectors expand in Greece as they have elsewhere in response to liberalisation). Most importantly, though, when dynamic longer-term effects are considered, the OECD's INTERLINK model predicts a cumulative output increase of 5-7% of GDP. Considering the significance of higher quality products and better budget balance, the total income gain could be 9-11% of GDP (OECD, 1998).

Reforms to date have demonstrated some of the expected benefits, although they vary among sectors. Rents have not changed much, despite deregulation; by contrast, deregulating domestic air service has led to lower fares. Opening the sale of securities to new entry stimulated extraordinary price competition, with one new entrant charging commission rates of 0 as an introductory offer.

It is difficult to quantify the likely effects of more effective competition policy. There are many restrictive agreements in place in Greece, but their net effect on competition may not be too great, because the structure of most Greek industries appears unconcentrated and because firms probably do not comply with these agreements in all respects. That is, they probably cheat on the cartels. Still, clearly enforcing the prohibition against horizontal agreements should stimulate price competition. The effects of improved competition enforcement on mergers and restructuring are also somewhat uncertain. There appears to be a trend toward somewhat higher concentration in Greek industry. Because many sectors are virtually atomised, this trend is probably healthy in most cases. Combinations could permit small firms to achieve economies of scale and operating efficiencies, and larger, healthier firms might even offer more jobs. Of course, not all mergers in every sector will necessarily be good for competition. But it is critical that competition policy focus on the handful of mergers that could present problems, and that it not hamper or delay other transactions that are likely to be beneficial.

6.4. Policy options for consideration

Expand staff resources at the Competition Committee, at least to the levels already authorised by statute. Authorise recruitment and compensation comparable to what has been authorised for other, high-profile agencies. Some other bodies, such as the Capital Markets Committee, evidently have authority to hire outside of the usual process and to pay up to 50% more than the standard pay scale in order to attract people with the qualifications they need. If competition policy is to have a significant role in reform, its institutions must get equivalent treatment. The recent amendments give the Competition Committee power to hire independently and double the authorised staff level.

Provide for independence of financial support, so that the formally independent Competition Committee is not subject to oversight by a ministry with inconsistent priorities. To ensure that competition policy institutions can operate independently, their source of funds must not be tied to such a narrow and changeable base. One way would be for the budget to be separately authorised by Parliament. Another, which was adopted by recent legislation, would be to establish an independent source of funding, such as fees for applications or small charges on capital market transactions and registrations.

De-emphasise merger review, by setting higher merger thresholds or otherwise changing the decision rules so the Competition Committee can concentrate only on the small number of mergers that may actually have anti-competitive effects and will no longer tie up other transactions for too long, or use too many of its resources processing them. Greater resources for the competition institutions would be wasted, if they continued to be spent on detailed reviews of mergers that are highly unlikely to present problems for competition. The law was recently amended to increase the thresholds. Another step would be to fundamentally change the decision process so that most mergers can be treated quickly under a more summary process, like that which applies to the "notification" category.

Shift attention to horizontal agreements. Additional resources in competition policy should be assigned to the endemic problem of excessive co-operation among Greek businesses. Clear enforcement of the statutory prohibition will help Greek businesses prepare for the vigorous competition of the wider European market.

Complete privatisation of structurally competitive services and industries. These include tourist facilities, travel agencies, airline catering, airlines, and petroleum product distribution. In this process, it must be clear that competition policy institutions have the ability, and the responsibility, to ensure that these transactions do not perpetuate market power in private hands but instead result in workably competitive markets.

Make advocacy possible. A formal change in the law has now made it clear that the Competition Committee can offer opinions on its own initiative, without waiting for a request from some other entity. In addition, though, the Competition Committee's prestige and credibility must be restored, through more effective enforcement, before policy advice and advocacy could be credible. A prime subject of attention could be the potentially anti-competitive effect of the extensive licensing requirements that are used to control entry into many businesses, which are administered principally by the Ministry of Development. For that to be effective, the Competition Committee must achieve full independence from that Ministry's influence or control. And the appearance of being tied to industry interests should also be overcome, by eliminating the power of business and industry associations to designate members of the Competition Committee. Normally, where there is a long tradition of state ownership and government control over market institutions, a high priority should be given to advocacy. That may prove true for Greece, too. But the Competition Committee has not been in a position to undertake effective advocacy. Experienced observers, and indeed some on the Competition Committee itself, believe that advocacy is not yet a priority, because no one in the government would listen to the Competition Committee's analysis and advice. Rather, they believe that resources must first be reinforced and redirected.

Give the Competition Committee responsibilities in the process of introducing competition into previously monopolised network industries. Such a role could increase its prestige as well as help ensure that the process promotes competitive outcomes. The relevant sectoral institutions, which are just being set up, appear to have had little contact with the Competition Committee so far. Both the Competition Committee and these sectoral institutions would profit from more extensive and formal interaction. The Competition Committee should be involved in the process of creating institutional responsibilities and relationships needed to achieve the appropriate division of labour.

Broaden the base of responsibility for supporting competition. Making other ministries as well as sectoral regulators responsible for eliminating constraints on competition within their own jurisdictions would extend the scope of competition policy and emphasise its broad, horizontal importance. The Competition Committee should play a central role. Thus, these other bodies should be held responsible for co-ordinating with the Competition Committee to promote expeditious enforcement. Ministries and sectoral regulators could establish antitrust offices to work with the Competition Committee and to advise industries about their compliance obligations.

6.5. Managing regulatory reform

The government is aware of the importance of market competition to long-term economic health. But it is also aware that, in the short run, free competition would not necessarily reduce the inflation rate. Moderating inflation would be a medium to long-term result of more effective competition. The top economic policy priority in Greece has been meeting the macroeconomic performance criteria for joining the euro zone. Keeping the measured inflation rate low in the short run has been considered more important than establishing institutions that will help moderate price increases in the long run. Reflecting these overall priorities, the Ministry of Development for many years did not agree to strengthen the competition policy institutions, but instead ascribed great importance to "gentlemen's agreements" to control inflation.

The priority of joining EMU, to make a credible, seemingly irrevocable commitment to fundamental reform, may well be understandable over a longer time horizon. Even some supporters of competition policy in Greece allow, reluctantly, that perhaps the time for strong competition policy in Greece may not come for another year or two. Reportedly, some expect that after Greece does join the euro zone, the "shock" of exposure to stronger competition may lead to demands for more effective competition policy and enforcement. Then, resources and staff would be increased to deal with "new" problems.

But the problems that result from weak competition policy institutions are present now, and they will continue to undermine reforms until something is done about them. Commitment to fundamental reform requires making an unambiguous commitment to effective competition policy, and doing so now, not at some undefined point in the future. The notion that the "shock" of stronger competition in the euro zone will elicit demands for stronger competition policy may be naive. Another likely response could be for the affected sectors to demand protection and even a reversal of the larger-scale process. Or, they might demand that the competition law be applied perversely, to cripple new, efficient competitors and protect established firms. It would be better to undertake the reform and strengthening of competition policy institutions before that happens, to ensure that the direction of policy is set and the resources are in place to implement it. Until the necessary changes are made, to shift attention from unnecessary merger reviews toward more important, albeit difficult, issues, and to provide sufficient independence and resources to do the job, competition policy will continue to impose undesirable costs that impede accomplishment of other policy goals, such as increased industrial efficiency and attracting foreign investment, while failing to accomplish its primary purpose, of promoting stronger competition to improve efficiency and benefit consumers. It is encouraging that recent appointments and amendments show an awareness of the need to shift priorities.

NOTES

1. Act 2836/3.8.2000.

2. Financial Times, 15 January 2000.

3. Government Gazette, issue 596/B/8.5.2000.

4. *Sikkens* II, case 38/1986.

5. *Hermes*, December 1999, ww.ana.gr/hermes/1999/dec.retail.htm.

BIBLIOGRAPHY

Christoforou, Theofanis (1990),
  "Competition Law in Greece," in *Competition Law in Western Europe and the* USA, Netherlands.

Clogg, Richard (1992),
  A *Concise History of Greece*, Cambridge.

Economist Intelligence Unit (2000),
  Country Profile: Greece 1999-2000.

Foundation for Economic & Industrial Research (IOBE) (1999*a*),
  Quarterly Bulletin No. 20, The Greek Economy 4/98, January.

Foundation for Economic & Industrial Research (IOBE) (1999*b*),
  Quarterly Bulletin No. 21, The Greek Economy 1/99, May.

Foundation for Economic & Industrial Research (IOBE) (1999*c*),
  Quarterly Bulletin No. 22, The Greek Economy 2/99, November.

Government of Greece (1999),
  Ministry of National Economy, *Progress Report on Reforms in the Product, Services and Capital Markets in Greece,* December.

Government of Greece (2000),
  Communication to OECD Secretariat.

International Monetary Fund (1999),
  Staff Country Report No. 99/131: Greece, November, Washington, D.C.

OECD (1997),
  The OECD Report on Regulatory Reform, Paris.

OECD (1998),
  Economic Surveys: Greece, Paris.

OECD CLP (1996),
  Annual Report on Competition Policy Developments in Greece (1995), Paris.

OECD CLP (1997),
  Competition Policy in OECD Countries (Annual Report of Greece, 1993-1994).

OECD CLP (1997*b*),
  Competition Policy in OECD Countries (Annual Report of Greece, 1994-1995).

OECD CLP (1997*c*),
  Annual Report on Competition Policy Developments in Greece (1996), Paris.

OECD CLP (1998),
  In-Depth Examination of Competition Policy in Greece (1997), Paris.

Tzouganatos, Dimitris (1998),
  "Protecting competition in Greece 1995-1998," *Global Competition Review,* p. 25, October-November

BACKGROUND REPORT ON ENHANCING MARKET OPENNESS THROUGH REGULATORY REFORM*

---

*   This report was principally prepared by **Evdokia Moïsé**, Administrator of the Trade Directorate. It has benefited from extensive comments provided by colleagues throughout the OECD Secretariat, by the Government of Greece, and by Member countries as part of the peer review process. This report was peer reviewed in September 2000 in the Working Party of the OECD's Trade Committee.

TABLE OF CONTENTS

List of Boxes

List of Tables

List of Figures

ACRONYMS

ACP	African, Caribbean and Pacific countries
BEST	Business Environment Simplification Task Force
CEN	European Commission for Standardisation
CENELEC	European Committee for Electrotechnical Standards
DECT	Digital Enhanced Cordless Telecommunications
DEH	Dimosia Epichirisi Ilektrismou (Public Power Corporation)
DEPA	Dimosia Epichirisi Photaeriou (Public Gas Corporation)
EA	European Co-operation for Accreditation
EC	European Communities
EDI	Electronic Data Interchange
EETT	Ethinki Epitropi Tilepikoinonion kai Tachydromion (National Telecommunications and Postal Commission)
EFTA	European Free Trade Agreement
ELKE	Elliniko Kentro Ependyseon (Hellenic Centre for Investment)
ELOT	Ellinikos Organismos Typopoiesis (Hellenic Organisation for Standardisation)
EMU	European Monetary Union
ERA	Energy Regulatory Authority
ESEE	Ethinki Synomospondia Ellinikou Emporiou (National Confederation of Greek Trade)
ESYD	Ethniko Symvoulio Diapistefsis (National Accreditation Council)
ETSI	European Telecommunications Standardization Institute
EU	European Union
FDI	Foreign Direct Investment
FESCO	Forum of European Securities Commission
FGI	Federation of Greek Industries
GATS	General Agreement on Trade in Services
GATT	General Agreement on Tariffs and Trade
GDP	Gross Domestic Product
GPA	Government Procurement Agreement
GSI	General Secretariat for Industry, Ministry of Development
GSP	General System of Preferences
IAF	International Accreditation Forum
ICIS	Integrated Customs Information System
IEA	International Energy Agency
IEC	International Electrotechnical Commission
ILAC	International Laboratory Accreditation Co-operation
IOSCO	International Organisation of Securities Commissions
IQNet	International Network of Quality System Certifiers
ISO	International Standardisation Organisation
ITU	International Telecommunication Union
MFN	Most Favoured Nation
MRA	Mutual Recognition Agreement
NSO	National Standardisation Organisation
OJEC	Official Journal of the European Communities
OKE	Oikonomiki kai Koinoniki Epitropi (Economic and Social Council of Greece)
OTE	Organismos Tilepikoinonion Ellados (Greek Organisation for Telecommunications)
PEDMEDE	Panhellenic Association of Engineers Providers for Public Works
RIA	Regulatory Impact Analysis
SATE	Syllogos Anonymon Technikon Etairion (Association of Technical Limited Companies)
SINCERT	Sistema per l'Accreditamento degli Organismi di Certificazione (Accreditation System of Certification Bodies)
SLIM	Simpler Legislation for the Internal Market
SME	Small and Medium Enterprise
SPS	Agreement on the Application of Sanitary and Phytosanitary Measures
TABD	Transatlantic Business Dialogue
TAXIS	Integrated Taxation Information System
TBT	Agreement on Technical Barriers to Trade
TEE	Techniko Epimelitirio Ellados (Technical chamber of Greece)
TRIS	Technical Regulations Information System database
UMTS	Universal Mobile Telecommunications System
UN-ECE	United Nations Economic Commission for Europe
WCO	World Customs Organisation
WTO	World Trade Organisation
YPETHO	Ypourgio Ethinkis Oikonomias (Ministry of National Economy)

Executive Summary

Background Report on Enhancing Market Openness through Regulatory Reform

As traditional barriers to trade have fallen, the impact of domestic regulations on international trade and investment has become more apparent than ever before. While regulations aim at improving the functioning of market economies in a range of fields, such as market competition, business conduct, the labour market, consumer protection, public health and safety or the environment, they may directly or indirectly distort international competition and prevent market participants from taking full advantage of competitive markets. Maintaining an open world trading system requires regulation that promotes global competition and economic integration, thereby avoiding trade disputes and improving trust and mutual confidence across borders. This report assesses how the Greek regulatory system performs from these perspectives and how regulatory reform may contribute to enhancing market openness and the benefits which consumers and producers can reap from open markets.

Over the last five years Greece has implemented an important programme of macroeconomic reforms, which contributed to substantial improvement of its economic performance and to its membership in the European Monetary Union as of January 2001. These efforts have provided a strong impetus for rethinking government practices and changing the role of the State in the economy. The momentum of and commitment to reform and the general policy stance towards international market openness have been largely shaped by the membership of Greece in the European Union. Although structural reforms complementing the macroeconomic stabilisation programme have been slower to come, there is broad consensus today between the government and the private sector that such reforms are necessary for sustaining the progress made. In particular, concerns are widely shared about the effects of a restrictive domestic environment, of important state control over the economy and of extensive recourse to command and control regulations, on the competitiveness of domestic enterprises and the attractiveness of the country to foreign investors.

When considering the efficient regulation principles for market openness defined by the OECD, non-discrimination, the use of internationally harmonised measures and the recognition of equivalence of foreign measures appear to be well integrated in the Greek regulatory framework, in part through the disciplines set by the European Union. On the other hand, transparency of decision-making, avoidance of unnecessary trade restrictiveness and application of competition principles still raise concerns relating to the market orientation of the Greek regulatory framework. Regulatory inflation and complexity has limited the predictability of the regulatory system and generated substantial costs of operation and entry, especially for foreign firms. The discretionary character of public consultation has inspired distrust by involved parties and undermined the efficiency of policymaking tools. The absence of prior assessment of regulatory impact on the economy often led to unduly restrictive regulation, affecting heavily productivity and competitiveness. Regulatory burdens have induced non-compliance while inadequate enforcement has further distorted market operation. Competition policy was hardly provided the means and support for ensuring effective protection.

Yet, over the last years all these areas have witnessed significant steps liable to enhance regulatory quality and promote a trade-friendlier regulatory environment. New procedures have been introduced to make regulatory information more widely available and to facilitate the access of individuals and businesses to administrative services. Administrative "one-stop-shops" have been created to simplify the issuance of licences and permits at the local level. The criteria used in public procurement procedures have been clarified. A new regulatory framework has just offered unprecedented impetus to the Competition Committee. Liberalisation in key sectors, like the telecommunications services is finally reaching the level of other EU countries. Other equally important steps still remain to be made, in particular as regards the further liberalisation of electricity and transportation, the introduction of regulatory impact assessment in the framework of the rulemaking process or the streamlining of existing regulation.

Most of the reforms are very recent, or still ongoing. Time is therefore needed for their effective results to be assessed. It is encouraging that the overall policy stance of the Greek government points towards a qualitative transformation of the role of the State in economic activity, entailing its withdrawal from direct involvement in production, the removal of excessive regulation of economic and social arrangements and a better focussing on those activities that are a clear government prerogative. The translation of this policy stance into concrete regulatory practices, will be the major challenge for years to come

The globalisation of production and the resulting deeper integration of national markets have reinforced the link between domestic policies and trade liberalisation. As traditional barriers to trade have fallen, the impact of domestic regulations on international trade and investment has become more apparent than ever before. While regulations generally aim at improving the functioning of market economies in a range of fields, such as market competition, business conduct, the labour market, consumer protection, public health and safety or the environment, they may directly or indirectly distort international competition and affect resource allocation and productive efficiency. Thus regulations should be made in a way consistent with an open trading system and support strong international competition. This report considers whether and how Greek regulatory procedures and content affect market access and presence in Greece. An important reverse scenario – whether and how inward trade and investment affect the fulfilment of legitimate policy objectives reflected in social regulation – is beyond the scope of the present discussion.

1. MARKET OPENNESS AND REGULATION: THE POLICY ENVIRONMENT IN GREECE

Greece is a small, import-dependent economy. In 1997 imports of goods and services accounted for 25.5% and exports for 16.1% of GDP.[1] Chronic trade deficits are roughly balanced by strong invisible receipts, mainly tourism and shipping. About 65% of total Greek trade is with other EU member states, while trade with Balkan countries and in particular Bulgaria and Albania has developed strongly in the recent years and represents today around 15%. Greece imports a large proportion of its energy, some food, virtually all its transport equipment and most of its machinery and electrical goods. Main exports are food (fresh and processed), raw cotton and tobacco, textiles (yarns, fabrics and ready-made clothing), chemicals, semi-processed mineral and metal products, cement and refined oil products.

Compared to other OECD economies, Greece has a relatively small industrial sector and an important agricultural sector. In 1998 agriculture (including forestry and fishing) represented 8.1% of GDP, against an EU average of 2.1% and 1.6% in the United States. Industry (including mining, manufacturing and construction) represented 22.4% of GDP, against an EU average of 30.4%, 25.2% in the United States and 35.6% in Japan. Within the industrial sector, construction was particularly important, accounting for 7.7% of GDP. The services sector (69.5% of GDP) is close to the EU average. In the services sector, tourism and transport services represent the most important share. The State plays a very important role in the economic activity. In 1997 the public sector accounted roughly for 49% of GDP (public spending represented 42%, public utilities 5% and public-owned banks and insurance companies 2% of GDP).[2]

The membership of Greece in the European Union and its participation in the multilateral trading system have played a major role in shaping the general policy environment toward international market openness and bringing momentum and commitment to reform. Multilateral trade agreements have resulted in historically low tariffs for products, and set trade in services on the path of progressive liberalisation. The development of the Single Market has led to the removal of regulatory barriers to trade among European Union countries. Tariffs, quotas, and other restrictive measures on industrial products, which amounted to 45% effective protection before EC membership in 1981,[3] have been totally removed by the early 1990s. The implementation of internal market directives is progressively opening key sectors, such as the telecommunications or energy sectors, to competition. However, Greece has frequently sought derogations that have delayed major reforms and the ensuing pro-competitive effects on the economy.

1.1. Overview of regulatory reform to date[4]

From 1950 to 1974, Greece underwent an important process of social and economic modernisation, driven by an average growth rate of 7%, and complemented by the reestablishment of democracy in 1974. However, *"the country's post-war "miracle" can be said to have been intimately linked with the emergence of a ubiquitous, over-interventionist, over-regulating, paternalistic and protectionist state"*,[5] which compromised economic progress during the following twenty years. From 1974 to 1995, the annual growth rate averaged 2%, industrial productivity growth 1.05% and inflation 18%. Accession to the European Communities in 1981 did not lead to the economic development experienced by other new Members after their accession. Redistributive economic policies between 1982 and 1985 brought the total government debt to 100% of GDP by 1989.

By the end of the 1980s, awareness that the Greek economy was in dire need of reform gained momentum. A policy of economic austerity, first launched in 1985-87, has been pursued since the early 1990s by all administrations, irrespective of which party was in power. Since 1994 Greece has adopted a series of convergence programmes to meet the criteria for admission to the European Monetary Union (EMU). Convergence policies aimed at reducing inflation and public sector debt through fiscal consolidation, tight monetary policy, broadening of the tax base and better tax collection, control on employment in the public sector and wage moderation. These policies were largely successful in bringing inflation down to 2.6% in 1999, public sector deficit to 1.5% of GDP and the general government debt to 104.2% of GDP, thus meeting the relevant criteria for EMU membership. Public investments, including EU fund transfers, boosted economic growth, which reached 3.5% in 1999. On 20 June 2000 the Porto European Summit confirmed that Greece would join the EMU in 2001.

Macroeconomic stabilisation has been complemented with a series of structural reforms. The banking and financial sectors have been liberalised considerably since 1987, mainly in order to comply with EU directives, and are now basically free of state interference. Foreign exchange controls have been gradually relaxed since 1985. Medium and long-term capital movements were fully liberalised in 1993. Most restrictions on short-term capital movements were lifted in 1994 and liberalisation was completed in 1997. Price controls have been abolished, except for pharmaceuticals and agricultural products. A privatisation program has been undertaken to reduce the dominant role of the government in the economy.[7] Devolution of powers from the central administration to the regional and local administrations was initiated in 1994, but took effect only in 1998-1999. On the other hand, reform of the regulated sectors, such as energy or transportation, is still at a very early stage. Structural reforms have been announced by the newly re-elected government as one of the central policy priorities for the next four years.

1.2. The role of foreign investment

Foreign direct investment has played a relatively limited role in the Greek economy. Among potential investors there has been limited interest in developing activities exclusively aimed at servicing the Greek market, mainly because of its small size.[7] In contrast, the main reason for establishing in Greece is obviously to gain access to other, wider markets, such as the European Union, or the broader Balkan and Eastern European area.[8] However, the direction of such strategy has changed considerably to adjust to the geopolitical and economic development in the region. Whereas in 1992 surveys indicated that 42% of investors viewed Greece as an entry point to the European Union markets and another 23% aimed primarily at the Balkans and Eastern Europe, these percentages were 3% and 80% respectively in 1997 (Hassid, 1997). The three most important factors limiting the attractiveness of Greece as a destination for FDI were reported in these surveys to be weak macroeconomic performances, shortfalls in infrastructure (in particular in telecommunications and transport) and the poor quality of public administration. The recent improvement of both macroeconomic performance and infrastructure has most likely played an important role in the increase of FDI inflows in the last three years. However, it is impossible to identify the respective contribution of these and other factors to FDI growth. In 1997 the Hellenic Centre for Investment approved 43 FDI applications totalling US$486 million, while the stock of FDI, which amounted to US$4 billion (market prices) by end 1996, had reached US$13.1 billion by end 1998.

Both local content and export performance are taken into consideration by Greek authorities in evaluating applications for tax and investment incentives, but they are not mandatory prerequisites for approving such incentives. Greece is divided into four investment zones, according to regional development and unemployment levels. Investments in the most disadvantaged regions can benefit from cash grants of 15 to 40% of the total sum invested or from tax allowances of 40 to 100%. The government encourages relocation of industries from Athens and Thessaloniki to less developed regions through tax breaks. Specific sectoral incentives exist for high technology, environmental protection services, and leisure facilities, as well as for manufacturing and mining companies engaged in export, or in import substitution.

Table 1.   Cumulative flows of FDI involving OECD countries 1990-98

Million US dollars

1. United States	605 052	8. Sweden	67 798
2. United Kingdom	240 513	9. Canada	66 888
3. France	178 323	10. Germany	60 260
4. Belgium-Luxembourg	105 859	11. Australia	55 603
5. Netherlands	101 028	12. Italy	31 278
6. Spain	84 039	13. Greece*	26 823
7. Mexico	68 576	14. Denmark	24 456

*   1990-97.
Source: OECD (1999), International Direct Investment Database.

2. THE POLICY FRAMEWORK FOR MARKET OPENNESS: THE SIX "EFFICIENT REGULATION" PRINCIPLES

An important step in ensuring that regulations do not unnecessarily reduce market openness is to build "efficient regulation" principles into the domestic regulatory process for social and economic regulations, as well as for administrative practices. "Market openness" here refers to the ability of foreign suppliers to compete in a national market without encountering discriminatory or excessively burdensome or restrictive conditions. These principles, which have been described in the 1997 OECD *Report on Regulatory Reform* and developed further in the Trade Committee, are:

- Transparency and openness of decision making;

- Non-discrimination;

- Avoidance of unnecessary trade restrictiveness;

- Use of internationally harmonised measures;

- Recognition of equivalence of other countries' regulatory measures; and

- Application of competition principles

They have been identified by trade policy makers as key to market-oriented, trade and investment friendly regulation. They reflect the basic principles underpinning the multilateral trading system, concerning which many countries have undertaken certain obligations in the WTO and other contexts. The intention in the OECD country reviews of regulatory reform is not to judge the extent to which any country may have undertaken and lived up to international commitments relating directly or indirectly to these principles but rather to assess whether and how domestic instruments, procedures and practices give effect to the principles and successfully contribute to market openness.

2.1. Transparency, openness of decision making and of appeal procedures

In order to ensure international market openness, the process of creating, enforcing, reviewing or reforming regulations needs to be transparent and open to foreign firms and individuals seeking access to a market, or expanding activities in a given market. From an economic point of view, transparency is essential for market participants in several respects. Transparency in the sense of information availabi-

213

lity offers market participants a clear picture of the rules on the basis of which the market operates, enabling them to base their production and investment decisions on an accurate assessment of potential costs, risks and market opportunities. It is also a safeguard in favour of equality of competitive opportunities for market participants and thus enhances the security and predictability of the market. Such transparency can be achieved through a variety of means, including systematic publication of proposed rules prior to entry into force and use of electronic means to share information, such as the Internet. Transparency of decision making further refers to the dialogue with affected parties, which should offer well-timed opportunities for public comment, and rigorous mechanisms for ensuring that such comments are given due consideration prior to the adoption of a final regulation. Market participants wishing to voice concerns about the application of existing regulations should have appropriate access to appeal procedures. Such dialogue allows market forces to be built into the process and helps avoid trade frictions. This sub-section discusses the extent to which such objectives are met in Greece and how. It also provides insights on two specific areas, technical regulations and government procurement, in which transparency is essential for ensuring international competition.

Relations between the State and civil society have long been fairly blurred in Greece. Decades of patronage relationships between the State and civil society have turned the special interests of various social groups into one of the most pervasive factors in policy making but at the same time have seriously undermined the position of civil society as an independent entity.[9] As they were able to obtain information or advance their interests through informal avenues, the most influential civil society groups did not feel compelled to push the State for greater transparency and accountability. This state of affairs has not only born potential for capture but has also de facto excluded "outsiders". It has further fostered a climate of distrust within civil society as regards the reliability and probity of the administration.[10] However, in recent years, a more mature Greek democracy has been gradually allowing market forces to play a greater role in the economy while favouring more open participation of civil society in the policy-making process. Both trends bode well for a progressive reinforcement of transparency procedures.

2.1.1. *Information dissemination*

Information with respect to adopted regulation is primarily provided through publication in the Government Gazette (E*fimerida tis Kivernisseos*) prior to entry into force, as required by the Constitution. Issues of the Government Gazette are also available online on the website of the National Printing House. Publication in the Government Gazette is a requirement for the validity of all regulations, including Acts of Parliament, Presidential Decrees and Ministerial Decisions. Article 77 of the Greek Constitution prohibits the retroactive effect of regulations other than authoritative interpretations by the Parliament of statutes already in force. Entry into force usually takes place ten days after the publication of the regulation in the Government Gazette, unless explicitly provided otherwise. Individual ministries occasionally publicise regulation in their respective areas of competence on their own websites, but this is not yet a standard government-wide practice. All these sites feature pages in English, although the text of regulations themselves is usually available only in Greek.

Apart from the Government Gazette, the most authoritative source for obtaining information on regulations is the "Code of Permanent Legislation" (*Kodikas Diarkous Nomothesias*), a loose-leaf edition regularly updated to reflect new or amended regulations. This publication is issued by the Ministry of Public Administration and is available on a subscription basis. An electronic edition of the Code is being developed. Electronic databases have also been elaborated through private or public initiatives. For instance, the National Printing House is currently completing an electronic collection of Greek regulation. Individual Ministries may also publish collections of regulation in selected areas of their competence.

Foreign firms that wish to obtain information about the regulatory and economic environment in Greece may also enquire at the Hellenic Centre for Investment (ELKE). ELKE was created in 1996 to seek, promote and support foreign investment in Greece, foster international ventures with Greek companies and contribute to improving the institutional framework for FDI. Jointly funded by the EU and the Greek government, it operates under the supervision of the Minister of National Economy and offers its services free of charge. ELKE provides in-depth information on the Greek regulatory and institutional framework for investment, identifies market opportunities, seeks partners and locations for firms wishing to establish in Greece and offers consulting services on the legal and financial preparation of greenfield investments and establishment of joint ventures. It also helps potential investors obtain the necessary licences and gain access to investment incentives, and supports them during the implementation stage of their projects (see below, section 2.3). Although its consulting and support services are available only to prospective investments above a certain threshold, its information services are available to all.

A limiting factor for the transparency of effective regulation is the existence of ambiguous or contradictory regulatory provisions, which frequently create the need for interpretative statements by the Parliament (in the case of laws), or interpretative Ministerial circulars (in the case of decrees). An additional factor may be the ever-increasing mass of regulation, which makes it difficult for citizens and firms to keep abreast and induces selective enforcement by the administration because of the increases in monitoring costs. Although not an exclusively Greek phenomenon, the frequent introduction of amendments in regulatory projects that are unrelated to the subject of these amendments further complicates the regulatory framework. These practices limit the predictability of the regulatory environment. Market players may on occasion have difficulty getting a clear idea of the applicable rules or a consistent reading thereof by the administration, so that professional help in doing so is often indispensable.[11] This seems to be particularly true of fiscal regulation.

In 1996, the Prime Minister issued a circular requesting Ministers to undertake the codification of regulation in their respective fields of competence and to suppress regulations that have become outdated, irrelevant or inoperative. Although this streamlining process has been advancing, it does not seem to be underpinned by consistent efforts to do away with regulations that are no longer warranted. Representatives of domestic constituencies feel this shortcoming may contribute to even greater confusion about applicable regulation.

There are no official channels for bringing prospective regulation to the attention of domestic constituencies and foreign parties at large. Although each Ministry forwards quarterly planning schedules and progress reports on prospective regulation to the General Secretariat of the Ministerial Council, these are not made officially available to the public. Information on prospective regulation is nonetheless publicised to a large extent, but this tends to happen through informal channels and private initiatives, such as the publication in the daily and professional press of general descriptions, excerpts or even the full text of the regulation. Information to the press is made available either by the administration itself through informal networks, or by the representatives of groups consulted by the administration during the preparatory stage. However, the process clearly lacks accuracy control on the part of the administration and entails a serious risk of misinformation.

The Greek regulatory system does not make use of formal "notice and comment" procedures whereby the entire text of the draft regulation would be made available to interested constituencies for information and comments. However, certain Ministries have taken initiatives in this direction. One recent example was the presentation on the website of the Ministry of Transport and Communications of the strategy paper and the draft law on telecommunications liberalisation. In December 1999, the Ministry invited public discussion on the project over a period of 45 days. This initiative elicited considerable interest from market players, including network and service providers, academic institutions, associations, as well as from other government entities. The Ministry received numerous constructive comments and found this endeavour generally positive and helpful. Following a major rethinking of the proposal, a new version of the law was publicised in June 2000, calling for public comments until the end of July.

2.1.2. *Consultation mechanisms*

Official consultation with concerned constituencies when preparing or reviewing regulations takes place through the Economic and Social Council of Greece (OKE). OKE was established by Act 2232 of 1994 and modelled on the Economic and Social Committee of the European Union. Its role is to provide the government with the opinion of social partners on important socio-economic issues prior to the enactment of relevant laws. The opinion of OKE is mandatory with respect to laws relating to *"labour relations, social security, taxation measures, as well as socio-economic policy in general, especially in topics of regional development, investment, export, consumer protection and competition"*.[12] The initiative for requesting an OKE opinion rests with the relevant government authority and the law does not seem to provide the possibility to challenge omissions. OKE can also formulate opinions on other issues of socio-economic policy on its own initiative or at the request of the competent Minister. In all three cases, the opinion is advisory. Since its inception, OKE has issued 40 opinions: of these, 25 concerned draft domestic or EU regulation, 7 dealt with socio-economic policy issues upon Ministerial request and 8 were formulated on OKE's own initiative.

OKE is organised along the lines of the typical tripartite model of representation, that is employers, employees and a third group representing farmers, liberal professions, consumers and local government. Its main aim is to contribute to maximising the social benefit by promoting social dialogue and facilitate the development of common positions on issues concerning Greek society as a whole or particular groups. It is therefore not intended as the avenue for voicing particular opinions or concerns, although such opinions and concerns are factored into the formulation of OKE's opinions. Its limited

---

Box 1.   **Transparency in the regulation of the Greek capital market**

Transparency and accountability of the supervisory authority are essential for building confidence in the operation of the Stock Exchange. In order to develop investors' trust and ensure that the regulation meets the market's needs, the Greek Capital Market Commission[1] has established a series of information dissemination and consultation practices. They are directly addressed to the concerned public and supplement the annual report that the Commission addresses to the Parliament. These practices include:

- Extensive consultation with the concerned constituencies at an early stage of the elaboration of regulation within the competence of the Commission. To begin with, the Commission issues a consultation paper presenting a preliminary version of the draft and distributes it to concerned professional associations, such as the Federation of Greek Industries, the Union of Brokers, the Union of Institutional Investors, or the Hellenic Bankers Association. Constituencies are given 30 days to react, but in practice this deadline is commonly extended to 45 days. After having received comments, which are usually quite extensive, the Commission organises a meeting between the associations and the Commission staff in order to discuss the comments and their eventual incorporation in the draft. This procedure has most recently been used for the elaboration of three Codes of Conduct on institutional investors, underwriters and brokerage firms and investment firms and on the upcoming regulation on public offers.

- Publication of all decisions on licenses and sanctions. These decisions, taken by the Board of Directors, are based on clear pre-established and publicised criteria and are subject to judicial review by the administrative courts.

- An open policy with respect to requests for information, comments or recommendations by foreign companies or institutions. The Commission endeavours to take appropriate account of such communications, both when they arrive in an *ad hoc* and informal way and through its participation to international fora, such as the Forum of European Securities Commission (FESCO) or the International Organisation of Securities Commissions (IOSCO).

- Public campaigns of information to educate inexperienced investors on the operation of the Stock Exchange.

- In addition, the Commission is in the process of instituting a Mediator for the Capital Market, responsible for arbitrating conflicts between investors and listed companies.

---

1.   The Capital Market Commission was established as a separate Public Law Legal Entity in 1991. It operates at arms length from the Ministry of National Economy and is accountable to the Parliament. It enjoys financial (through fees on Stock Exchange transactions and on Initial Public Offerings -IPOs-) and functional independence, as it has regulatory powers on the capital markets, can issue and revoke licences and impose administrative sanctions and financial fees without Ministerial intervention.

membership is a de facto further obstacle to the expression of opinions and concerns by foreign partners.

In parallel to the formalised consultation mechanism of OKE, consultation with concerned constituencies when preparing or reviewing regulations takes place in an informal way. Each Ministry establishes its own informal networks and sets up standard practices for the exchange of views with respect to prospective regulation. Informal consultations are primarily addressed to existing professional associations, national chambers of commerce and trade unions, many of which are also represented in OKE. However, the choice of participants is tailored more closely to the specific competence area of the consulting Ministry. By way of example, the Ministry of Public Works elaborates regulation in informal working groups composed of civil servants, representatives of the Technical Chamber of Greece (TEE) and of professional associations like the Panhellenic Association of Engineers Providers for Public Works (PEDMEDE) or the Association of Technical Limited Companies (SATE) and sometimes academics. These same associations receive the draft proposal for comments, and the TEE publishes it in its weekly Information Bulletin for comments by its members. The main avenue for foreign parties to participate and make observations is through domestic associations and entities, although it is not uncommon for foreign enterprises to directly contact the concerned Ministry, especially when their views dissent from the opinion expressed by domestic associations.

The level of satisfaction of parties involved in these informal consultative processes appears in general rather low. Constituencies frequently complain about not being heard, not being given sufficient time to react, or not being consulted at all. Regulation is often prepared under pressure, especially with respect to the transposition and implementation of EU Directives.[13] However, the key problem seems to arise from different (and sometimes divergent) expectations of the parties involved as to the purpose of the consultation, their respective role therein and what the process should ultimately yield. Long-established mutual distrust between the administration and the market has fostered paternalistic attitudes by the civil service and often pushed the private sector to pursue narrow, corporatist agendas. A more transparent consultation practice, with clear timetables and participation criteria, subsequent reporting of debates and respective positions, and publication of motivated policy conclusions from the administration would go a long way towards building confidence and enhancing the efficiency of consultation.

2.1.3. Appeal procedures

By virtue of Article 10 of the Constitution, market participants wishing to voice concerns about administrative measures or the absence thereof have the possibility to appeal in a first instance either directly to the competent administrative authority or to its superior authority. Alternatively, the appeal can be brought directly to the administrative courts and in particular the Council of State. Where administrative recourse is specifically provided for, judicial recourse is possible only after exhaustion of available administrative remedies or in the absence thereof (such as when the decision emanates directly from a Minister or the Head of a regulatory agency). The appellant can request the suspension of the measure until the court decision is issued.

Access to administrative or judicial remedies is available to all parties whose rights or interests are affected by an administrative decision, action or omission irrespective of citizenship or domicile. Equality before the law in public administrative procedures is enshrined in Article 20 of the Constitution. However, access to judicial remedies suffers from considerable delays, as the Council of State, which is competent for the main share of all types of administrative appeals, is constantly overloaded.

Complaints or objections in relation to specific measures of regulatory authorities, to the absence thereof, or more generally to the quality of service provided by the administration can also be submitted to the Citizen's Advocate (Ombudsman). The Ombudsman may invite the authorities to motivate their decision, put forward recommendations for amendments, or call upon them to withdraw a decision in breach of the law. It can also suggest policy reforms in order to improve the quality of administrative services.

2.1.4. *Transparency in the field of technical regulations and standards*

Transparency in the field of technical regulations and standards is essential to firms facing diverging national product regulations, as transparency reduces uncertainties over applicable requirements and thus facilitates access to domestic markets. In this field Greece provides information to its trading partners and gives them the opportunity to comment as part of its notification obligations to the European Commission and the WTO. Draft product regulations that are not pure transpositions of EU harmonising directives, as well as draft standards that are distinct from international or European standards, are notified to the European Commission by virtue of Directive 98/34. The EU notification system has enhanced the transparency of the process, as it allows for a strong scrutiny of trading partners over domestic regulatory activities and provides for an early-warning mechanism on any potential obstacles to trade stemming from product regulations.

Responsibility for prompt notification of Greek draft technical regulations and standards lies with ELOT, the national standardisation body (see below Section 2.4). By virtue of Presidential Decrees 206/87 and 523/88, all draft Laws, Decrees and Ministerial Decisions containing technical specifications are transmitted to the Information Centre of ELOT by the regulatory authority in charge. The Information Centre of ELOT is also responsible for receiving notifications from the other EU Members, dispatching them to the competent authorities in Greece, and bringing together any Greek comments on the notified regulations and standards. In order to make sure that government authorities and private sector alike are well aware of all developments in the field, ELOT has established an information network of public and private entities. Information dispatching takes place online, as well as by means of a fortnightly publication mailed to all members of the network. Membership to this information network is open to all on subscription.

To the extent that notified prospective regulations are not based on relevant international standards, the European Commission transmits the information to the WTO Secretariat and other WTO Members in accordance with the obligation laid down by Article 2.9 of the WTO Agreement on Technical Barriers to Trade. Similarly, notification required under other WTO provisions (such as Article 7 of the WTO Agreement on the Application of Sanitary and Phytosanitary Measures, or regular notifications in the framework of WTO Agreements on agriculture, rules of origin, import licensing, etc.) is made to the WTO by the European Commission on behalf of Member States.

2.1.5. *Transparency in government procurement*

Transparency in government procurement is essential for ensuring the effective opening of the markets for public works, supplies and services to international competition. In Greece important reforms have been undertaken in this policy area during the last years, primarily under the momentum provided by the European regulatory framework (see Box 3), but also on account of observed dysfunctions of the system. Public procurement markets are now open to European suppliers in accordance with EU rules, although the implementation of these rules has been very slow, even with respect to the deferred deadlines granted to the Greek government. For instance, rules with respect to utilities, overdue since 1998, were finally transposed in April 2000, although they were already enforced *de facto*.[15] Third country suppliers enjoy the rights afforded by virtue of the WTO Government Procurement Agreement, which entered into force in the European Communities on 1st January 1996. However, some foreign partners believe that, in Greece as in other EU countries, "... *firms from other* EU *Member States have an automatic advantage over non*-EU *contenders in winning Greek Government tenders.*"[16] Implementing legislation concerning third country access to procurement by utilities was due in Greece by mid-February 2000, but has not been introduced yet.

Government procurement in Greece is under the responsibility of the Ministry of Environment and Public Works for works,[17] of the Ministry of Development for supplies, and of the Ministry of National

Box 2. **Provision of information in the field of technical regulations and standards: Notification obligations in the European Union**

In order to avoid erecting new barriers to the free movement of goods which could arise from the adoption of technical regulations at the national level, European Union Member States are required by Directive 98/34 (which has codified Directive 83/189) to notify all draft technical regulations on products, to the extent that these are not a transposition of European harmonised directives. This notification obligation covers all regulations at the national or regional level, which introduce technical specifications, the observance of which is compulsory in the case of marketing or use; but also fiscal and financial measures to encourage compliance with such specifications, and voluntary agreements to which a public authority is a party. Directive 98/48/EC recently extended the scope of the notification obligation to rules on information-society services. Notified texts are further communicated by the Commission to the other Member States and are in principle not regarded as confidential, unless explicitly designated as such.

Following the notification, the concerned Member State must refrain from adopting the draft regulations for a period of three months during which the effects of these regulations on the Single Market are vetted by the Commission and the other Member States. If the Commission or a Member State emit a detailed opinion arguing that the proposed regulation constitutes a barrier to trade, the standstill period is extended for another three months. Furthermore, if the preparation of new legislation in the same area is undertaken at the European Union level, the Commission can extend the standstill for another twelve months. An infringement procedure may be engaged in case of failure to notify or if the Member State concerned ignores a detailed opinion.

Although primarily directed at Member States, the procedure benefits private parties by enhancing the transparency of national regulatory activities. In order to bring draft national technical regulations to the attention of the European industry and consumers the Commission publishes regularly a list of notifications received in the Official Journal of the European Communities, and since 1999 on the Internet. Any firm or consumer association interested in a notified draft and wishing to obtain further information or the text may contact the Commission or the relevant contact point in any Member state. The value of the system for private operators has been enhanced with the initiative of the Commission in 1999 to publish notifications on the Internet. A searchable database of notifications (Technical Regulations Information System -TRIS-) going back to 1997 gives access to the draft text and the notification itself, including the rationale of the regulation and the status of the proposal.

The incentive of countries to notify, and thus the efficiency of the system, has been strongly reinforced by the 1996 Securitel decision of the European Court of Justice (Decision of 30 April 1996, CIA Security International SA versus Signalson SA and Securitel SPRL). The decision established the principle that failure to comply with the notification obligation results in the technical regulations concerned being inapplicable, so that they are unenforceable against individuals.

As far as standards are concerned Directive 98/34 provides for an exchange of information concerning the initiatives of the national standardisation organisations (NSOs) and, upon request, the working programmes, thus enhancing transparency and promoting co-operation among NSOs. The direct beneficiaries of the notification obligation of draft standards are the European Union Member States, their NSOs and the European Standardisation Bodies (CEN, CENELEC and ETSI). Private parties can indirectly become part of the standardisation procedures in countries other than their own, through their country's NSOs, which are ensured the possibility of taking an active or passive role in the standardisation work of other NSOs.

Notification obligations in the field of technical regulations and standards are complemented by a procedure requiring Member States to notify the Commission of national measures derogating from the principle of free movement of goods within the EU. The procedure has come in response to the persistence of obstacles to the free movement of goods within the Single Market. Member States must notify any measure, other than a judicial decision, which prevents the free movement of products lawfully manufactured or marketed in another Member State for reasons relating in particular to safety, health or protection of the environment. For example Member States must notify a measure which imposes a general ban, or requires to modify the product or withdraw it from the market. So far, this procedure has produced limited results.

---

1. http://europa.eu.int/comm/dg03/tris/.
2. This procedure was established by a December 1995 Decision of the European Council of Ministers and the European Parliament (Decision 3052/95) and came into effect on 1st January 1997.

Economy for services. These Ministries have also a monitoring role for the overall coherence of procurement activities and the compliance with procedural requirements, including transparency. In addition to procurement centralised through these Ministries,[18] tenders can be directly organised by other public administration services, local authorities, utilities and other public undertakings, as well as private enterprises with a minimum of 50% state or public utility ownership or which are financed at a minimum of 50% by the state or a public utility. Procurement tenders are published in a special issue of the Government Gazette and transmitted to the related Chambers of Commerce. Summaries are also published in national economic dailies and in local newspapers in the case of local procurement. In case of violation of the publication requirements any award contract is null and void. Publication requirements imposed by the EU framework are very widely observed. Despite its small size, Greece has actually the highest number of procuring entities publishing their tenders at the Official Journal of the European Communities, 3186 entities in 1998. During that same year tenders published at the OJEC represented 6.39 billion Euros out of 14.31 billion of total public procurement in Greece, that is around 44.5%, against an average of 13% for the European Union countries.

Box 3. EU rules on public procurement

Public procurement in the European Union represents today approximately 1 000 billion Euros, or around 14% of EU GDP. Because of its economic importance it has been considered as one of the cornerstones of the Single Market[1] and led to the adoption of a series of rules aimed at promoting a climate of openness and fairness and securing enhanced competition in the area of public works, supplies and services. A special framework is applied to utilities (energy, water, telecommunications and transport). Some of the major requirements of EU rules on public procurement are the following:

Information: Contracting authorities must prepare an annual indicative notice of total procurement by product area, that they envisage awarding during the subsequent 12 months. The annual indicative list and any contract whose estimated value exceeds specific thresholds must be published in the Official Journal of the European Communities. Tenders must indicate which of the permitted award procedures is chosen (open, restricted or negotiated) and specify objective selection and award criteria. Contracting authorities must also make known the result of the tender procedure through a notice in the Official Journal of the European Communities. Provisions setting minimum periods for the bidding process ensure effective opportunity of interested parties to participate in the tender.

Remedies: Member States must provide appropriate judicial review procedures of decisions taken by contracting authorities. In particular, they must provide for the possibility of interim measures, including the suspension of procedures for the award of public contracts, for setting aside decisions taken unlawfully and for awarding damages to parties affected by the infringement. The EU Directives require that these procedures be effectively and quickly enforced. Effectiveness and speed may however be difficult to judge in practice, given the diversity of judicial systems across EU member states.

Non-discrimination: This principle, applicable among EU member states, is set by the Treaty of Rome which prohibits any discrimination or restrictions in awarding contracts on the grounds of nationality and prohibits the use of quantitative restrictions on imports or measures with equivalent effect.

Use of international standards: EU rules require the use of recognised technical standards in defining specifications, with European standards taking precedence over national standards.

In May 2000 the European Commission introduced proposals aimed at consolidating and modernising the regulatory framework on public procurement. Their main features are the consolidation of the directives on public works, supplies and services into a single text; incentives for a wider use of information technologies in public procurement; and an improved and more transparent dialogue between awarding authorities and tenderers in determining contract conditions. In addition, as utilities, starting with telecommunications, are opened to effective competition, they will be progressively excluded from the regulatory coverage.

---

1. European Commission, *The cost of non-Europe in public procurement* (Cecchini Report), 1988.

However, despite a thorough observance of publication requirements, the openness of public procurement in Greece has been significantly obstructed in the past by the use of "... *loosely written specifications which are subject to varying interpretation.*"[19] Inadequate technical preparation of the tenders is believed to have been the main reason behind conflicting requirements, incomplete supporting studies and frequent miscalculations of the projected costs, which in turn have led to regular reconsiderations of the procurement financing. This state of affairs de facto reduced transparency of the tenders, even giving rise to allegations of corruption. It also indirectly encouraged less competitive suppliers to put forward underrated bids in order to win the contract, knowing that the renegotiation of the costs was easy to obtain.

The adequacy of specifications has been progressively improved through the increasing use of internationally harmonised technical standards, while particular attention has been paid to avoiding design-oriented standards mirroring specific suppliers. Furthermore, recent amendments of the regulatory framework aimed at tightening the procedures for drafting pre-selection and award criteria, attributing and making publicly available a mark for each criterion and clearly disconnecting the technical assessment from the economic assessment. In the area of public works, new provisions introduced arithmetical formulas for discarding particularly low-priced bids that would not be justified by the use of innovative cost-effective technologies and limited the possibility to reconsider the cost of the project in the absence of additional works that could not have been foreseen. A practical guide of all procedures, bodies, documents and remedies involved in tender and award procedures is now available on line and aims to help in particular SMEs and new entrants in the Greek market. The effect of amended procedures on the openness and cost-effectiveness of procurement markets has purportedly started bearing its first fruit.

Appeals related to the publication and running of the tender, the exclusion of a bidder or the award of the procurement contract have to be lodged as a first instance with the authority that supervises the procuring entity, in most cases the Minister in charge.[20] In the area of public works aggrieved parties can also address to the Body of Inspectors of Public Works, which are responsible for undertaking regular monitoring, as well as random inspections of the award, implementation and final delivery of public works. If the appeal is accepted the procedure has to resume at the point of the violation. Judicial appeals can be lodged with the Council of State for procurement by the State or by public undertakings, while procurement by private undertakings under state ownership or funding are subject to the jurisdiction of civil courts. The prospect of obtaining effective relief through judicial proceedings had been hampered on the one hand by the ambiguity of selection and award criteria and on the other hand by the delays commonly observed in such proceedings, which could range from one and a half or two years, to five years in case of appeal to a superior court. As courts were generally reluctant to order interim suspension of the procurement procedure because of the public interest to have the procurement carried out, especially in the case of public works financed through EU funds, by the time a court decision was issued the procurement could even be completed. However, in the context of the new procurement procedures, strict deadlines were introduced for judicial relief, which can no longer exceed 30 days for interim measures and 5 months for the final order. This has greatly enhanced the opportunities of affected parties to obtain effective relief.

2.1.6. *General overview*

Significant efforts have been made by the Greek authorities over the last years to reinforce the transparency of the regulatory framework. Formalised actions, like the establishment of the Economic and Social Council, the creation of the Hellenic Centre for Investment or the streamlining of public procurement procedures, have been supplemented by informal initiatives, such as the increasing use of informal consultation procedures and of the Internet. EU rules have also promoted transparency, particularly in the area of product regulations and of government procurement. However, more could be done to ensure that complete, accurate and timely information, as well as real and deliberate opportunities for comment are offered to all market players and in all circumstances. The introduction of more systematic and formalised prior notice and public consultation procedures would bolster the confidence of the citizens and the market to a rules-based and predictable operation of the economy. Access to the domestic market would also be greatly enhanced by concerted efforts to streamline the regulatory framework.

2.2. Measures to ensure non-discrimination

Application of non-discrimination principles, Most-Favoured-Nation (MFN) and National Treatment (NT), in making and implementing regulations aims at providing effective equality of competitive opportunities between like products and services irrespective of country of origin and thus at maximising efficient competition on the market. The extent to which respect for those two core principles of the multilateral trading system is actively promoted when developing and applying regulations is a helpful gauge of a country's overall efforts to promote a trade and investment-friendly regulatory system.

2.2.1. Non-discrimination in domestic regulation

There are no overarching requirements in Greek legislation to incorporate non-discrimination principles into the regulatory decision-making process, other than the general equality provisions contained in articles 4 and 5 of the Greek Constitution. However, in the specific field of economic relations, Greece has subscribed to the MFN and national treatment principles *inter alia* in the context of its membership to the WTO. These WTO commitments form an integral part of the Greek legal system by virtue of Article 28 of the Constitution and override any conflicting provisions in domestic regulation. The observance of these principles is supervised by the Ministry of National Economy, which has the responsibility of identifying regulations incompatible with Greece's international commitments and co-ordinating with the relevant Ministry their amendment or withdrawal.

Overtly discriminatory regulatory content is quite exceptional. Existing measures that discriminate against foreign ownership tend to be fairly limited in scope, while the ongoing deregulation across a number of sectors of the economy is likely to further enhance international market openness. However, enduring exceptions to this general trend remain. These often concern the need for non-EC residents to obtain an authorisation for certain types of investments, such as the acquisition of real estate in border regions,[21] or the establishment of a representative office or a branch of a foreign bank. Limitations of ownership to a minority share apply to domestic airline companies, domestic flag vessels and television and radio broadcasting companies. Expressly discriminatory elements against non-resident foreign companies were also contained in fiscal legislation, which taxed less heavily domestic companies listed in the Athens Stock Exchange as well as subsidiaries of foreign companies. Following complaints at the European level, the Greek government has recently revised the Law to suppress its discriminatory elements. The level of taxation of listed non-resident foreign companies is reduced to the level of listed domestic companies, while the taxation differential between listed and non-listed companies will be gradually removed over the next two years.

As other OECD countries, Greece maintains some exceptions to the non-discrimination principle in the area of services and in particular of professional services. In the context of the GATS Agreement, the list of exemptions to MFN treatment as well as the schedule of commitments to market access and national treatment have been decided at an EU-wide level and have been submitted to the WTO by the European Commission. These are composed of EU-wide exemptions and commitments as qualified by the additional restrictions attached by individual Member States (often replacing full commitments by partial commitments or unbound limitations). EU-wide commitments are generally considered to be among the least restrictive in the WTO context.[22] However, additional restrictions attached by EU Member States increase significantly the restrictiveness of the European Union market for services towards third countries.

Additional limitations introduced by Greece and affecting non-EU nationals concern principally the presence of natural persons, where conditions of nationality apply to legal practitioners, statutory auditors, engineers, urban planning and landscape architects, doctors, dentists and midwives, nurses, physiotherapists and paramedical personnel, pharmacists,[23] real estate services, teachers for primary and secondary education, employees in public hospitals, and tourist guides. Furthermore, cross-border supply is unbound for accounting services, bookkeeping services, engineering services, urban planning and landscape architectural services, while commitments with respect to public voice telephony and facilities-based telecommunications services will only be enforced as of 1st January 2003. Greece also maintains some additional limitations relating to the commercial presence of service providers. These are conditions of nationality for the managers of construction companies supplying the public sector and for the majority of members of the Board in private primary and secondary education schools. There are no commitments granted as regards the establishment of higher education institutions granting recognised State diplomas.

of the weight of the services sector in the Greek economy, the reduction of barriers to entry in regulated professions is bound to have a very important pro-competitive effect overall. The regulatory framework with respect to professional services is currently reconsidered by the Greek government in this perspective. An interministerial committee under the co-ordination of the Ministry of National Economy has undertaken to identify and assess entry barriers and operation formalities hampering the exercise of professional services or imposed on business activities. This review will be based on an analysis of the conditions applicable to all professions regulated by permits and licences and is expected to lead by the end of the year to the elaboration of a general policy framework. This framework will then be submitted for consultation to concerned constituencies.

2.2.2. *Preferential agreements*

While preferential agreements give more favourable treatment to specified countries and are thus inherent departures from the MFN and NT principles, the extent of a country's participation in preferential agreements is not in itself indicative of a lack of commitment to the principle of non-discrimination. In assessing such commitment, it is relevant to consider the attitudes of participating countries towards non-members in respect of transparency and the potential for discriminatory effects. Third countries need access to information about the content and operation of preferential agreements in order to make informed assessments of any impact on their own commercial interests. In addition, substantive approaches to regulatory issues such as standards and conformity assessment can introduce potential for discriminatory treatment of third countries if, for example, standards recognised by partners in a preferential agreement would be difficult to meet by third countries.

The most important preferential agreement in which Greece participates is obviously the European Communities, while all other preferential trade agreements that it applies form an integral part of the common European Union trade policy (namely the agreements with EFTA countries, the association agreements with Central and Eastern European countries and Mediterranean countries,the post-Lomé Agreement with ACP countries and the General System of Preferences for developing countries). The European Union manages these Agreements in a highly transparent manner. Information is readily available to interested non-parties through a variety of avenues, including the Internet or publications such as the *European Bulletin*. In addition, information on preferential agreements is made available to third through notifications to the WTO. The WTO Committee on Regional Trading Agreements reviews all preferential agreements, in a process that consists among other things of written questions and answers. Within this context recourse is available for third countries which consider they are prejudiced by these agreements. In considering proposals for new preferential agreements, the European Council addresses a number of strategic questions, including compatibility with all relevant WTO rules, the impact on the Community's other external commitments and the likelihood that the agreement would support the development of the multilateral trading system.

2.2.3. *General overview*

Discriminatory elements in the Greek regulatory framework are therefore mainly limited to the services area. The effect of such restrictions on the openness of the market may be considerable, given the importance of the services sector in the economy. The Greek government is currently reconsidering domestic policy with respect to professional services.

2.3. Measures to avoid unnecessary trade restrictiveness

To attain a particular regulatory objective, policy makers should favour regulations that are not more trade restrictive than necessary to fulfil a legitimate objective, taking account of the risks non-fulfilment would create. Examples of this approach would be to use performance-based rather than design standards as the basis of a technical regulation, or to consider taxes or tradable permits in lieu of regulations to achieve the same legitimate policy goal. At the procedural level, effective adherence to this principle entails consideration of the extent to which specific provisions require or encourage regulators to avoid unnecessary trade restrictiveness and the rationale for any exceptions; how the impact of new regulations on international trade and investment is assessed; the extent to which trade policy bodies as well as foreign traders and investors are consulted in the regulatory process; and means for ensuring access by foreign parties to dispute settlement.

2.3.1. *The impact of regulations on trade*

In Greece there are no explicit provisions requiring or encouraging regulations or administrative practices to be trade and investment friendly. Accordingly, it is up to individual ministries, agencies and the administration in general to apply regulations and administrative procedures in ways that do not affect the free flow of trade and investment. However, the interventionist and over-regulating tradition of the Greek State has not promoted the use of market-based approaches in the elaboration and the enforcement of regulation. Most government actions still rely on legalistic and procedural approaches with little attention to economic perspectives and policy performance. Regulatory inflation has made it particularly difficult to ensure coherent policies, especially in the absence of an efficient mechanism for assessing the impact of regulation on the economy. Above and beyond this, the widespread risk-aversion of the public service has often led to enforcement that was even more restrictive than required by the letter of the law. The negative impact of this state of affairs on FDI attractiveness, the competitiveness of Greek firms and economic development in general has been repeatedly highlighted by researchers and businesses and is increasingly recognised by the government and the administration.[24] In response to these concerns, several simplification projects have been initiated across the administration, some of which start now bearing their first fruits.

The potential impact of proposed regulations on trade and investment is not formally assessed when preparing new or modifying existing regulations. More generally there are no established mechanisms for undertaking prior cost-benefit analysis or assessing the expected social and economic impacts of proposed regulation, other than the constitutional requirement for a budgetary impact report supplementing all regulations with an impact on the public budget (for a detailed discussion on regulatory impact analysis see background report to Chapter 2). Likewise, the process for developing and amending regulations does not comprise a concrete appraisal of the prospects for proper enforcement, or the availability of alternative, more appropriate policy instruments for attaining the desired objective. Suboptimal consultation mechanisms, as described above, further deprive the administration of valuable insights on the potential effects of the regulation on the economic activity, and on the capacity of concerned constituencies to comply. As a result, regulation tends to impose burdens that are disproportional to its aims and induces non-compliance. When regulation fails to achieve its objectives or no longer corresponds to changed circumstances, the lack of a comprehensive assessment of the reasons behind regulatory failure may drive the regulator to just fill the gaps in a fragmented manner rather than envisaging a complete streamlining of the regulation.

In the absence of a formalised RIA system, the sole possibility for identifying and preventing trade and investment restrictive regulation is through the intervention of concerned Ministries in the framework of interdepartmental co-ordination. The co-ordination of regulatory production is conducted by the General Secretariat of the Ministerial Council, which centralises all draft laws and regulations forwarded by respective Ministries in order to be commented and approved by the rest of the government. The approval of the whole government is requested for proposals to proceed. More specifically, proposed regulation that may affect foreign economic relations and in particular the implementation of the country's obligations arising from international economic agreements is within the ambit of the Ministry of National Economy (YPETHO). YPETHO has the possibility to request the withdrawal of a regulation that violates international obligations or the redrafting of a regulation that may cause adverse trade effects. Any disagreement has to be arbitrated by the government in plenary. However, it can be very difficult for the interdepartmental co-ordination to correctly assess and rule out trade and investment restrictive regulation because of the lack of substantiated information on the necessity, efficiency and proportionality of the proposal and on alternatives.

2.3.2 Regulatory burdens on business operation

Surveys conducted in 1997 among foreign enterprises in Greece have shown that the bureaucracy and more generally the contacts with central or local authorities are perceived as one of the most significant problems faced by businesses operating in Greece, along with insufficient infrastructure, fiscal legislation, and labour and social security legislation.[25] According to the 1997 surveys bureaucratic burdens related more particularly to the lack of operational flexibility of the administration and the considerable delays in handling matters, namely on account of insufficient co-ordination between implicated services or between the centre and the periphery. Recurrent complaints also concerned the emphasis established procedures put upon form over content and the lack of a client-oriented culture within the civil service. In addition, the absence of a long-term perspective and the frequent changes in procedures and policies, in particular in the fiscal area,[26] were seen as seriously limiting predictability and inhibiting the possibility of strategic planning by the firms. Administrative burdens are obviously not unique to Greece, but the substantial role played by the Greek State in the economy confers on them a particular influence over private investment decisions.

Seventy percent of the surveyed firms considered that the type and degree of problems do not significantly differ among foreign and domestic firms, although it could be assumed that foreign firms might find those problems more difficult to overcome. However, the considerable amount of discretion that characterises the implementation process enables selective enforcement in favour of insiders. Especially where regulatory requirements are too complex to monitor and too costly to implement, the administration will often allow some leeway for established firms. Regulatory burdens are thus particularly demanding on new entrants, be they domestic or foreign, which have to devote considerable effort to adjust.

They are also quite exacting on small firms because they entail fixed costs, which do not vary significantly with the size of the firm. These non-productive costs have been partially quantified by the National Confederation of Greek Trade (ESEE)[27] in the framework of an investigation conducted in 1999 among commercial SMEs operating in 6 major Greek cities. The assessment focussed on a series of administrative formalities relating to fiscal and social security requirements and the delivery of the related clearance certificates from the concerned authorities. It concluded that such formalities could take up to 30 hours per month and even completely disrupt economic activity for certain micro firms. The situation is expected to improve considerably in the fiscal area with the completion of the Integrated Taxation Information System (TAXIS),[28] which rationalised the whole process through the use of modern communication systems. After a pilot operation at the beginning of the year, the system became fully operational as of May 2000, with 231 connected tax offices (over a total of 301), representing 95% of expected fiscal revenues. At that date TAXIS recorded 8 200 registered users, the majority of which are tax-consulting firms.

2.3.3. The example of licensing procedures

One of the areas that have attracted considerable criticism is the licensing of industrial activities where overlapping, redundant and time-consuming requirements hinder new entrepreneurial activi-

225

ties. The Federation of Greek Industries has estimated that it could take up to 45 different "steps" to set up a business activity. Some of these steps may concern duplicative permit requirements by different authorities, while others relate to assembling the various certificates requested from the applicant. Formalities can take very long depending on the services. Furthermore, each step is usually considered as a prerequisite for the next, so that it is difficult to speed up the formalities by parallel processing of the licensing requirements. Particular problems seem to be observed at the local government level, especially as regards zoning regulations. FGI believes that a couple of major greenfield investment projects in recent years may have been driven out of Greece because of excessive delays that prevented them from meeting their own time constraints. A recent research project commissioned by the European Commission[29] concluded that in four cases investigated in Greece 2 to 8 licences were required, involving 3 to 9 different authorities. The time elapsed from the submission of the file to the granting of the authorisation varied from 4 months for the simplest case (renewal of mechanical equipment) to 33 months for a case including an approval for traffic connection.

In recent years the Greek government has made several attempts to contain the hindrance of administrative formalities, the most important of which were the creation of ELKE in 1996 (see above, Section 2.1.1) and the adoption of Law 2516 on the establishment and operation of industrial activities in 1997. One of the main functions of ELKE as a promoter of investment activities is to help potential investors secure the necessary licences for setting up their activity. ELKE assists the firm in understanding all licensing requirements, pulls together the required certificates, checks that the file is complete and takes care of all formalities and contacts with relevant administrations. On the other hand, ELKE has no competency to issue any of the necessary licences or grant investment incentives, and in that sense it is not really a "one-stop-shop". In case of excessive delays in the processing and in particular where conflicts arise between involved administrations, ELKE can convene these administrations to a special meeting in order to expedite the issue. Its ability to offer an efficient solution against administrative burdens is circumscribed by the fact that it has been given no real power to urge involved administrations for prompter service and that its assistance is not available for smaller investment projects nor for prospective investors that do not apply for cash grants or other incentives.

Law 2516 of 1997 aimed at simplifying industrial licensing procedures and at synchronising industrial development and environmental protection. It consolidated permits for the establishment of industrial activities into a single licence, issued by the regional department of the General Secretariat for Industry in each Prefecture. Each regional GSI department is responsible not only for formalities related to industrial policy but also for obtaining the necessary permits from environmental or zoning authorities and incorporating them into the single licence. GSI departments have to issue the licence or notify the reasons for rejecting the request within a period of 40 to 60 days depending on the type of activity, renewable once by Ministerial Decision. In case of non-respect of the deadlines, responsibility for issuing or refusing the licence is with the Ministry of Development, the silence of all other administrations equalling consent. Silence of the Ministry beyond a total of 3 months can be taken to the administrative courts. Permits for the operation of industrial activities were also consolidated into a single licence, applied for after the granting of the establishment licence. An interim authorisation has to be delivered within two months, valid until the definitive licence, or refusal thereof, is issued. In case of non-respect of the deadline the firm can start its activities without an authorisation.

Despite the introduction of a streamlined procedure, the law has not initially produced the efficiency gains anticipated, because the lack of appropriate resources and co-ordination with other Departments did not allow GSI services to meet prescribed deadlines and requirements. The judicial recourse provided in case of non-respect was hardly an efficient relief, since delays in judicial procedures are generally longer than licensing procedures. Moreover, the law did not provide for a simplification of requested certificates, which can be very complex and time-consuming to obtain. In order to deal with these problems, the Ministry of Development launched in May 2000 a major initiative to better translate the new regulatory framework in practice. This initiative included the codification of all requirements with a view to displaying them on the Internet together with an interactive guide to help applicants; the suppression of several unnecessary requirements; the development of industrial zones with attractive infrastructure conditions, in which no zoning permits are needed; the establishment of precise descriptions of all requirements introduced by other administrations so as to help GSI departments meet them; and the training of regional GSI departments to improve qualifications, co-ordination, service attitude and motivation. By way of example, formalities for establishing stock companies now take 4 to 8 days, down from 45 to 50 before the streamlining of superfluous requirements. Five prefectural offices started operating one-stop-shops on a pilot basis since June 2000. Lessons learned from their experience will serve to shape the project on a national basis.

Box 4.   **Promoting competitiveness through the improvement of the business environment. Simplification initiatives in the European Union**[1]

Efforts to improve the business environment by enhancing regulatory quality and reducing the regulatory burden have been central to the European strategy for the achievement of the Single Market. Initiatives aimed at simplifying the business environment in Europe include the *Simpler Legislation for the Internal Market (SLIM)* project, the *Business Environment Simplification Task Force* (BEST) and the *European Business Test Panel*.

SLIM, which was launched in 1996, consists of an ex post regulatory impact assessment and consolidation mechanism. Small teams, composed of Member State officials and of users of the legislation, review Community legislation in particular sectors with a view to identifying concrete suggestions for simplification. These suggestions, which are not binding, may then be used as a basis for amendments proposed by the Commission to the Council. The focus is on provisions that give rise to excessive implementation costs and administrative burdens, diverging interpretations and national application measures and difficulties in application. Areas for review may be proposed by regulators or business associations, who should indicate what are the problems to be addressed and the benefits anticipated from simplification. Reviewed legislation is usually at least 5 years old in order to allow its strengths and weaknesses to be properly identified.

Since 1996, SLIM reviews have taken place in 14 sectors, including ornamental plants, classification of dangerous substances, pre-packaging, construction products, fertilisers, electromagnetic compatibility, banking, insurance and company law, recognition of diplomas, social security rules, VAT, internal trade statistics and nomenclature for external trade. The Commission has proposed amended legislation on six of these and three have been adopted by the Council and the Parliament. Proposals on the remaining sectors are underway. The effectiveness of the project has recently been reviewed by the Commission, which highlighted the importance of an appropriate follow up by EU institutions of the concrete suggestions put forward by the SLIM teams. Indeed, SLIM recommendations are formulated on average within six months but the process afterwards is quite protracted. As regulatory costs and red tape related to national and regional regulation, were estimated at 3-5% of the EU GDP, some SLIM teams have tried to incorporate parallel reviews of national implementation of the reviewed Community legislation. However, these attempts were too ambitious for the means and resources of the teams to ever be successful. It was thus proposed to complement SLIM reviews with co-ordinated parallel exercises in the Member States.

BEST was created in 1997 to investigate the regulatory and administrative environment and support measures that directly affect the competitiveness of SMEs. It was composed of business representatives, public officials and academics. Recommendations focussed on access to financing, human resources management and training, innovation and technology transfer, as well as all aspects of public administration and its contacts with the enterprises. As regards the improvement of public administration it was particularly stressed that the assessment of regulatory impact on business should be central to the decision-making process; that the launching of SMEs should be facilitated by simplifying applicable procedures; and that the transparency and efficiency of rules of operation should be enhanced. An Action Plan was established in 1999 on the basis of the BEST report. Most of its actions are currently underway.

© OECD 2001

Promoting competitiveness through the improvement of the business environment. Simplification initiatives in the European Union (*Cont.*)

European Business Test Panels were first set up in 1998 as a pilot tool in the framework of the European Commission business impact assessment system. The Panels were designed as a complement to the existing consultation procedures and aimed at assessing compliance costs and administrative burdens, especially in the area of trade and industry, and identifying alternative solutions. They would be set up at the national level in each Member State that volunteered to participate, and operate according to the Member's consultation traditions and procedures. Panels would bring together representative firms from the concerned sectors and work under very short timescales to avoid delaying the legislative process. Their conclusions would then feed into the cost-benefit analysis undertaken by the Commission.

During the trial phase Business Test Panels were convened to assess proposals on VAT fiscal representation, Accounting and Waste from Electrical and Electronic Equipment. They allowed consulting from 1067 to 1744 businesses around Europe. The response ratio to the questionnaire was from 35% to 43%. After each consultation a report was issued explaining the opinions of respondents and the steps the Commission envisages in view of these opinions. After two consultations on less contentious matters, the Panel on Electrical and Electronic Waste showed that 77% of the affected businesses found the proposal to be an administrative burden and around half of them that it would require additional investments. The Commission will take into account these concerns when finalising its proposal.

---

1. See European Commission, "*Communication from the Commission to the European Parliament and the Council. Review of SLIM: Simpler Legislation for the Internal Market*" COM(2000)104 final; European Commission, "*Communication from the Commission to the European Parliament and the Council. The Strategy for Europe's Internal Market*" COM(1999)464; European Commission, "*Action Plan to Promote Entrepreneurship and Competitiveness*" COM(1998)550 final; European Communities, "*Report of the Business Environment Simplification Task Force*", Vol.I and II, 1998; European Commission, "*Communication from the Commission to the European Parliament and the Council, The Business Test Panel. A Pilot Project*", 1998.

2.3.4. *The example of customs procedures*

As tariff levels have declined through GATT/WTO rounds, the costs imposed by customs procedures have attracted growing attention from businesses. Customs procedures encompass formalities and procedures in collecting, presenting, communicating and processing data requested by customs for and related to the movement of goods in international trade. Costs are generated by compliance with documentary requirements (acquiring and completing the documents and paying for their processing) and by delays of cargo processing at borders. The aims of customs procedures (to collect revenue, to compile statistics, to ensure that trade occurs in accordance with applicable regulations, such as those aiming at protection of human safety and health, protection of animal and plant life, environmental protection, prevention of deceptive practices, etc.) should be pursued so as to ensure that the procedures do not create unnecessary obstacles to international trade. In other words, the lowering of trade barriers may not achieve the full efficiency of liberalisation without harmonised, simplified, fast and secured customs procedures.

Customs services in the Greek Ministry of Finance have taken measures to simplify customs procedures in the framework of the European rules set in the EU Common Customs Code. Greece has not acceded to the World Customs Organisation (WCO)'s revised Kyoto Convention,[30] as there remains legal-technical issues to be resolved within the European Union. However, along with other EU customs authorities, the Greek authorities have implemented trade facilitation measures provided by this international convention, such as pre-arrival import declarations. These measures have significantly improved transparency in customs regulations and operations, and accelerated customs clearance, without compromising regulatory objectives, such as revenue collection.

Until recently, the customs system made only limited use of electronic means. Computerisation of the system was organised and financed in the framework of successive Community Support Framework

Programs. This involved the establishment of an electronic data interchange system (EDI system),[31] called Integrated Customs Information System (ICIS). The main objectives of the system were to avert custom duty evasion, improve the service to customers, facilitate transactions, improve public health protection through better monitoring of shipments, and facilitate the performance of trade statistics. Infrastructure work for ICIS and basic training of customs officers were completed in April 2000. In May 2000 ICIS was launched on a pilot basis and is progressively expanded to other customs offices as computer equipment is put in place and applications' training is proceeding. It is expected that 90% of customs offices will be connected by spring 2001. The totality of customs declaratives offices in Greece have already been equipped and connected to the system, as well as an increasing number of major importing firms.

ICIS enables importers to submit import declarations and to receive customs clearance electronically. Through its implementation it helps harmonise the interpretation and implementation of customs regulations across all border points and ensures equality of treatment for all customers. Its effects on the speed of the clearance process is considerable, since for connected customs offices the average clearance time fell to 30 minutes down from 5 to 6 hours previously.

2.3.5. Overview of measures to avoid unnecessary trade restrictiveness

Unnecessary trade restrictiveness of regulations, regulatory enforcement and administrative practice seem to be one of the major shortcomings of the Greek regulatory framework. The government and the administration have neither the experience nor the tools for assessing the potential impact of regulation on the business activity in general. Regulatory burdens are perceived to be widespread and to impact heavily on productivity and competitiveness alike. Several simplification and facilitation measures have been directed at these burdens in recent years, including the computerisation of tax and customs procedures, the rationalisation of licensing procedures or the creation of an investor's "help desk". Given the complexity of the Greek regulatory system, these measures need time to produce tangible results. However, neither these nor future endeavours can succeed without properly targeting the roots of the problems and avoiding piecemeal approaches. The development of regulatory impact assessment tools will thus be critical for devising a successful simplification policy.

2.4. Measures to encourage use of internationally harmonised measures

The application of different standards and regulations[32] for like products in different countries – often explained by natural and historical reasons relating to climate, geography, natural resources or production traditions – presents firms wishing to engage in international trade with significant and sometimes prohibitive costs. Hence, when appropriate and feasible, reliance on internationally harmonised measures, such as international standards, as the basis of domestic regulations can facilitate trade flows. National efforts to encourage the adoption of regulations based on harmonised measures, procedures for monitoring progress in the development and adoption of international standards, and incentives for regulatory authorities to seek out and apply appropriate international standards are thus important indicators of a country's commitment to efficient regulation.

2.4.1. The European influence

The current Greek policy with respect to technical regulations is shaped to a large extent by Greek membership in the European Union. This entails not only a clear commitment towards harmonisation, but also limits government intervention wherever possible to the setting of essential requirements, leaving technical details to be worked out by means of standardisation, testing and certification by and for industry (see Box 5). These principles are part of the institutional framework for standardisation activities as laid down in Law 372 of 1976, subsequently amended to reflect Greek obligations under EU directives and the WTO TBT Agreement.

A basic principle, which underlies European standardisation, is subsidiarity with respect to global standards, based on the assumption that conformity of European standards to global standards is likely

---

Box 5. Harmonisation in the European Union[1]

The New Approach and the Global Approach

The need to harmonise technical regulations when diverging rules from Member States impair the operation of the common market was recognised by the Treaty of Rome in Articles 100 to 102 on the approximation of laws. By 1985 it had become clear that relying only on the traditional harmonisation approach would not allow the achievement of the Single Market. As a matter of fact, this approach was encumbered by very detailed specifications which were difficult and time consuming to adopt at the political level, burdensome to control at the implementation level and requiring frequent updates to adapt to technical progress. The adoption of a new policy towards technical harmonisation and standardisation was thus necessary to actually ensure the free movement of goods instituted by the Single Market. The way to achieve this was opened by the European Court of Justice, which in its celebrated ruling on Cassis de Dijon[2] interpreted Article 30 of the EC Treaty as requiring that goods lawfully marketed in one Member State be accepted in other Member States, unless their national rules required a higher level of protection on one or more of a short list of overriding objectives. This opened the door to a policy based on mutual recognition of required levels of protection and to harmonisation focusing only on those levels, not the technical solution for meeting the level of protection.

In 1985 the Council adopted the "**New Approach**", according to which harmonisation would no longer result in detailed technical rules, but would be limited to defining the essential health, safety and other[3] requirements which industrial products must meet before they can be marketed. This "New Approach" to harmonisation was supplemented in 1989 by the "Global Approach" which established conformity assessment procedures, criteria relating to the independence and quality of certification bodies, mutual recognition and accreditation. Since the New Approach calls for essential requirements to be harmonised and made mandatory by directives, this approach is appropriate only where it is genuinely possible to distinguish between essential requirements and technical specifications; where a wide range of products is sufficiently homogenous or a horizontal risk identifiable to allow common essential requirements; and where the product area or risk concerned is suitable for standardisation. Furthermore, the New Approach has not been applied to sectors where Community legislation was well advanced prior to 1985.

On the basis of the **New Approach** manufacturers are only bound by essential requirements, which are written with a view to being generic, not requiring updating and not implying a unique technical solution. They are free to use any technical specification they deem appropriate to meet these requirements. Products, which conform, are allowed free circulation in the European market.

For the New Approach, detailed harmonised standards are not indispensable. However, they do offer a privileged route for demonstrating compliance with the essential requirements. The elaboration at European level of technical specifications which meet those requirements is no longer the responsibility of the EU government bodies but has been entrusted to three European standardisation bodies mandated by the Commission on the basis of General Orientations agreed between them and the Commission. The CEN (European Committee for Standardisation), CENELEC (European Committee for Electrotechnical Standards) and ETSI (European Telecommunications Standards Institute) are all signatories to the WTO TBT Code of Good Practice. When harmonised standards produced by the CEN, CENELEC or ETSI are identified by the Commission as corresponding to a specific set of essential requirements, the references are published in the Official Journal. They become effective as soon as one Member State has transposed them at the national level and retracted any conflicting national standards. These standards are not mandatory. However conformity with them confers a presumption of conformity with the essential requirements set by the New Approach Directives in all Member States.

The manufacturer can always choose to demonstrate conformity with the essential requirements by other means. This is clearly necessary where harmonised European standards are not (or not yet) available. Each New Approach directive specifies the conformity assessment procedures to be used. These are chosen among the list of equivalent procedures established by the Global Approach (the so-called "modules"), and respond to different needs in specific situations. They range from the supplier's declaration of conformity, through third party type examination, to full product quality assurance. National public authorities are responsible for identifying and notifying competent bodies, entitled to perform the conformity assessment,

---

Harmonisation in the European Union (*Cont.*)

but do not themselves intervene in the conformity assessment. When third party intervention is required, suppliers may address any of the notified bodies within the European Union. Products which have successfully undergone the appropriate assessment procedures are then affixed the CE marking, which grants free circulation in all Member States, but also implies that the producer accepts full liability for the product.[4]

The strength of the New Approach and the Global Approach lies in limiting legal requirements to what is essential and leaving to the producer the choice of the technical solution to meet this requirement. At the same time, by introducing EU-wide competition between notified bodies and by building confidence in their competence through accreditation, conformity assessment is distanced from national control. The standards system, rather than being a means of imposing government-decided requirements, is put at the service of industry to offer viable solutions to the need to meet essential requirements, which however are not in principle binding. The success of the New and Global Approaches in creating a more flexible and efficient harmonised standardisation process in the European Union heavily depends on the reliability of the European standardisation and certification bodies and on the actual efficiency of control by Member States. First, European standardisation and certification bodies need to have a high degree of technical competence, impartiality and independence from vested interests, as well as to be able to elaborate the standards necessary for giving concrete expression to the essential requirements in an expeditious manner. Second, each Member State has the responsibility to ensure that the CE marking is respected and that only products conforming to the essential requirements are sold on its market. If tests carried out by a notified body are cast in doubt, the supervisory authorities of the Member State concerned should follow this up.

---

1. See Dennis Swann "*The Economics of the Common Market*", Penguin Books, 1995; European Commission, "*Documents on the New Approach and the Global Approach*", III/2113/96-EN; European Commission, DGIII Industry, "*Regulating Products. Practical experience with measures to eliminate barriers in the Single Market*"; ETSI "*European standards, a win-win situation*"; European Commission, "*Guide to the implementation of Community harmonisation directives based on the new approach and the global approach* (first version)", Luxembourg 1994.
2. Decision of 20 February 1979, Cassis de Dijon, Case 120/78, ECR, p. 649.
3. Energy-efficiency, labelling, environment, noise.
4. See the Council Directive 85/374/EEC of 25 July 1985 on the approximation of the laws, regulations and administrative provisions of the Member States concerning the liability for defective products.

to facilitate access of European products to world markets. Apart from the standardisation work mandated by the Commission (see Box 5), most standards are prepared at the request of industry. On the one hand, a growing number of European and national standards are in fact transpositions of international standards produced by ISO, IEC and ITU; on the other hand, various initiatives have been developed at the European level to promote transparency and co-operation at the international level:

– The standardisation process is undertaken in close co-operation with all parties involved, such as the Member States (through the membership of all European Union national standardisation bodies), industry and consumers (through the representation of industry, consumers, and trade unions associations on the technical committees and working parties responsible for the preparation of the standards) and trading partners (through the association with EFTA and other countries and the co-operation agreements described below); the standards produced are publicly available by means of paper and electronic publications of the standardisation bodies, as well as of official publications of the European Commission.

– The numbering of European standards clearly indicates the relationship with international standards, for instance, whenever a CEN standard is a transposition of an ISO standard it will be referenced by the same number by simply adding the EN prefix in front of the ISO prefix (f.i. EN-ISO 5079 on textile fibres); the same applies for national references (f.i. ELOT-EN-ISO 5079).

- Co-operation agreements have been signed between ISO and CEN (Vienna Agreement) and between IEC and CENELEC (Dresden Agreement) to secure the highest possible degree of approximation between European and international standards and avoid duplication of work. A similar agreement is being prepared by ETSI and ITU to take into account the specificities of telecommunications.

- Furthermore, the European Union is a party to the UN-ECE 1958 Agreement on Automotive Standards. This agreement provides a basis for the technical approval of motor vehicle equipment and parts. It has been supplemented by additional regulations developed by the UN-ECE Working Party on the Construction of Vehicles. UN-ECE regulations have played a major role in the harmonisation process of regulations within the European Union. Thirty five of them have been recognised equivalent to EU directives that specify technical requirements for the type approval of motor vehicles.

2.4.2. *Standardisation activities*

Law 372/1976 established the Hellenic Organisation for Standardisation (ELOT), which is the national central standardisation and certification body. ELOT is a state-owned, non-profit, limited company under the supervision of the General Secretariat for Industry of the Ministry of Development. Its operations are based on 155 technical committees and working groups bringing together representatives of the producers, the consumers, scientific institutions and the administration. ELOT is financed on the one hand by the contributions of its members, the sale of standards and the remuneration of its testing, quality control and certification services and on the other hand by the Greek government. With the progressive development of ELOT activities, own resources, which represented 29% of the ELOT budget in 1995, have risen to 59% in 1999.

ELOT standardisation activities are clearly geared towards the adoption of European and international standards, resulting in an easier access of foreign products to the domestic market as well as an additional competitive edge in the global market for Greek producers. This commitment was already present in the founding Law, which stipulates in its present version that *"Greek standards and specifications shall be harmonised, where appropriate, to those of the European and international standardisation organisations."* The breakdown of ELOT standardisation activities demonstrates its international orientation. By the end of 1999 ELOT had published 8772 finalised standards, only 1594 of which were purely national standards. The rest of them were transpositions either from European standards (CEN, CENELEC and ETSI) or from international standards (IEC and ISO) not yet adopted at the European level. The number of purely national standards has steadily declined over the years as the scope for European harmonisation has increased and limited the need for national standards. Similarly ELOT has only a limited activity of harmonisation against existing international standards as this work is mainly carried out by the European standardisation bodies. The adoption of harmonised standards is thus increasingly related to the European Single Market.

At the national level technical rules continue to be devised in areas where there is an absence of European harmonisation as well as in areas where there is EU legislation, but European standards are not available. In addition, ELOT has a particular standards-setting activity in the area of Greek *"cultural requirements"*,[33] producing national standards which are then promoted as international ones. In order to speed up the pace of harmonisation, ELOT can propose the interim direct use of existing international standards, pending their translation into Greek standards. This practice is widely applied by many EU countries as regards European standards. Although technical specifications produced by ELOT are of course voluntary, in line with the European regulation, some of them may be ascribed a mandatory character by means of Ministerial Decision for particular reasons pertaining to human health and safety or the protection of the environment.

In parallel to its commitments towards the adoption of harmonised standards, ELOT is bound by its founding Law to actively participate to the activities of foreign and international standard-setting bodies and to fulfil the related international obligations of Greece. ELOT thus maintains close-working relationships with national standards and certification bodies of other countries and participates actively in the work of the European standard-setting bodies (CEN, CENELEC and ETSI) and of ISO and IEC. It has concluded memoranda of co-operation with standard-setting bodies in neighbouring countries (including Armenia, Bulgaria, Cyprus, the Former Yugoslav Republic of Macedonia, Romania and Ukraine) providing for technical assistance to help these bodies upgrade their infrastructure and proceed with the adoption of harmonised standards. ELOT is designated as the Greek contact point for notifications of draft technical standards and regulations under Directive 98/34/EEC, as well as under the WTO TBT Agreement. It has accepted the WTO TBT Code of Good Practice for the preparation, adoption and application of standards and is thus committed to operate according to the principles set therein.

Figure 1. **ELOT standardisation activities**

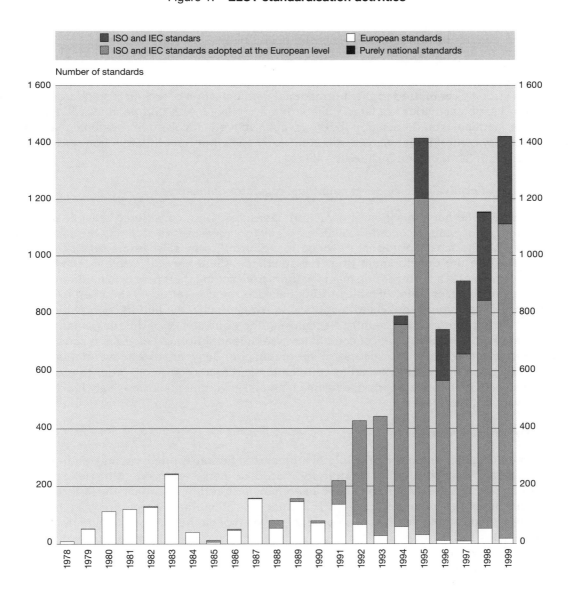

Source: OECD on the basis of figures provided by ELOT.

ELOT is also active in the areas of testing and certification and is the national body for conformity assessment activities in the framework of the Global Approach. As its infrastructure capacities to perform testing and certification are insufficient to meet growing market needs,[34] it operates in parallel to several private organisations (among others VERITAS, Lloyd's and VDE) which have set up certification operations in Greece. Although annual certification output of ELOT (including certification of quality systems, environmental management control and health and safety control) has expanded from 137 certificates in 1995 to 554 certificates in 1999, this represents a drop from 70% to 50% of market share. The importance of certification activities is growing not only in the private but also in the public sector. Tendering authorities have only recently introduced the systematic use of certification as an additional qualification or even a prerequisite for participating in government tenders, as in the past such condition would de facto eliminate most Greek firms. A series of programs to promote the concept of quality among Greek firms have been developed by the Ministry of Development. By 1999 there were 1685 firms certified to ISO 9000 management system standards (from 20 only in 1993) and 21 firms certified to ISO 14000. Since 1998 even a number of public administration services have sought ISO 9000 certification, but the number of certified services is still negligible.

2.4.3. General Overview

Greece is strongly committed to the international harmonisation of technical standards and regulations. Standardisation activities are largely shaped in accordance with European standardisation policies and the national standardisation body is also actively involved in regional harmonisation initiatives. Quality control initiatives are still at an early stage but benefit lately from increased attention from the administration and businesses alike.

2.5. Recognition of equivalence of other countries' regulatory measures

In cases where the harmonisation of regulatory measures is not considered feasible or necessary, the recognition of equivalence of other countries' regulatory measures in attaining the same regulatory objective may be the most appropriate avenue for reducing technical barriers related to regulatory divergence. Despite the development of global standards, there are still many areas where specific national regulations prevail, preventing manufacturers from selling their products in different countries and from enjoying full economies of scale. Additional costs are also raised by the need to demonstrate the compliance of imported products with applicable regulations in the import country through testing and certification accepted in that country. Recognising the equivalence of differing standards applicable in other markets, or of the results of conformity assessment performed elsewhere can greatly contribute in reducing these costs. The success of international endeavours to achieve mutual recognition is naturally reliant on the quality of testing, certification and accreditation. In order to ensure the adequacy of these activities to the needs of evolving markets, governments increasingly leave them in the hands of private entities.

2.5.1. Intergovernmental initiatives

Within the European Union the principle of mutual recognition applies among Member States (see Box 3). This means that all products lawfully produced or marketed in one Member State must be accepted by the others even when they have been manufactured in accordance with technical regulations differing from the domestic ones.[35] The principle of mutual recognition has helped build progressively a Single Market for European products, even though the European Commission considers that much remains to be done and has developed mechanisms to better monitor and enhance the application of the principle.[36] Greece has been among the few EU Members to have complied with the monitoring requirements and its record with respect to mutual recognition infringement cases is rather good (10 cases out of a total of 228 for the period 1996/98).

Beyond its effect on the movements of European products, the principle of mutual recognition in the framework of the Single Market has perceptibly benefited third country manufacturers, which no longer need to face the requirements of each and every EU member they seek access to, as long as they satisfy the requirements for one. Access to European markets is further assisted by European policies aimed at recognising the equivalence of regulatory measures and results of conformity assessment performed in third countries. These policies are elaborated at the European Union level, although their implementation is partly incumbent on national authorities or institutions. They are based on the negotiation and adoption of Mutual Recognition Agreements (MRAs), which are for the time being limited to mutually recognising the results of conformity assessment performed in third countries.

Table 2. **Mutual Recognition Agreements concluded or under negotiation by the E.U.**

	Mutual Recognition Agreements							PECAs[d]			
	Australia	New Zealand	United States	Canada	Israel	Japan	Switz-erland	Czech Republic	Hungary	Estonia	Latvia
Construction plant & equipment							✓				N
Chemical GLP[a]			✓	N							
Pharmaceutical GMP[b]	✓✓	✓	✓		N	✓			N	N	
Pharmaceutical GLP[a]					✓		✓			N	N
Medical devices	✓✓	✓	✓		N	✓		N			
Veterinary medicinal products			N								
Low voltage electrical equipment	✓✓	✓	✓			✓	N	N	N	N	
Electromagnetic compatibility	✓✓	✓	✓		N	✓	N	N	N	N	
Telecom terminal equipment	✓✓	✓	✓		N	✓			N		
Pressure equipment	✓N[c]	✓N[c]				N	✓	N			
Equipment & systems used in explosive atmosphere							✓	N			
Fasteners			N								
Gas appliances & boilers							✓	N			
Machinery	✓✓				N	✓	N	N	N	N	
Measuring instruments							✓				
Aircraft	N	N									
Agricultural & forestry tractors							✓				
Motor vehicles	✓					✓					
Personal protective equipment							✓	N	N		
Recreational craft			✓	✓							
Toys							✓				
Foodstuffs										N	N

✓ Concluded
N Under Negotiation
a Good Laboratory Practices
b Good Manufacturing Practices
c The Agreement covers simple pressure equipment. Extension to other pressure equipment is considered.
d Protocols on European Conformity Assessments. In February 1997 the European Commission signed an agreement with Poland regarding preparatory steps on conformity assessment, precursor for a real PECA.

Source: European Commission.

235

Each MRA includes a general framework agreement and a series of sectoral annexes. The framework agreement specifies the conditions under which each party accepts the results (studies and data, certificates and marks of conformity) of conformity assessment issued by the other party's conformity assessment bodies, in accordance with the rules and regulations of the importing party. These rules and regulations are specified on a sector-specific basis in the sectoral annexes. A certification by a conformity assessment body in the exporting country that a product covered by a MRA is in conformity to the rules and regulations of the importing party has to be accepted as equivalent by the importing party. This is particularly beneficial to small-and-medium sized enterprises that will be able to use less costly local testing facilities for the examination and certification of products for export. On the basis of negotiating directives issued by the Council in 1992 the European Commission has signed agreements on the mutual recognition of conformity assessment with the United States, Canada, New Zealand and Australia. By June 2000, the European Commission had also completed negotiations with Switzerland and Israel and undertaken negotiations with Japan and central and eastern European countries.

2.5.2. Accreditation mechanisms

Accreditation is a procedure whereby an authoritative body gives formal recognition that a body or person is competent to carry out specific tasks.[37] Accreditation mechanisms are used to assess and to audit at regular intervals laboratories, certification and inspection bodies by a third party as to their technical competence against published criteria. They provide confidence on the competence of conformity assessment bodies, which is essential for the success of mutual recognition. In that sense, international co-operation on accreditation is seen as an important supporting measure to promote recognition of equivalence in regulatory systems.

Accreditation mechanisms have been developed only recently in Greece. A National Accreditation Council (ESYD) was instituted in 1995, but has been inactive until 1999. Accreditation activities were thus exclusively undertaken by foreign institutions until recently. ELOT itself is certified since 1997 by the Italian accreditation body SINCERT. In June 2000 ESYD has delivered its first accreditation certificate to the drug-testing laboratory for the 2004 Olympic Games. Six other laboratories expected accreditation before the end of the year 2000. The Secretariat of ESYD is provisionally held by ELOT. On the other hand, ELOT is a member of the IQNet (International Network of Quality System Certifiers), which provides for the mutual recognition of quality certificates issued by any of the 29 participating national certification bodies in the world. The lack of accreditation mechanisms has proved a serious hindrance for certification activities, as the reliability of non-accredited laboratories was widely questioned by the private sector[38] A strengthening of accreditation mechanisms would be essential for improving business confidence.

2.6. Application of competition principles from an international perspective

The benefits of market access may be reduced by regulatory action condoning anti-competitive behaviour or by failure to correct anti-competitive private actions that have the same effect. It is therefore important that regulatory institutions make it possible for both domestic and foreign firms affected by anti-competitive practices to present their positions effectively. The existence of procedures for hearing and deciding complaints about regulatory or private actions that impair market access and effective competition by foreign firms, the nature of the institutions that hear such complaints, and adherence to deadlines (if they exist) are thus key issues from an international market openness perspective. These issues will be the focus in this sub-section, while a more detailed discussion of the application of competition principles in the context of regulatory reform can be found in the background report to Chapter 3.

Under the Greek Competition Act, the basic decisions and actions on competition matters (with the exception of the telecommunications sector)[39] are taken by the Greek Competition Committee, an independent authority under the supervision of the Ministry of Development. The Competition

Committee is competent for competition issues related to private behaviour, including clearing notified conduct, granting exemptions, issuing merger authorisations, initiating investigations *ex officio* and hearing complaints. On the other hand, it has no competence for dealing with competition problems raised by regulatory policies and decisions. Mergers prohibited by the Competition Committee can be subsequently approved by a joint decision of the Ministers of National Economy and of Development on grounds of public and general economic interest.

The Competition Committee has jurisdiction over all anti-competitive behaviour that has or may have effects within the country, even if it concerns agreements, mergers or collusive practices of firms taking place outside Greece or if it relates to firms that have no establishments in Greece. This includes abuse of dominance or of economic dependence that affects the Greek market. In parallel, the European Commission can take action against practices that limit the access of foreign firms to domestic markets. Many notified transactions are among foreign firms, whose turnover in Greece is sufficient to require them to file there. On the other hand, there seems to be no particular provision in the law for the case where a firm with market power in Greece impairs competition in other markets. The Competition Act could be read to apply in such cases only to the extent that the incriminated market conduct has a noticeable effect on the Greek market. No complaint of this kind has been made yet. Given the relative size of firms that might enjoy dominant position in Greece in relation to third markets where they operate, this has presumably not been an issue in the past. The situation could however change with the growing penetration of Greek firms in Balkan and Eastern European markets.

Firms wishing to advance complaints against alleged anticompetitive horizontal or vertical agreements, abuse of dominance or abuse of economic dependence must take their complaints to the Competition Committee. The complainant has the right to attend the hearings, examine the file and present his arguments before the Committee. The Committee must reach a decision on the complaint within six months, but can prolong this deadline by two months under exceptional circumstances calling for further investigations. Decisions of the Competition Committee, as well as Ministerial decisions on mergers can be appealed to the Athens Administrative Court of Appeal within 20 days from their notification. Further recourse is possible against the decision of the Court of Appeal by writ of error to the Council of State. There is no legal provision for an independent private suit under the Competition Act. However, civil or administrative courts can reach a decision on alleged anti-competitive behaviour on which there is no previous ruling by the Committee or on the validity of Committee or Ministerial decisions that have not been appealed on time in the framework of cases that are contingent upon them. Such court decisions are not binding on the Committee, the Court of Appeal or the Council of State. Foreign firms have the same rights as domestic firms to bring a case before the Competition Committee or the courts and enjoy equal treatment in every respect.

Thus far competition policy has had low priority in Greece and the Competition Committee has lacked resources and political support to be able to operate in a meaningful way (see background report to Chapter 3). A considerable shift in policy has taken place after the elections, but the announced amendments in the regulatory framework and the reinforcement of means and resources of the Competition Committee are too recent to have yet produced tangible results. Although Greek regulatory procedures for initiating and advancing complaints about alleged anticompetitive private behaviour offer equal opportunities for action between foreign and domestic firms, the limited capacity of the Competition Committee to provide effective protection overall and in particular as regards transnational effects or regulatory actions that restrict competition is not supportive today of a market open to global competition. How satisfactory the application of competition principles from an international perspective will be under the new regulatory framework remains to be seen.

3. ASSESSING RESULTS IN SELECTED SECTORS

This section examines the implications for international market openness arising from current Greek regulations in four sectors: telecommunications services; telecommunications equipment; automobiles and components; and electricity. For each sector, an attempt has been made to draw out the effects of sector-specific regulations on international trade and investment and the extent to which the six efficient regulation principles are explicitly or implicitly applied. Particular attention is paid to product standards and conformity assessment procedures, where relevant. Issues addressed here include efforts to adopt internationally harmonised product standards, use of voluntary product standards by regulatory authorities, and openness and flexibility of conformity assessment systems. Electricity and telecommunications are reviewed in greater detail in background reports to Chapters 5 and 6 respectively.

3.1. Telecommunications services

The telecommunications sector is currently one of the most dynamic sectors of the Greek economy. Reforms of the regulatory framework have been driven on the one hand by Greek obligations under the EU telecommunications regulatory package, and on the other hand by the two main objectives of recent Greek telecommunications policy: to modernise the network and reorganise the incumbent operator so as to cope with increased international competition; and to extend activities to Balkan and Black Sea countries with a view to becoming a telecommunications hub for the wider area.[40] Modernisation of the sector has started rather late, supported by EU financing through the 1st Community Support Framework (1989-1993); despite the substantial expansion of the sector during the last ten years, the prospects for further rapid development remain promising. Fixed-line connections have reached 53.3% connections per 100 inhabitants by the end of 1999, close to the EU average. Digitalisation of the network has passed from 42.7% in 1998 to 92% in 2000. Mobile phone subscriptions rose from 32500 in 1993 to 2.057 millions in 1998 and 3.9 millions in January 2000.

Until 1992, all telecommunications services were supplied by a state-owned monopoly, the Greek Organisation for Telecommunications (OTE). In 1992 Greece began services in the cellular telephony market through licences for GSM cellular phones to two private operators, PANAFON, majority-owned by British Vodafone,[41] and TELESTET (owned by the Italian Stet, Interamerican and Bell-Atlantic-Nynex). The licences provided for special rights in the market for mobile phones for 8 years. In December 1995, a third mobile licence was awarded to OTE. In April 1997 70% of the license was transferred to OTE's subsidiary COSMOTE and the remaining 30% to the Norwegian Telenor. At the beginning of 2000 the three operators held 42.7%, 30.4% and 26.9% of the market respectively and had invested a total of close to 1 billion dollars. Internet provision services, electronic data interchange services and other value added networks have been liberalised since 1994, but restrictions of access to OTE leased lines for providing the liberalised services were only lifted in 1996 and the incumbent has delayed access of other operators until 1998. Parts of OTE were offered for sale through public flotation or direct sale of stock in different stages (the last sale in July 1999 reduced government holding to 51%).

Complete liberalisation of the market for EU nationals in accordance with EU requirements, and in particular termination of the OTE monopoly on voice telephony, will only take effect on January 2001 because of the special exemption negotiated between the European Commission and the Greek government. Liberalisation of the market for non-EU nationals will take effect on January 2003, because of limitations Greece introduced to EU-wide commitments on telecommunications. After that, MFN and national treatment will apply, as trade in this sector is regulated by the WTO Agreement on Basic Telecommunications under which the European Union did not ask for any exceptions. There are no foreign ownership, size of shareholding or other ownership restrictions on individuals or corporations investing in public telecommunication operators.

Responsibility for telecommunications policy and the establishment of the regulatory framework of the sector rests with the Ministry of Transport and Communications. In addition an independent regulator, the National Telecommunications and Postal Commission (EETT), was founded in 1994 to implement the telecommunications policy and supervise the market with particular regard to the competition and user protection issues. During its first years of operation, some trading partners have claimed that the allocation of responsibilities between EETT and the Ministry was not clear-cut.[42] The new draft framework law on telecommunications, which was publicised by the Ministry of Transport and

Communications in June 2000, provides that EETT would be responsible *inter alia* for licensing, numbering, domain name regulation, universal service, setting of price-caps, unbundling of the local loop, spectrum allocation, type approval of terminal equipment, imposing sanctions and arbitrating disputes. It could refer cases of anti-competitive behaviour to the Competition Committee or ask for assistance from it. The Ministry, beside its policy-making and regulatory responsibilities, would hold direct responsibility for the National Allocation Table for frequencies and satellite orbits assigned to Greece by ITU.

Other concerns raised by domestic market players and foreign trading partners related to the insufficient staffing of EETT and the seconding of staff from the incumbent operator.[52] In particular, new entrants have felt that the Commission was not sufficiently proactive in dispute resolution and have found dispute resolution procedures too long. They have also reported delays in the licensing procedures for liberalised services. Staffing problems were mainly due to the former obligation of EETT to hire through very strict bureaucratic procedures and are now practically solved. Greek authorities also hope to address these problems through the new framework law, which confirms the administrative and financial independence of EETT and offers it hiring flexibility, a sizeable staff with appropriate scientific qualifications and a clearer allocation of responsibilities. Practical implementation of the new regulatory framework will be the main challenge in the near future.

Since 1999, the telecommunications regulators have taken some significant steps towards increased transparency, by facilitating access to information and setting up consultation mechanisms. The Ministry of Transport and Communications is one of few Greek authorities to have instituted "notice and comment" procedures when preparing regulation (see above, Section 2.1.1). EETT has developed a comprehensive website that contains information on applicable regulations and decisions.[44] Issues under the responsibility of the Commission are systematically displayed in the site and open to comments by all interested parties. Public consultations have been launched to date on the allotment of spectrum in the frequency bands of 2nd generation mobile telephony and the granting of relevant individual licenses; on the licensing of public telecommunication networks based upon DECT technology; and on the licensing for fixed wireless access (FWA). A different type of public consultation and opinion exchange has been undertaken on the issue of the introduction of UMTS third generation mobile telecommunications systems in Greece. EETT entrusted the organisation of the consultation to a team of scholars from the National Technical University of Athens, who addressed to all parties active in the field of telecommunications and computer sciences in Greece, including businesses and academics. As all these consultations are still very recent, it is not clear yet what the practice of the regulator will be in managing the process and reacting to opinions received.

3.2. Telecommunications equipment

Domestic production of telecommunications equipment is mainly directed to infrastructure equipment (71.3% of total production) to meet the needs of the incumbent operator in particular as regards digital line systems.[45] Domestic production supplies 92% of domestic infrastructure demand. This segment is dominated by two major industrial companies, Intracom and Siemens. The demand for infrastructure equipment has been boosted by the ongoing conversion of analog telephone networks to digital networks. The remaining 28.7% of domestic production covers private use equipment, mostly telephone parts. The demand of telecommunications equipment for private use, and in particular the increasing demand for mobile phone devices, is met mainly by imports, representing 78% of the market. This segment is characterised by strong competition between several firms (Lucent, Intertech, Doxiadis, Nokia, Motorola, Ericsson) but Ericsson covers about half of the market for mobile phone devices.

Regulations relating to telecommunications equipment have been mainly driven by the harmonisation process at the EU level. The main framework has been set with two "New Approach" Directives, Directive 98/13/EC on telecommunication terminal and satellite earth station equipment superseded by Directive 99/5/EC on radio and telecommunication terminal equipment. Standards to meet the Directives requirements are currently being developed by the European Telecommunications

239

Standardisation Institute (ETSI). By July 2000, 65 out of 73 standards had been published in support of Directive 98/13 and 10 out of 99 standards had been published in support of Directive 99/5, with another 54 finalised and under approval. The Hellenic Organisation for Standardisation (ELOT), in co-operation with the Ministry of Development General Secretariat for Industry, and the Ministry of Transport and Communications and OTE as ETSI members for Greece, participates in the development of these standards and is in charge of transposing European standards into Greek standards.

In accordance with EU provisions, all terminal equipment connected to the Greek telecommunications network must meet the essential requirements set by the EU Directives. The placing of the product to the market is no longer subject to type approval. The manufacturer can draw up a declaration of conformity either on the basis of harmonised standards, or, where such standards are not available, through the provision of technical documentation demonstrating the conformity of his product to the requirements. On the other hand, a number of MRAs with non-EU countries, which also apply to telecommunications equipment, allow under certain conditions for the acceptance of results of conformity assessment performed in Australia, New Zealand, the United States, Canada and Switzerland.

3.3. Automobiles and components

Concerns about market openness and domestic regulation of automotive industries around the world are not new. Due to the historic dynamism of global economic activity in the sector and traditionally interventionist policies of some governments aimed at protecting domestic automotive industries, trade tensions related to domestic regulatory issues in general, and to standards and certification procedures in particular, have long figured on bilateral and regional trade agendas. This reflects the fact that automobiles remain among the most highly regulated products in the world, primarily for reasons relating to safety, energy conservation and the environment. Divergent national approaches to the achievement of legitimate domestic objectives in these key policy areas are therefore likely to remain a significant source of trade tensions as global demand for automobiles continues to rise.

There is no automobile manufacturing industry in Greece, other than fairly limited spare parts and components manufacturing activities. Local production of tyres by Pirelli and GoodYear was terminated in 1991 and 1996 respectively. The needs of the local market for automobiles and components are thus almost entirely met through imports. The near total of the Greek passenger car market is shared between EU and Asian car manufacturers (in 1998 57.8% and 40.6% respectively, the latter figure covering 27.5% of Japanese and 13.1% of Korean cars). As a country wholly dependent on imports, Greece maintains no restrictions on the import of cars. Products imported from non-EU countries are subject to the EU common external tariff schedule.

However, until recently the automobile market has been overburdened and distorted by very high vehicle registration tax rates.[46] Transactions in passenger and utility vehicles have been one of the most important sources of fiscal revenue for the Greek State. In contrast, utilisation fees are extremely low. On the other hand, the engine capacity of passenger vehicles is used by the fiscal authorities as a non-contestable element of evidence in order to calculate the level of taxable income. Until recently this fiscal treatment kept passenger vehicle transactions below real needs, heavily oriented the market towards small to medium sized vehicles and slowed down considerably the renewal of the fleet. The situation changed considerably in 1998,[47] when serious reductions in the vehicle registration fees (ranging from 31 to 57%), adopted in the framework of the overall government policy to reduce inflation, resulted in a 10% drop in average car prices. Following this reduction, new car registrations surged by 60.4% during the first quarter of 1999, 31.5% and 36.4% in the second and third quarters and 65% in October 1999 after a further tax reduction.

A sluggish automobile market kept the average age of the car fleet at around 11 years. This in turn created serious air pollution problems, especially in the metropolitan Athens area, and increased the rate of traffic accidents. From 1991 to 1993 the government introduced a series of fiscal incentives for withdrawing old polluting cars and replacing them with environmentally friendly technology cars. The measures brought the average age down to 8.84 years in 1993 but after their termination it returned to

10 years by 1996, with 26% of vehicles older than 15 years. The withdrawal programme was complemented with exhaust emission regulations in 1992, and inspection programmes including fines for non-conformity since 1995. The 1998 reform of the registration tax involved a reshuffling of the calculation of the fiscal value, determined in the past only on the basis of engine capacity, to take into account the environmental performance of the vehicle. Latest technology vehicles are taxed from 7% to 88% according to the engine capacity and the fiscal burden gradually increases for older technology cars to reach from 41% to 385% for conventional technology cars. Following the adoption of the new fiscal policy, conventional technology cars (which numbered 1 300 000, against 1 109 000 catalytic converter cars in December 1997) dropped to 1 300, against 2 868 000 catalytic converter cars as of April 2000.

As an EU Member, Greece applies harmonised EU safety standards for motor vehicles based on a type-approval system and abides by the mutual recognition requirement of type-approval certification applicable among EU Member States. Within the EU, technical requirements for motor vehicles have been fully harmonised since 1993. Unlike the areas covered by the New Approach Directives, detailed technical requirements are specified in various EU Directives and applicable throughout the EU and EFTA countries. In its Framework Directive (92/53/EEC), the EU has also recognised the equivalence of 35 UN-ECE Regulations to relevant EU technical Directives. The certification of technical requirements is done through a system of type-approval of motor vehicles. Before it can be marketed, each vehicle model, whether domestically produced or imported, must be brought to a national Regulatory Body – in Greece the Ministry of Transportation – that will test it and certify whether the vehicle or separate technical units satisfy the technical requirements as specified in relevant EU Directives.

Since 1996, EU type – approval certification for a passenger vehicle in one Member State is valid in all other Member States and the vehicle can be registered or marketed in all EU States. Since 1998, mutual recognition of EU type-approval certification is extended to all vehicles except large vehicles. Type-approval procedures are usually initiated by automobile importers before the marketing of a model in any EU market. The procedure is extremely complicated and lengthy, so that an individual wishing to import directly a car originating from a third country and not yet type-approved in the EU cannot realistically expect to go through it successfully.

3.4. Electricity

In Greece, power generation, transmission and distribution are dominated by the Public Power Corporation (DEH), a state-owned enterprise. It controls 100% of transmission and distribution services and owns more than 97.5% of the total domestic generating capacities. In 1994, Law 2244 authorised autogeneration, provided it used renewable energy sources or generated electricity through combined heat and power producing systems. Law 2244/94 also provided for the preferential treatment of auto-producers by the system operator. Total commitments of such plants amount today to approximately 450 MWs, while there exists a much larger amount of applications. Imports accounted for about 2% of Greek demand in 1998.

Reform in the electricity sector is mainly driven by Greek obligations under EU rules for the internal market for electricity, whereby Greece must open at least 30% of its electricity demand to competition by 19 February 2001. In this context a new energy law was adopted in 1999, removing the legal prohibition on entry of new generators and liberalising supply for certain customers. DEH retains its vertically integrated structure, ownership of existing generation and supply facilities, transmission and distribution grids, and the monopoly in the supply of captive customers. 49% of the company will be capitalised, while the State will retain majority ownership. Regulatory responsibility remains with the Ministry of Development for licensing, tariff setting, and the imposition of public service obligations. Two new entities are also created: the Energy Regulatory Authority (ERA) which has monitoring, advisory and referral responsibilities, especially with respect to competition and consumer protection; and the System Operator which will operate, ensure the maintenance and development of, and interconnections with other networks of the transmission system.[48] (For more details on the reform in this sector, see background report to Chapter 5).

Large-scale domestic entry is unlikely because entrants face high barriers, in particular access to fuel, switching costs of potential customers, and low prices to large industrial customers. Lignite, representing 68% of generation, and hydroelectric power plants, representing 9.8%, are state-owned. Natural gas, accounting for 12% in 1999 and expected to develop further in the coming years, will be under state monopoly until 2006.[49] In addition, although effective and non-discriminatory access to transmission and distribution is statutorily guaranteed by the System Operator, its de facto dependence from DEH in the first years after liberalisation should make such access difficult to ensure.

Greece has no direct electricity connections with other EU or IEA Member countries. Connections with other Balkan countries are used only for transactions between electricity monopolists. A memorandum for the interconnection of the power systems between Greece and Turkey has recently been signed, while an interconnection link with Italy is expected to begin commercial operations after 2001. However, the impact of this link will be limited because of its small capacity and engineering and geographical constraints. Beyond interconnection constraints, imports would face quite burdensome conditions on supply authorisations. Applicants must own adequate generating capacity, installed in an EU Member State, and provide "satisfactory long-term confirmation" that they have access to sufficient transmission and interconnection capacity to transmit the electricity they will supply. Within the regulatory framework to be enforced from February 2001, competition to generate and supply electricity is thus not likely to develop in Greece in the foreseeable future.

4. CONCLUSIONS AND POLICY OPTIONS FOR REFORM

4.1. General assessment of current strengths and weaknesses

Over the last five years Greece has undertaken serious macroeconomic reforms with a view to improving economic performance and meeting the criteria set for membership in the European Monetary Union. These efforts have provided a strong impetus for rethinking government practices and changing the role of the State in the economy. They have produced considerable results, which should put Greece on the path towards a more open and competitive business environment. Structural reforms associated with the macroeconomic convergence program have been more timid until now. Although the vicious economic cycle of the previous twenty years, from 1974 to 1994, has been broken, the improvement cannot be sustained unless market principles are introduced more boldly into the regulatory environment.

According to summary indicators on product market regulation developed by the OECD in 1999 (Nicoletti *et al.*, 1999), the regulatory environment in Greece appears as one of the less friendly to market mechanisms among OECD economies. This largely reflects a restrictive domestic environment and in particular important state control over the economy (relating to public ownership of business enterprises and the involvement of the state in the operation of private businesses) and strong recourse to command and control regulations and price controls. The overall picture is now steadily improving as privatisation and liberalisation are progressing, but the cultural leap away from past regulatory practices remains to be made.

Not all of the six efficient regulation principles examined in this review are expressly codified in Greek administrative and regulatory oversight procedures to the same degree. Available evidence suggests that the principles of use of harmonised standards and of recognition of equivalence of foreign measures are given ample expression in practice. WTO and EU disciplines have played a key role in giving them prominence in the Greek regulatory environment, but Greece has also been active in promoting them and broadening their effects to the wider Balkan area. Regulatory practices also generally abide by the principle of non-discrimination, although numerous exceptions still exist with respect to professions.

As regards the other efficient regulation principles, several formal or informal steps have been made in the right direction lately. They include *inter alia* the increasing use of electronic means to make regulatory information more widely available and to facilitate the access of individuals and businesses to administrative services; the informal "notice-and-comment" procedures newly introduced in the rulemaking process; the creation of an "investors' desk" and of administrative "one-stop-shops" for licences and permits at the local level; the clarification of criteria used in public procurement procedures; the development of a computerised system for customs procedures; and the strengthening of the Competition Committee. All these steps are liable to enhance regulatory quality and promote a trade-friendlier regulatory environment, but are still too recent for their effective results to be assessed.

Figure 2. **Restrictiveness of regulatory approaches in OECD countries**

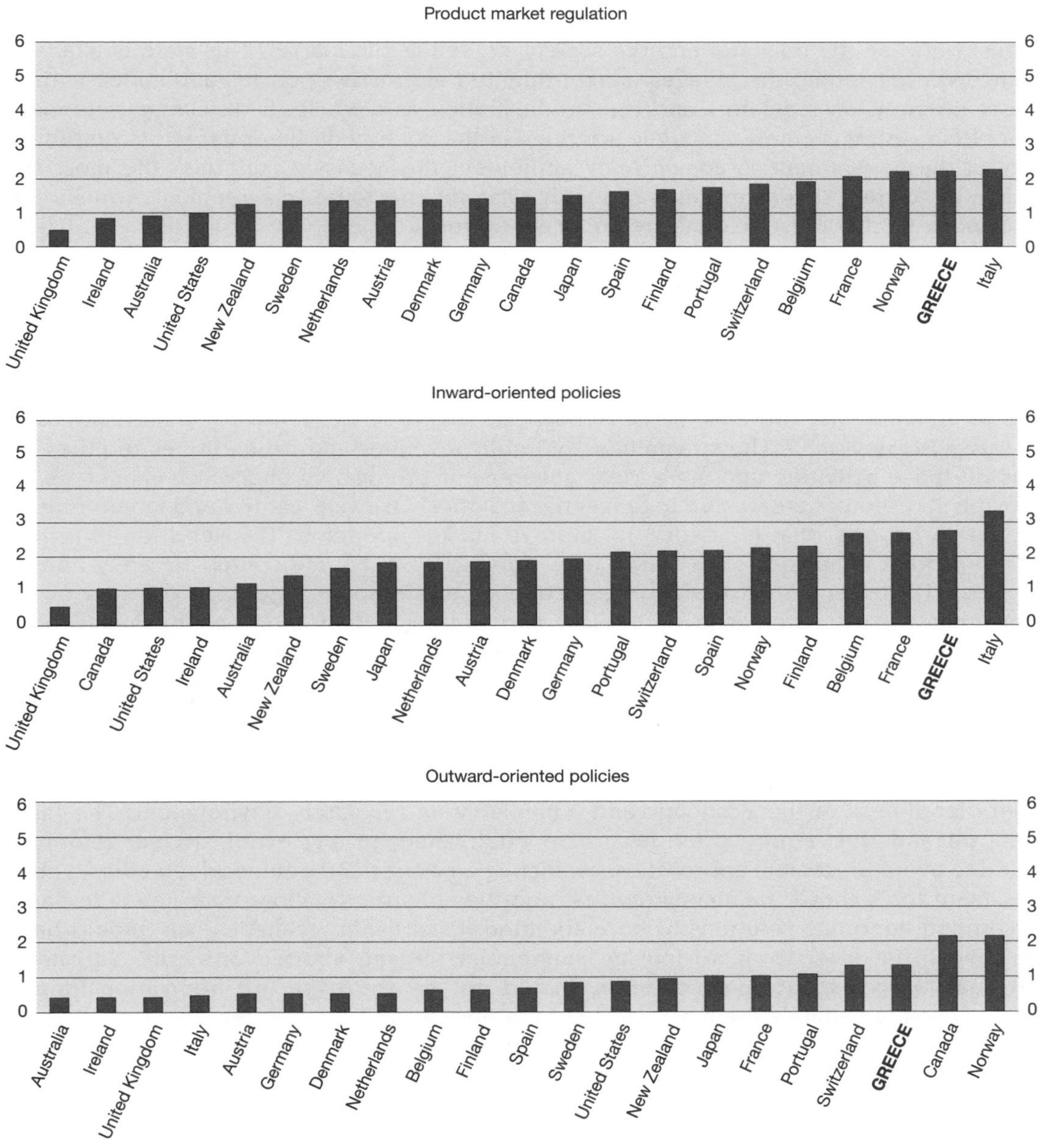

Product market regulation

Inward-oriented policies

Outward-oriented policies

Source: Nicoletti Giuseppe *et al.* (1999), reproduced from *OECD Economics Department Working Papers* No. 226.

243

Several concerns relating to the market orientation of the Greek regulatory framework have been dealt with only partially. The discretionary character of public consultation and the ensuing distrust of involved parties seriously undermine the efficiency of what could be a valuable tool for better policy-making. Only little progress has been made in improving the coherence and user-friendliness of the body of existing regulation and plans to repeal unwarranted regulation have not materialised. Rules to simplify the licensing procedures for industrial firms have not yet produced tangible results for lack of accompanying enforcement measures. The implementation deficit, due to the inherent flaws of regulations, as well as the deficiencies of enforcement mechanisms, offers little incentives to comply with regulations and penalises individuals and businesses that do. Several sectors, including telecommunications and electricity, are not yet open to competition. Moreover, Greece has yet to consider introducing regulatory impact assessment in the framework of the rulemaking process.

Overall, the most important weakness of the current regulatory framework seems to be the climate of mistrust between the regulator and the society, as well as the market. This state of affairs not only maintains over-regulation, discourages market-oriented alternative policies and stifles initiative, but also casts discredit on regulators and the administration as a whole. It dissuades potential foreign investors from setting up new economic activities in the country. In the long run it compromises the capacity of the government to convincingly implement the necessary reforms. The most important strength in the current circumstances is probably what appears to be an agreement virtually across the political spectrum that these reforms are no longer optional.

4.2. The dynamic view: challenges for future reform

The qualitative transformation of the role of the State in economic activity, entailing its withdrawal from direct involvement in production and the removal of excessive regulation of economic and social arrangements, will be a major challenge for years to come. It is very encouraging that the government henceforth assumes that *"the State should no longer get involved in the operation of private enterprises, neither pretend to be a businessman"*.[50] The streamlining of public revenues and expenditures requires the State to focus on those activities that are a clear government prerogative and which cannot be assumed satisfactorily if resources are wasted in tangential activities. Likewise, control and monitoring activities should not go beyond what is needed to improve market operation. The need for all governments to address market failures through sound regulatory action is an undisputed sovereign prerogative. Nonetheless, ill-conceived, excessively restrictive or burdensome regulation exacts a heavy price on commercial activity, domestic or foreign, and places a disproportionately heavy burden on small-and medium-sized enterprises. Given the large percentage of small and micro domestic firms in the Greek private sector, remaining regulatory burden is likely to be even more detrimental to these firms than to larger foreign-owned enterprises that can avail of larger staff and expertise and wider financial basis.

A second major challenge relates to the move towards effective transparency, consistency and user-friendliness of the economic and administrative regulatory environment. The task ahead is significant and will require priorities to be established. In any event, a clear reform strategy is needed to avoid piecemeal approaches, conflicting measures and equivocal remedies. The mastery of assessment tools should be among the first priorities in order to allow other needs to be properly prioritised and adequate solutions to be elaborated. Establishing realistic goals should be another central concern in order to avoid loosing momentum through aborted attempts. Yet, in order to identify realistic goals, the main criterion should not be the expected opposition from vested interests; these are certainly the most vocal but not necessarily the most representative of the needs and opinions of the Greek society. The communication deficit of the administration has been high enough in the past to suggest that conflicts with society would be reduced if only sufficient transparency efforts were made.

The third major challenge is to incorporate market principles not only in regulation, but also in the everyday operation of the administration. This requires adequate training of civil servants, both at national and local levels, as well as transparent monitoring mechanisms. Rethinking such central concepts as performance, incentives and accountability of the civil service is a long-term task, but in the meanwhile improvement can be achieved through the generalisation of tools such as the silent consent or the liability for non delivered service.

4.3. Policy options for consideration

This section identifies avenues for future action. The following recommendations are based on the assessment presented above and the policy recommendations set out in the 1997 OECD Report to Ministers on Regulatory Reform. Founded on international consensus on good regulatory practices and on concrete experiences in OECD countries, they are likely to enhance the adaptation of the regulatory environment in Greece to the conditions of a global economy.

- *Make information on applicable regulations more easily accessible.*

Informal and occasional initiatives to display information on the Internet should be formalised and applied in a systematic manner across the administration. Efforts should be made to display elements of interest to foreign partners in English. Information desks and call centres should also be more widely used across the administration. Local gateways allowing access to information at the prefectural and municipal level should be further developed. Authorities initiating new regulation should have the responsibility to consistently bring local or central information desks, such as the ELKE, up to date with regulatory requirements.

More attention should be paid to the clarity and quality of regulation. Regulations should be complemented with a better developed preamble clarifying the grounds for adoption of the regulation, so as to obviate the need for subsequent interpretative statements and ensure consistent enforcement. Once RIA tools are developed, they could serve as a basis for developing preambles.

The ongoing efforts for improving the clarity of pre-selection and award criteria for public procurement should be actively pursued and given concrete expression in practice. The recent improvement of opportunities of affected parties to obtain effective judicial relief through speedy and low-cost appeal procedures is an important step in this direction and should be further encouraged.

The Greek government should intensify endeavours to streamline existing regulation by consolidating all applicable provisions on a specific policy issue under a single text and by repealing regulations that have become outdated, irrelevant or inoperative. The development of electronic inventories could greatly assist such endeavours. Moreover, while regulatory consolidation and simplification is not yet completed, allowing public access to the inventories will improve the transparency of the regulatory framework in a useful manner. In this case attention should be paid to present inventories in a user-friendly manner and to update them on a regular basis.

- *Improve the transparency of the rulemaking process and widen the opportunities of concerned constituencies to provide input.*

Prospective regulation should be made available to concerned constituencies for information and comments through formal channels. Although informal channels may usefully enhance the transparency of the rulemaking process, responsibility for bringing regulatory proposals to concerned constituencies should rest with the administration. Efficient "notice-and-comment" procedures would greatly enhance the predictability of the market and enable strategic planning by the firms. They would also provide the regulators with valuable input from market players, allowing them to better adapt regulations to the needs of the market. Recent examples of "notice-and-comment" procedures used by the Ministry of Transport and Communications could serve as a model for expanding and formalising this tool across the administration. Other forms of dissemination, such as formal publication to the daily and professional press, should also be envisaged in order to reach constituencies that have not access to electronic means of communication.

Consultations with respect to proposed regulation should be organised in a timely manner so as to allow meaningful interaction between concerned constituencies and the administration. Such consultations should take place sufficiently early in the rulemaking process so that they can have an incidence on the proposed regulation. They should allow sufficient time for consulted groups to reflect constructively and formulate an opinion.

In order to improve the efficiency of consultation, it is essential to promote the confidence of the private sector and the citizens in general in the consultation mechanisms. Confidence-building measures mainly consist of clear rules of the game and transparent outcomes. Consultation timetables and participation criteria should be clearly identified. The positions of various participants in the consultation process should be made publicly available and the policy conclusions drawn by the administration following the process should also be publicised and motivated. This would urge the administration to reflect more methodically on the incidence of proposed regulatory action; improve the prospects of compliance on behalf of the concerned parties; and provide serious safeguards against regulatory capture by specific interests.

- *Reduce discriminatory elements in the regulatory framework for services.*

The ongoing review of the applicable regulatory framework for professional services is a good opportunity for reconsidering existing discriminatory elements. Constraints on entry into regulated service markets, and in particular limitations on foreign service providers, should be assessed and their effect on the domestic competitive environment clearly documented.

- *Introduce a coherent regulatory impact analysis (RIA) system for the whole range of regulations, including administrative rules; develop a consistent practice for the assessment of trade and investment effects of proposed regulations.*

Regulatory impact analysis should be introduced for all new and amended regulation. An efficient and cost-effective analysis should include an initial screening stage whereby regulation warranting further scrutiny would be identified on the basis of predetermined criteria. The screening would prevent holding up resources, which could be used on a more efficient assessment of scrutinised regulation. Expertise in assessing the impact of proposed regulation and identifying alternatives should be progressively build through training in all rulemaking parts of the administration. Useful models for developing such expertise could be drawn from the participation of the Greek administration to European projects like the SLIM reviews and the Business Test Panels.

RIA procedures should explicitly cover impacts of proposed regulations on business activity and in particular on trade and investment. A valuable basis for identifying impacts and costs on the business activity is the input provided by concerned constituencies during the process of prior consultation. The efficiency of trade impact assessment procedures would thus be enhanced by further promoting the incorporation of market players concerns through the improvement of consultation procedures. Intra-governmental co-ordination should be further strengthened to allow trade policy makers to be an active part in this process.

The outcomes of RIA procedures should be made publicly available before the regulatory proposal is finalised. This would greatly enhance transparency of the rulemaking process, improve the democratic legitimacy of the regulatory framework, enhance the quality of RIA procedures through external scrutiny and assist parliamentary control.

- *Strengthen the administrative capacity for the enforcement of applicable regulation and reinforce a client-oriented culture*

The staffing of services in everyday contact with users should be enhanced both in terms of quantity and of quality. The overall distribution of human resources across the administration should be rethought to allow for increased staffing for certain services and a clearly defined accountability for "front-line" civil servants. A client-oriented culture should be promoted through training and performance-linked incentives.

- *Accelerate efforts to rationalise administrative procedures affecting businesses and eliminate unnecessary restrictions to business operations and trade flows*

The authorities have engaged in a series of projects to rationalise administrative procedures affecting citizens in general and businesses in particular. Some of them, like the TAXIS project, are now operational, while others, like the simplification of industrial licensing procedures, are still in the process of being set up. The Greek government will have to monitor the operation of these projects in close consultation with affected parties, in order to check their efficiency, single out failures and gaps and identify further needed improvements. On the basis of lessons learned, simplification endeavours should progressively be extended to other areas of the economy.

Attempts to rationalise procedures should not be limited to simplifying the compliance process through the use of novel technologies but should involve a rethinking of all administrative requirements to ensure that nothing is asked that is not indispensable. Such rethinking should take into account not only the implementation cost for the administration and the compliance cost for the citizen but also the real prospects of perfect enforcement and the consequences of non-enforcement. An ongoing monitoring would be necessary to ensure that requirements that were once justified but no longer warranted are regularly repealed.

Beyond the regulatory streamlining of administrative burdens, the very attitude of implementing authorities needs to be made more efficient. The experience of past simplification reforms shows that a simple amendment in regulation to require swifter procedures is not enough if implementation in the field does not follow suit. For instance, in the area of licensing procedures, strict deadlines should be introduced for regulatory action, after the expiry of which silence of the administration should be interpreted in favour of the applicant. Deferral of a decision should not be allowed without communicating duly motivated grounds or clearly defined conditions upon which the decision will ultimately be taken. Particular attention should be paid to improving the co-ordination between various involved parts of the administration or between the central and the local level. Personnel staffing the prefectural "one-stop-shops" currently developed should benefit from appropriate training to learn assessing the impact of their actions on business activity.

- *Continue to encourage the use of international standards as a basis for national standardisation activities and to promote international harmonisation at the European, regional and international level.*

The widespread use of internationally harmonised standards not only facilitates the access of new and innovative foreign products to the domestic market for the benefit of Greek consumers but also enhances the market opportunities of Greek firms and products world-wide. Assisting neighbouring countries to move towards harmonised standardisation systems will help consolidate efficient and transparent markets in the wider Balkan and Black Sea area, where many Greek businesses actively seek to expand activities. The increased reliance on market-driven specifications will offer domestic firms the necessary flexibility to pursue the most efficient business strategies and promote innovation.

Quality control and certification need to gain more prominence in business culture for the Greek market to benefit fully from the use of internationally harmonised standards. Ongoing information campaigns by the government and major professional associations to promote the concept of quality control should be actively pursued. Domestic firms, and especially SMEs, should be encouraged and assisted in resorting to certification. ELOT should continue its efforts to reinforce its quality control and certification mechanisms.

As part of a wider endeavour to build market confidence in the operation of harmonisation and mutual recognition systems, the Greek government should step up efforts to activate domestic accreditation mechanisms. The National Accreditation Council should intensify operations and should be given the means to establish rapidly a reputation of reliability.

- *Promote the application of competition principles from an international perspective.*

The new regulatory framework adopted recently aims at reinforcing the importance of competition policy among the overall economic policy priorities of the Greek government. As this new framework hopefully grows up to become an efficient remedy against anti-competitive behaviour, it should pay sufficient attention to potential trans-national effects.

247

4.4. Managing the reform

The objective environment in which Greece operates as a result of its membership to the European Union and its integration into an increasingly global economy makes structural reform an inescapable policy option for the country. The problem thus is on the one hand how to bring about the subjective awareness that the option is unavoidable and very broadly beneficial to help foster and shape the process of change and make it more acceptable to the large social strata affected by it; and on the other hand how to formulate policies that minimise the social and political costs of structural change.

While the effects of macroeconomic convergence and the accession of Greece to the EMU have received large publicity, too little attention has been paid so far to communicating with the public and all major stakeholders with respect to the short and long-term effects of opening the markets and on the distribution of costs and benefits. Citizens can see clearly the impact of an inefficient administration on their everyday lives and can readily appreciate reforms aimed at improving service to the citizen. It is more difficult for them to have a comprehensive picture of the incidence of market opening reforms on their jobs, quality of life and future prospects. Communication strategies have to include the early delivery of visible benefits for the consumer, like the drop in prices brought about by the telecommunications or financial services liberalisation, which concern the totality of the Greek population.

The most dynamic segments of the Greek economy, such as certain services or export-oriented manufacturing sectors, which are held down by current inefficiencies, are likely to be the major reform allies. However it is equally important to overcome the resistance of the segments most affected by change by a balanced reform programme emphasising both liberalisation to allow market forces more space, and a more efficient regulation of such forces to protect consumers, health, safety and the environment, and prevent anti-competitive behaviour. In addition, a particular focus should continue to be given to the integration of SMEs into the new domestic economy and to their prospects for successfully competing in a global economy.

NOTES

1. Figures in this and the following paragraph come from the OECD Main Economic Indicators of July 2000, and the National Statistical Service of Greece.

2. Centre of Planning and Economic Research (KEPE), "*The Size and Role of the Public Sector in Greece. Developments and Comparisons with other Countries*", Athens 1999.

3. Economist Intelligence Unit (1999-2000), *Country Profile Greece.*

4. For a detailed overview see Chapter 1 on the macroeconomic perspective of the reform.

5. Nikiforos Diamandouros, "Greek Politics and Society in the 1990s" in *The Greek Paradox. Promise vs. Performance, The* MIT *Press,* 1997. The author identifies three structural weaknesses explaining in part the underperformance of the economy from 1974 to 1995: the discriminatory political system in post-war Greece, which introduced political non-meritocratic and clientelistic criteria for state employment, causing deficiencies in civil service skills and the impossibility of effective quality control; the particularistic logic of distribution of social and economic benefits in society, reducing the accountability of the State and producing perceptions of inequity; and the resulting fragmentation of productive structures, which made them dependent on State protection for their continued growth and survival.

6. Recent privatisations included five public-sector banks, ELVO (Greek Arms Manufacturers), Hellenic Petroleum, Olympic Catering, the Athens Water company, large shares in the National Bank of Greece, the Athens Stock Exchange and the Greek Organisation for Telecommunications (OTE) (although the government retains voting control on all three), and assets of the National Tourist Organisation (EOT). The Duty Free Shops were sold to the Agricultural Bank of Greece, still under State control.

7. Surveys conducted by the Athens American Chamber of Commerce in 1992 and 1997 among foreign investors in Greece showed that only 10 to 14% of investors in the sample had chosen Greece in order to service the domestic market.

8. According to the World Markets Research Centre "*it is as a base for expansion into the Balkans that the country will lay claim to further foreign direct investment.*" http://www.worldmarketsonline.com.

9. See also Spanou, Calliope (1996), "On the Regulatory Capacity of the Hellenic State: a Tentative Approach Based on a Case Study" in *International Review of Administrative Science,* Vol. 62.

10. Spraos (1998), *Quality in Public Administration: Recommendations for Changes,* financed by the National Bank of Greece.

11. According to the US Department of Commerce "*Foreign companies consider the complexity of government regulations and procedures -and their inconsistent implementation by the Greek civil administration- to be the greatest impediment to operating in Greece.*" (Country Commercial Guides. Greece FY 2000 "*Investment Climate*"). See also the World Markets Research Center Country Assessment for 1999.

12. Act 2232/1994, Article 1:2.

13. At 15 April 2000, a total of 109 EU Directives were overdue in Greece (the EU average transposition deficit at the same date was 52 Directives), while there remained a total of 159 Directives to be implemented before end of 2000. EU Single Market Scoreboard No. 6, May 2000 at http://europa.eu.int/comm/internal_market/.

14. This notification procedure is separate from that of Directive 83/189/EEC.

15. However, 192 framework contracts were concluded in the utilities sector in 1997, just before the expiry of the dispensation period, predominantly with domestic suppliers. These contracts will have the practical effect of foreclosing new entrants from this market for several years.

16. USTR 1999 National Trade Estimate Report on Foreign Trade Barriers – European Union.

17. The Ministry of Environment and Public Works is the most important procuring entity in Greece, responsible for

around one third of total public procurement. This covers public works of national importance, such as highways, airports and major ports, irrigation, sewage and flood-protection systems. All other works are managed at the prefectural or municipal level. The importance of public works in total procurement reflects the major share of infrastructure projects in the Greek economy in the recent years, both for catching up with the domestic infrastructure deficit and for meeting the needs for the 2004 Olympic Games.

18.	For example, in the area of supplies approximately 10% of total procurement, corresponding to the needs of the various Ministries, is handled by the Ministry of Development, General Secretariat of Commerce. All such needs are registered once a year to the Single Program for Government Procurement, so as to enhance transparency and enable potential suppliers to take advance notice. The Program is available online (http://www.gge.gr), but only in Greek.

19.	USTR 1999 National Trade Estimate Report on Foreign Trade Barriers – European Union.

20.	Appeals against public works tenders organised by the local authorities can be lodged with the Minister of Public Works since 1999. According to the Ministry most appeals introduced during the first year concerned tenders at the municipal level.

21.	According to the EU Schedule of Commitments to the GATS Agreement, such authorization is easily obtained in practice when the acquisition is part of a direct investment project.

22.	See, for instance, USITC (1995), *"General Agreement on Trade in Services: Examination of Major Trading Partners' Schedules of Commitments"*, Publication 2940, December.

23.	Greece, like several other EC Members, restricts access to the profession to natural persons only. In addition it imposes a monopoly for pharmacists on the supply of pharmaceuticals to the general public. Hence, the limitation on the presence of natural persons amounts to a *de facto* closed market for commercial presence too.

24.	See, *inter alia*, Spraos (1998), *Quality in Public Administration: Recommendations for Changes*, financed by the National Bank of Greece.

25.	See Hassid, Joseph, *Strategies for the Attraction of Foreign Direct Investment in Greece*, Study commissioned by the Ministry of Development to the University of Piraeus, July 1997 and *Foreign Enterprises in Greece*, Survey conducted for the American Chamber of Commerce in Greece, September 1997. On the problems related to the fiscal legislation and to labour and social security legislation, see Chapter 1 on the Regulatory Reform in Greece, covering macroeconomic issues.

26.	*"The complexity and excessive amount of regulation … are due to the frequent changes of the fiscal regulation, its innumerable cross-references and exceptions and the absence of popularisation informative material for the taxpayer."* Spraos (1997), A More Efficient Management of Public Revenues, Commission for the Review of Long-term Economic Policy, Athens.

27.	National Confederation of Greek Trade (ESEE) (1999), *The increase of the functional cost of a commercial enterprise because of the necessary bureaucracy procedures*, Athens.

28.	The Integrated Taxation Information System (TAXIS) is one of the major computerisation programs of the Ministry of Finance in the framework of the Operational Project for the Modernisation of the Public Administration ("Kleisthenis" Project), co-financed by the European Communities. It aims at speeding-up procedures and reducing operational costs by "de-materialising" (through fax, Internet and mobile phones) the contacts between the citizen and the administration. This includes general and detailed fiscal information and assistance manuals, and the possibility to submit fiscal declarations or deliver compliance certificates. It is also designed to allow electronic payment of taxes in the future.

29.	Austrian Institute of Economic Research (WIFO), *"Benchmarking Licensing, Permits and Authorisations for Industry, Emphasising SMEs"*, Background Document for the Industry Council of 18 May 2000.

30.	The objective of the "International Convention on the Simplification and Harmonisation of Customs procedures" (the so-called "Kyoto Convention") that entered into force in 1974 was to simplify and harmonise customs procedures across countries. In June 1999, the Council of the World Customs Organisation (WCO) adopted a revised text in order to adapt the convention to the development of international trade. The new procedures will increase transparency and harmonisation of customs procedures by using new information technology and modern clearance techniques based on risk analysis. The revised convention is now open for signatures. It shall enter into force three months after forty contracting parties will have signed the amendment protocol without reservation. As of end June 2000, ten members of the WCO have signed it.

31.	The establishment of a computer network between customs offices and traders allows the latter to submit customs declarations electronically, which are then automatically processed by the customs computers. This addresses bottlenecks and cuts back communication time.

32. In accordance with established terminology in the WTO TBT Agreement, mandatory technical specifications are referred to as "technical regulations", while voluntary technical specifications are referred to as "standards".

33. In the area of standardisation the term *"cultural requirements"* refers to a series of language parameters used in computer science, including fonts, coding of characters, keyboard setting, sorting of words, date and time formats, etc.

34. ELOT has established four laboratories to perform certification tests for low voltage electric and electronic appliances, electric cable, toys, and polymers and plastics, all areas where external testing capacity was not available. All other certification testing is subcontracted to external laboratories in Greece or abroad. The policy of ELOT has thus been to rely to available external laboratories offering satisfactory guarantees of reliability. However, the lack of appropriate accreditation mechanisms in Greece has, until recently, restricted the trust of the business sector to this system. The development of a more satisfactory network of testing laboratories and the establishment of a Greek Metrology Institute in 1999 have been among the major axes of the 1994-1999 Operational Programme for Industry conducted by the Ministry of Development and co-financed by the 2nd Community Support Framework.

35. The limits of this principle, such as the exception in Article 36 of the EEC Treaty, led to the efforts for harmonisation of technical specifications for products and subsequently to the adoption of the "New Approach".

36. Such as the notification of all derogations, according to European Parliament Decision 3052/95 and the drawing of evaluation reports. See European Commission, "Principle of mutual recognition: Working towards more effective implementation", *Single Market News*, No. 17, July 1999.

37. ISO/IEC Guide 2, EN45020.

38. See Nikos Kastrinos and Fernando Romero (1997), "Policies for Competitiveness in Less-favored Regions of Europe: a Comparison of Greece and Portugal" in *Science and Public Policy*, 24(2), June.

39. In the telecommunications sector primary responsibility on competition issues lies with the National Telecommunications and Postal Commission (EETT). However, EETT can refers a matter to the Competition Committee or request assistance from it.

40. In the last years, OTE has made several foreign direct investments in telecommunications operators in the wider region, such as Telekom Serbija, ArmenTel, RomTelecom, etc.

41. Data Holdings S.A and Intracom own each 10%. France Telecom owns another 20% share but announced end 1999 its intention to sell it.

42. USTR (1999), *National Trade Estimate Report on Foreign Trade Barriers*, and European Commission (1998), *Fourth Report on the Implementation of the Telecommunications Regulatory Package*. The Ministry has always rejected these claims.

43. European Commission (1999), Fifth *Report on the Implementation of the Telecommunications Regulatory Package*, COM(1999) 537 final, November.

44. The address is http://www.eett.gr. The first decision of the EETT to have been displayed is the decision on the management of the domain name [gr].

45. Data in this paragraph are drawn from Panagopoulos, Yiannis (1998), *Telecommunications Equipment*, Sectoral study, Foundation for Economic and Industrial Research (IOBE), July.

46. Registration taxes are imposed on all vehicles, new or second hand, when they are brought into service in Greece for the first time.

47. Act 2 682 of 1997.

48. The Greek Electricity Transmission Operator will be owned 51% by the State and 49% by power generators. The 49% share will initially belong to DEH and will be transferred progressively to new entrants.

49. Greek Public Gas Corporation (DEPA) is owned directly by the State, except for a blocking 35%, owned by Hellenic Petroleum, itself 80% state owned.

50. Minister of Development, Press Conference on 11th May 2000. Reproduced in the website of the Ministry at www.ypan.gr. Unofficial translation by the Secretariat.

BIBLIOGRAPHY

Allison, Graham T. and Nicolaïdis, Kalypso (eds.) (1997),
   The Greek Paradox: Promise vs. Performance, The MIT Press, Cambridge, Massachusetts.

Austrian Institute of Economic Research (WIFO) (2000),
   "*Benchmarking Licensing, Permits and Authorisations for Industry, Emphasising SMEs*", Background Document for the EU Industry Council of 18 May 2000.

Centre of Planning and Economic Research (KEPE) (1999),
   "*The Size and Role of the Public Sector in Greece. Developments and Comparisons with other Countries*", Athens.

Economist Intelligence Unit (1999-2000),
   Country Profile Greece.

European Commission, *Infringement Procedures involving Greece*, http://europa.eu.int/comm/dg15/en/update/inf/index.htm.

European Commission (2000a),
   Single Market Scoreboard, n°6, May, at http://europa.eu.int/comm/internal_market/.

European Commission (2000b),
   Economic Reform: Report on the functioning of Community product and capital markets, COM(2000)26 final, Brussels, 26.1.2000.

European Commission (2000c),
   "*Communication from the Commission to the European Parliament and the Council. Review of SLIM: Simpler Legislation for the Internal Market*", COM(2000)104 final.

European Commission (1999a),
   Single Market Scoreboard, n°5, November, at http://europa.eu.int/comm/internal_market/.

European Commission (1999b),
   Fifth Report on the Implementation of the Telecommunications Regulatory Package, COM(1999)537 final, Brussels, November.

European Commission (1999c),
   "*Communication from the Commission to the European Parliament and the Council. The Strategy for Europe's Internal Market*" COM(1999)464.

European Commission (1999d),
   "Principle of mutual recognition: Working towards more effective implementation", *Single Market News*, No. 17, July.

European Commission (1998a),
   "*Action Plan to Promote Entrepreneurship and Competitiveness*" COM(1998)550 final.

European Commission (1998b),
   "*Communication from the Commission to the European Parliament and the Council. The Business Test Panel. A Pilot Project*".

European Communities (1998c),
   "*Report of the Business Environment Simplification Task Force*", Vol. I and II, Brussels.

Giannaros, Ioannis (1997),
   The automobile market, Foundation for Economic and Industrial Research (IOBE), May.

Hassid, Joseph (1997),
   Strategies for the Attraction of Foreign Direct Investment in Greece, Study commissioned by the Ministry of Development to the University of Piraeus, July.

Hassid, Joseph (1997),
   Foreign Enterprises in Greece, Survey conducted for the American Chamber of Commerce in Greece, September.

International Monetary Fund (1999),
    IMF Staff Report on Greece, Article IV Consultation.

IOBE (1999),
    The Greek Economy, 2/99, No. 22, November.

Kastrinos, Nikos and Fernando Romero (1997),
    "Policies for Competitiveness in Less-favoured Regions of Europe: a Comparison of Greece and Portugal" in
    Science and Public Policy, 24(2), June.

Mertzanis, Harilaos (2000),
    The Regulatory Framework for the Operation of the Greek Capital Market, Ministry of National Economy, Working Group
    for the Review of the Regulatory Framework, Athens.

Mertzanis, Harilaos (1999),
    "Growth and Regulation of the Capital Market in Greece" in Emerging Markets Quarterly, winter.

Ministry of the National Economy (2000),
    Team work for the Study of Regulation, Greece.

National Confederation of Greek Trade (ESEE) (1999),
    The increase of the functional cost of a commercial enterprise because of the necessary bureaucracy procedures, Athens.

Nicoletti, Giuseppe, Stefano Scarpetta, and Olivier Boylaud (1999),
    "Summary Indicators of Product Market Regulation with an Extension to Employment Protection Legislation",
    OECD Economics Department Working Papers No.226, Paris.

OECD (2000),
    Environmental Performance Reviews: Greece.

OECD (1999),
    "Recent Trends in Foreign Direct Investment", Financial Market Trends, June.

OECD (1998),
    Economic Survey of Greece.

OECD (1997),
    Economic Survey of Greece.

Panagopoulos, Yiannis and Vorlow, Costas (1998),
    Telecommunications Networks, Sectoral study, Foundation for Economic and Industrial Research (IOBE), January.

Panagopoulos, Yiannis (1998),
    Telecommunications Equipment, Sectoral study, Foundation for Economic and Industrial Research (IOBE), July.

Spanou, Calliope (1996),
    "On the Regulatory Capacity of the Hellenic State: a Tentative Approach Based on a Case Study" in International
    Review of Administrative Science, Vol. 62.

Spanou, Calliope (1998)
    "European Integration in Administrative Terms: a Framework for Analysis and the Greek Case" in Journal of
    European Public Policy 5:3, September.

Spraos (1997),
    A More Efficient Management of Public Revenues, Commission for the Review of Long-term Economic Policy, Athens.

Spraos (1998),
    Quality in Public Administration: Recommendations for Changes, Commission for the Review of Long-term Economic
    Policy, Athens.

Social and Economic Committee, Greece (OKE) (1998),
    Report on the Draft Law on Incentives for Private Investment.

US Department of Commerce, Country Commercial Guide, Greece Fiscal Year 2000, Chapter Investment Climate, http://www.usa-
    trade.gov/website/CCG.nsf/byuid/.

USTR (1999), National Trade Estimate Report on Foreign Trade Barriers – European Union.

World Markets Research Centre (1999),
    Country Assessment, Greece, http://www.worldmarketsonline.com.

BACKGROUND REPORT ON
REGULATORY REFORM IN ELECTRICITY,
DOMESTIC FERRIES AND TRUCKING*

* This report was principally prepared by **Sally Van Siclen**, Principal Administrator, of the OECD's Division for Competition Law and Policy. It has benefited from extensive comments provided by colleagues throughout the OECD Secretariats, by the Government of Greece, and by Member countries as part of the peer review process. This report was peer reviewed in June 2000 by the Working Party on Competition and Regulation of the Competition Law and Policy Committee of the OECD.

TABLE OF CONTENTS

List of Boxes

List of Tables

List of Figures

REGULATORY REFORM IN ELECTRICITY, DOMESTIC FERRIES AND TRUCKING

In its 1998 Economic Survey of Greece, the OECD reported that almost all public enterprises had been poorly managed, and had often been used to implement multiple policy objectives unrelated to their primary objective of efficiently providing quality goods and services. As a result, public enterprises were usually inefficient, provided low service quality, and were a costly drain on the public purse. From 1996, however, the need for change, to respond to the demands of market opening under EU Directives, and the desire to meet the Maastricht public finance criteria to join the European Monetary Union, spurred concrete reforms.

This chapter reviews regulatory and competition issues in Greece in the transport (road and ferry) sector and electricity sector. The electricity company, Public Power Corporation (PPC), is the largest Greek corporation, and improving its commercial performance will support the continued growth of the Greek economy. The other sectors reviewed in this chapter, domestic ferries and trucking, are privately owned but the regulatory regimes for these sectors can also be improved so that they operate more efficiently. Both sectors provide key inputs into large parts of the economy.

REGULATORY REFORM IN ELECTRICITY

1. INTRODUCTION TO THE ELECTRICITY SECTOR

The electricity sector in Greece is comprised almost completely of a single state-owned corporation, Public Power Corporation, or PPC. PPC is vertically integrated in all aspects of the electricity sector, from lignite mining to selling power. Only trivial amounts of power are supplied by others or imported. The Greek gas sector, too, is monopolised by a vertically integrated state-owned company.

The most immediate spur to reform of the Greek electricity sector is its obligations under the EU Electricity Directive.[1] Under this Directive, Greece must *inter alia* open at least 30% of its electricity demand to competition by 19 February 2001. Greece's 1999 Law (Law No. 2773 Liberalisation of the Electricity Market – Regulation of energy policy issues and other provisions, 22 December 1999) was adopted to comply with the Directive.

The 1999 Law establishes the Energy Regulatory Authority (ERA), an advisory body attached to the Ministry of Development. The Minister for Development continues to regulate the sector. PPC remains intact, but must separate accounts for its electricity activities. Its legal monopoly in generation and supply of liberalised customers is removed. Conditions to supply liberalised consumers are set out, and Greece will liberalise 30% of demand, meaning that those customers will be free to choose their electricity supplier. The establishment of a System Operator, owned by the state, PPC and, later, other generators, is provided for. The criteria defining liberalised customers will be set out in further regulation.

These reforms are clearly positive. The relationship between PPC and the State is now formalised. A professionally-staffed advisory body is established. Provision is made for privatisation of up to 49% of the company. Under the right conditions, consumer choice could help promote market efficiency. But, unless the industry structure and regulatory regime are reformed further, competition to generate and supply electricity is not likely to develop in Greece in the foreseeable future. The Government chose not to split PPC to create competing generators. Entry is discouraged by access conditions for fuel, the governance of access to transmission and distribution, and low tariffs to the largest customers. Conditions for supply from outside the European Union are sufficiently burdensome to preclude such supply.

For Greece to enjoy significant efficiency gains, it will need to take additional steps to promote the development of effective competition. These steps include reducing barriers to entry for generators, splitting PPC into competing generating companies with distinct ownership, transferring regulatory responsibility to an effective regulatory authority that is independent of the industry and of the day-today political pressures of government, and improving the corporate governance of PPC. These steps would improve economic performance in Greece, and make easier attainment of its environmental objectives.

1.1. Description of the electricity sector

PPC (Public Power Corporation) is, essentially, the Greek electricity sector. PPC was a state-owned corporation in private law until 1 January 2001, when it became a *société anonyme*. It is vertically integrated into all aspects of the electricity sector – generation, transmission, distribution and supply – as well as lignite mining. Only 2% of electricity is generated by others, electricity that is mainly used by the industrial companies that generate it, with the rest sold to PPC (IEA, 1998).

The Greek mainland and a number of islands are served by an interconnected grid. Other islands – of which the largest are Crete and Rhodes – have isolated systems. Lignite, mined domestically, accounts for two-thirds of generation, in seven power plants. Oil-fired (43 plants) and hydroelectric stations provide the remainder, primarily for peak and mid-load both on the mainland and islands. Natural gas has been available via pipeline since 1997: Four gas-fired units (1 107 MW capacity) are in operation and one other is under construction.

PPC faces no competition from abroad. Net electricity imports in 1998 accounted for about 3.7% of Greek demand, but this dropped to 0.4% of demand in 1999 and, in the first four months of 2000, Greece was a net exporter of electricity. Greece has no direct electricity connections with other EU or IEA Member countries. The substantial links to other Balkan countries are used only for balancing and back-up transactions amongst the electricity monopolists. If, in future, the Bulgarian nuclear plant is closed, or other plants are closed for environmental reasons, capacity constraints in the Balkan area will be exacerbated. Investments that would increase generation capacity in the Balkans have been announced. There is no interconnection with Turkey, but PPC and TEAS, the Turkish utility, are studying one under the Transeuropean Energy Networks Programme of the European Union. After 2001, a small 500 MW link to Italy, co-owned by PPC and ENEL, may provide limited competition.

Box 1.   Greek electricity sector at a glance

Installed capacity (1998): 10.5 GW, of which 1.1 GW is on islands with independent systems and 0.2GW autoproducers

Annual generation (1998): 42.7 TWh of which 0.9 TWh autoproducers

Annual PPC sales (1998): 39.2 TWh

Peak demand (1998): 7.4 GW

Growth rate: about 4% per annum (1997 to 1998 was 4.8%)

Fuel mix (capacity, 1998): lignite (47%), hydro (28%), oil (20%), gas (5%), other (0.2%)

Fuel mix (generation, 1998): lignite (68%), hydro (9%), oil (19%), gas (4%), other (0.1%)

Interconnections: Albania (1 540 MVA), Bulgaria (1 400 MVA), FYROM (1 540 MVA)

Imports/exports: net imports equal to about 4% of total supply (1998)

Source: *PPC Annual Report 1998.*

While the 1999 law removes the legal prohibition on entry of new generators, only two companies, both with independent access to fuel, have expressed much interest. Hellenic Petroleum may construct a plant at one of its refineries. Prometheus Gas may build a plant to export electricity. This company is 50% owned by Gazprom and has the right, under certain conditions not currently fulfilled, to use part of the gas pipeline. Other possible entrants are auto-generators who, by definition, would use most of the electricity themselves, and combined heat and power producers. Other companies have also expressed some interest in building or participating in power projects in Greece, but have not announced any specific project.

Transmission, distribution, supply to captive consumers, and supply on the non-connected islands is reserved to PPC (Art. 24).

Access to fuel is a key requirement for entry into generation. Most new generating plants use natural gas. Greek Public Gas Corporation (DEPA) is the vertically integrated monopolist in the Greek gas sector. DEPA is owned directly by the State, except for a blocking 35%, owned by Hellenic Petroleum, itself 80% state owned. DEPA has the exclusive right to import, transport and supply large customers – such as power plants – with gas. The Greek gas sector will not be liberalised before 2003, three years before Greece's derogation from the EU Gas Directive ends. Gas is a "developing sector" in Greece, with the first gas deliveries only in the late 1990s.

Box 2. Description of the electricity sector

The electricity sector has four main stages of production, which vary in terms of their scope for competition and the regulation that can be applied. These stages are:

- Generation – the production of electric power using a variety of fuels and technologies;

- Transmission – the high-voltage "transport" of electric power over distances from generators to distribution networks and large industrial customers;

- Distribution – the low-voltage "transport" of electric power to smaller customers;

- Retailing or supply – a set of services including metering, billing and sale of electric power to final consumers.

A fifth component is system operation. The electricity system must remain in balance, with demand and supply equal at each moment in time. Demand varies unpredictably. Hence to remain in balance, supply must respond immediately to changes in demand. System operation is the control of the generating units and other equipment attached to the transmission grid to ensure this demand-supply balancing, as well as to maintain other quality attributes of electricity.

Transmission and distribution are, for the foreseeable future, natural monopolies at any given geographic location. Further, even where a transmission grid has different owners in different geographic regions, the physical properties of electric power imply not that the sections of the grid could compete but rather that they would each "transport" a share of the power. Consequently, competition in transmission and distribution is infeasible.

By contrast, both generation and retailing are potentially competitive activities and indeed are competitive in many countries for at least some final consumers. It should be noted that generators may be located on either the same or the opposite side of an international border from the users of the electric power.

Behaviour by one user of an electricity system can change the costs of other users. These externalities imply that, at least up to relatively large geographic areas, system operation over a larger area is more effective than over a smaller area. This implies that system operation at any given geographic location is a natural monopoly activity and competition is infeasible.

Lignite is, at present, the most important fuel for electricity generation in Greece. While the Greek State owns the lignite deposits, PPC exploits the deposits under license from the state. (Private mines extract and sell to PPC less than 5% of total lignite mined.) The state does not collect royalties on lignite (although a 0.4% levy goes to local authorities).

The 1999 law largely retains the structure of PPC. PPC remains vertically integrated, retains exclusive ownership of transmission (Art. 12) and distribution (Art. 21), and retains ownership over its generation and supply facilities. While formally PPC loses control over the operation of the transmission grid and dispatching of generation – it must develop and maintain the system according to instructions of the Transmission System Operator (Art. 12) – the ownership and staffing of the System Operator mean that there will be no immediate *de facto* change. PPC may use the transmission system for non-energy related activities, such as for a telecommunications system, so long as the energy objectives are not impeded (Art. 13). PPC must produce separate accounts for generation, transmission and distribution and, for non-electricity activities, consolidated accounts (Art. 30).

Figure 1. **International price comparisons**

Industrial electricity prices in selected OECD countries, 1998

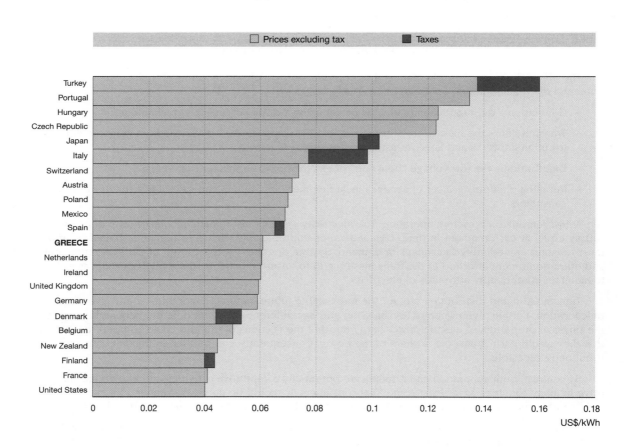

Note: Data not available for Australia, Canada, Korea, Luxembourg, Norway, and Sweden.
Source: IEA/OECD (2000), *Energy Prices and Taxes*, 3rd quarter, Paris.

Figure 2. **International price comparisons**
Household electricity prices in selected OECD countries, 1998

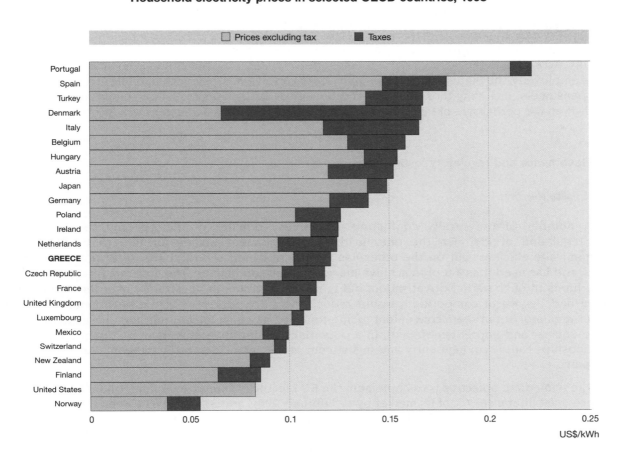

Note: Ex-tax price for the United States. Data are not available for Australia, Canada, Korea and Sweden.
Source: IEA/OECD (2000), *Energy Prices and Taxes*, 3rd quarter, Paris.

Average industrial prices of electricity in Greece are low, and household prices are about average, compared with other European IEA countries. But these price comparisons do not reflect PPC's relative efficiency: input prices are distorted and the company has non-commercial public service obligations, such as supplying some consumers below cost. Electricity prices were used as an anti-inflation tool, hence the real (inflation-adjusted) price fell 24% in the decade to 1999. Average industrial prices are distorted because PPC supplies large quantities of electricity at about half price to the aluminium and nickel firms (OECD, p. 119). These subsidies are due to be phased out in 2006 and 2003, respectively. Commercial and small industrial customers pay prices well above their cost of supply. Revenues collected from households covered in 1997 only about 60% of the costs attributed to them, and agricultural and other special categories of customers pay even less. The Greek government states that by 1999 household revenues covered about 90% of their costs.

Transfer prices for fuels are not necessarily market prices. Besides lignite, described above, other fuels are bought from other predominantly or wholly state-owned firms, although in some cases, PPC pays market-based prices. Personnel costs are high – one informed observer estimates that a reduction of 20% would be easily obtainable – and rose through the 1990s from 16% of revenues to 23% by 1999. Return on equity has been far below normal. PPC has received DR212bn (Euro 0.65bn)

263

between 1981 and 1998 of EU grants, and E29m in 1999. PPC has a high debt to equity ratio for a company without recent acquisitions – its gearing was 185% at the end of 1999. In sum, PPC has used financial resources that might have been put to better use elsewhere, and has charged higher prices to those parts of the economy that are normally responsible for the greatest job creation.

A major challenge to restructuring and liberalising PPC was the company's under-funded pension liability. According to the 30 July 1999 agreement between the Government and the union representing PPC's employees, the State as sole owner of PPC takes on all PPC's insurance liabilities to its employees and pensioners, including those not covered by annual contributions. Also, a certain fraction of pro-ceeds from the partial sale of PPC would be put into this fund. This agreement was incorporated in the 1999 Law.

1.2. Governance and regulatory institutions

1.2.1. Policy objectives

A number of potentially conflicting objectives coincide in the governance, ownership, and regulation of PPC. On the one hand, the government wishes for PPC to become more economically efficient, but on the other hand it has assigned to PPC a variety of non-commercial tasks, and has used it as a tool to achieve macroeconomic objectives. The government might seek to raise funds through partial privatisation, but more competition, or uncertainty over the future regu-lation and degree of competition, would reduce the price received. In the government's role as owner-regulator, it can seem convenient to fine-tune PPC's behaviour, but this sort of regulation tends to be unclear and unpredictable and, in a potentially competitive environment, opaque regulatory relationships can discourage entry and investment in the sector, and reduce the market value of the company.

The immediate objective is to implement the EU Electricity Directive on time. Under the Directive, Greece must liberalise 30% of its market by 19 February 2001, and 33% by 2003 (Greece had a two-year derogation.). If Greece liberalised all consumers whose annual consumption exceeds 1.5 GWh, this would correspond to 30.26% of demand and about a thousand customers. Individual Member States retain discretion in how they implement the Electricity Directive.

The new law sets out the objectives of the Minister of Development and the ERA as including:

– To protect the environment from the consequences of electricity activities

– To satisfy the total energy needs of the country

– To control whether the recipients of authorisations for generation and supply can fund those authorised activities

– To promote sound competition in generation and supply of electricity, as well as any other forms of energy

– To protect the interests of consumers, particularly as regards prices, terms of supply, security of supply, regularity and quality of service

– To promote the use of efficient and economical methods and practices by authorisation holders, as well as the efficient and economical use of electricity and other forms of energy supplied to consumers (Art. 3(4)).

1.2.2. Corporate governance

PPC is a corporation under private law. It will be transformed into a *société anonyme* by a Presidential Decree. In 2000 it is entirely state-owned, but the 1999 Law foresees eventual partial privatisation in that it requires that the state retain at least 51% of the voting shares (Art. 43).

PPC is managed by the Managing Director, the Board of Directors and the Management Board. The Board of Directors consists of six members (including the Managing Director) elected by the General Assembly of company's shareholders, two representatives elected by the employees, two members representing minority shareholders and one member appointed by the Economic and Social Committee. If there are no minority shareholders, the General Assembly of company's shareholders elects eight members instead of six. The Management Board consists of the Managing Director and the company's General Directors. The managing Director and the Management Board run the utility day-to-day. The company is subject to external financial control.

The State has financial and operational responsibility. The State appoints most of the board of directors and the top management. The Ministry of National Economy approves the company's financing programmes. The Ministry of Development controls total revenue, as well as some individual tariff classes. The Ministry of Development controls tariffs to captive customers, after the opinion of the ERA has been given. The Ministry of Development otherwise exercises formal control, such as through review of investment plans. It has been the practice, however, for PPC to supply the Ministry with key personnel.

1.2.3. *Regulatory institutions under the 1999 Law*

The 1999 Law provides for the creation of two new entities, the Energy Regulatory Authority (ERA) and the System Operator. Primary regulatory responsibility remains with the Minister for Development: Licensing, tariff setting, and the imposition of public service obligations are assigned to the Minister. The ERA will have monitoring, advisory and referral responsibilities. It will be able to impose fines, revoke licenses, and settle disputes. It is to enjoy a certain degree of independence from the Minister of Development. The various Codes – Grid, Power Exchange, Distribution and Consumer Protection – will be drafted by the System Operator or PPC acting as Distribution Network Operator, evaluated by the ERA, approved by the Minister, and enforced by ERA. The Competition Committee retains authority over competition matters in this sector but has not been active.

Ministry of Development

The Minister of Development has primary regulatory responsibility, but before he exercises that power he generally must receive the opinion of ERA, though he is not bound to follow that opinion. The Minister has three main regulatory responsibilities: issuing authorisations, setting tariffs, and specifying public service obligations. Under the 1999 law, tariffs must cover costs and reasonable profits; consequently, the Minister may no longer use electricity tariffs to control inflation.

Table 1. Assignment of regulatory powers

	Minister of development	Energy regulatory authority	System operator (51% State-49% PPC*)	PPC
Final tariffs (for captive consumers)	Approves	Provides opinion		
Authorisations				
Generation	Grants	Provides opinion		
Supply	Grants	Provides opinion		
Impose fines		Decides		
Public service obligations	Decides			
Transmission access				
non-tariff terms	Included in Grid Code			
tariffs	Approves	Provides opinion	Proposes	
Distribution access				
non-tariff terms	*Included in Distribution Code*			
tariffs	Approves	Provides opinion		Proposes
Grid Code	Approves	Provides opinion	Drafts	
Power Exchange Code	Approves	Provides opinion	Drafts	
Distribution Code	Approves	Provides opinion		Drafts

* PPC's initial share would decrease as other generators receive authorisations and buy shares in the System Operator.

Participation in the electricity sector requires authorisations. The Minister issues authorisations for generation for the mainland and connected islands (Art. 9) and for suppliers to liberalised customers. For generation on non-connected islands, the Minister issues a call for tender and, after a specified procedure carried out or monitored by ERA, awards the corresponding authorisation (Art. 11). The Ministers of Development and Finance, by common decision, set a fee for the issuance, as well as annual fees for the usage of, authorisations (Art. 28(2)). Tariffs and public service obligations, which can take the form of restrictions on tariffs, are set by the Minister after he has received the opinion of ERA (Art. 29(3), 28(3)(a)).

Box 3. **Main features of Law No. 2773/99: Liberalisation of the electricity market – regulation of energy policy issues and other provisions, 22 December 1999**

The law:

– Establishes the objectives of the Minister of Development and the Energy Regulatory Authority in this sector.

– Provides for the establishment, of an Energy Regulatory Authority, an administratively independent agency within the Ministry of Development, to advise and monitor the energy markets, and impose fines.

– Retains regulatory powers in the Minister of Development, notably with respect to authorisations for any electricity activities, tariffs, and public service obligations, in all cases after receiving the opinion of the Energy Regulatory Authority

– Sets out regulatory principles, notably that tariffs must cover all costs, including public service obligations, as a reasonable profit, and that PPC cannot cross-subsidise between liberalised and captive customers.

– Requires PPC to keep separate accounts for its generation, transmission, and distribution-supply activities

– Removes PPC's legal monopoly on generation by introducing an authorisation regime for the mainland and interconnected islands and a tendering process for non-interconnected islands.

– Removes PPC's legal monopoly on supply by introducing an authorisation regime, but retains PPC as the unique supplier to captive consumers.

– Retains PPC as the exclusive owner of transmission, and exclusive owner and operator of distribution.

– Requires that a supplier own adequate generation capacity in an EU Member state, and prove long-term access to the necessary transmission and distribution capacity.

– Provides for the establishment by June 2000 of a system operator, Greek Electricity Transmission System Operator, S.A. to operate, manage, secure the maintenance of, and plan the development of the transmission system. It also procures ancillary services. It will be owned 51% by the state and 49% by generators connected to the system, initially only PPC. PPC is obliged by the Law to sell equity at a price fixed by the Minister, to independent power generators connected to the system.

– Provides for access to the transmission and distribution grids at tariffs set by the System Operator and PPC, respectively, which must be approved by the Minister after receiving the opinion of ERA.

– Provides that, on 19 February 2001, consumers totalling 30% of demand, including all customers with annual consumption over 100GWh, will become eligible to choose supplier.

– Provides that the cost of commitments or guarantees of operation given before the entry into force of the Directive may be included by PPC in its tariffs. [The Government has applied to the EC for transitional regime ("stranded cost") treatment].

Energy Regulatory Authority

ERA will have the following powers and responsibilities:

– Monitor and control the operation of the energy market and propose to the competent bodies the necessary measures required to comply with competition rules and consumer protection.

– Provide opinion regarding the granting of authorisations and control the exercise of rights granted under the authorisations

– Collect and evaluate information required for the fulfilment of its duties regarding entities active in the energy sector

– To impose fines on violators of this and other acts issued in accordance with this law, including the Grid Code and other Codes

– To co-operate with corresponding authorities in other countries or international organisations.

– ERA acts and decisions are entered into a special official book, easily accessible to the public, except in cases involving national defence or public security (Art. 5).

Decisions of ERA can be appealed within 30 days to ERA. The next levels of appeal are to, respectively, the Athens Administrative Court of Appeal and the Supreme Administrative Court.

ERA will be governed by five members. The members are appointed by the Minister of Development, through a published invitation, after the competent Parliamentary Committee has expressed its opinion. The term of office is five years, and may be renewed once. Members cannot be removed, unless they commit offences that would require the dismissal of a civil servant. Members may not have any ties with energy companies (Art. 4).

The budget of the ERA is attached to the budget of the Ministry of Development (Art. 6), but it is not included within the overall budget envelope of the Ministry. The law provides for 50 employment positions in the Secretariat of the ERA (Art. 7). Employees of state corporations in the energy sector may be transferred to serve in these positions, by specific decision of the Minister of Development and the competent Minister (Art. 7, para. 6), provided ERA agrees. These employees thus change their employer and enter a new employment contract with ERA.

1.3. Analysis

1.3.1. *Rate of return regulation*

PPC has not been subject to formal regulation, such as rate of return or price caps. Rather, its tariffs are affected by national policies, for social and development reasons. Similar considerations prevail on the cost side, notably as regards staff levels and joint hydropower-irrigation investments. PPC has not, historically, been run as a profit-making entity. Rather, in addition to the above objectives, it has had the objective of providing electricity at the lowest possible cost, an objective that has been pursued in part by manipulating input costs.

The 1999 law specifies some of the principles of economic regulation that will be applied to electricity companies. Tariffs (for captive customers) are to take into account the recovery of a reasonable profit and costs, including operational costs, investment depreciation and return on invested capital (taking into account the risk and capital cost of similar activities), and cost of compliance with public service obligations (Art. 29).

1.3.2. *Public service obligations and cross-subsidies*

Although only PPC may supply captive customers, any holder of supply authorisations may be required to differentiate tariffs for groups of customers (Art. 29(3)) or to offer specific tariffs or terms for categories or classes of customers (Art. 28(3)(a)). Each authorisation holder would be able to recover all costs incurred, and PPC cannot cross-subsidise between eligible and captive consumers (Art. 29).

Competition problems can arise where PSOs, or indeed any "reserved activity," are not thoroughly separated from competitive activities. It can be difficult to distinguish between those revenues which are intended to cover the cost of PSOs and those which are profits from commercial activities, or indeed to distinguish between costs incurred to comply with PSOs and costs of assets that also can be used to supply the competitive market. Although PPC cannot cross-subsidise between eligible and captive consumers, the required accounting separation – between generation, transmission and distribution (Art. 30) – is insufficient to detect this sort of cross-subsidy because many of the assets are used both to supply eligible and captive customers. It may be less costly to insist on appropriate separation from the beginning, than to rely upon ERA to collect and scrutinise accounting data.

1.3.3. Foreign entry

Other countries or regions have increased competition in their markets through competition from imports. The Netherlands, countries in NordPool, and the German *Länder* are examples. However, Greece has erected barriers to competition from imports.

The conditions to receive a supply authorisation are burdensome. An applicant must own adequate generating capacity, installed in an EU Member State, and provide "satisfactory long-term confirmation" that it has access to sufficient transmission and interconnection capacity to transmit the electricity it will supply (Art. 24). These conditions foreclose supply from Greece's immediate neighbours. Requiring PPC to provide this reserve capacity, at a price reflecting the cost of providing it, would allow generators in neighbouring countries to overcome this near-absolute entry barrier. The weak links through the Balkan Peninsula and weak legal framework for transit make that route difficult for EU generators. Thus, competition from imports is virtually precluded, except from Italy.

A small interconnector with Italy is expected to begin commercial operations after 2001. Its capacity, 500 MW or about 4 000 GWh, would allow the supply of about 8% of total Greek demand, or less than a third of demand to be liberalised in 2001. Actual deliveries would likely be reduced by engineering constraints and commercial incentives. The link is intended and designed to reinforce the EU grid, as its financing by the EU indicates. Since electricity prices are higher in Italy than in Greece, the flow is likely to be westward. Southward capacity constraints across the Alps imply that only Italian generators would be able to supply through the link. The competitive impact of the link will be limited.

While the Italian Authority for Electricity and Gas allocates access to supply liberalised customers over the alpine interconnectors, the allocation and pricing mechanisms for the Italy-Greece link have not been announced. Access to the Italy-Greece interconnection should be allocated and priced to maximise the competitive impact of Italian generators. If the access price is high, then competition from Italy can be blocked. If access is limited to specific firms, then they can offer high prices secure in the knowledge that other firms cannot undercut them.

1.3.4. Domestic entry

Large-scale domestic entry is unlikely because entrants face high barriers. Sources of these barriers include access to transmission and distribution, access to fuel, switching costs of potential customers, and low prices to large industrial customers.

One key concern of entrants is non-discriminatory access, at efficient prices and terms, to transmission and distribution. PPC owns 49% of the System Operator, itself staffed by personnel seconded or transferred from PPC. PPC remains wholly vertically integrated – except for the state owning directly 51% of the System Operator – and must accounting separate its electricity activities. Access conditions – set out in the Grid and Distribution Codes – will have been drafted by the System Operator or PPC itself as Distribution Operator. While both Codes must be approved by the Minister, the law does not provide for review of access price by ERA or the Minister. However, the ERA does monitor access prices. That is, the System Operator and PPC set the access prices to transmission and distribution, respectively (Articles 18(7) and 22(4)).

All access terms and prices for transmission and distribution should be subject to independent regulation. High but non-discriminatory access pricing is just as harmful of competition as high and discriminatory pricing, since the price a company "charges" itself has no economic effect. While it is commendable that the law includes a provision to limit the duration of access negotiations, the law provides for arbitration by ERA to be established by Presidential Decree (Art. 8) or the Minister. Hence, it seems that a generator offered only anti-competitive transmission access prices and terms may have to request the ERA to refer the complaint to the Competition Commission, under Art. 5(1)(a). This could involve considerable delay until final resolution. Delayed access benefits the incumbent.

The continued vertical integration of PPC leaves intact its incentives to discriminate. Other countries have experienced problems in ensuring non-discriminatory transmission access. Accounting separation is ineffective in preventing discrimination against non-integrated companies. Divestiture, that is, separation of ownership of generation from transmission, is the only form of separation that eliminates incentives to discriminate. Lesser forms of separation can reduce the ability to discriminate, provided appropriate regulation is in place and the regulator is vigilant.

Box 4.   Access regulation to the Greek grids

Access to the transmission and distribution grids is essential to the development of competition. The law provides for the establishment of a new entity – the System Operator – a new role for PPC as Distribution Network Operator, and the writing of several Codes that will govern grid access.

The System Operator (Greek Electricity Transmission System Operator, S.A.) shall operate, use, ensure the maintenance and development of, and interconnections with other networks of the transmission system. The SO shall publish transmission tariffs, and will draft the Grid Code. The SO shall contract for electricity only as needed to provide ancillary services.

The SO will initially be owned 51% directly by the State, 49% by PPC. As other generators arrive, the share owned by PPC will be decreased as transfers of SO shares – at prices decided by the Minister – to those other companies are made. The law makes provision for the secondment of PPC personnel to the SO, with confidentiality agreements (Articles 14-17). The SO will pay PPC for the operation and use of the transmission system, where this payment includes a reasonable profit and covers reasonable expenses including a reasonable return on invested capital (Art. 18). The SO must protect commercially sensitive information.

PPC is the distribution network operator (Art. 21). As such, PPC sets the tariffs (Art. 22(4)) and draws up the terms and conditions of access to the distribution network by generators, suppliers, and eligible customers (Art. 23(1) and 23(2)(b)). PPC draws up, also, the criteria for the calculation of expenses attributed to access to the distribution network (Art. 23(2)(g)).

Three codes governing access to the transmission and distribution grids, and settlement, will be written.

– The Grid Code regulates access to transmission and dispatch. The price and other access terms must be non-discriminatory, and the System Operator sets the access price (Arts 18-19). Dispatch priority may be given to generating units that use indigenous sources (lignite, up to 15% of the total), as well as renewable energy sources, and co-generation (Art. 19).

– The Power Exchange Code governs the economic relationships among the sector participants. *Inter alia*, it provides the basis for calculating the System Marginal Price at which settlement takes place (Art. 20).

– The Distribution Code sets the terms of access by generators, suppliers, and eligible customers to the distribution network (Art. 23).

The fuel arrangements discourage entry. With respect to gas, a potential entrant must negotiate price with the monopolist, DEPA. The "most favoured customer" arrangement between DEPA and PPC implies not only that the entrant cannot buy gas on more favourable terms than PPC, but also that DEPA has reduced incentives to lower its price to an entrant since it would have to apply any price decrease to PPC's purchases. Both of these raise the price of gas to customers. If the state is involved in DEPA's commercial decision-making, then the price DEPA charges to competitors of PPC may reflect the state's ownership interest in PPC. The structure of the gas supply sector is unlikely to change before 2003, three years before Greece's derogation from the EU Gas Directive ends.

PPC's favourable access to lignite may discourage competitive entry, not only because an entrant might want to use lignite-fired plants, but also because the entrant would have to be able to supply electricity that can compete successfully against power generated using low-cost lignite. Offering to sell lignite to other generating companies would allow the state to set a market price for the extraction royalties, which would also end concerns that the zero-royalty practice might constitute State aid.

Entrants are discouraged if liberalised customers incur costs to switch suppliers. Under the law, PPC can charge liberalised customers who are supplied by another company for additional expenses incurred by PPC because that customer was or is supplied by another company (Art. 26). While this additional charge cannot discriminate between liberalised customers, and its amount is regulated, it does increase the customer's uncertainty about the benefits and cost of switching his business to a new entrant. This reduces his willingness to switch.

Figure 3. **One and two firm concentration levels for selected countries or regions, 1998[1]**

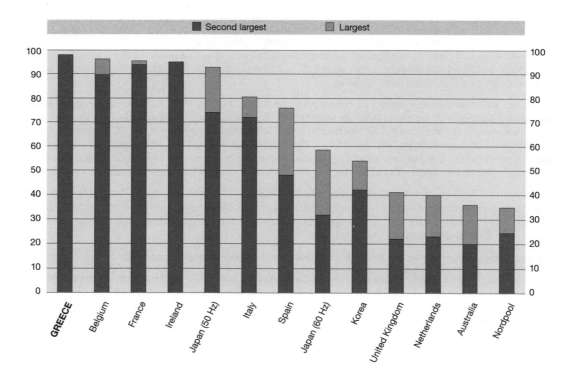

1. Data refers to 1999 for Greece and Ireland.
Source: OECD, IEA, Electrabel annual report (Electrabel + SPE), EdF and Charbonnage de France annual reports, Edison April 1999 presentation to shareholders, Spanish and Korean Ministry of Industry and Energy, Ofgem (NatPower and PowerGen in England and Wales 97/98), NEMMCO, Macquarie and Delta annual reports (SE market only), Nordpool annual report and Vattenfall, Statkraft.

Low prices to large customers discourage entry. In many countries under the old regulatory regimes, large industrial companies had been paying above their cost of supply. Thus, after liberalisation, new entrants had incentives to seek them as customers. In Greece, the existing contracts with the aluminium and nickel companies provide for prices below the cost of supply. Matching those prices would be unprofitable for an entrant. By reducing the size of the potentially profitable liberalised market, entry is less attractive. (These subsidies are scheduled to be phased out in 2006 and 2003, respectively.)

1.3.5. *Structural change*

Since entry is unlikely to have a significant effect on the Greek electricity sector for the foreseeable future, the objectives of efficiency, competition, and sufficient investment must be sought in a different manner. Structural change, in the form of creating competing generating companies, promotes these objectives. Other countries have created competing generating companies both before and after privatisation because that promotes greater efficiency and private investment into the sector. This has been done in the United Kingdom (England and Wales), New Zealand, Australia (three largest States), some States of the United States, and Argentina, and it is planned in Italy and South Korea.

Efficiency is promoted by competition. Endesa, in Spain, estimates it can cut operating costs by half between 1996 and 2006 (OECD, 2000). ENEL, in Italy, is expected to be able to reduce the number of its employees by a quarter by 2004, largely through incentived early retirement (CNN, 1999a). There is significant scope for reducing costs in PPC, partly by reducing investments in unprofitable activities and partly by reducing the number of employees (up to 20% according to one valuator). These efficiency gains are passed onto consumers in the form of lower prices, or taxpayers in the form of lower subsidies.

Some might object to splitting up PPC's generating capacity, claiming that the resulting firms would be "too small." However, small generating companies persist, or are being deliberately created, elsewhere. In Denmark, the two partnerships, Elsam and Elkraft, owned 6.7 GW and 4.8 GW capacity, respectively, primarily coal-fired. In Spain, Union Fenosa and Hidrocantabrico, own 5.2 and 1.7 GW capacity, respectively. In Hungary, the generating companies have capacities of 2.1, 1.8, 1.3, 0.8, 0.4, 0.4 and 0.3 GW, respectively. (However, these are not all independent companies.) In Nordic countries, there are several small hydropower based generators. The generating spin-offs from ENEL will have capacities of about 7, 5.4, and 2.6 GW, respectively. The total installed capacity of PPC is 10.5 GW, or 9.4 GW excluding capacity on islands with independent systems. There are tens of generating plants on the Greek mainland. Thus, it would be feasible to spin-off for several competing generating companies from PPC.

Box 5.   Effects of competition in electricity

Significant time series on efficiency and prices are only available for the UK. Since 1990, productivity has skyrocketed (as output rose by 8% from 1988 to 1995, employment was reduced by 50%), and prices have plummeted. In real terms, over the 1990-1997 period, household ("domestic") prices decreased by 20%, and prices to other consumers fell 19 to 27% (Littlechild, 1998, cited in IEA, 2000). In 1998, in real terms, the standard domestic tariff in England and Wales was 26% lower, and for industrial customers the price was 23 to 32% lower than in 1990 (Office of Electricity Generation, 1998, p. 58). Only shorter time series are available for other reforming countries. For example, 1997 prices in the Australian state of Victoria fell to less than half their 1995 level, reflecting the introduction of competition, privatisation, and excess capacity. However, prices in Norway and New Zealand, where the sector remains state owned and there is a high reliance on hydropower – thus subjecting the system to cost variations due to hydrological variations – did not fall with the introduction of competition (IEA, 2000).

271

The predominance of lignite-fired plants in the PPC portfolio makes designing an effective "split" more difficult. It may be difficult to find buyers of such plants: the plants cannot operate without their adjacent mines, or long-term contracts with the mines, and the demonstration of the lack of cost-competitiveness of lignite plants in other highly competitive markets would be discouraging.

Selling the two gas-fired plants along with their long-term gas supply contracts, to two separate companies, would give an immediate boost to competition. The single gas-fired plant in operation alone accounts for 6% of total capacity. Together, these two plants, along with imports, would be able to supply a significant fraction of liberalised demand. This step alone would not create effective competition in Greece, but it would be the necessary first step and would enable the regulatory system to develop. However, opponents of such a sale have pointed out that these are PPC's best generating plants, being new and gas-fired, and located in areas of heavy load.

A less intrusive policy would be to cap PPC's generation capacity at its current level. However, simple calculation shows that, if all new demand were met by new entry – that is, if PPC did not increase or decrease the amount it generates – then even after six years, new entrants would account for only one-quarter of the market. Only after more than a decade would PPC's share fall below half, assuming a total demand growth rate of 4% per annum. This is a very long time to wait, especially as other members of the European Union are enjoying the benefits of competitive electricity markets.

Some might claim that the cost of capital of non-integrated electricity companies would be higher than for a single large company. Differences in firms' cost of capital reflect differences in their exposure to uncertainty. Uncertainties to which electricity companies are exposed include, in general, regulatory uncertainty (that changes in regulations will change profits), uncertainties in related markets like capital and fuel, and electricity market uncertainty. By splitting PPC into several competing companies, some of these risks are reduced because the resulting companies would follow different strategies. While other large electricity companies have a lower cost of capital, this is often because they "spread their risks" across a number of countries. Any "size of company" effect would be swamped by the effect of regulatory risk on the cost of capital. The major uncertainty, which gives rise to a regulatory risk premium, can only be reduced by strengthening the regulatory framework, and increasing its credibility and predictability.

Another way to consider this risk premium is in the stock market value of a company. Sophisticated potential investors will form their own expectations in valuing PPC when it is floated. In particular, they will have knowledge of the path of electricity sector reforms in other countries over the past two decades, so in bidding for shares, they will assign a discount to the sale of an intact monopoly subject to economic regulation by a non-independent regulator. This discount is an expression of the regulatory risk premium of the cost of capital.

Another possible claim is that a monopoly provides more security of supply. However, supply security is provided in competitive markets. Sufficient investment must be attracted so that sufficient supply is available for the quantity of demand, at the relevant price, and liability for failure must be assigned. The attractiveness of an investment opportunity depends, partly, on the regulatory regime to which that investment will be subject. If the regime does not allow an adequate return, then the private capital will be invested elsewhere. In the 1990s, PPC reported returns on equity of 1-2% for 1991, 1994 and 1998, but 3.44% for 1999. Any potential investor would of course estimate his own expected returns based on his own forward-looking costs and revenues. But a return of 1-2% would be unlikely to attract private investment, hence the improvement toward the end of the decade is promising. By contrast, when the United Kingdom had one of the most liberalised electricity sectors in the world, some observers felt that there was excess investment in generation during the "dash for gas." Thus, competition can reinforce security of supply by promoting investment in generation.

Security of supply, in another meaning, is provided by the flexible prices in electricity spot markets. When demand nears capacity, market price rise. This price rise chokes off some demand – some users shift their heavy usage of electricity to other times, when electricity prices are lower. This type of supply security requires that at least a portion of demand be exposed to short-term price fluctuations that, in turn, reflect short-term cost fluctuations. Another benefit from the resulting demand smoothing is lower total cost for the whole system, since peak capacity can be smaller. A third meaning of security of supply relates to continuity of access to fuel. So long as such a large share of generation is fuelled with lignite, security of supply in this sense is unlikely to change.

The creation of competing generation companies in Greece would promote the goals that are set out in the law. Relying on entry to create competition delays the arrival of the benefits of competition for several years, if not decades.[2] The link with Italy will not allow much competition from generators located in Italy, and the law as written, combined with Greece's physical location, almost precludes supply by other foreign generation. In order to meet the stated goals, the fastest and easiest route for Greece to follow would be to make the structural splits in PPC's generation.

Regulatory framework

A greater reliance on independent regulation can reduce regulatory barriers, promote entry and investment, and accelerate the development of competition in the Greek electricity sector. Other OECD countries have independent regulators, including Australia, Finland, Italy, the United Kingdom and the United States. Germany and New Zealand use the competition authority to regulate electricity. While specific arrangements differ in each country the main features of independent regulation are: complete independence from the regulated companies, a legal mandate that provides for separation the regulatory body from political control, a degree of organisational autonomy, and well defined obligations for transparency (*e.g.*, publishing decisions) and accountability (*e.g.*, appealable decisions, public scrutiny of expenditures). Key to independent regulation is independent expertise and sources of information.

There are three sources of concern about the Greek regulatory framework. First, the Minister of Development, rather than the ERA makes regulatory decisions. The Minister controls authorisations, sets tariffs, and can impose tariff and other conditions on all authorisation holders under the rubric of "public service obligations." The concern is that ministers, whether in Greece or in other countries, tend to be subject to greater day-to-day political pressure, and to be replaced more frequently, than are regulators who are given a specific public mandate and appointed for fixed terms. Ministers may also make trade-offs that discourage investment: in Greece, there would be concern that the Minister might continue the practice of using electricity prices to influence inflation. Thus, ministers find it more difficult to maintain predictable policies over longer periods of time, whereas regulators maintain policies unless Parliament instructs them otherwise. Unpredictable regulation discourages private investment, and changing regulation renders investment less efficient.

Second, PPC itself retains substantial influence over regulation. The System Operator and the Distribution Network Operator have regulatory powers associated with granting access and operating their respective grids. PPC will own, initially, 49% of the System Operator and the law provides that PPC personnel may be seconded to the System Operator. PPC is assigned the role of the Distribution Network Operator. Each of these is a route for PPC influence. To the extent that the aim of regulation is to protect consumers and promote competition, this influence is inappropriate. In other countries, the objectives of the regulator and the policy-maker differ from those of the regulated firms. Thus, the influence of PPC can influence policy and regulatory outcomes in ways detrimental to consumers and competitors.

Third, the Ministry needs to develop an independent ability to make energy policy. The practice of transferring and seconding PPC personnel is indicative of this need. In Greece, state-owned energy companies provide an important source of information, expertise and advice in relation to energy policy matters on an *ad hoc* basis if not formally (IEA, pp. 28, 30). This practice discourages the development of independent expertise within ERA and the Ministry. In other countries, the regulatory institutions – both independent authorities and ministries – hire or train their own personnel to perform the regulatory functions and to make policy. The expertise of companies is tapped during public hearings or public comment periods. The transparency provided by public hearings and consultation also ensures that the views of all affected parties are heard, rather than only those that the ERA or the Ministry have chosen to consult. Greece needs to develop the expertise of its agencies, and broaden the consultation process, in order to develop the credibility of its regulatory regime.

The establishment of a non-discriminatory, stable regulatory framework in Greece starts with the establishment of appropriate institutions. Providing for the establishment of the Energy Regulatory Authority is a sound first step, if it will be strong enough. However, once the ERA is functioning, final regulatory authority for generating and supply authorisation, tariffs, and access to transmission and distribution need to be transferred to ERA. ERA needs to regulate the electricity sector independently of PPC, with its own dedicated employees as far as that is possible. Both the Ministry and ERA need to develop expertise to regulate and to make policy. If it was once efficient to integrate the company, the regulator and the policy-maker, and make use of a common pool of expertise for each task, it no longer is. Such practices can leave the interests of consumers underrepresented, and can discourage entry by competing firms that may believe that their concerns will not get the same consideration as the incumbent's.

Part of building a stable regulatory framework, in the Greek case, is improving the corporate governance of PPC. The Ministry, as owner, retains a deep control over decisions that would normally be made by corporate managers. Listing on the Athens Stock Exchange will force some changes in this relationship, but following yet more stringent principles of corporate governance would make this relationship more arms' length. This, too, would reassure potential entrants that they would be treated by the Ministry in a way similar to the treatment of PPC.

1.4. Conclusions and policy options

The economic objectives of the electricity sector are to satisfy demand, to promote "sound competition" in generation and supply of electricity and to ensure that generators and suppliers can fund their activities, to promote efficiency, and to protect consumers particularly as regards price, security and quality of supply. These objectives are linked, because competition promotes efficiency and protects consumers as regards price and, if an appropriate liability system is in place, security and quality of supply as well. A sound regulatory regime would help attract sufficient investment to ensure that demand is satisfied and that competition is sustainable.

The Greek electricity sector is an example of the importance of domestic support for structural reform. Many of the changes incorporated in the 1999 law are made to comply with Greece's obligations under the EU Electricity Directive. The liberalisation of 30% of demand, the creation of the Energy Regulatory Authority and System Operator, and the formalisation of the relationship between PPC and the Ministry of Development are positive steps. However, as a package, they are half-way steps, and do not create a dynamic for reform. Market entry and the vigorous competition needed to provide pressure for greater economic efficiency are impeded by the sector's structure and by the regulatory framework. Instead, under present arrangements, any pressure to improve the economic efficiency of the monopolist, PPC, is more likely to arise through partial privatisation. This will create external stakeholders who will have incentives to advocate for regulation that allows greater efficiency and thus profitability. Accounting reforms will also make better information available, and thus make better decision-making feasible. However, shareholder and consumer interests are not identical. Reliance on shareholder interests would place too little emphasis on promoting efficiency and greater resistance to subsequent creation of effective competition. For the latter reason, competition should be established before privatisation.

The Greek authorities have made several policy choices whose effect is to ensure that the sector remains a stable monopoly, such as not creating immediate competition by splitting generation. Some of these choices will discourage entry. Without entry or the creation of competing companies, the regulatory framework will not be developed and modified to sustain a competitive sector. Potential entrants cannot learn what the regulatory framework would be were they to enter, and hence entry is discouraged and the structure of the sector is perpetuated.

These policy choices include those related to access to transmission and distribution, and access to fuel. Self-regulation of transmission and distribution access prices, albeit monitored by the ERA, and virtual self-regulation of other access terms, imply that an entrant would not be offered access to all of these essential facilities at efficient prices and terms. In other countries, access to transmission, especially, has been a source of discrimination if not carefully regulated. Sorting out disputes are likely to be lengthy, as the energy law does not provide a mechanism for expedited resolution. (Establishment of arbitration at the ERA by Presidential Decree is foreseen, however.) Access to fuel, particularly gas, constitutes a further barrier to entry, since gas is sold on negotiated terms by a monopolist until 2003, and there is not yet a framework for access to lignite. Entry from abroad is virtually precluded, at least until the link to Italy is completed.

The reduction of entry barriers, creation of competing generating companies, and significant strengthening of the regulatory regime, provide a way toward the Greek objectives of greater efficiency through the development of competition. Competition in generation and supply has worked in other countries to deliver efficiency gains and prompt private investment in the sector. Competition is feasible in Greece, too, but requires a stronger regulatory regime, and more skilled human and other resources. Resources and regulatory powers must be placed in a regulatory body, independent of Ministry and the regulated companies. These conditions, combined with the steps already taken in the 1999 Law, will bring Greece substantially closer to its goals in the electricity sector.

1.4.1. Policy options

1. Develop effective competition in generation and supply.

- Effective competition requires an adequate number of competitors and efficient, non-discriminatory access to essential networks. Separate ownership of the networks from the potentially competitive activities of generation and supply reduces incentives for discrimination, whereas separate operation of the system from generation reduces the ability to discriminate. An Independent System Operator, with a governance structure that ensures the reflection of consumers and generators' interests, is more likely to operate the system in an efficient and non-discriminatory manner. *Therefore, separate the ownership of the networks from that of generation and supply. Where this is not feasible, create an Independent System Operator with a governance structure to ensure efficient and non-discriminatory access.*

- Even where ownership, or operation, of the networks is separated from that of generation, there remain incentives to price access above efficient levels. Independent regulation can ensure that the access terms are efficient. *Therefore, access to transmission and distribution grids should be subject to regulation by an independent regulator.*

- The structure and small size of the Greek electricity market imply that foreign competitors will be important in reducing market power. *Therefore, ensure efficient and non-discriminatory access to international transmission links. Reduce barriers to foreign supply, including specifically by requiring PPC to make available reserve capacity at regulated, cost-reflected prices.*

- Domestic entry, also, would increase the number of independent competitors. There are a number of features of the regulatory regime that discourage entry. Among these are the self-regulation of transmission and distribution access prices, and the limited enforcement regime for access. *Therefore, take steps to reduce barriers to domestic entry, notably regulate access to the grids so that access is granted on terms that are efficient and non-discriminatory. Also, provide an expedited procedure to resolve access disputes.*

- Splitting generation into competing companies, sold separately, would create a healthier competitive environment. It would also reduce the need to rely on competitors from outside the European Union. *Therefore, create competing generating companies, without common ownership, designed to create effective competition.*

275

- One of the safeguards of competition in this sector is the competition law. *Therefore, ensure that the application of competition law to the electricity sector prevents abuse of dominance or anti-competitive agreements, mergers, and long-term contracts that risk frustrating the development of competition.*

2. **Develop regulatory institutions that promote investment, efficiency, and competition.**

- Greece needs to establish a non-discriminatory, stable regulatory framework. The first step is to establish the institutions of this framework. Among the requirements is for the regulator to be independent of day-to-day political pressures, and independent of the regulated companies. *Hence, transfer to the Energy Regulatory Authority final regulatory authority for generating and supply authorisation, tariffs, and access to transmission and distribution. Endow the ERA with human and other resources that enable it to independently and effectively regulate the sector. Ensure that the budget, personnel and other internal decisions, of ERA are independent of the Ministry. Ensure that the ERA decision-making process is transparent, such as through public consultation processes, and that it is accountable.*

- The Ministry, also, needs independent policy-making capabilities. Hence, ensure that the Ministry of Development acquires or develops the technical expertise, independent of any company, to make electricity policy.

3. **Improve the corporate governance of PPC.**

- Developing a more arms' length relationship between the Ministry and the regulator, and the entry of new competitors into the market, imply developing a more arms' length relationship between the Ministry and PPC. *The government should transform the relationship between itself and PPC to a more commercial basis. The government should expect to receive dividends at the same rate as a private shareholder and should not be responsible for guaranteeing any new debt of PPC. The management and board of directors of PPC require sufficient autonomy so that they can make investment and other decisions on commercial criteria. Finally, after PPC is partially privatised, to enhance the board's decision-making process, the government should make appointments to the board of directors that would represent the interest of the minority shareholders.*

4. **Evaluate the state of the sector, after some time, with a view to further reform.**

- Reform of the electricity sector is an on-going process, with experience prompting demand for further reform or fine-tuning. *Therefore, review the sector in the short term (e.g. two to three years) to* judge whether effective competition is developing and electricity companies are increasing efficiency. Comparisons with other countries would be particularly valuable.

REGULATORY REFORM IN DOMESTIC FERRIES

2. INTRODUCTION TO THE DOMESTIC FERRY SECTOR

Domestic ferries ply the waters of the Greek seas, linking the economies of the islands and mainland. About 114 Greek islands are inhabited. There are about 150 ports, and about a thousand ferry links are made a day. Piraeus, the main port for Athens, is the centre of the ferry network.

Demand for ferry services is highly seasonal and demand among the routes is highly skewed. Some islands would not be served at all without subsidies. The sector has recently consolidated, coalescing around three corporate groups. However, a fringe of smaller companies remains. The main innovation in the past few years has been the introduction of higher speed ferries, financed through partial floatation on the Athens Stock Exchange. The ferry companies are entirely privately owned, but ports are in public ownership.

The domestic ferry sector is at present highly regulated by the Ministry for Merchant Marine (MMM or YEN for its Greek acronym). Licenses, specific to the vessel, are granted for specified itineraries at specified, invariant frequencies. Licenses for service to islands for which service is non-profitable are often bundled together in the same itinerary with islands for which service is profitable, or are imposed on companies as conditions for receiving profitable routes. Licenses are granted by the MMM on the basis of criteria that are not transparent, and it is difficult to get a new license. Fares are also set by MMM. Many details of running the hotel aspects of the ship are specified (for safety reasons, details of running the engineering aspect of the ship are also specified.) A research analyst called the institutional framework "complex, rigid, outdated and cumbersome" (Psaraftis, p. 3). The European Commission characterised the legal and regulatory framework for domestic ferries as "rigid…particularly as regards the grant of operating licenses and the fixing of fares by the Ministry for the Merchant Navy" (EC, par. 105).

Full application of the EU Directive on cabotage[3] should begin in November 2002, pending adoption of the draft law currently being developed by the Greek government. Under the EU Directive, the latest date to begin is 1 January 2004. This may mean that entry restrictions or regulation of frequency and fares will be lifted, which is preferable, but it may mean that the existing regulatory framework, perhaps slightly modified, would be applied equally to Greek- and other EU Member state-flagged ships.

There is tremendous scope for freeing ferry companies to serve customers better. One of the broad objectives of the Government of Greece is to improve the relationship between the state and its citizens. Changing the regulatory framework to enable consumer wishes to be met more closely, more flexibly, and at a lower price, would respond to this goal. The role of the Ministry, in the area of domestic ferries, could move to one of protecting competition and ensuring safety. Flexibility and resiliency could be built into the regulatory system, in order to deal better with uncertainty. Competition would also provide incentives for innovation, which would result not only in lower costs and prices, but also in the introduction of services that better meet consumer wishes. Public policy objectives, primarily related to sufficiently frequent service to designated islands and to safety, can be met in ways that do not unnecessarily impede competition.

Reform to the regulation of the sector is urgently needed, as recognised by market participants and by the responsible ministry, which has launched a programme of reform. In late 2000, the government developed a draft law to liberalise the domestic ferry sector, aiming at free and fair competition and protection of public interest, that should be the basis for further reform. The ministry's earlier move toward an integrated approach to the sector, focusing on passenger transport needs and the interactions with port infrastructure, is another positive development.

2.1. Policy objectives

This sector is regulated to secure the territorial integrity of the country and the cohesion of the Greek islands and mainland. This implies that designated islands should receive service of specified frequency. Regulation is also aimed at improving the quality of service, renewing the fleet, and securing existing jobs and creating new jobs. As a member of the European Union, Greece also must adapt the regulatory regime to the requirements of the relevant EU Directives. These objectives are set in a safety-ensuring framework.

The Ministry for the Merchant Marine has, over the past two years, moved toward a focus on the satisfaction of the passenger transport needs, viewing all of the constituent parts (network, ships, port infrastructure, institutional infrastructure, shipyards, communication services) as parts of a single integrated system of domestic marine transport. This contrasts with the former focus on ships, in isolation from demand and the complementary infrastructure. As part of this effort, the Ministry has drafted an action plan to revise the institutional framework, and plans to put into place a System of Internal Sea Transports (SETHAM) to enable objective criteria to be used as input into the management of the domestic marine transport system. A contract has been awarded to a consulting consortium for the analysis and design of SETHAM.

2.2. Description of the sector

Piraeus is the main port for Athens and forms the central hub of the ferry system. Thessaloniki in the north, Patras in the Peloponnese, and Rafina and Lavrio near Athens are the other large mainland ports. The Aegean Islands, which compose the majority of the islands, are rather compact. Rhodes, to the Southeast and nestled within sight of the Turkish coast, is 260 nautical miles from Piraeus. The Aegean Islands are conventionally grouped into the Saronic, Cyclades, Dodecanese, Sporades and Northern Aegean. Crete is a major ferry destination with several ports. The Ionian Islands lay to the west of the Greek mainland.

Demand for ferry services is highly seasonal, with August accounting for some 23% of total annual passengers, and February for only 2%. Some routes have much higher demand for travel than others. *e.g.*, in 1990 almost one-fifth of all traffic was accounted for by travel between nine ports at Athens/Piraeus, Mykonos, Santorini and Crete (Psaraftis, p. 5). This disparity is caused not only by differences in tourism at the island destinations but also by differences in permanent population on the islands. Although the single island cluster with the most traffic in passengers is the Agrosaronikos system near Piraeus, most of the traffic in passenger-miles is between Piraeus and Crete. Some islands have fewer than 100 residents; Crete has half a million. The largest islands have airports, which provide alternative transport for passengers and certain goods.

In addition to the domestic ferry sector, the subject addressed here, there is substantial ferry traffic between Greece and Italy. The three largest companies in the Aegean are three of the four large companies in this Adriatic Sea trade. The Adriatic has been the proving ground of some of the innovation that is now arriving to the domestic sector. However, the two networks are governed by different regulatory frameworks, with the international routes of the Adriatic under European Commission competence and subject to liberalisation of entry, pricing, and frequency since 1993. International traffic between Greece and Italy does not come under the Greek domestic cabotage institutional and legal umbrella, except that part that links Greek ports, *e.g.*, among Patras, Igoumenitsa and Corfu. Also, international routes are subject to enforcement of European Union competition laws by the Commission.

After a recent spate of consolidations, three groups dominate the domestic sector. These groups are Minoan Lines, ANEK, and, indirectly, Attica Enterprises through its alliance with Strintzis Lines. Many much smaller ferry companies also remain in the Greek domestic market. Total turnover in Greece, which includes revenues from international routes, notably to Italy, was about DR200bn in 1999 (*Kathimerini*, 13 December 1999). All ferry companies are privately owned. Also, Minoan Lines owns 28% of the merged Aegean Airlines and Air Greece, the largest private air carrier in Greece (*Kathimerini*, 30 December 1999) and other private airlines are owned by other ship owners.

The companies specialise in particular routes, often reflecting their historical roots on particular islands. For example, Minoan and ANEK, both based in Crete, have all the licenses for routes to Crete from the mainland (*Kathimerini*, 8 March 2000). Minoan Flying Dolphins has been buying the majority of smaller companies operating in the Cyclades (*Kathimerini*, 24 January 2000), under the name of its Hellas

Table 2. Structure of the Greek ferry sector

Parent or leading company	Subsidiaries or alliance members	Share of combined international and domestic ferry revenues
Attica Enterprises	Superfast (38%) Strintzis Lines	45%
Minoan Lines	Minoan Flying Dolphins (MFD) Hellas Ferries (subsidiary of MFD) (46%) GA Ferries	30%
ANEK (Cretan Maritime Company)	(50%) LANE (16.5%) NEL (Lesvos Shipping Company) (43.3%) DANE (Dodecanese Company S.A.) (50%) ETANAP	12%

Source: *Kathimerini*, 13 December 1999 and 15 February 2000; ANEK, 2000*a*.

Table 3. Earnings and sales of Athens stock exchange-listed shipping companies

Company	Sales 1998	Earnings 1998
Minoan Lines	48 560	10 113
Attica Enterprises	26 802	9 067
ANEK	30 343	5 055
Strintzis Lines	18 266	2 375
NEL (Lesvos Shipping Company)	9 052	1 046

Source: "Review of Attica Enterprises Holdings SA," an article by Invest in Greece, available at <http://www.invgr.com/members/attica_enterprises.htm> on 27 April 2000.

Ferries subsidiary, whereas ANEK focuses on the northern Aegean and Dodecanese routes (Inv.gr, 2000*b*). The small Rhodes-based company DANE operates in the Dodecanese and Cyclades, and to Thessalonika.

The main innovation in this sector is faster ferries. The new ships are half again or twice as fast as the ships they replace, and often have larger capacity. Hence, it is sometimes feasible to replace two older ships with one new ship. These vessels greatly reduce travel time, *e.g.*, between Patras, Greece and Acona, Italy to 20 hours from 30 hours, Piraeus to Rhodes via Kos to 10 hours from 18 hours, and Piraeus to Chania to 5¼ hours from 10 hours. Since one of the costs passengers bear is the value of their time, the reduction in travel time made possible by faster ferries significantly reduces passengers' total cost. However, to date, with the exception of hydrofoils and some catamarans that cannot carry vehicles, there are very few high speed ferries in the Greek domestic market: The MFD High Speed I (catamaran) and the fast mono-hull AEOLOS by NEL. MFD expects to add another high speed catamaran in the summer 2000.

The introduction of faster ferries significantly affects markets and market structure. For example, the two 27-knot ships that entered the Patras-Bari via Igoumenitsa route in the Adriatic won about two-thirds of the market in less than a year, increased the size of the market by 5 to 36% (depending on whether trucks, private vehicles, or passengers are measured) and shifted traffic toward Bari from other southern Italian ports (Attica Enterprises 1999*b*, pp. 30, 31, 33).

Faster ferries were introduced first in the liberalised Adriatic market. In 1993, Gerasimos Strintzis introduced a "fast ferry" in this market, innovating also by raising funds for this ship in the Athens SE (ANA, 1998, p. 4) Pericles Panagopoulos (Attica Enterprises) followed in 1995, with initially two 27-knot but later four 27-knot ferries operating in the Adriatic. Then, in summer 1998, Minoan Lines entered the Adriatic with two 27-knot ferries (Minoan Lines, 2000*a*) ANEK has announced that it, too, will introduce two faster ferries on Patras-Italy routes in 2001.

In the Aegean, the introduction of faster ferries has been delayed. In September 1997, Panagopoulos (Attica Enterprises) applied to the Ministry of Merchant Marine for a license to operate a faster ferry between Piraeus and Heraklion, Crete. The new ferry would have cut the journey time from 11 to 6 hours, and the price would have been cut by 20%. MMM turned down the request on the grounds that the port facilities could not accommodate the ship, existing ships served demand adequately, and that the proposed lead time, 18 months, was too long. Attica Enterprises found the reasons for the rejection "truly unfounded," and pointed out that the port was vacant at the times proposed and that no businessman would build a ship for domestic service without an operating license in hand (Forbes, Attica Enterprises 1998, pp. 8-9). Instead, the incumbent licensee, Minoan Lines, promised to introduce a newly built ship on the route by spring 1999. It takes delivery of the new ship for this route in autumn 2000 (Lloyd's List). In general, faster ferries are being introduced into the domestic market under the threat of loss of protection from foreign-flagged ships, and with the expectation of growth in demand.

Individual companies use their newer and faster ships on the longer, liberalised Adriatic routes and slower, older ships on the Aegean. For example, Minoan Lines uses ships with maximum speed of 27 knots on its Patras-Igoumenitsa-Ancona route, but ships with maximum speed of 19 knots on its Piraeus-Heraklion route, and 20 knots on its routes to islands from Thessaloniki or Crete (Minoan Lines, 2000a). For ANEK, the difference is smaller, with the Adriatic routes served by ships with speeds of 25 and 23 knots, and Aegean routes served by ships with speeds of 16 to 22 knots (ANEK, 2000a). Attica Enterprises was reportedly looking for "room" in the Aegean for the "superfast" ferries to be delivered by August 2001 – it has not yet been able to get licenses to serve the Aegean routes – but would operate them on new routes in the Mediterranean if none appears (Athens News Agency, p. 5, *Kathimerini*, 24 January 2000).

In parallel, passenger-only catamarans are being introduced to the Aegean. In 1998 Strintzis began service with a catamaran to the Cyclades. In mid-1999 it announced it would serve two other domestic routes, in the Cyclades and Northern Aegean, with new high-speed ships (Strintzis 1999). Other high-speed ships operate in the Aegean (*Kathimerini*, 26 April 2000). And NEL has just launched a ship capable of carrying cars and passengers at 36 knots (*Kathimerini*, 20 April 2000). The route specifications, with their multiple stops, do not allow the speed advantages of catamarans to be exploited.

These programmes of investment in new ships are closely linked with the development of the Athens Stock Exchange as a source of capital. Traditionally, shipping companies were family owned, and they are still mostly family run and owned. However, the capital requirements for fleet modernisation are large. In one case a $125m ship is replacing a $10m to $15m ship. One estimate is that the investment programme of Minoan totals close to $1bn since 1995, (*Kathimerini*, 24 January 2000) and the investment programme of Superfast, part of Attica Enterprises, totals $ 1 billion for eight more ferries (Superfast, 2000).

2.3. Regulatory regime

2.3.1. *Institutions*

Domestic ferries are under the responsibility of the Ministry for the Merchant Marine (MMM). The Ministry is responsible for regulating and overseeing the whole of the sector – market entry, licensing, pricing, route scheduling, manning (hotel as well as engineering), imposition of public service obligations, determination of and tendering for unprofitable routes, enforcement of licence terms, certification, control, vetting and inspection of ferries for navigational and environmental safety. The Minister issues *inter alia* licenses and decrees controlling prices.

The Minister is aided by an advisory body, the Coastal Transport Advisory Committee (CTAC).[4] The CTAC makes non-binding recommendations about licenses and prices which, in practice, the Minister has always followed. For inter-island routes, the Ministry of the Aegean is also involved. Before September 2000, six of the twelve members of the CTAC were government officials or appointed by the Minister. The remaining six were split among four representatives of shipping, a representative of the Piraeus Chamber of Commerce and Industry, who arguably could also be expected to support shipping interests, and the National Tourist Organisation (to represent consumers).

This institutional arrangement seems ill-suited to the announced focus on passenger needs. The arrangement seems to correspond more with self-regulation, and industry participants seem to have influence over the economic regulation enforced by the Ministry (discussed below). In this situation, new investors, whether Greek or foreign, would have a basis for concern that their potential competitors would be making decisions about, *e.g.*, licenses. This concern would discourage entry.

Increased representation of consumer interests on the CTAC, whether tourist, island resident or non-marine transport companies, would help offset the influence of producer interests. Indeed, in September 2000, membership in the CTAC was expanded to include more consumer groups, both commercial and island residents. More use of public hearings in the decision-making process would also increase transparency. At least as important would be for each Ministerial decision to be accompanied by a public, reasoned explanation of the objective criteria applied, as well as the policy objective driving the decision. It may or may not be appropriate for CTAC recommendations to be made public. However, a consistent public record, along with clear policy objectives against which the record can be viewed, would help provide assurance to market participants and potential investors that the market was a level playing field.

2.3.2. *Economic regulation*

European Union

European Union level legislation also governs the Greek domestic ferries sector. The European Union Regulation 3577/92 on cabotage [Applying the principle of freedom to provide services to maritime transport within Member States (maritime cabotage), 7 December 1992, OJ L 364 12.12.92 p. 7] lifted cabotage[5] restrictions for EU Member States for any ship flying the flag of an EU Member state. This Regulation defines how the principle of freedom to provide services has to be applied to maritime transport within Member States.

This Regulation includes a derogation for Greece, until 1 January 1999 for cruise ships and vehicle ferries over 650 tons sailing between mainland ports, and until 1 January 2004 for regular passenger and ferry services and services under 650 tons. The eleven-year delay, of which eight years have already passed, was intended to allow Greece to prepare for the opening of the market to competition.

Provided certain conditions are met, the Regulation allows the Member State to conclude public service contracts with or to impose public service obligations as a condition for the provision of cabotage services on shipping companies participating in regular services to, from and between the islands. Also, the Regulation establishes manning conditions (European Commission 1999, pp. 168-9). Reimbursement of operating losses incurred as a direct result of fulfilling certain public service obligations is not, as a matter of general practice, considered to be State aid by the Commission, provided an adequately public tender is made, the contract duration is reasonable and not over-long, the reimbursement is directly related to the calculated deficit, and there is no cross-subsidisation (*Ibid*, p. 173).

Despite the liberalisation of cabotage in the northern Member States, as late as 1998 there was no non-national flag involvement in domestic passenger trades of EU Member States (European Commission, 2000, p. 18). In Greece, there has been no impact to date from the lifting of cabotage restrictions on EU-flagged vessels over 650 tons at the beginning of 1999.

The scope for public service obligations is particularly wide in Greece. In the electricity sector, for example, public service obligations can take the form of charging specified prices.

The MMM has indicated that it will implement the same rules for all ships, Greek or EU, and it contends that this uniform approach will comply with EU regulations (Athens News Agency, p. 1). Thus, the lifting of the cabotage restrictions does not necessarily imply that other aspects of the regulatory framework will change, nor that new entrants will actually be licensed.

Ministry for Merchant Marine

The Minister for Merchant Marine issues licenses to a specific vessel for a specific itinerary.[6] The licenses have an indefinitely long duration. The licenses impose a number of economic conditions on the licensees, *inter alia* with respect to frequency, service to uneconomical islands, pricing, and employment practices. It had not been unusual for license applications to be turned down. After the reform of the CTAC in 2000, however, almost all requests for licenses have been granted.

The economic conditions attached to the license protect a number of cross-subsidies. First, the licensed itinerary that must be followed may include islands for which the cost of providing the service exceeds the revenues gained. Second, the crews must be employed and on the payroll throughout the year, whether the vessel is operating or idle, and regardless of the seasonal variation in traffic. The crew must be nationals of Member States of the EU or of the European Economic Area. Third, there are only two levels of frequency of service – winter and summer – except that there is a statutory right to remain idle for 60 to 90 days annually for dry docking, maintenance, repairs, surveys, and inspection. Fourth, fares charged must be equal to those issued in the Ministerial decree. Finally, the vessels must carry mail free of charge and must be made available to the State during times of war for military purposes. These economic conditions are discussed below.

Licences

The licenses have a long duration because the system is designed to assign routes to particular ships for the ships' complete working lifetime. Licenses are vessel-specific and the entry and exit regulations are based on the ship's age. No vessel entering the domestic market can be older than 20 years, and the license is valid, if its terms are respected, until the ship is 35 years old. Recently, the Minister has quit granting licenses for ships over 10 years old. Thus, new licenses are valid for at least 25 years. (The Greek Coastal Shipping Association has asked for the 35-year limit to be scrapped) (*Kathimerini*, 25 February 2000).

License applications require information about the vessel's technical characteristics, including carrying capacity of vehicles and passengers, as well as a feasibility study, including data on operating costs, transportation flows on the requested route, capacities of the ports of call and other data to prove the commercial viability of the proposal. The date on which the vessel could begin serving the requested route must be provided.

New licenses are not issued on demand. Instead, the CTAC examines the request in light of the needs and current level of service, and considers *inter alia* the age of the vessel, the credibility of the company, and the speed with which the vessel can enter the requested service. In the formulation of its opinion, the CTAC takes into account many others' views on the feasibility of the requests, many times of those in direct competition with the company requesting the licence. However, the evaluation does not include a review of the economics of the proposal. It does not include the objective criteria that would promote competition among companies serving the same route or would discourage monopolistic or oligopolistic situations. It should be noted that there currently exist sectors of the domestic ferry market, such as in Argosaronikos or certain segments of the Cyclades where all maritime services are provided by only one company, MFD and its subsidiaries.

It is not always clear how these objective criteria are weighed. Negative licensing decisions have been controversial, and obtaining a new license had been called "difficult" (Athens News Agency, p. 3). There seemed, in practice, to be a tendency to maintain the *status quo*, enabling incumbent companies to remain unchallenged. This was the case in 1997, when an applicant to provide faster and cheaper service on the Piraeus-Heraklion, Crete route was turned down while the incumbent was pressured to

---

Box 6. Prices in the Aegean vs. Adriatic

The Adriatic has had free pricing for several years. Fares in the Adriatic are much lower, per unit distance, than fares in the Aegean. Two very popular routes are Piraeus-Heraklion, Crete, a distance of 175 nautical miles, and Patras-Ancona, Italy, a distance of 510 nautical miles. As the table shows, the price per unit distance is much lower for the Adriatic route.

	Piraeus-Heraklion		Patras-Ancona	
	Fare (GRD)	GRD/nautical mile	Fare (GRD)	GRD/nautical mile
Passengers	63 000	360	145 600	285
Car	33 700	193	31 200	61
Truck	156 750	896	140 000-170 000	275-333

Assumptions: Passengers: two persons in a double outside cabin; Truck: 16.5 meters (price includes tax, which is normally rebated).

upgrade its ship (Athens News Agency, p. 3, *Forbes Global*, p. 45, Attica Enterprises 1998 pp. 8-9, 14, Lloyd's List). Another example involves NEL. When NEL learned that competitors had attempted to enter the Piraeus-Hios-Lesvos route, where it had the license, it ordered a new ferry (Athens News Agency, p. 6). However, later the MMM did award three new licenses on that route (*Kathimerini*, 11 February 2000). And since the CTAC was reformed in 2000, it has granted almost all requests for licenses, 32 as of mid-February 2001.

The restrictions on route entry harm consumers. Companies who wish to enter a route can offer lower prices and better quality of service than customers are now receiving. (If they could not, then they would not apply to enter.) Even if the incumbents eventually upgrade their offerings, consumers suffer in the interim. By contrast, entry is free on the Adriatic routes: The quality of service has risen, the number of passengers has grown, and prices are lower, per kilometer, than in the Aegean. Passengers on Adriatic routes have benefited from liberalised entry.

Labour regulation

Under MMM regulation, crews must be maintained year round, even when a ship is idle, thus insulating labour from the seasonal fluctuation of demand for ferry services. Other MMM regulation is quite specific. For example, the hotel composition, including number of cooks and stewards, is specified as a function of ship size (ORMS Today). These rules apply to all ships in the Greek market, since the EU Directive provides that the host state's rules on manning for island cabotage are imposed on all ships (EC, 1999, p. 10).

The Ministry has explained some of its crewing requirements as aimed at increasing employment. Other crewing regulations relate to safety. The effect on employment may well be the opposite of that intended, since the rule on year round employment discourages seasonal expansions in capacity – with its associated employment – by raising the cost of that expansion. The hotel manning rules discourage the introduction of new year round capacity by raising the cost of using that capacity.

Unprofitable service to islands

Under the current regulatory framework, two sets of islands are served despite such service being labelled unprofitable. One set, called "public service" islands, are islands that are served as intermediate stops in a licensed itinerary to or from a mainland port, as a condition of the license. An example of this is the packaging together of daily service between Piraeus and Rhodes, one of the most lucrative domestic routes, with weekly service to a number of small islands along the way, in such a way that the whole package may be uneconomic (Lloyd's List).

The other set of islands that are served despite the service being unprofitable are islands that are served over "unprofitable routes." By definition, these routes are inter-island routes. The routes are designated by joint Ministerial decree (Ministers of Finance, Development, and Merchant Marine) issued on request or proposal of the local authorities or other interested parties, and after CTAC's opinion has been pronounced. This designation is reviewed every five years. The obligation to provide services on unprofitable routes is allocated by annual tender, where companies bid for minimum subsidy. However, the amount of subsidy appears to be subject to some negotiation.

The shift of focus to inter-island routes is to be applauded. It may well be more cost-effective to provide services to low demand islands from a local hub, itself linked to Piraeus, rather than directly from Piraeus. This shift in focus promotes the development of such hubs. However, the shift in concept could go yet further, for example by designing transversal or circular routes that link the spokes of radial lines emanating from major hubs.

The focus should be on islands rather than routes. Islands now served, unprofitably, as a license condition and those now served over "unprofitable routes" would be combined into a single concept, with a common policy framework for all. In this way, the MMM does not pre-judge the route over which each island would be most economically served, that is, which island would be the local hub. The commercial decision about where to locate a hub would normally take a number of features into account.

283

These features, such as location and availability of labour, port facilities, and others, influence the cost and reliability of the hub, especially under a variety of weather conditions. It is not clear that the MMM would have available better information, or compelling commercial incentives, to make a better choice of hub than the companies themselves.

The shift to focus on islands for which there is low traffic demand would have a number of positive effects. The development of hub-and-spoke service to "public service" islands would enable them to be served at lower cost. The (profitable) destination islands could be served at greater speed – time would not be spent at intermediate stops, and it may be economic to use faster ships – and thus lower total cost to those passengers. It would eliminate the problem of a ship being too large to enter a port that it is obliged, by its license, to serve.

The development of a hub-and-spoke network would, as it has in liberalised airline industries, probably benefit most those passengers on heavily travelled routes with hubs at both ends. These passengers would see greater frequency, lower prices and faster service. Residents of low demand islands may see a reduction in travel time to the mainland, if higher speed ferries offer service between their local hub or hubs to the mainland. They may also experience improved scheduling, as it may be feasible to shift some middle of the night service to more convenient times of day. On the other hand, just as with the liberalised airline industry, residents of low demand islands might experience an increase in total travel time, particularly if connections at the hubs are not well co-ordinated or the service between their hub and the mainland is not provided by faster vessels. This inconvenience may be greater if vehicles also transit at hubs. There should be a role for the Ministry, along with the ports, to facilitate schedule co-ordination and optimisation of capacity utilisation, as well as to provide a legal framework to facilitate passengers using two or more ferry companies on the same trip.

Funding and providing non-profitable service

Service to islands with low demand is subsidised. Service to islands as part of a licensed itinerary are cross-subsidised by passengers on other routes, and service to those on "unprofitable route" are subsidised by the State and, perhaps, other passengers. The annual State subsidy is 2.5 billion drachma. A more flexible framework for providing these services would lower their cost. Indeed, with lower costs, some services may become profitable and subsidies to those services could be withdrawn. Nevertheless, there would remain some islands to which service of adequate frequency must be subsidised.

The provision of service to islands with low demand has two aspects, funding and identifying the provider. Usually, funding such subsidies from the general government budget causes the least economic distortion. However, an alternative, common in other sectors in other countries, is to fund such subsidies out of a small fee, acting like a tax, on the price of all tickets. Thus, as at present, other passengers would fund this service. An advisory body to the MMM has already suggested this type of funding for service to some islands.

The most efficient way to identify the least-cost provider is to competitively tender (for a subsidy out of the above-described fund) the obligation to serve a low-demand island. The Ministry already uses such a method for "unprofitable routes." However, the MMM uses a different method to assign the provider of service to "public service" islands. The licensee whose vessel passes by an island is not always the lowest-cost supplier: the value of the time lost in making an intermediate stop, particularly for an expensive and fast ferry, can be quite large. By extending the tendering process to all low-demand islands, the Ministry would in general reduce the cost of service. This would reduce the total amount of subsidy needed.

Hence, the first step in implementing this new system is to define precisely the public policy requirements for service to low-demand islands in terms of frequency, price, and perhaps minimum travel time to the mainland. The second step is to identify which islands are low-demand. That is, some islands will receive service that meets or exceeds the public policy criteria because shipping companies find it profitable. The remaining islands, those that will not receive service meeting the public policy criteria, are defined to be "low-demand islands." The third step is to hold competitive tenders for subsidies. The tenders are to provide the service to low-demand islands that was defined in the public policy requirement, but which was not provided by commercial decision by the companies in the second step. In this system, companies would make their own, independent commercial decisions about routes and islands served, much as these same companies are already experienced in doing in the Adriatic and other seas.

Seasonal fluctuations in demand

Several license provisions are aimed at moderating the effect of seasonal fluctuations in demand. One requirement is that there be only two levels of frequency of the service – winter and summer – except for the statutory right to remain idle for 60 to 90 days annually for maintenance, repair and inspections. Another requirement, mentioned above, is that crews be employed and on the payroll throughout the year, regardless of whether the vessel is operating or idle. Both of these have the effect of raising the cost of providing ferry services.

Ensuring a minimum frequency of service, of appropriate quality and price, year round, contributes to securing the cohesion of the Greek islands and mainland. Ensuring sufficient winter service is equivalent, conceptually, to the task of ensuring sufficient service to low-demand islands. Indeed, it is as though during winter more islands fall into the low-demand category.

The policy response to ensure sufficient winter service at minimum cost is also the same as for ensuring service to low-demand islands. In particular, if the companies that make the commercial decision to serve an island during the summer do not make the commercial decision to serve that island during the winter (or they choose to serve it too infrequently), then holding a tender for minimum subsidy to provide the required service would both identify the lowest-cost provider of that service, and the lowest subsidy that will induce that service. It may well be that the winner of the tender is the same company who provides summer service, perhaps because his costs are lower than his competitors', or perhaps because there are benefits, like building consumer loyalty, that justify a bid for lower subsidies.

The value of holding the tender for winter service, and allowing free commercial decision-making year round, is that the winter and the summer service are provided at lowest cost and companies are forced to find ways to appeal to consumers. Under the present system, the winter service is subsidised by the summer service, and this cost is hidden. The incumbent, protected by entry barriers and price constraints, may not even know the lowest cost way to provide the services. By forcing him to be alert to possible entry by a competitor in summer, he must seek ways to keep his consumers – lower prices, better quality, more convenient sailing times – and ways to keep his costs down. For winter service, if the politically-determined level of service is not commercially interesting, then the service is put up for tender for minimum subsidy, and the funds to pay the subsidy to the winner of the tender come from the above-described fund. Because the obligation to provide winter service is put out for tender, the lowest-cost company will win, and all bidders will have had incentives to seek ways to lower their costs.

Unbundling winter and summer service makes possible additional cost-saving through allowing flexibility of vessel and route network during winter, in order to better match demand conditions.

Fares

The Ministry regulates fares and freight rates of all services and companies in the domestic sector. The Ministry sees its involvement as aimed at protecting consumers, especially island residents. The fare setting process involves exchanges of information between market participants and the regulator, as well as among market participants themselves. A hearing at the CTAC is required. Finally, a Ministerial decree is issued.

The same price formation scheme is applied throughout the country, but a large number of variables can be used to adjust the price for a specific route. Fares may be adjusted downwards by 10% during

October-March and 10% upwards during April-September. Further, a company can discount its fares by submitting a request to the Minister in September of each year. The discount requires CTAC's consent and the Minister's approval. The discount is subsequently published in the Official Gazette.

The institutional framework provides substantial scope for collusion. Competition officials usually see three conditions as needing to be met in order for collusion to work: The competitors can reach agreement, they can detect cheating on the agreement, and they can punish cheating. The commercial information that must be disclosed in the license application, and then discussed by CTAC and other interested parties during its review, ensures the first condition is met. The second condition seems to be met, since prices and discounts are published in the Official Gazette and there seems to be no secret discounting. The third condition is met when the Ministry enforces its own decrees.

It is not clear why the commercial data need to be submitted with a license proposal. If the Ministry of CTAC uses the data to judge the commercial feasibility of a proposal, then it is difficult to imagine conditions under which they would be able to – or have the role to – protect a company from a commercially disadvantageous proposal. If the Ministry does not use the commercial data to judge commercial feasibility, it is not clear why the data should be required or submitted.

In its decision on price-fixing from the late 1980s to 1997 by seven ferry companies on routes between Italy and Greece,[7] (EC, para. 97, 153-154) the European Commission published some information about price-fixing by ferry companies in the domestic market. During the period of the Commission's investigation, there was a usual practice of fixing domestic ferry fares in Greece. The consultation process of the MMM involved all domestic operators submitting a common proposal, and the Ministry making an ex post decision (para. 163). The companies knew in detail the relevant economic components to analyse the operational costs of the ships, because of the publication of their operational licenses and the meetings held under the aegis of the MMM (para. 71). It has been suggested that the process of agreeing prices, before the meeting of the CTAC, has continued into the present.

Box 7.   Destructive competition

The MMM is concerned that "destructive competition" is against the long-term interests of consumers and producers. Competition, it fears, would reduce profits from the high season that are used to subsidise services in the winter and to fund new investments. The MMM sees regulation as creating less uncertainty than competition.

The risk of destructive competition in the Greek domestic ferry market does not seem high. First, those who would be injured by such an outbreak, the incumbent ferry companies, are in favour of liberalisation – or "playing by European rules" – of routes, fares, and frequency. Second, the market does not have the characteristics to engender this rare phenomenon: excess capacity can easily exit the market by switching to any number of other Mediterranean routes.[1] This sort of route-shifting is expected as faster ferries are delivered and begin operating in the Adriatic, and the replaced vessel moves to domestic operations (*Kathimerini*, 24 January 2000). Third, competition, rather than "destructive competition," eliminates excess profits that can be used for cross-subsidies. The provision of unprofitable services can be assured by a transparent combination of competition, "tax" or "fee" on the competitive services to fund the subsidy, and tendering for subsidy to provide the unprofitable service.

---

1. "Indeed, destructive competition would be inconceivable except for the presence of market imperfections. In particular, it is the inability of capital readily (that is, in the short run) to move out of a situation of excess capacity once it has become embodied in that capacity, that creates the possibility of gross returns on investment remaining for extended periods of time below the minimum required in the long run to maintain it." Kahn, pp. 175-176.

The asymmetric regulatory structure between the Adriatic and the domestic routes creates anomalies. For example, while domestic prices are regulated, companies operating on both routes can – and do – offer discounts on the combined tickets (Minoan Lines brochure 1999, ANEK Lines brochure 1999). While these 10-15% discounts are signs of competition in the Adriatic, it also reduces the efficiency of that competition since the discounts represent a subsidy from the non-competitive, price-regulated markets.

By freeing fares over potentially competitive routes from Ministerial control, and thus automatically making them subject to the competition law prohibition against collusion, the Ministry could greatly increase the efficiency with which vessels are used. The large difference between peak and off-peak demand, combined with few alternative uses of the ships during winter and the year round manning requirements, mean that companies would find it profitable to seek ways to increase the use of their ships during winter. Just as airlines in liberalised markets offer different prices at weekend and mid-week, and mid-winter and school vacations, or combine their offers with hotels or car rentals, so too would the ferry companies have an incentive to find ways to increase passenger numbers in winter. This would have a positive effect not only in this sector, but also for others. Any increase in the number of ferry passengers would have a positive effect on demand for complementary tourist services such as hotels, restaurants and car rentals. Each of these has an impact on job creation. Hence, liberalisation of prices on potentially competitive routes would aid the economy as a whole.

Within the Greek ferry system, there are severe capacity and environmental problems at a number of mainland and island ports. Certain ports are clearly at a saturation point. The three mainland ports, Igoumenitsa, Patra and Piraeus have clearly reached capacity in one or more dimension; indeed, all three are now operating beyond capacity in important aspects. In two cases, Rafina and Lavrio, further expansion of the port is not contemplated and alternatives are needed. The completion of the Rio/Antirio bridge will relieve some congestion at Patra by shifting some ferry routes to Rio.

In 2004, an increase in the number of ships wanting to use the ports must be expected. Thus, a detailed survey of the ports, to identify both the urban factors on the landward side of the port, such as road congestion and quality of life for the residents, and the berthing capacity on the seaward side, is indicated. Until the survey is completed, and indicated increases in ports' capacities are made, then there would need to be a system of slot allocation, comparable to take-off and landing

---

Box 8.   Predatory pricing

Predatory pricing, cutting prices to drive rivals out by forcing them to lose money, is only profitable if the rivals exit the market and do not re-enter. After the rivals are forced to exit, the company would have to raise the price to a monopolistic level and then gain more than enough profits to repay the losses it incurred while driving out the rivals. But this will not work if the rival – or any other firm – can re-enter the market to share in those high prices and, by doing so, reduce the predator's profits.

Concern is sometimes expressed about predatory pricing in network transport sectors, since firms without extensive networks are thought to be vulnerable to predation by those with such networks. On the other hand, concern is also sometimes expressed that tough competition can be mistaken for predation, since in both cases higher cost firms suffer. In the case of tough competition, though, consumers benefit.

One way to reduce the possibility of predation is to ensure that entry and exit are low-cost and rapid. Exit can be facilitated by a wide range of alternative uses of vessel and crew, *i.e.*, by low entry barriers across all routes. Ubiquitous low entry barriers would, paradoxically, have a stabilising influence as firms would recognise the pointlessness of predation, and perhaps turn to value-creating product differentiating strategies, as airlines in liberalised markets have generally done.

287

slots at congested airports. As at airports, slots would need to match the realistic expectations of arrival and departure, taking into consideration actual sea speed, including acceleration and deceleration, time to enter, manoeuvre within, and clear the port, and time to load and unload. Some problems that would need to be overcome include slow loading and unloading, perhaps due to an excessive number of vehicles. Tradable slots would provide incentives for faster loading and unloading, since longer slots – or two adjacent slots – would be more valuable. They would also ensure that more congested ports are more costly to use, thus providing incentives to some ferry routes to switch to less congested ports.

The Ministry of Merchant Marine has launched a programme of reform. In late 2000, the government developed a draft law to liberalise the domestic ferry sector, aiming at free and fair competition and protection of public interest, that should be the basis for further reform. The ministry's earlier move to expand the representation of consumer interest on the CTAC, and toward an integrated approach to the sector, focusing on passenger transport needs and the interactions with port infrastructure, are other positive developments.

Box 9. Creating a new regulatory framework for domestic ferries

In mid-2000, the Greek government took the first steps to reform of the domestic ferry sector by expanding participation in the Coastal Transport Advisory Committee and by convening law-drafting committees. The draft law under discussion in early 2001 aims to create non-discriminatory conditions for competition and to otherwise protect the public interest. Public interest objectives include securing the safety and quality of service, and safeguarding the country's territorial integrity and the economic and social cohesion of the island parts of Greece. The Minister for Merchant Marine will be able to impose public service obligations, such as ports served, capacity to provide transport service, freight rates, and manning. For those routes where entry does not occur in a free market, a Europe-wide tender for a contract to provide service will be issued. An independent Regulatory Authority for Domestic Maritime Transport will be established to monitor the sector, impose fines, and submit its opinion to the Minister on issues falling within its competence. Transparent assessment procedures and proposal selection will be introduced. Licensing procedures will be abolished, and controls limited to ship safety, capacity and reliability of the ship owner and quality of service. These steps are in line with many of the OECD's recommendations on reform of the sector.

2.4. Conclusions and policy options

Domestic ferries are vital to the economic life of Greece's islands and, through their role in tourism, the health of the national economy. Demand for ferry services has grown rapidly through the 1990s, and further growth is expected. However, reform to the regulation of the sector is urgently needed, as has been recognised by market participants and by the Ministry, which has launched a programme of reform. The move toward an integrated approach to the sector, focusing on passenger transport needs and the interactions with port infrastructure, is a positive and thoughtful development.

More extensive reform of the sector in three main directions would benefit consumers. First, regulatory institutions need to be modernised. At present, institutions are more appropriate to a system of self-regulation than a regime of transparent, accountable regulation focused on the needs of passengers and ensuring equitable treatment of all market players. Second, economic regulation needs to be eased, so that the companies make choices about their own commercial operations in response to consumer wishes and developments in the marketplace. As producers make more commercial decisions, the Ministry should ensure that the regulatory framework is transparent, accountable, and pro-competition. Third, criteria that would encourage competition and discourage monopolistic or oligopolistic situations should be devised.

The reforms recommended here would fundamentally change the relationship between the MMM and the domestic ferry companies.

– The Ministry and its advisory committee, CTAC, would withdraw from regulating routes entry, prices, and other dimensions of competition. The MMM would ensure service to low-demand islands. The Ministry would retain its monitoring role, and take on greater responsibility to prevent collusion and, carefully defined so as to distinguish it from tough competition, predation.

– The CTAC would have greater consumer representation, but economic liberalisation and greater use of broader consultation methods would diminish its role.

– Transparency and accountability of regulation would be increased by publishing explanations of regulatory decisions, both in terms of the objective criteria used and the way in which the decision promotes public policy objectives. This would assure both consumers and market participants of the reliability, effectiveness, and neutrality of the new regulatory framework.

Experience in the routes across the Adriatic Sea shows that competition and liberalised entry speeds innovation – faster ferries were introduced sooner – and lowers prices. Entry should be liberalised in the domestic market by changing the economic licensing system from authorisation to notification (safety-related licensing is not addressed in this report). Licenses should cease to be route-based, so that companies can design their own networks on the basis of commercial criteria. Fares and frequencies should be decided on a commercial basis by individual companies, so that capacity can be better utilised throughout the year. The competition thus engendered would provide incentives for fleet modernisation, just as competition across the Adriatic does today.

These recommended reforms are a package, the effectiveness of one part depending on the others. For example, the flexibility of routes is necessary to use the threat of competitive entry as a tool to limit abusive pricing, as well as the feasibility of predatory pricing. If this flexibility is absent, for example if an authorisation must be granted, then the abusive pricing may go on for some time.

The Greek ferry sector is, as the Ministry has recognised, a network. Like other transport networks, an optimal shape may involve hubs and spokes, and like those other networks, it may involve feeder lines and main lines. In liberalised airline markets, such networks have developed as an outcome of competition among several companies. There was no central planning, but rather each company extended and withdrew its network in response to commercial pressures. In those markets, too, the network is ever-changing not only in terms of routes served but also in other dimensions, since companies have equipment flexibility and fare flexibility to respond to changes in consumer demand. It is a resilient system built upon flexibility. And in those markets, giving firms the freedom to design their own services has led to the reappearance of point-to-point systems, too, in competition with hub-and-spoke systems.

One of the main policy objectives for this sector is ensuring service to all the designated Greek islands. The recommended reform would expand the public tendering system to ensure service to all islands that would be left unserved, under-served, or served only at high price under free commercial decision-making. Service to some islands would continue to require subsidy, and the subsidy of service to additional islands in winter would be made explicit. By holding a public tender, competition in bidding ensures that the subsidy is no higher than necessary to provide the service, and it ensures that the service is provided at lowest cost. Funding for these subsidies would come either from general funds, or from a fee, acting like a tax, on all ticket sales, so that, as now, other passengers support these vital services.

These reforms would likely have a long-term positive effect on employment. More demand for ferry services means more demand for seamen as well as more employment in destinations. More shipbuilding means more employment in shipyards, including perhaps those in Greece. To the extent that hub-and-spoke networks develop, the increase in inter-island traffic would mean more employment on the islands. If year-round employment requirement were eased, this would introduce greater seasonal variation in employment, but expand the average. The introduction of more modern ships, which require smaller crews, will however negatively affect the number of jobs for seamen. This report has not

289

addressed safety regulation, which is of primary concern to consumers, regulators, and ship owners alike. It can be noted, however, that the safety regulations as regards crewing would continue to imply that Greek crews would be required on Greek domestic routes.

2.4.1. Transitional period

The time needed to implement a change in regulatory regime influences its acceptance, the preparedness of institutions and market participants, and the value of the change for consumers. The further in the future it is, the easier change is to accept but it is of lower value. In Greece, reform did not advanced very far, as illustrated by the absence of institutional change, relatively minor policy changes, and the limited changes by market participants in the purely domestic market, during the first seven years of the eleven-year transitional period for the EU Directive. Yet the economic value to consumers of the reform of the regulatory regime of the domestic ferries sector is higher, the sooner it is implemented.

Operating, during a transition period, two regulatory systems simultaneously can be costly, difficult, and risky with respect to regulatory failures. And there are situations where only one system can prevail, such as entry restrictions: either service to a particular island is subject to free entry rules or not, but it cannot be both simultaneously.

Too-rapid change of a regulatory regime, which decreases the value of capital invested in a sector, might be considered "unfair". But determining what rate of change is excessive is a matter of judgement, which would have to consider both the seven-year transitional period since the EU Regulation on maritime cabotage entered into force elsewhere in Europe, and the experience Greek ferry companies have gained in liberalised markets throughout European waters. Notably, the Adriatic routes did not have an eleven-year transition period. The transition period would also take into account the economic impact of reform, in light of the fact that ships can be used to provide services in other markets, so that much of their capital costs are recoverable.

2.4.2. Policy options

The recommendations are divided into two parts, those addressing the institutions and those addressing economic regulation.

1. **Reform the institutions to reflect the shift in focus toward consumers and viewing the domestic ferry sector as an integrated system.**

   - Increase transparency and accountability of regulation, establish objective criteria by which the Ministry's regulatory powers will be exercised, ensure a public comment period or public hearing for major decisions, and ensure that Ministerial decisions are accompanied by public reasoned explanations of how the decision conforms with the objective criteria, as well as the responses to public comments.

   - To increase the focus on consumer interests, expand the representation of consumers – whether tourist or island residents or non-marine transport companies – on the CTAC.

   - Adopt in the Ministry of Merchant Marine practices of good regulation identified in the OECD *Report on Regulatory Reform*, such as regulatory impact analysis, that help to ensure that regulation is of good quality. Good regulation *inter alia* is regulation that is needed to serve clearly identified policy goals, effectively achieves those goals, minimises costs and market distortions, promotes innovation, is consistent with other regulations and policies, and is compatible as far as possible with competition, trade and investment-facilitating principles.

2. **Reform the regulatory system to stimulate competition, while preserving service to all designated islands.**

   Reduce barriers to entry.

   - A centrally planned network has a number of inefficiencies compared with one that is the outcome of decentralised decision-making by profit-seeking companies. In order to free ferry companies to design their own most efficient route networks, and to enter into service to islands of their choice, *replace the authorisation principle of the economic licensing system by a notification principle. Allow companies to serve islands in any combination or order.*

Promote competition and efficient commercial decision-making.

- Competition takes place in a number of dimensions. Two key dimensions where competition can be effective are price and quantity. Hence, *eliminate licensing provisions regarding fares and constancy of frequencies.*

- Competition can be reduced or eliminated by collusion, and consumers suffer as a result. Reducing information exchange can reduce the risk of collusion. Hence, *eliminate the license requirement for a commercial feasibility study.*

- Consumers benefit when companies find ways to reduce costs, which still maintaining safety and environmental standards. Hence, eliminate licensing provisions regarding manning, particularly the hotel staff, that do not affect levels of safety or compliance with international standards or agreements. Review licenses for other provisions that intervene into normal commercial practices, with a view to eliminating those not required to achieve safety, environment, or other public policies.

Protect service to low-demand islands.

- It is a public policy objective to maintain service to low demand islands. The efficiency of such service can be improved at the same time route entry can be liberalised, which in turn will increase both efficiency and the satisfaction of consumer demands. To achieve this requires the simultaneous institution of a number of related reforms.

- *Define the public policy requirements for service to all potentially low-demand islands.*

- *Replace the licensing provisions regarding "public service" islands with an expansion of the tendering process for "uneconomic routes" to include all islands that are not served – to the standards set out in the requirements – as a commercial decision by the ferry companies. This includes not only unserved islands, but also those islands where the price charged exceeds a maximum determined by the Ministry, or where the frequency of service is below a minimum determined by the Ministry. Some islands may have low traffic demand for only the winter season, but be in the commercial domain in the summer season.*

- *Establish a fund for service to low-demand islands. It may be a combination of funds from the central budget, or a fee, acting like a tax, on each ticket the proceeds of which go into a central fund, administered by the Ministry, for the sole purpose of this service.*

REGULATORY REFORM IN TRUCKING

3. INTRODUCTION TO THE TRUCKING SECTOR

The geography of Greece profoundly influences its land transport sectors. Other countries can rely more heavily on rail, but the islands, as well as Greece's location without a direct land connection to the main part of the Single Market of the European Union, give trucks a greater importance.

The regulation of the trucking sector is consistent with the regulation of other sectors in Greece. There is a heavy reliance on traditional, command-and-control methods. There are numerical restrictions on entry, and prices are regulated. These constraints unnecessarily raise costs. If EU influence were not so pervasive in this sector, these constraints would also protect incumbents. However, competitors from other countries, operating under different rules, have been able to enter the Greek market and take away customers. The current regulatory regime, therefore, is unsustainable. In March 2001, a formal joint committee was set up by a ministerial decision, published in the Official Gazette. This committee consists of representatives of ministries, hauliers, unions, and transport experts, and aims to map out a reform of the entire sector.

Greece should follow the path of other countries that have reformed their trucking sectors by freeing domestic entry and prices while enforcing safety and environmental standards by direct regulation and inspection. Greek truckers would then be able to compete on a level playing field and be subject to the same rules as truckers from other Member States.

3.1. Regulation

The regulatory framework in Greece combines both European Union and Greek elements.

3.1.1. *European Union regulation*

The first major reform of road freight transport markets at the EU level was limited to international markets. That is, it was limited to services in which a vehicle is loaded in one Member State and unloaded in another. Under Council Regulation 881/92 of 26 March 1992, any carrier registered in a Member State could provide bilateral or transit services if it had an authorisation for international service. These authorisations were not restricted by quota (European Commission 1999, p. 33).

The next major reform (Council Regulation 3118/93 of 25 October 1993) gradually liberalised national or "cabotage" markets, that is, where a vehicle is loaded and unloaded in the same Member State. During the transition period, trucks could receive an authorisation to perform cabotage services in another Member State. These authorisations were valid for only one or two months and were subject to an increasing quota. Since 1 July 1998, the system of cabotage authorisations was abolished and any truck authorised to perform international transport services under regulation 881/92 may perform cabotage services in any Member State.

Council Regulation 3118/93 introduced an anomaly. Whereas truckers who carried goods between two points in the Member State where they were registered were subject to that State's rules, truckers who performed the same service but were registered in a different State were subject to Community rules (I*bid*, p. 35).

Important aspects of regulation of this sector relate to driver safety. Council Regulation 3820/85 of 20 December 1985 establishes driving time maxima and rest time minima (I*bid*, p. 49). Council Directive 88/599/EEC specifies how regulators should check that these standards are indeed met, specifying road-side checks and inspection visits to the offices of the transport companies. (I*bid*, p. 52).

A later directive (Council Directive 96/26/EC) harmonised entry standards. A licences can only be denied on the grounds of a lack of a good repute (as measured by criminal convictions), financial standing (the undertaking must have specified capital and reserves) or professional competence (the manager of the undertaking must pass an examination). Short-haul truckers are exempt (I*bid*, p. 53).

3.1.2. *Greek regulation*

Greek domestic regulation is aimed at ensuring "balance in the market." Laws and regulations in Greece, as elsewhere, distinguish between two parts to the road freight sector:

–   Transport on one's own account (which is covered by Law 1959/91) and

–   Transport of goods for another party in return for remuneration (which is covered by Law 383/76).

Road freight transport in Greece is also divided into prefectorial, national, and international. Prefectorial transport is outside the scope of restrictions on entry (moral character, capital, professionalism). There are also separate licenses for dangerous goods, for carrying fresh fruits and vegetables, and so on. These are not addressed here.

Those who transport on their own account, account for the vast majority of truckers in Greece, and their number has been increasing.

Table 4. Trucks registered in Greece

Type of permit	Number (1994)
Own account	812 538
Third party	36 495
Total	849 033

Source: Greek National Statistical Service.

Prefectoral authorities issue permits to companies for trucks to provide transport for that company, if the company can prove need. The amount of turnover determines the number of trucks permitted. This is a binding constraint – there are companies that would like more permits. These permits are not transferable. However, under Directive 84/647 and Presidential Decree 91/89, a company may hire or hire out trucks, with gross weight up to six tonnes, for which the company has a permit to transport goods on its own account.

Permits for trucks to haul goods for third parties are, by contrast, subject to a numerical limit and are transferable. The permits are bought and sold freely, if a transfer fee is paid to the Ministry. The current law allows the number of permits to increase, if the need were pinpointed. The need can be pinpointed only after a study is conducted. Since no study has been conducted, the number of permits for third party trucking has not increased.

Prices for trucking services within Greece are regulated according to Law 383/76. The law specifies both a minimum, set to cover operating costs, and a maximum, to limit the profits of the trucker. The difference is 18 to 20%. Under the law, the parties to a particular contract negotiate the price within these limits. However, actual transaction prices are, reportedly, often below the minimum due to competition.

The degree of competition from non-Greek registered trucks can be seen in the following table. In 1997, almost 16% of national and international hauling was done by trucks not registered in Greece, thus subject to European Union rules.

3.2. Conclusions and policy options

The deregulation, in other countries, of third-party haulage, has resulted in lower prices, improved quality of service and more flexibility. The general trend throughout Europe is to shift away from own-account to third party provision of trucking services. Deregulation has been partly responsible for the shift. But also, in competitive manufacturing and service sectors, companies are moving toward out-sourcing non-core activities, including own-account trucking (OECD, 2000, p. 6). Outsourcing trucking, or indeed the entire logistics chain, allows companies to have access to an entire network and pay only for usage. This, in turn, lowers barriers to entry into the markets for which transport is an input, which increases competition in those markets. Thus, the development of a flexible, reliable trucking or logistics sector has significant positive effects throughout an economy.

The trend toward outsourcing trucking services, however, cannot be followed among Greek registered trucks since the number of permits for third party transport is fixed. Instead, the number of trucks registered for own-account transport is growing. This suggests inefficiency: Presumably Greek manufacturing and service companies would make the same shift as other European companies if they had the same choices. Another indicator of efficiency is the number of empty back-hauls: Truckers for third-parties tend to have fewer empty back-hauls than own-account truckers.

If the objective of the regulation is to protect the third party truckers, then it is failing. Under EU rules, other European truckers can, provided they have an authorisation to operate internationally from any Member State, unrestrictedly enter the Greek national market. Competitors – own-account transport, EU registered trucks, non-EU trucks that nevertheless carry goods within Greece – are in law

Table 5. Development of goods transport in Greece
(in thousand million tonne-kilometres)

| | Rail | Road (Haulage on national territory, national and international) | | |
| | | Total | Haulage by vehicles registered in the country | |
			National	International
1970	0.7	4.9	n.a.	n.a.
1980	0.8	7.3	n.a.	n.a.
1990	0.6	10.9	n.a.	n.a.
1994	0.3	12.8	10.8	0.6
1995	0.3	14.8	12.4	0.9
1996	0.3	15.9	12.5	0.8
1997	0.3	16.5	13.0	0.9

Source: European Commission at *http://europa.eu.int/en/comm/dg07/tif/4_goods_transport/*.

or in practice able to expand their capacity in the Greek market. They will continue to operate there so long as it is feasible and profitable. Hence, they will continue to put pressure on Greek third party truckers' prices and costs. Indeed, actual prices allegedly sometimes lie below the legal minimum.

If the purpose of the regulation is to increase safety levels and reduce environmental effects, then the regulation is mis-directed. Even if the regulation could increase truckers' profits, increasing profits does not change the cost of compliance with these standards, the penalties for non-compliance, nor the enforcement practices of the regulator. In order to cause a shift in investment and practices to support environmental and safety standards, then the cost of compliance must fall, or the penalty for non-compliance rise, or enforcement increase.

The current regulatory framework is unsustainable. Liberalised foreign truckers compete against Greek truckers who are hampered by national restrictions on entry and pricing. Greece should follow the path of other countries that have reformed their trucking sectors by freeing entry and prices. Safety and environmental standards are enforced by direct regulation and inspection. Most recently, Laws 2800/2000 and 2801/2000 enforce these inspections at national and prefectoral levels. These changes would increase efficiency of the sector. And these changes would allow Greek truckers to compete, under the same rules, with foreign truckers. The establishment in March 2001 of a formal joint committee, with representatives of ministries, hauliers, unions, and transport experts, to map out a reform of the entire sector is a positive development.

Therefore,

– *Greece should, within the constraints of European Union rules on entry, liberalise entry by domestic trucks, whether for transport on their own account or for third parties. It should, in particular, abolish quotas and other numerical restrictions.*

– *Greece should remove price regulation for domestic trucks.*

NOTES

1. Directive 96/92 of 19 December 1996 concerning common rules for the internal market for electricity, OJ 1997, L 27/20.

2. Simple calculation shows that, if all new demand were met by new entry – that is, if PPC did not increase the amount it generates – then even after six years, new entrants would account for only one-quarter of the market. Only after more than a decade would PPC's share fall below half, assuming a total demand growth rate of 4% per annum.

3. Council Regulation No. 3577 of 7 December 1992 applying the principle of freedom to provide services to maritime transport within Member States (maritime cabotage) OJ L 364 of 12.12.92, p. 7.

4. The composition of the Coastal Transport Advisory Committee is: the Secretary General of the Ministry of Merchant Marine (Chairman), the Director of the Domestic Sea Transport Directorate of the MMM, the General Director of Merchant Ships Control General Directorate of MMM, a shipping expert appointed by the Minister, and one representative each from the following organisations: Ministry of the Aegean Sea, Ministry of Transport and Communications, Greek National Tourist Organisation, Hellenic Chamber of Shipping, Piraeus Chamber of Commerce and Industry, and three shipowners (one from short coastal shipping, one from Mediterranean cargo shipping, and one from passenger coastal shipping).

5. Cabotage means transport between two points within the same country.

6. If a commissioned ferry is to be sold, then it must be decommissioned by exiting the route it serves. Exiting a route requires the permission of the Minister. Nevertheless, in practice a company can buy a ferry along with the expectation that it will be licensed to continue to operate on the same route (Source: Kathimerini, 12 November 1999 and 8 March 2000).

7. The Greek government's primary concern, in 1995, with respect to the Italian-Greek routes was the viability of the route and the avoidance of any possible "price war" which could possibly hinder the smooth promotion of export and import trade or the transport of vehicles and passengers (EC para. 103)

BIBLIOGRAPHY

Athens News Agency, 1998.
> *Hermes Magazine*, "Shipping: A sea of profit amid highly competitive waters", http://www.ana.gr/hermes/1998/dec/shipping.htm, December 1998, No. 29.

ANEK Lines (1999),
> *Ellada-Italia* [Greece-Italy] (brochure).

ANEK (2000a),
> Available at http://www.anek.gr on 27 April 2000.

Attica Enterprises, SA. (1999),
> Press release 12 October at http://www.superfast.com/english/attica/1210.html on 4 April 2000.

Attica Enterprises, S.A. (1999b),
> *Annual Report and Accounts* 1998.

Attica Enterprises, S.A. (1998),
> *Annual Report and Accounts* 1997.

CNN (1999a),
> "Italian energy IPO on track," 11 October 1999, at <http://www.cnnfn.com/199/10/11/europe/enel> on 23 October 1999.

Copelouzos, Dimitrios (2000),
> Speech before the 4th Economist Government Roundtable discussion in Athens, 18 April 2000 available at < http://www.invgr.com/members/copelouzos_speech.htm >.

European Commission Decision of 9 December 1998 relating to a proceeding pursuant to Article 85 of the EC Treaty (IV/34466 – Greek Ferries), OJ L 109 27.4.1999, pp. 24-50.

European Commission (1999),
> *Guide to the Transport Acquis*, October. <http://europa.eu.int/en/comm/dg07/enlargement/guide2acquis/en.pdf> on 27 April 2000.

European Commission (2000),
> *Third Report on the Implementation of Council Regulation 3577/92 Applying the principle of freedom to provide services to maritime cabotage* (1997-1998), COM(2000)99, 24 February, at http://europa.eu.int/eur-lex/en/com/pdf/2000/com2000_0099en01.pdf on 3 April 2000.

Forbes Global (2000),
> "Athens at the Crossroads," pp. 42-45, 17 April. Also available at http://www.forbes.com/forbes/00/0417/6509088a3.htm on 26 April 2000.

Greek Ministry of Foreign Affairs, http://www.mfa.gr/aboutgr/brief_on_greece.htm on 1 April 2000.

Greek National Tourism Organisation http://www.vacation.net.gr/p/crete.html on 1 April 2000.

Hermes Magazine (1998a),
> "A sea of profit amid highly competitive waters", December, at http://www.ana.gr/hermes/1998/dec/shipping.htm on 23 January 2000.

International Energy Agency (2000),
> *Competition in Electricity Markets*, Paris.

Invest in Greece (2000*b*), "Attica Enterprises Holdings SA agreed to acquire an approximate 38% equity stake in Strintzis Lines Shipping SA," August 31st, 1999, at < http://www.invgr.com/members/attica_strintzis.htm> on 27 April 2000.

Kahn, Alfred (1970-71), *The Economics of Regulation: Principles and Institutions*, Vol. 2, "Destructive Competition and the Quality of Service," Ch. 5, pp. 172-250.

Kathimerini (1999),
"Record-breaking profits for shippers," 13 December 1999 at http://www.k-english.com/news.asp on 9 March 2000.

Kathimerini (1999),
"Aegean Airlines completes its acquisition of Air Greece" 30 December 1999 at http://www.k-english.com/news.asp on 1 April 2000.

Kathimerini (2000),
"MFD makes a tactical retreat from partnership with Lesvos," 8 March 2000 at http://www.k-english.com/news.asp on 1 April 2000.

Littlechild, S.C. (1998),
"*Contribution to the European Electricity Regulation Forum*," 6 February, Florence, Italy.

Lloyd's List (1999),
"Ferry license system in firing line," 5 February 1999.

Minoan Lines (1999),
Greece-Italy (brochure).

Minoan Lines (2000*a*),
http://minoanl.minoan.gr/corporat.html on 27 April 2000.

OECD (2001),
Roundtable 115: Road Transport for Own Account in Europe, Paris, May.

Office of Electricity Regulation (1998),
Annual Report 1998, at http://www.ofgem.gov.uk/elarch/index.htm on 10 May 2000.

Psaraftis, Harilaos N. (1996),
"Changing Tides: Countdown to 2004: Greek coastal shipping prepares for deregulation and colossal changes," ORMS *Today*, Vol. 23, No. 3, June at http://lionhrtpub.com/orms/orms-6-96/greece.html on 14 February 2000.

Public Power Corporation (PPC) (1998),
Annual Report 1998.

Public Power Corporation (PPC) (2000*a*), "Management and Organization" at http://www.dei.gr/company/managem.htm on 15 February 2000.

Strintzis Lines Shipping S.A. (1999),
Press Release, "Strintzis Lines Shipping S.A. announces that it has obtained two licenses from the Ministry of Merchant Marine for 2 New Buildings for the Chios – Mytilini & Andros – Tinos – Myconos – Ikaria – Samos routes," Piraeus, 13 May. at http://www.strintzis.gr/ on 4 April 2000.

Superfast Ferries Maritime S.A. (2000),
"Superfast Ferries Maritime S.A.Files Application for Listing at the Main Market of the Athens Stock Exchange,"15 February at http://www.superfast.com/english/deltia.html on 4 April.

BACKGROUND REPORT ON
REGULATORY REFORM IN
THE TELECOMMUNICATIONS INDUSTRY*

* This report was principally prepared by **Natasha Constantelou** of the National Technical University of Athens with the participation of **Dimitri Ypsilanti**, of the Directorate on Science, Technology, and Industry. It has benefited from comments provided by colleagues throughout the OECD Secretariat, by the Government of Greece, and by Member countries as part of the peer review process. This report was peer reviewed in December 2000 by the OECD's Working Party on Telecommunication and Information Services Policies with the participation of the Competition Law and Policy Committee.

TABLE OF CONTENTS

List of Tables

List of Figures

Executive Summary

Background Report on Regulatory Reform in the Telecommunications Industry

The telecommunications sector in OECD countries has seen significant regulatory reform in recent years. Twenty-seven OECD countries had, in 2001, unrestricted market access to all forms of telecommunications, including voice telephony, infrastructure investment and investment by foreign enterprises, compared to only a handful just a few years ago. The success of the liberalisation process depends on the presence of a transparent and effective regulatory regime that enables the development of full competition, while effectively protecting other public interests. There is a need to promote entry in markets where formerly regulated monopolists remain dominant and to consider elimination of traditionally separate regulatory frameworks applicable to telecommunications infrastructure and services and to broadcasting infrastructures and services.

Greece has committed to open its market to full competition on 1 January 2001. Since 1990 Greece has been making progress, albeit slowly, in adopting pro-competitive regulatory principles. Greece's programme for regulatory reform in telecommunications has been steered and reinforced by the principles prescribed by European Union (EU) directives and the 1997 WTO agreement on basic telecommunications. In 1996, Greece initiated the first phase of the privatisation of the Hellenic Telecommunication Organisation (OTE), the state-owned, incumbent monopoly. The privatisation is expected to continue during 2001 and the government has stated that they are looking for a foreign strategic partner for OTE.

Greece's market liberalisation is occurring several years after most EU countries have fully opened their markets (on 1 January 1998) and established new regulatory frameworks. This relatively late start could have provided Greece with a unique opportunity to draw on the experience of these countries so as to be able to apply best practice methods of regulatory reform. Unfortunately this window of opportunity has not been used. As of the beginning of the third quarter of 2000 a number of key pieces of legislation and regulation had yet to be implemented, including the new draft law and the licensing framework. Although it is clear from the EU's 1999 Communication Review that during 2000-2003 there will be a new emphasis on streamlining regulations, including the licensing procedures, insufficient foresight has been given to implementing new best-practice regulations. The licensing regime needs to be streamlined to facilitate quick market entry at the expiry of the exclusive provision period. Interconnection charges need to be cost-based with accounting separation introduced. From 2001 there will be a need to promote effective competition in all communication markets. The nature and extent of universal service obligations has been defined in the new Law, however, a method of funding and delivering them in a cost-effective, technologically neutral, way needs to be established. The new telecommunications law, that has recently been adopted by the Greek Parliament (published in the Official Journal of the Hellenic Republic on 19 December 2000) and came into force in January 2001, offers a timely opportunity to install such pro-competitive regulatory principles. But while appropriate pro-competitive legislation is an important step, it is only *one* necessary step. The regulatory rules must then be promptly and effectively implemented by a well-empowered independent regulator to develop a fair, transparent and stable competitive environment for all market players. The new draft law provides a framework for this to occur. Unfortunately there are signs that in some areas like price regulation and licensing conditions, the rhetoric of reform has not been backed up by decisions made by government. This must change.

Technological change and 'convergence' are also further complicating regulatory reform. Greece has not yet recognised that, like other OECD counties, it must now address the challenge of not only completing the move to an effectively competitive telecommunications market, but also of preparing for the 'next generation' regulatory regime which convergence will necessitate.

This report examines Greece's regulatory reform effort thus far and its impact on the performance of telecommunications markets. The report concludes that there needs to be an accelerated effort to ensure that Greece's framework for regulation in telecommunications is at best practice levels and provides the dynamism necessary to support network based services necessary for an electronic commerce environment. The adjustments that have been made in anticipation of the opening of the market to competition, such as in the area of price rebalancing, have had positive benefits.

1. THE TELECOMMUNICATIONS SECTOR IN GREECE

1.1. Development of telecommunications in Greece

The Hellenic Telecommunications Organisation was founded in 1949 and given exclusive rights for the operation of telecommunication service in the country. Table 1 presents a brief account of major events in the history of Greek telecommunications.

In Greece, as in most OECD countries until the late 1980s, the traditional organisational structure of the telecommunication sector has been a monopoly market. Since the early 1990s, however, this structure has gradually come into question for a number of reasons. First, the poor performance of the public network was inhibiting the recovery of the domestic economy, the attraction of foreign capital, and the expansion of new production activities. Second, Greece's membership in the European Union required it to comply with European telecommunication policy Directives and shift to a more liberalised market environment. In this context, as well, unless the country was willing to show some progress towards telecommunication market liberalisation, the flow of Commission funds to the increasingly troubled Greek economy would be seriously delayed. Last, but not least, the emergence of advanced communication networks and services called into question the prevailing formal institutional set-up of the sector. These technological innovations offered 'windows of opportunity' for entry into new service areas, which had started to become increasingly appealing to both Greek and international investors.

Three phases in the history of Greek telecommunication policy-making can be identified.[1] The first phase (1949-1980) was characterised by massive investment in network infrastructure in an attempt to provide universal telephone service across the country. Given the economic euphoria the country

Table 1. Major events in Greek telecommunications (1930-2000)

Date / Event	Comments
1930	Establishment of the Greek Telephone Company S.A. (GTC) with Siemens-Halske as its main shareholder. GTC developed local networks in 23 Greek towns. In 1946, 75% of GTC's foreign shares were handed over to the Greek State as compensation for war reparations.
1949: Law 1049/1949: Foundation of OTE	OTE was founded as a merger of GTC and Cable & Wireless and had exclusive rights over the operation of telecommunication services in the country.
1973: Presidential Decree 165/1973	The Decree extended Law 1049/1949 and specified OTE's relationship with the State. In particular: • The State should not interfere in OTE's management; • OTE's investment programmes should conform to the annual and five-year government investment programmes; • International agreements, contracts, and tariffs should be approved by the Ministry of National Economy and the Ministry of Transport and Communications.
1982: Presidential Decree 1256/1982	OTE and its subsidiaries became parts of the public sector.
1985: Presidential Decree 58/1985	The Decree provided for the 'socialisation' of OTE as a public utility company allowing employee representatives to participate in OTE's Board of Directors.
1990: Law No. 1892/90	Liberalisation of value-added services and of mobile telephony.
1992: Law No. 2075/92	Opening of market to mobile services – OTE excluded from mobile market.
1994: Law No. 2246/94	Liberalisation of all telecommunication services, except public voice telecommunication, and full liberalisation of mobile market allowing OTE to participate.
2000: New Law on Telecommunications	The law has five basic aims: protect the consumer; safeguard free and healthy competition; safeguard personal information; the provision of universal service; and the growth of telecommunications. The law was passed by the Greek Parliament in early December 2000.

enjoyed in the 1960s and 1970s, financing network expansion was not particularly problematic. However, the Hellenic Telecommunications Organisation (OTE) was covering its needs for switching and transmission equipment through imports, primarily from East European countries. Thus, the 1980s found OTE with an amalgamation of 12 types of increasingly obsolete analogue switches from different vendors, a situation that started to cause problems in the operation and maintenance of the network.

The second phase (1981-1990), marked by a radical shift in the national political scene, resulted in OTE becoming a 'socialised' enterprise, which essentially meant an increased representation of employees on the Board of Directors (BoD). Its performance indicators, however, were deteriorating. Not only was investment in infrastructure modernisation less than the OECD average, but also traditional ties with the government left no room for autonomy in OTE's day-to-day operations and management.

The third phase began in 1991 and has been characterised by a continuous improvement in network infrastructure and a slow shift towards a more liberalised regulatory environment. In 1990, the deregulation of value-added services and mobile telephony services was enacted by Law No. 1892/90, according to which, apart from the Hellenic Telecommunications Organisation, other public and private operators could provide the aforementioned services.

In 1992, the legislative framework for the partial opening of the telecommunications market was enacted by the framework – Law No. 2075/92, which *inter alia* provided that mobile telephony services could only be provided by private operators, excluding OTE from the mobile telephony market. Following a public tender, two mobile telephony licenses were granted to "STET Hellas SA" and "PANAFON S.A".

In 1994, Law No. 2075/92 was replaced by the framework-Law No. 2246/94, which enacted *inter alia* the liberalisation of all telecommunications services, with the exception of voice services and the provision of public switched telecommunication networks. Additionally, this Law provided for the full liberalisation of the mobile telephony market, allowing OTE to enter this market segment. The Law also defined the responsibilities of the Ministry of Transport and Communications (MTC, hereafter called 'the Ministry') and provided for the establishment of an independent regulatory authority for the sector, the National Telecommunications and Post Commission (EETT).[2] A new telecommunications Law, submitted to Parliament in September 2000 and approved in early December 2000 replaced Law 2246 in the light of full liberalisation on 1 January 2001.

1.1.1. *Derogation from* EU *market opening*

In June 1996, the Greek State (currently the majority shareholder of OTE) and OTE itself applied for an extension of the EU's 1 January 1998 deadline for full liberalisation in the provision of voice telephony and the associated network infrastructure until 1 January 2003. The request was made on the grounds that OTE needed further time and revenues for the digitalisation and modernisation of its public network infrastructure. Thus:

> *The authorities of the Hellenic Republic maintain that due to constraints on national financial resources, the high cost and the size of OTE's modernisation programme, aggravated by the burden of delivering telecommunications services throughout the Hellenic Republic, full digitalisation by the year 2003 can only be achieved if OTE is further guaranteed sufficient revenues via the continuation until that date of its current exclusive rights.*[3]

The European Commission, in rejecting most of the arguments used by the Government to justify an extended derogation, granted the Greek State an extension until 31 December 2000 to remove all restrictions on the provision of voice telephony and the underlying public network infrastructure (Decision 97/607). The Commission agreed to this derogation solely on the basis of a single justification, that is to allow OTE sufficient time to rebalance its tariffs. However, this derogation was conditional on the Greek government following a timetable and implementing the following provisions:

- Notification to the European Commission by 1 October 1997, instead of 1 July 1996, of all measures necessary to liberalise the provision of services on (a) networks established by the provider of the telecommunication service, (b) infrastructures provided by third parties, and (c) the sharing of networks, and other facilities and sites;

- Notification to the European Commission by 18 March 1998, instead of 11 January 1997, of all legislative changes necessary to implement full competition by 31 December 2000, including proposals for the funding of universal service;

- Notification to the European Commission by 31 December 1999, instead of 1 January 1997, of draft licenses for voice telephony and/or the underlying network providers;

- Publication by 30 June 2000, instead of 1 July 1997, of the licensing conditions applicable to public voice telephony and of interconnection charges, as appropriate and in both cases in accordance with applicable EU directives; and

- Award of new licenses and amendment of existing licenses by 31 December 2000 to enable the competitive provision of public voice telephony services.

In most cases the deadlines set by this timetable were met. Several of these conditions had either not fully been met by the third quarter of 2000 or had been considerably delayed. This applies in particular to the requirement to award licenses before 31 December 2000, which only materialised in late December, and to the requirement to make any necessary modifications in OTE's license by 31 December 2000. In addition, although a new operating licence for OTE had been drafted and was sent to the Commission for approval, no new licence for the incumbent has yet been published providing for the abolition of its exclusive rights.[4] These delays have serious implications for the rapid development of competition in the Greek market since, as new entrants claimed the late publication of licensing terms and conditions would not allow them to be fully operational by 1 January 2001. The delay in implementing these requirements is symptomatic of the period 1995-1999 in Greece as concerns telecommunications policy. This period was characterised by significant delay in adopting and formulating required policies and taking decisions to help the process of liberalisation.

This refusal of the prolongation of the derogation until 2003 by the EC can be justified. However, given the extent of the external investments by OTE in recent years, one can question whether a derogation was necessary at all. Secondly, external investments have implication for domestic universal service since domestic revenues are being leveraged to finance such investment. OTE seems to be well positioned to bear the cost of universal service in Greece given spare resources for external investment and its profitability (its net income margin[5] ranged from 24.3% to 16.4% during the period 1995-99). The diversion of investment effort, while possibly undertaken for longer-term strategic reasons, nevertheless had implications for domestic investment. In particular, it slowed down the upgrading of the network towards best-practice technology. In turn this will have longer-term impacts on consumers, using industries and the Greek government's plans to develop the information society in Greece. If OTE were operating in a competitive environment there would be no reason to question external investments.

1.2. The national context for telecommunication policies

Unlike most other OECD PTOs that had long ago shifted their strategies from the 1980s model of achieving high teledensity to the 1990s model of establishing sophisticated intelligent networks, OTE throughout the 1990s put more emphasis on the expansion of basic network infrastructure and the satisfaction of pending demand than on the modernisation of public network. As a result, the provision of all advanced network features was considerably delayed and started to materialise only after 1997. The strategic focus on expansion of the fixed network has achieved considerable success. Teledensity for fixed-line connections has steadily increased and, digitalisation of the public network has reached 90.6% in December 1999 compared to 37.1% at the end of 1995 (see Section 3).

In the mobile sector a duopoly regime was introduced in 1993 for the provision of digital mobile telephony. OTE, with its subsidiary company COSMOTE, entered the market as the third player in April 1998, despite the contention by Panafon and Stet Hellas who challenged the validity of COSMOTE's mobile license before the Council of State as being contrary to the Greek constitution and EU Law. Since 1998, the take up of mobile services in Greece has increased dramatically reaching 41% penetration rate in mid-2000, a figure comparable to the OECD average.

Value-added networks and services began to be offered in Greece in the early 1990s. These were either national networks built on leased lines for the provision of data and other value-added services to closed user groups, or international value-added networks which had established local points of presence in Greece to serve their international clientele. Moreover, unlike the situation in other OECD markets where data and satellite communication markets have been opened to competition as early as 1994, OTE was given special permission by the European Commission to maintain its exclusive rights over public data networks and services until 1997.

The use of alternative network infrastructure was liberalised in October 1997, but only for the provision of liberalised services. Although Greek utility companies, such as the National Railways and the Public Electricity Company started fairly early to investigate the possibility of utilising their infrastructures to enter the telecommunication market, none of them took the initiative at that early stage to enter as a network provider. In the satellite segment, independent suppliers expressed an early interest in market entry soon after the pending legislation set the environment for competition.

On the institutional side, the National Telecommunications Commission was established in 1995 as the independent regulatory authority for the sector. The Commission's tasks included the enforcement of sector-specific regulations, the monitoring of the telecommunication market, the provision of consultation to the Ministry, and the resolution of disputes arising out of the provision of telecommunications services. In 1999, the Commission undertook under its jurisdiction the supervision of Posts and has thus been renamed National Commission for Telecommunications and Posts (hereafter EETT). Since its establishment, however, EETT has remained severely understaffed due to the lengthy bureaucratic procedures required for the recruitment of personnel in the wider public sector. In addition, there has not been a clear division of responsibilities between EETT and the Ministry as EETT's advisory role to the Ministry has often been tangled up with regulatory duties.

On the regulatory side, over the last several years the transposition of key EC Directives proceeded under pressure from the EC at a relatively fast pace after long delays in adopting national measures. Currently, all major EC Directives have been transposed into National Law. However, this transposition has remained to a large extent inactive as secondary legislation and other necessary pre-conditions (*e.g.* licensing frameworks, interconnection frameworks and prices, an appropriate accounting system and a costing model for OTE) are still pending. Since the EC Directives are relatively general, transposition needs to be accompanied by more detailed regulatory decisions to flesh out how a Directive will be implemented.

EETT has begun to take an open approach in decision-making by initiating public consultation processes on telecommunication development matters, such as the unbundling of the local loop, the allocation of fixed-wireless access licences, etc. Such an approach, however, has been criticised by some market participants as cumbersome and time-consuming at a time when speedier decision-making procedures need to be established in the light of the forthcoming market liberalisation. While there is an urgent need to catch-up on the years of indecision and delay, it is also necessary to have and maintain an open and effective consultative procedure.

The new government that was formed after the April 2000 parliamentary elections appears to have the political will to promote the necessary structural changes in the Greek economy and to put an end to the administrative difficulties that have burdened competition in the telecommunication sector. For example, it rapidly drafted a new Telecommunication Law and submitted it to Parliament in September 2000. The law, is a major step in the right direction. However, as is noted below, other decisions, such as that pertaining to the allocation of fixed wireless licences to the incumbent, indicate the need for further efforts to create open and non-discriminatory regulatory frameworks.

In the light of the upcoming full liberalisation in the telecommunication market and the emergence of an information society, Greece should take any action necessary to speed up the practical implementation of the institutional framework for the sector. In addition, experience from other OECD countries shows that reliance on market forces accelerates the building of modern communication infrastructures and the diffusion of new technologies. In this respect, Greece should limit government intervention and allow more room for market mechanisms in order to create a more vigorous environment for competition and the development of information society.

The delay in implementing key measures is also having repercussions in other key economic policy areas. For example, the government has placed high priority in its policy agenda on the Information Society, as outlined in the 1998 'Green Paper on the development of the Greek Information Society'.[6] If adequate measures are not in place to enhance public access to broadband communication infrastructures and thus allow Greece to participate in the emerging Information Society, these goals will not be attained.

1.3. General features of the regulatory regime

Since 1995, observed progress has been made in delivering secondary legislation for the sector (*i.e.* Presidential Decrees and Ministerial Decisions). The main Laws and Presidential Decrees issued include:

The regulatory framework has been supplemented by a number of Ministerial Decisions which define, for example, the terms and conditions for the granting of Licenses and Declarations, the fees associated with their granting, etc. All this secondary legislation stems from Law 2246/94, which remained for a long time the primary source of regulation for the sector. Notwithstanding, the content of all legislative acts, and by implication their policy objectives, are borrowed from the EC and essentially represent translations of the text of the EC Directives.

The main driving force behind the fast compliance of the Greek regulatory framework with the EU Directives has in fact been the financial pressure exercised by the EC upon the Greek government. More specifically, in one of its routine reviews in the telecommunications regulatory and licensing regime in EU member states, the European Commission has found that Greece is seriously behind in its compliance with key EC directives. In this context, the Commission suspended subsidies in 1997 to OTE of approximately ECU 49.9 million for network modernisation and personnel training, pending harmonisation of Greek law with EC Directives. This decision put extra pressure on the Ministry to harmonise the Greek regulatory framework at a faster pace than originally envisaged.

This effort, however, was not always followed by the practical implementation of provisions included in these Directives. For example, despite its full transposition, Directive 96/2/EC with regard to the liberalisation of mobile and personal communications remained inactive in that the Greek State did not consider the option to issue additional licenses for mobile services. Two infringement proceedings against the Greek State for failure to implement Directive 96/2/EC are currently pending before the European Court of Justice in connection with the granting of licenses for DCS 1800 and DECT systems.[7] However, the Ministry has recently declared its intention to award a fourth mobile license by the end of 2000. In July 2000, the EETT initiated a consultation process seeking the views of new and existing market participants regarding the number, conditions of award, and duration of potentially new mobile licenses.

Similarly, there is a Ministerial Decision based on Law 2246 that specifies the procedure to be followed by an applicant for the provision of services that require the use of frequency spectrum. This remains to a large extent inactive due to the fact that neither the Ministry nor EETT have taken any decisions regarding the most suitable method for the allocation of available frequency spectrum.[8]

In the experience of the OECD, a bold shift in policy to ensure that telecommunication competition develops rapidly has yielded important economic benefits to industry and users. The telecommunications laws and regulations of a country are thus crucial in providing the future framework for the Information society and electronic commerce, which will require an adequate infrastructure.

Box 1. Developments in the Greek telecommunications regulatory regime

1. 1992: Law 2075/92 (A129): Constituted the regulatory framework of the telecommunications sector, transposing Directives 90/387/EEC and 90/388/EEC.

2. 1994: Law 2246/94 (A 272): Replaced Law 2075/92 and constitutes the Framework Law for the sector. It has been replaced by Law 2867/00 (A 273) on the Organisation and Operation of the Telecommunication Sector in Greece.

3. 1997: Law 2465/97 (A 28): Amended, partially, Law 2246/94 as regards the granting of licenses and declarations.

4. 1998: Law 2578/98 (A 30): Partial transposition of Directive 96/19/EC, in accordance with the derogation period granted to Greece for full competition in the telecommunication sector.

5. 1997: Law 2472/97 (A 50): Transposition of Directive 95/46/EC with regard to the processing of personal data.

6. 1999: Law 2774/99 (A 287): Transposition of Directive 97/66/EC with regard to the protection of personal data and privacy in the telecommunications sector.

7. 2000: Law 2840/00 provides EETT with regulatory powers over the award of both general and individual licences as well as over the relevant criteria for their award.

8. 2000: Law 2867/00 (A 273) on the Organisation and Operation of the Telecommunication Sector in Greece, replaced Law 2246/94.

Presidential Decrees (P.D):

a) 1995: P.D 424/95 (A 243): Transposition of Directive 91/263/EEC concerning telecommunications terminal equipment, including the mutual recognition of their conformity.

b) 1995: P.D 437/95 (A250): OTE's license according to Law 2246/94 and 2257/92.

c) 1996: P.D 40/96 (A 27): Transposition of Directive 92/44/EEC on the application of ONP to leased lines.

d) 1997: P.D 212/97 (A 166) Transposition of Directive 94/46/EEC with regard to the liberalization of satellite communications.

e) 1998: P.D 122/98 (A 103): Transposition of Directive 93/97/EEC with regard to satellite earth station equipment.

f) 1998: P.D 123/98 (A 103): Transposition of Directive 95/51/EC as regards the use of cable networks for the provision of liberalized telecommunications services.

g) 1998: P.D 124/98 (A103): Transposition of Directive 96/2/EC with regard to the liberalization of mobile and personal communications.

h) 1999: P.D 9/99 (A5): Transposition of Directive 95/47/EC on the use of standards for the transmission of television signals.

i) 1999: P.D 156/99 (A 153): Transposition of Directive 97/51/EC as regards the implementation of ONP to a competitive environment in telecommunications.

j) 1999: P.D 157/99 (A153): Transposition of Directive 97/13/EC as regards the common framework for general authorizations and individual licenses.

k) 1999: P.D 165/99 (A 159): Transposition of Directive 97/33/EC on interconnection.

l) 1999: P.D 181/99 (A 170): Transposition of Directive 98/10/EC with regard to liberalization of voice telephony, universal service with the application of ONP.

In this context, the Ministry prepared a new Framework Law to replace Law 2246/94 with the aim to provide the legal and regulatory framework for the development of competition. In late-1999, a draft text of the Law was put on the Ministry's Website to allow interested parties to submit their comments and suggestions. The consultation showed that many potential market participants believed that the draft Greek law, although covering the main issues necessary to transform the telecommunication sector from a monopoly to a competitive market following the general requirements of the European Union, did not sufficiently provide for the means to create such a market. In particular, there were several major weaknesses in the draft 1999 Law:

a) The draft law did not clearly clarify the responsibilities of the different government bodies with a role in the sector. In this respect, it did not provide the regulator (EETT) with sufficient independence or power to meet its proclaimed objectives, that is to 'establish a regulatory framework for the development of telecommunications in an open and competitive environment'.

b) It foresaw a number of bodies for the organisation and supervision of the sector that would complicate rather than simplify decision-making.

c) It included restrictions in the organisation of EETT that would limit its flexibility to meet changing market structures.

d) It contained too much detail on regulations, which would be better addressed in secondary legislation implementing the law.

The second draft of the Law, which was submitted by the newly appointed Minister in early July 2000, incorporates most of the comments and suggestions received during the consultation process and, to a certain extent, has addressed the aforementioned inadequacies. The new Law is more precise and does not enter into practical details that are more appropriately dealt with in regulations. Its most distinct feature is that it reinforces EETT by transferring powers to it from the Ministry, as mandated by the EC regulatory provisions regarding national regulatory authorities (NRAs), in relation to licensing, supervision of interconnection, universal service, the implementation of cost-accounting systems, numbering, frequencies, and rights of way. Details of the main provisions of the new draft Law in some of these key areas are included in respective sections below.

1.4. Telecommunications market and participants

Several companies have sought to enter the liberalised segments of the Greek market to provide advanced communications and services. Overall, although the number of service providers in the liberalised segments has increased, the structure of the market has not undergone major changes as the public voice segment of the market is still under OTE's monopoly.

Currently, apart from the major market players (*i.e.* OTE and the 3 mobile operators), there are over 200 telecommunication service providers operating in the Greek market. Most of them are active in the

Table 2.   Structure of the Greek telecommunication market

Services	Number of providers
Voice services to closed user groups, pre-paid telephone cards	30
Audiotex	9
Data services	17
Fax services	17
Resale of mobile services	6
Internet access	143

Source: EETT Annual Report 1999.

market for Internet services, while a significant number of companies offer value-added and voice services to closed user groups. The changing structure of the Greek telecommunication market is summarised in Table 2.

In mid-July 2000 the Ministry announced its plans to award 9 licenses for Fixed-Wireless-Access. This resulted out of a public consultation process initiated by EETT among interested parties. By late November 2000, EETT had already started preparing the auction procedure for the award of licenses among the list of seven prospective bidders, including the Greek cellular market operator Panafon, the Public Power Corporation (DEH) and a consortium between STET International Netherlands NV, a holding company owned by Telecom Italia, and Forthnet. Five licenses were awarded to successful bidders in early December 2000.

1.4.1. Mobile

A duopoly had been established in the market for digital mobile services since 1993, when GSM services were first introduced into Greece. Prior to that, there was no analogue mobile system in operation. The two companies with licenses to operate in the market were Panafon S.A. and STET Hellas S.A., a subsidiary of the Italian STET International. Each company paid a license fee of GRD 32 billion (USD 102 million) to the Greek State. According to their licenses, the mobile operators had to construct their own wireless networks and were allowed to resell any excess capacity. Today, both companies offer wireless leased lines for the set up of virtual private networks (VPNs) for corporate customers and closed user groups. Table 3 presents the current ownership structure and market share of mobile operators in Greece.

Panafon was established in 1991 as a joint venture between Vodafone (45%), France Telecom Mobile International (35%), Intracom S.A. (10%) – the largest IT company in Greece – and Databank (10%) – the leading Greek information services provider, which is 50% part of the Intracom Group. The strategy pursued by the company has been one of rapid expansion of mobile network infrastructure in order to meet the required service targets and be ahead of its competitors. The company maintains a group of 5 service providers for its GSM services. In 1998 a minority stake of the company was floated on the Athens Stock Exchange. In late 1999, France Telecom withdrew the majority of its shares and Vodafone became the main shareholder.[9]

STET Hellas (known as Telestet) started off as a subsidiary company of the Italian STET Mobile Holding. At a later stage, NYNEX Network Systems and the Greek Insurance group of companies, Interamerican acquired a 20% and 5.2% stakes respectively. Italian managers head the company. The strategy pursued by STET Hellas has been one of slower network expansion in favour of better service quality. Initially, STET Hellas had only one service provider/distribution partner, Mobitel, a company established for this purpose. At end of 1998, Mobitel joined the Panafon group. STET Hellas changed its retail strategy and gradually established a network of 7 service providers and 14 direct retail points. In June 1998 a minority percentage of Stet Hellas floated into the NASDAQ and Amsterdam Stock Exchanges.

During the first three years of operation, the duopoly regime resulted in very similar tariff structures being offered by both companies. It was only after 1995 that companies started to promote service 'packages' of customer tailored solutions as well as value-added services in collaboration with local service providers.

OTE was granted the right to provide mobile telephony services pursuant to the Telecommunications Law and its operating license. However, it did not pay for the license an amount equal to the one paid by the other mobile operators. Instead, it paid GRD 15.5 billion to the State as an 'investment in kind' for the use of frequency spectrum in order to launch the DCS 1800 technology and transferred this right to its subsidiary COSMOTE during 1997. In May 1997, a subsidiary of Telenor AS, the Norwegian Telecommunications Company, acquired a 30% interest in COSMOTE. COSMOTE began commercial operation in April 1998. COSMOTE currently markets its services through exclusive COSMOTE sales points, OTE sales points, and five other non-affiliated service providers.

Table 3. Mobile operators and their current ownership status

Operator and market share (as in March 2000)	Ownership status (as in September 2000)
Panafon (41%) (10%), public investors (32%).	Vodafone Europe Holdings (55%), France Telecom Mobile International (3%), Intracom
Stet Hellas (30%)	Stet Mobile Holding NV (Telecom Italia) (58.1%), Bell Atlantic-NYNEX (Verizon) (20%), public investors (16.7%), Interamerican Group (5.2%).
COSMOTE (29%)	OTE (70%), Telenor B-Invest AS (22%), W.R. Com Enterprises 8%.

Source: Company Websites and MTC (2000).

An initial public offering of COSMOTE took place in late September 2000 offering 15% of its share capital in its IPO. COSMOTE began trading on the Athens and London exchanges in early October with a market capitalisation of between GRD1.029 and 1.15 trillion (USD 2.6 billion – USD 2.97 billion).[10]

OTE's attempt to break the duopoly in the mobile market was considered by the two other GSM operators as a violation in the terms of their licenses, which guaranteed a duopoly regime until the year 2000. To justify the uneven cost of license between COSMOTE and the other two operators, COSMOTE argued that a number of factors were taken into account by the State, such as (a) that GSM companies in a duopoly regime kept prices (and profits) too high; (b) that the level of investment for GSM was much lower than for DCS, and (c) that GSM companies had significant revenues from roaming services whereas COSMOTE could not offer roaming from the start. Both Panafon and STET Hellas challenged the validity of COSMOTE's mobile license before the Council of State and the European Commission but have since withdrawn their complaint.

In 1999, both Panafon and STET Hellas were designated by EETT as organisations with significant market power (SMP) in the mobile services market.[11] This allows the regulator to mandate access to the network of these operators. However, no specific obligations have been imposed on them legally. It is expected that COSMOTE will also be designated as having significant market power in 2000.

In mid-July 2000, the Ministry announced that a fourth mobile license will be awarded by the end of 2000 for the development of a DCS 1 800 system, following a public consultation led by EETT. No final decisions have yet been made regarding the award of UMTS licenses. According to State officials, any decision on this matter will be a co-decision between the Ministry of National Economy, the Ministry of Communications and Transport and EETT.[12] In late September 2000, EETT made a provision call for tender for the selection of an experienced consultant organisation to advise it on this matter.

1.4.2. *Privatisation of* OTE

In April 1996 the Government began the privatisation of OTE through public subscription and private placement of a minority 7.5% of the company's share capital. Discussions on the privatisation of OTE had started as early as 1992, but were blocked due to political discord and the opposition of OTE trade unions. Table 4 summarises milestones in OTE's privatisation process.

Presently the State through the Ministry of National Economy holds 51% of OTE. The Government has announced its intention to seek a strategic partner for OTE in exchange for a significant number of OTE shares. The Ministry intends to maintain some control in key areas where co-decisions will be required but does not envisage maintaining a golden share. However, keycontrol of OTE through the company's charter is equivalent to a golden share and would likely lack transparency. There are provisions in the new Law which provide the State with sufficient powers in the case of national emergencies – there should be no need for any further control over OTE. It appears that the Minister is determined to proceed fast with the process of finding strategic partners so that they are in place by spring 2001. The first step was made in late September 2000 when the Greek parliament voted overwhelmingly in favour of allowing the government to sell its controlling stake in OTE.

Table 4.   Milestones in OTE's privatisation

Date	Event	Comments
November 1992	First privatisation attempt announced	*The plan*
		The Conservative Government introduced the 'strategic investor initiative'.
		This involved the sale of up to 49% of OTE shares as follows:
		• 35% shares plus management responsibilities for a decade to an experienced foreign strategic investor.
		• 7% shares floated in international stock markets.
		• 7% shares floated in the Athens Stock Exchange.
		The motives
		• 'Shock therapy' as remedy for OTE's increased managerial and organisational inefficiencies.
		• Exclusive financing of OTE's modernisation programme by foreign investors without the Commission's support.
		• Privatisation revenues expected to alleviate State budget deficit and aise international interest in the domestic stock market.
		The timetable
		Completion by September 1993
September 1993	Freezing of privatisation negotiations	The Conservative Government lost its marginal majority of one vote when an MP decided to withdraw his support. The affiliated press related the event with an earlier Government decision to halt procurement negotiations with local suppliers so that the strategic investor could take the decision. The country was led to premature elections and the Socialists returned to power.
November 1994	Second privatisation attempt cancelled	The Minister of National Economy found no interest from international investors.
January 1996	New Socialist Prime Minister	As soon as the new Prime Minister was elected he gave immediate priority to State restructuring, including OTE privatisation.
April 1996	OTE's initial public offering (IPO) took place	The primary offer involved the issue of 31.6 million shares representing 7.5% of the company's share capital. State's share in the company was reduced to 92%.
June 1997	2nd Public offering	The Government sold 12.6% through private placement to institutional investors in Greece and abroad and through public subscription in Greece only. The company was also listed in the London Stock Exchange.
April 1998	Block Trade	The Government sold another 3.3% of its stake. through block trading to institutional investors.
November 1998	3rd Public offering and entry into the NYS	Another 10% of state-owned shares were offered through public subscription and private placement reducing the State's participation in OTE to 65%. At the same time, OTE became the first Greek company to be listed on the NYS.
July 1999	4th public offering	Another 14% of state-owned shares were offered through public subscription and private placement reducing the State's participation to 51%.

Source: Greek press (various) and OTE (2000).

2. REGULATORY STRUCTURES AND THEIR REFORM

2.1. Regulatory institutions and processes

Under the provisions of the early Law 2246/94, the Ministry of Transport and Communications, and more specifically its General Secretariat for Communications, and EETT shared regulatory tasks for the sector. According to the Law, the Ministry was responsible for exercising policy and regulatory functions and for initiating proposals for legislation (*i.e.* Presidential and Ministerial Decisions) in the field of telecommunications. In particular, the Ministry was responsible for:

– Designing appropriate policy measures for the sector;

– Enacting primary and secondary legislation;

– Managing the radio frequencies and eliminating harmful interference;

– Promoting standardization in the sector;

– individual licenses, and

– Granting recognition of conformity assessments.

The same Law established EETT, which came under the responsibility of the Ministry. EETT was entrusted with the task to monitor the telecommunications market and to implement the legislative and regulatory framework, with a view to promoting the development of the market, ensuring fair competition and protecting consumers' interests. In addition, according to the Law, EETT had an advisory role in that it could provide opinions to the Minister on Ministerial Decisions to be issued and make proposals to the Minister with regard to the granting, renewing, suspending or withdrawing of individual licenses, universal service, and other policy issues. However, it was the Ministry that awarded licenses to telecommunication operators. EETT was also responsible for the resolution of disputes arising out of the provision of telecommunications services and had the power to impose fines for violations.

Apart from the Ministry and EETT, the Law provided for additional institutions to be involved in the regulation of the Greek telecommunication sector. These included:

– The Authority for the Protection of Personal Data;

– The Ministry of National Defence, and

– The Ministry of National Economy.

2.1.1. *The National Commission for Telecommunications and Posts (EETT)*

Article 2 of Law 2246/94 contained basic provisions for the set-up and organisation of EETT. The organisational structure and financial resources of EETT were further defined in subsequent secondary legislation issued in 1995 and 1997. In 1998, Law 2668 allocated EETT additional responsibilities over the monitoring and regulatory supervision of the Greek postal market.

According to Law 2246/94, EETT was an independent authority supervised by the Ministry, with functions of consultative, supervisory, and enforcement nature. If during its normal supervisory duties a case arose which fell within the jurisdiction of other administrative or legal entities, EETT was required to pass the case on to them.

EETT was structured around a Commission with a total of nine members, consisting of one President and eight Commissioners. Two of the Commissioners were appointed as Vice-Presidents, one responsible for telecommunications and the other for posts. The Minister through a Ministerial Decision appointed the President and the Commissioners for a period of five years.[13] Any Commissioner, unjustifiably absent from more than three subsequent assemblies was *de jure* discharged. EETT was supposed to be staffed with a total of 70 employees, of whom 50 were required to be qualified scientists and engineers with expertise in particular areas described in the Law. Their appointment had to be approved by the Ministry.

During the period of service, all members of EETT have the status of civil servants and report to the Minister on the results of industry developments and the achievement of policy objectives. EETT was given the obligation to submit to the Minister an annual report of activities and a financial report of accounts every six months.

The legal framework also determined that EETT's financial resources should come from the revenues it obtained from license and frequency fees, fines, fees for equipment type approvals, etc., imposed on telecommunication operators and service providers operating in the market. However, the Minister of Finance and the Minister of Transports and Communications was given the authority to decide upon the way EETT administers its financial resources. However, according to the Law, the Minister of National Economy, the Minister of Finance and the Minister of Transports and Communications, could determine through a joint Decision that any unspent funds held by EETT should pass on to the General Secretariat of Communications of the MTC to fund its operations, as well as to fund universal service objectives, or relevant studies for the sector.

2.1.2. Deficiencies of Law 2246/94 with regard to conflict of responsibilities and the role of EETT

The EC, although with considerable delay, noted in its December 1999 report on Greece's progress on the Implementation of the Telecommunication Regulatory Package, that the boundaries between EETT's powers and those of the Ministry had not always been clearly defined and called the Ministry to address issues of division of power through the new Framework Law. Most market participants have raised similar concerns. They attributed this phenomenon to (a) the large number of provisions (mainly secondary legislation) that have created considerable confusion for market participants, and (b) to EETT's weakness stemming from its insufficient human resources and lack of relevant expertise.

In fact, both EETT and the General Secretariat of Communications (GST) suffered because of the lack of personnel. Under the early Framework Law, GST should have had 62 employees but existing staff is about 50. The EETT should have had 70 employees, but after 5 years of operation it remains severely understaffed. Recently, it appointed 10 new employees with limited expertise whereas the initial target was to appoint 28. It appears that the majority of candidates decided not to join EETT due to the low salaries offered. Almost all experienced people at EETT have been seconded from OTE but have recently been recalled to that Organisation. Due to personnel shortages, external experts and advisors have often assisted EETT in its duties. The fact that EETT has been severely understaffed, however, resulted in slow decision-making in certain areas, such as dispute resolutions and licensing. The use of OTE personnel by the EETT did not serve to enhance the reputation of EETT's independence among market participants.

The sharing of responsibilities between the Ministry and the regulator has created problems in a number of OECD countries (including a number of European Union countries). It has been recognised that while the Ministry obviously needs to be responsible for overall policy and areas such as the determination of a radio spectrum plan, the regulator needs to have overall responsibility for the implementation of the Law, especially where this has implications for improving the competitive situation in the industry. The experience from telecommunication market liberalisation has shown that a key to successful creation of competitive conditions has been the establishment of an independent telecommunication regulatory body, separate not only from the telecommunication operators but also from line-ministries, which maintain responsibility for policy-making and separate from the incumbent. An important requirement to achieve independence is clear clarification of responsibilities of the different government bodies with a role in the sector. In this context, the provisions of Law 2246/94 and of subsequent secondary legislation have been inadequate since they gave insufficient powers to EETT and reduced its role to an advisory body. In addition, without the ability to make and implement binding decisions the regulator remains in a weak position.

The regulator cannot be responsible for the sector when a number of important areas are left outside of its control. According to the regulatory framework in existence in Greece prior to the adoption of the new Law, responsibility for action was left to the Ministry, while the regulator provided only advice to the Ministry. This effectively resulted in the regulator becoming a tool of the Ministry. It limited its responsibilities and more importantly its independence of action as stipulated by the regulatory framework. This placed the regulator in a difficult position since it was not be able to effectively carry out its tasks if, for example, the Ministry does not fully take its advice into account.

For example, starting in 1998 EETT took the initiative to undertake the necessary preparatory work on important policy matters, such as the preparation of a new draft Telecommunication Law, the drafting of a new operating license for OTE and for new entrants, as well as a study on the costs and financing of Universal Service. However, the Ministry did not fully endorse EETT's pro-active approach. On the contrary, on certain occasions, the Ministry took parallel initiatives, such as the launch of a separate study on the costs of Universal Service in early 2000, and the formation of a separate group of experts to undertake the preparation of a new Telecommunication Law, thus causing further delays and confusion to market participants.[14]

EETT needs sufficient powers to manage the transition of the sector from monopoly to competition. It must actively contribute to promoting competition in the telecommunication sector with the aim of giving consumers, enterprises, etc. access to a wide and varied range of telecommunication services, at low prices and of high quality, while ensuring the necessary consumer protection. So far, EETT could not fulfil these objectives since it did not control important areas such as the provision of licences, or the capacity to decide when to abolish individual licensing and allow entry on the basis of general licensing. If EETT is responsible to review and comment on individual license applications, for example, then it should also have the responsibility of granting these licenses. To impose a split jurisdiction in the individual licensing regime is inefficient, and can lead to delays and reduce transparency.

Furthermore, not only is it important for EETT to be provided with the power and independence to effectively carry out its tasks, but also with the flexibility to meet the changing market structure and requirements. For example, the regulator may need to expand activities because of market developments and the licensing of new service providers (*e.g.* in Wireless Local Loop, UMTS, etc.) and should have some flexibility in its recruitment policy. The skills that the EETT's staff requires to possess to regulate effectively in a competitive environment may change over time due to the globalisation of telecommunication markets. The mixture of skills should be decided by EETT and should not be pre-defined in the Law. In this respect, EETT should be allowed to design its own recruitment policy, and training programmes, as well as have a certain freedom in setting salary scales outside of civil service constraints.

Last, but not least, the independence of EETT is also jeopardised through its resource dependency. This is evident not only in the provisions of the Law imposing limits on EETT in terms of human resources but also in not allowing EETT to retain and administer any unspent funds. The General Secretariat for Communications is subject to funding through the central government budget, therefore it should not seek indirect funding via EETT. Rather, EETT should have the right to retain any unspent funds and use them for training purposes, universal service objectives, etc. If EETT has a continuous surplus, then it should review the level of administrative charges it imposes on operators in the market and consider reducing these charges as appropriate.

The set up of EETT has been an important step in the organisation of the institutional structure for the sector. Yet, further steps are required in order to create appropriate conditions for effective competition and the maximisation of consumer welfare. A clear separation of responsibilities between EETT and the Ministry should be the first policy objective in this direction. In line with the experience of most OECD countries and the main provisions of the European Commission Directives, EETT should have the authority to exercise its powers to the full: in terms of budget and staff, in relation to licensing, interconnection, price controls, universal service, numbering, the taking of binding decisions, and the implementation of other regulatory safeguards.

2.1.3. The new Framework Law

The new Framework Law announced by the Minister in early July 2000, and adopted by Parliament in early December 2000, is a significant improvement over drafts that had been under consideration over the last several years. The law has five basic aims: protect the consumer; safeguard free and healthy competition; safeguard personal information; provide for universal service; and encourage the growth of telecommunications.

The concerns expressed above about the present framework have, to a large extent been addressed in the law, which reinforces EETT by transferring powers to it from the Ministry. It is the intention of the Law to safeguard the independence of EETT and to provide a clear demarcation of responsibilities between EETT and the Ministry. To this end, the overall policy-making for the sector rests with the Ministry while EETT, apart from monitoring the operation of the telecommunications market and safeguarding consumers' best interests, is entrusted with full responsibilities over

- Licensing, including the award, amendment, withdrawal, and transfer of individual and general licenses;

- Management and allocation of frequency spectrum;

- Interconnection negotiations and resolution of disputes, in particular following the provisions of a forthcoming Presidential Decree that will specify the arbitration procedure to be followed in each case;

- Telecommunication tariffs, and in particular their cost-orientation in relation to interconnection, local loop unbundling, and leased lines, as well as the implementation of proper cost accounting systems;

- Leased lines and their availability in accordance to Community regulations;

- The definition, costing, and financing of universal service;

- The administration of National Numbering Plan and the allocation of numbers;

- Administrative procedures regarding the installation of antennae; and

- Administrative procedures that facilitate 'one-stop-shopping' to new entrants, in order to safeguard timely access to rights of way to public and private land for the parties concerned.

According to the new Law, the Ministerial Council will appoint EETT's President while the Minister of Transport and Communications will appoint the Commissioners. The period of service of all members can only be renewed once.

In addition, EETT will have the right to issue regulatory acts and publish them in the Official Gazette i.e. to take and implement binding decisions without prior approval of the Minister. Furthermore, its authorised staffing level will increase from 70 to 180 employees, of which 120 should be highly qualified scientists and engineers. For an initial period of four years EETT will also be allowed to employ employees from other public organisations for a maximum period of two years. The Law defines the categories of personnel EETT should have, their professional qualification, and the number of employees in each category, but also includes a provision that allows EETT the right to change these categories and the number of personnel, and allows it to deviate from the salary rates of civil servants. Still, EETT will continue to be resource dependent as it is not allowed to retain and administer any unspent funds.

Although improvements in the new Law regarding the structure and operation of EETT are appropriate and pro-competitive, it is doubtful whether the relevant provisions will effectively be in place by the time the market opens to competition in January 2001. In particular, the empowerment of EETT with qualified personnel will take time to materialise. The difficult question for EETT is twofold: First, how can it increase its staff rapidly from 13 employees to 180 and second, how soon can new employees be trained to issue regulatory acts and mandates for the development of a fair, transparent and stable competitive environment. The Vice-President of EETT expressed the view that with the relaxation of the lengthy bureaucratic procedures required for the recruitment of personnel and the shift of such responsibility to EETT,[15] they are ready to proceed to the selection of 26 additional people by November 2000. When the new Law is ratified, it will open the way to further recruitment. It is of utmost importance that the recruitment and training of new personnel take the minimum time possible. There is already plenty of experience Greek regulators could draw on from other countries in order to organise their Authority effectively without further delays. Any delays in this respect would be unjustifiable.

2.1.4. *The role of other institutional players*

Under Law 2246/94, apart from the Ministry and EETT there are a few other institutional players with responsibilities for the sector.

– *The Authority for the Protection of Personal Data* plays a role in the telecommunications sector in that it has the authority to inspect the records and files of all telecommunication operators, including OTE, in order to investigate whether there has been any violation of the rules on the protection of personal data, following Commission Directive 97/66. The Authority reports annually and on a case-by-case basis to the Greek Parliament and comprises members of each political party, the Vice-President of the Parliament, and one communications expert appointed by the President of the Parliament.

– *The Ministry of National Defense* plays an active role in spectrum planning.

– *The Ministry of National Economy* (MNE) remains the major shareholder of OTE and, even after the sale of shares to a strategic partner, it is expected to maintain some control in key areas where co-decisions will be required. Up till the end of 1997, any change in OTE's tariffs had to be reviewed and approved by the MNE. It has been reported that any decision on UMTS licenses will be a co-decision between the Ministry of National Economy, the Ministry of Transport and Communications, and EETT.

The following Table summarises the responsibilities of each institutional player as defined in Law 2246/94 and as are currently envisaged in the new Law.

Table 5. Greece: division of responsibilities among main actors (1994-2000)

Area	MTC 94	MTC 00	MNE 94	MNE 00	EETT 94	EETT 00	OTE 94	OTE 00
Policy making	●	●			○			
Tariffs			○		○		●	●
Frequency management	●				○	●		
Frequency allocation	●				○	●		
Numbering	●				●		○	
Interconnection (tech.)					○	○		
Interconnection charges					○	○		
Licensing	●				○	●		
Terminal equipment type approval	●				●	●		
Industrial policy	○	○			○			
Customer information					○	○		

Notes:
○ = Intervention/Arbitration;
● = Overall responsibility; MTC = Ministry of Transport and Communications;
MNE = Ministry of National Economy;
EETT = National Telecommunication Commission.

In contrast to other countries where industry associations, and particularly large users groups, have been actively engaged in the reform process and the design of a pro-competitive regulatory framework for the sector, the Federation of Greek Industries (SEV) has played a relatively small role in the policy process. An exception has been its involvement in the *Telecommunication Forum*, an informal body set up in 1998 comprising academics, policy-makers, users representatives and members of EETT whose purpose was to work on the design of a new Telecommunications Law. Users should be instigated to become more actively involved in policy reforms. In this respect, the new Law should have included provisions that would call for the formal set up of consumer associations to represent the interests of all users, including industry and residential users, in policy formation.

Similarly, the Competition Authority is not as actively involved in the regulation of anti-competitive conduct in the Greek telecommunication market, as is the case with similar agencies in other countries. At present, the Competition Authority does not play a role in the sector in terms of advocacy and EETT has displaced it in relation to competition issues except for mergers, which remain under the jurisdiction of the Competition Authority. Although there is no formal link between EETT and the Competition Authority, there is well-established informal co-operation between the two agencies. According to EETT officials, there is concurrent jurisdiction between them on matters of mutual interest. EETT asks the opinion of Competition Authority for nearly every matter that arises in relation to competition in the sector and, despite the lack of clarity in the division of responsibilities and the potential for overlap between them, no practical problems have arisen yet. This could be due to the fact that the two agencies are complementary to each other, as officials at the Competition Authority appear to have limited knowledge of the telecommunication sector. The situation in respect to the role of Competition Authority is expected to change with the new Competition Law that was adopted by Parliament in August 2000. The involvement of Competition Authority in the regulation of the telecommunication sector up till now and the new role envisaged for it in the future are discussed later.

2.2. Telecommunication regulation and related policy instruments

2.2.1. *Regulation of entry and licensing*

Table 6 summarises the status of market liberalisation in Greece as of December 2000. At present all market segments are open to competition except the markets for public fixed switched voice telephony services and public fixed telecommunications networks.[16] OTE has exclusive rights in these areas until 1/1/2001, following its official request to the EC for derogation on the basis of pending network modernisation and price re-balancing. In particular, OTE's exclusive rights in voice services involve exclusivity in the provision of local, long-distance, and international voice telephony as well as ISDN services to the public.

Table 6.   State of competition (as in December 2000)

Public Voice telephony	Public fixed network for the provision of public voice services	Public fixed network for the provision of VAS	Voice to Vclosed-user groups	Leased Lines	Mobile	Paging	Cable TV	Satellite	VAS
M	M	C	C	C	C	C	C	C	C
Until 1/1/2001	Until 1/1/2001	Since October 1997					N/A		

Notes:
VAS = Value-Added Services;
M = Monopoly;
C = Competition;
N/A: Not Available.

The wisdom or need for a two-year derogation can be questioned on the basis of experience in other EU countries that opened their markets to full competition even before full re-balancing had been achieved. Competition allowed for a more rapid re-balancing of prices, while at the same time bringing more immediate benefits to users. Although, as shown in Section 3, good progress has been made in network modernisation, competition would have also speeded-up the modernisation of OTE's network. OTE's international investment programme (especially in the Balkans) has sidetracked OTE's domestic investment efforts. While such strategic investments may be important in the longer term for OTE, they are being undertaken on the basis of leverage obtained from its exclusive monopoly position and the profits gained from this position. Domestic users would have benefited far more from acceleration of domestic investment in new services and the upgrading of technology.[17]

According to the Licensing regime that was introduced in 1995 based on Law 2246/94, all liberalised services were subject to Declaration except for those entailing the use of scarce resources. The latter were subject to a License. In particular, according to EETT's practical guide on the provision of tele-communication services in Greece, the 'license regime' applied to services whose provision involved one or more of the following:

– Establishment, operation and/or exploitation of telecommunication networks for the provision of telecommunication services;

– Use of scarce resources, in particular, radio-frequencies, the geostationary-satellite orbit, and numbers from the national numbering plan;

– Compliance with specific conditions related to the essential requirements or other special requirements related to National Defence and Security, and

– Award of special or exclusive rights (as is the case with OTE).

According to this licensing system, Declarations were issued by EETT within three months following the submission of a formal request, otherwise the Declaration was considered to be, *de facto*, endorsed. Further submissions were required each time one or more of the conditions referred to in a declaration were modified. The Ministry, following a recommendation by EETT, issued licenses within six months following the submission of an application to EETT.

A Ministerial Decision issued in July 1995 specified that the applicant putting a request for a license had to provide the regulator with the following information:[18]

1. A detailed description of the services to be provided.

2. A full presentation of the typology of infrastructure and the geographical area of coverage.

3. A description of how the applicant intends to use the radio frequencies to provide the service (where applicable).

4. The requested numbering space (where applicable).

5. The proposed duration of the license (could not exceed 10 years).

6. The total capacity of leased lines required within Greek territory and between Greece and other countries (in Kbps).

7. A feasibility study along with the business plan and the timetable for its implementation.

8. Provisions related to the licensee's relations with users (repair time, conditions for interruption of service, etc.).

Similar information had to be submitted by operators in their application for a declaration. An application for a declaration should include a detailed description of the services, the typology of infrastructure and the geographical area of coverage, the technical specifications of any terminal equipment (TTE), the requested numbering space (where applicable); a brief business plan; the total capacity of leased lines in use, and a statement of commitment against anti-competitive behaviour and compliance with the arbitration procedures set by the EETT.

Law 2246/94 set a number of general, and somewhat vague, criteria, which had to be taken into account for granting a license. These included the general state of national economy, the needs of the market, the strengthening of competition, the potential effect on the of development telecommunication infrastructure in the country, as well as the amount, origin, and method of financing of the required investment. The credibility and relevant experience of the applicant were also taken into account.

This licensing system was maintained until the transposition of Licensing Directive in 1999. According to officials at the Ministry, the requirements for obtaining an individual license, including a license for the provision of mobile telephony service, are included in a Ministerial Decision issued in late 1999.[19] General licenses are issued by EETT following a request for registration submitted to EETT by the applicant companies[20] In their request applicants should explicitly state that they would comply with the essential requirements. According to EETT, there are several categories of general licenses according to the type of services on offer. Similarly, if it is voice telephony services, then there are separate types of licenses for local, long-distance, or voice over IP services and in each case the prospective licensee needs to clearly specify which type of service it wishes to offer. The development and exploitation of alternative networks, including radio, mobile, and satellite networks are subject to individual licenses. The criteria to obtain an individual license include the requirement that the applicant company is incorporated in the form of *société anonyme* and that the company is registered in an EU member state and is formally represented in Greece.

The obligations imposed on license holders are according to the provisions of the Licensing Directive 97/13/EC that was transposed in the Greek Law. According to the Ministry, in the case of individual licenses, non-compliance with the data submitted by the applicant, especially when public works are concerned, may result in the full or partial loss of the financial guaranty deposited by the applicant, whereas for general licenses no consequences are foreseen for not respecting the time schedule or for not providing the services specified.

As in a number of OECD countries, the legal framework imposes fees on telecommunication operators to cover the administrative costs of examining an application for a license. A Ministerial Decision also imposes annual fees on license holders. These are calculated according to a formula that is based on the gross revenues they earn from activities that are included in their license.

Unlike the Ministry, which believed that licensing matters were settled following the transposition of the Licensing Directive, the majority of new players in the market expressed their dissatisfaction with licensing procedures. In particular, they have complained that licensing procedures have been extremely lengthy and bureaucratic. In one case, it was reported that a company received the first individual license to deploy a fibre optics alternative network 15 months after it had submitted their application.[21] In 1998, the same company had filed an application for a license to offer international facility-based services and intended to buy capacity for this purpose, but the Ministry revoked its application due to a lack of secondary legislation.

Part of the problem relates to the difficulties encountered by new entrants over access to rights of ways. An interviewee reported that for a company to lay a fibre optic cable in the sea it needed about 40 different licenses from public authorities. The case of satellite services is worse. New entrants have reported extreme delays in licensing to establish transmitter and/or receiver antennae due to difficulties encountered in obtaining rights of way. The first company to obtain a license to build and operate a satellite network was granted the license in December 1999, almost three and a half years after it first filed an application in summer 1996. According to company officials, they need permission to set up earth stations from a range of public authorities. Given that they need permission for each earth station they install, this results in considerable delays.[22] With the ratification of the new Telecommunications Law and the involvement of EETT in establishing procedures for 'one-stop-shopping' these conditions should change and there should be no more unnecessary delays in licensing due to difficulties in the exercise of rights of ways on public land. A first positive step has been made with a recent law (Law

2840/00) which provides EETT with regulatory powers over the award of both general and individual licences as well as over the relevant criteria for their award.

Some market players have also complained that the Ministry systematically delayed the award of licenses for the provision of services that require use of frequency spectrum. In particular, it has been reported that only OTE and the three mobile operators enjoy the right to use radio frequencies to provide services beyond those for which they were initially granted frequencies, whereas other companies have repeatedly asked for the right to use microwave frequencies without any success. This is despite the fact that the requirements for the provision of mobile and radio services are covered by the Ministerial Decision issued in late 1999. Part of the problem has been due to the absence of appropriate regulations for the management of frequency spectrum and the unauthorised use of certain frequency bands. In 1999 the Ministry in collaboration with EETT made a positive step by setting up a Committee to manage the frequency spectrum.

The Ministry recently announced the Government's intention to grant a fourth mobile license by the end of 2000 and has been negotiating with the mobile operators to grant more frequencies. In this context, on 29 June 2000 EETT initiated a public consultation seeking the views of interested parties in relation to the type of mobile services they intend to offer, the frequencies they wish to get access to, the number and duration of prospective licenses, and the preferred system to be implemented for their allocation (*i.e.* competition tender or auction). Similar public consultations were launched in June 2000 for the award of licenses for DECT services and for individual licenses for fixed-wireless access.

Hellas and Panafon each began their operations in 1993.

In 1995, OTE was awarded an operating license after paying a lump sum of GRD 160 billion. Its licence allowed OTE to provide mobile communications services using the DCS-1800 technology. In addition, it specified that OTE should pay an additional charge of GRD 90 billion, adjusted annually relative to the Consumer Price Index, for the use of all frequency spectrum allocated to the Organisation. The Ministry issued Decision 92093/1995 which granted OTE the right to use the radio spectrum of the 1710-1785 and 1805-1880 MHz frequency bands in the DCS 1800 system for mobile telephony. Subsequently, in 1996, COSMOTE was established for the purpose of providing mobile telecommunication services. Pursuant to Law 2465/97, OTE transfer its right to develop and provide personal communications services using DCS 1800 technology to its subsidiary COSMOTE. However, COSMOTE never paid for a mobile licence. Instead, OTE paid a lump sum of GRD 15.5 billion for the frequency bands required for the operation of the DCS 1800 system. Both established mobile operators complained to the Greek State and to the EC about unfair treatment since there was no open bidding procedure in the licensing of COSMOTE. However, there has never been a formal investigation to these claims and the matter has been buried since.

According to its operating licence, OTE has also been enjoying certain privileges with respect to frequency allocation, including the right to request use of certain frequencies as part of its network expansion and modernisation programme. In the light of the upcoming new operating licence of OTE, these provisions should be reviewed and modified accordingly so as not to weaken competition in the market for wireless services.

A recent positive development that opened the way to new entrants in the market for wireless services has been EETT's decision in June 2000 to launch two public consultation debates: one regarding the allocation of a fourth mobile operating licence, and the second regarding the licensing of operators offering fixed-wireless access (FWA) in the local loop market.

With regard to licences for fixed-wireless access, EETT published its conclusions of the public consultation in July 2000. A total of 26 companies participated in the consultation process. The majority of these companies expressed interest in bidding for a FWA licence and opted for a nation-wide licence. In addition, it was suggested that licences should be allocated through a competitive tender procedure and that established operators (either wire-based or wireless) should be excluded from the tender process in order to stimulate competition and open the field to new entrants.

In September 2000, EETT issued an Information Memorandum, which opted for an auction procedure for the allocation of FWA licences. The memorandum essentially prepared the ground for the issue of an Invitation to Tender in late October 2000. According to the memorandum, the number of individual licences to be granted are four (4) national Licences in the 3410 – 3600 MHz band, and five (5) national licences in the 24500 – 26500 MHz band. These will have a 15 year duration. An auction procedure has the advantage of ensuring transparent allocation of licences, and it would allow the NRA to impose certain minimum requirements, *e.g.* in terms of network rollout, on potential licensees.

However, a Ministerial Decree was issued in early September 2000, stating that the auction procedure would take place for the allocation of 3 (instead of 4) national licences in the 3 410 – 3 600 MHz band, and 4 (instead of 5), national licences in the 24 500 – 26 500 MHz band. The government decided that the two pending licences in the 3.5 GHz and the 25 GHz bands would be granted to OTE without an open bidding procedure. The only condition was that OTE would pay an amount equal to the bandwidth that OTE will be granted multiplied by the maximum price per MHz that will result from the auction for each band. The memorandum also contained an indicative timetable for the award of licences and a list of reserved prices for each of the licences under auction. The authority to award the licences and the responsibility to run the auction lies with EETT.

The granting of a licence without a competitive evaluation to the incumbent must be condemned. It is discriminatory, negates the principal rationale of holding an auction (or competitive tender), and places the regulator in a difficult position in terms of a neutral and independent arbitrator in the market. Neither is the procedure in line with WTO commitments that, in the Reference paper to the WTO agreement, state that any procedures for the allocation and use of scarce resources will be carried out in an objective, transparent and non-discriminatory manner.

In addition, the proposed allocation of two FWA licences to OTE is not consistent with the stated policy objectives of promoting effective competition to the benefit of all relevant parties and preventing anti-competitive practices. On the contrary, it is expected that such an approach will enhance OTE's dominant position in the market. The incumbent has no inherent right to such fixed wireless licences. On the contrary, since the licences are crucial in generating competition at the local level where the incumbent already has essential facilities, a case can be made to exclude the incumbent from the auction. Experience from other OECD countries has shown that competition has been the key driver to the rapid and efficient modernisation of the network since it provides incentives for investment in physical infrastructure.

Eventually, the auction procedure took place in early December 2000 and EETT announced the award of six fixed wireless access (FWA) licences to five successful bidder at an auction which raised GRD 15.7 billion ($41 million). The successful consortia include (a) Europrom, made up of Eurocom Networks Ltd and Prometheus Gas, which bid GRD 2.2 billion for a licence in the 3.5GHz band; (b) the mobile market operator Panafon, with GRD 2.77 billion; (c) The consortium formed between Greece's Public Power Corporation (DEH) and three Greek banks with a bid of GRD 3.01 billion; (d) The Mediterranean Broadband Services, a joint venture between Telecom Italia and Greek ISP Forthnet, with GRD 2.92 billion; and (e) Quest Wireless consortium, a joint venture between Infoquest, the constructing Hellenic Technodomiki, Starcom and CV Romania with GRD 1.5 billion. There were no offers for the third licence in the 3.5 GHz band. In the light of these events, EETT's role in preparing the environment for competition is crucial.

Further improvement in the licensing system is envisaged in the proposed new Telecommunication Law, in particular with regard to the time required for reviewing an application and granting the license. More specifically, the Law determines that a general license should be granted within 15 days of application and an individual license within 6 weeks. Although these new timeframes represent a considerable improvement, further streamlining in the classification system is necessary.

For example, the new Telecommunication Law in Greece retains the system of general and individual licences and considers that any company that wishes to install, operate, and/or exploit public telecommunication networks is subject to an individual license. This implies that even if a company has no facilities of its own but provides facility-based services to the public it is subject to an individual license. In addition, according to the new law, the Minister may decide to impose a limit on the number of licenses should this prove necessary on the grounds of non-availability of frequencies and/or numbers. Since it is the regulator that provides licences and administers numbers, it should be the same body that decides on whether there are resource constraints requiring a temporary suspension of licensing.

In regard to restrictions on licensing, the Ministry argued that any restrictions imposed on licensees relate mainly to competition rules and are in accordance with the relevant provisions of the EC Treaty. There are no explicit ownership restrictions in the regulatory framework for telecommunications. However, according to the Ministry, ownership restrictions may be imposed before granting new licenses on a case by case basis. This practice is deemed necessary as long as such restrictions aim to prevent the adverse effects of cross-ownership. Cross-ownership between competing telecommunication operators can lead to collusion and should be discouraged to ensure fair and transparent competition in the market. Yet, any such restrictions should be imposed following the provisions of specific regulation to protect competition and should not be arbitrary. The new Law has indicated that a forthcoming Presidential Decree will set upper limits in the shareholdings a single person can have in similar companies operating in the same geographical market. This policy objective is considered as essential and should be undertaken as soon as the market opens to competition in order to avoid collusive behaviour and conflict of interest among companies.

According to the new Law, EETT should issue specific regulations to define the details for obtaining each type of license, the requirements for data submitted by potential licensees, the conditions included in the various licenses, as well as the administrative fees imposed on operators. It is expected that EETT's regulations will not differ from the Ministerial Decisions already in place that determine these issues. However, some market players are confused over which of the existing legislative acts will continue to apply and which are going to be replaced by new ones. Here again the government should immediately implement new EU proposals set out in the proposed *Directive on the authorisation of electronic communications networks and services*, which stresses the importance of simplicity in licensing and the information required from market entrants.

Licensing is one area where the Greek authorities should take advantage of their delay in opening the market to competition and implement streamlined procedures that meet best practice regulation. In this context a number of OECD countries have introduced simple authorisation schemes that do not require explicit approval by the regulator for market entry. These market entry procedures have worked well and have facilitated the development of competition. The European Union is also in the process of proposing streamlined market entry procedures based on general authorisation.[23]

In the creation of competition, EETT's mandate and market entry are inextricably interlinked. In the context of EU requirements and WTO commitments market entry must be unhindered except where objective resource constraints impose limits. With the exceptions of the incumbent, that is OTE, which will be subject to asymmetric regulation and of mobile companies using scarce spectrum resources, there is little justification in maintaining an individual licensing regime. The use of individual licenses encourages the inclusion of many detailed conditions that can delay entry. The EC in its 1999 Communications Review stresses that individual license can 'create administrative barriers, which may be disproportionate…' and, as noted above, foresees a new framework which would use general authorisations. Such streamlining would allow Greece somewhat to catch-up on its delay in creating a competitive market resulting from the 2-year derogation period by stimulating new market entry. In this respect, there is a need for Greek authorities to begin from now to formulate a new streamlined licensing framework and minimise licensing procedures. In the context of regulatory streamlining, also stressed by the present government in its policy platform, general licenses ensure greater transparency and reduce the administrative burden on market participants. The responsibilities of telecommunication operators offering public telecommunication networks and services could have been specified either in a separate article in the new Telecommunications Law or by EETT through regulation, rather than through individual licenses. A bold step forward would be to abolish the requirement for individual licenses for fixed infrastructure and services. Such a step would be in accordance with the spirit of the regulatory framework proposed by the EC.

2.2.2. *Interconnection and regulation of interconnection prices*

Interconnection has been the first regulatory matter that required EETT's intervention. Given that OTE has maintained exclusive rights over the provision of local, long-distance and international services, mobile and other operators had to rely on OTE for interconnection to the fixed public network. Since 1993, operators have had to rely on an interconnection regime that was established under Law 2246/94, and later on multilateral negotiations among the parties concerned that often made reference to various Articles in the Interconnection Directive. In this respect, interconnection charges have not been based on costs, nor on an commonly agreed objective methodology.

The first phase of the interconnection regime in Greece began in 1993, when OTE entered into interconnection agreements with the two mobile operators at the time, STET Hellas and Panafon. The terms and conditions of those interconnection agreements were included in the licenses awarded to the GSM operators. According to these licenses, mobile companies had to pay for interconnection charges for calls from a mobile to a fixed network, while they received payments for fixed to mobile calls on a revenue sharing basis. More specifically, according to the licenses, interconnection charges paid by mobile operators to OTE for mobile to fixed traffic should be calculated as a percentage of revenue (not on a call per minute basis) and had to be equal to the highest of either of the following amounts:

a) 5% of mobile operators' revenue from all national calls originating from OTE's fixed network to the telephone network of mobile operators and vice versa; or

b) 3.35% of mobile operators' gross revenue from providing cellular telecommunication and roaming services in Greece.

OTE followed the second formula and charged the mobile operators accordingly.

For fixed to mobile calls, the mobile companies received approximately 80% of the tariff while OTE retained the agreed interconnection fee per minute plus an administrative fee of 4% to cover the costs of accounting, billing customers, etc.

These interconnection charges were due to apply for the first eight years of the commercial operation of the two mobile operators, a period during which they were granted a duopoly. However, the licenses included a condition under which the interconnection charges could be revised anytime if OTE was obliged by EC regulations to base its charges on cost. In addition, it is worth mentioning two other provisions that were included in GSM licenses. First, mobile operators were prohibited from charging their customers lower tariffs than OTE's highest long distance rates. This restriction certainly did not help create appropriate conditions for competition to develop and should be rescinded in 2001 when new operating licenses for the GSM operators should be issued. Second, mobile operators were given the right to determine call charges for both originating and terminating traffic to their network.

The second phase began in 1995, with OTE appealing to EETT against the formula set out in the operating licenses of mobile companies. OTE claimed that interconnection charges were too low and that EETT should require that they should reflect the actual costs incurred. EETT relied on the results of a study conducted by a team of independent experts and academics and in July 1997 it set new interconnection charges at a rate of GRD 11.5 per minute instead of GRD 6.5 that was the rate following the formula proposed in the licenses. Both STET Hellas and Panafon appealed against this decision claiming that it was beyond EETT's authority and initiated legal proceedings before the Council of State. A public hearing of the case was scheduled for October 2000. The new increased rate was applied retroactively starting from the second half of December 1995. OTE collected the interconnection charges for 1996 and 1997 also based on this rate. However, in March 1998, EETT informed OTE that it had set the interconnection charge for 1996 at a lower charge of GRD 10.54 per minute. Subsequently, in October 1999, EETT issued a third decision by which the interconnection

325

charge for 1997 was set at GRD 9 725 per minute. OTE has refunded both Panafon and Telestet the difference for 1996 and 1997.

The experts that undertook the study on behalf of EETT calculated the interconnection charge per minute for all traffic passing through OTE's network. For this purpose they used traffic and cost data provided by OTE and the mobile operators. Most OECD countries, along with the EC, have realised that the fully distributed cost (FDC) methodology is inappropriate to determine interconnection prices as it is subject to manipulation in the allocation of joint and common costs across different services and does not discount for inefficiencies of former monopolies. For this reason, the methodology proposed by regulators and the EC is that of the long-run average incremental cost (LRAIC), based on forward looking costs and a sufficient return on investment for the incumbent.

However, at that time, OTE's cost accounting system was based on historic data while the cost allocation methodology used by OTE followed the fully distributed cost (FDC) model. In addition, the EETT experts were often faced with OTE's inability or unwillingness to provide the required data to allow for service costs to be estimated. With regard to operating costs, for example, no proper costing data existed. Despite these inherent difficulties the experts developed a model following the principles of the recommended long run average incremental cost methodology. EETT used this model as a basis to decide on the interconnection charges for 1995, 1996, and 1997 respectively.

Since then the Interconnection Directive was transposed into the Greek law in 1999 (Presidential Decree 165/99). Although no accounting methodology is specified in the existing legislation, the Ministry expects that the methodology to be applied will be in line with the European Commission's recommendations, that is the LRAIC methodology. OTE claims that it is in the final stage of adopting and implementing a comprehensive cost accounting system which will enable it to determine the costs of interconnection conforming to the EC requirements.

Figure 1. **Comparison of EU peak interconnection rates based on a call duration of 3 minutes**

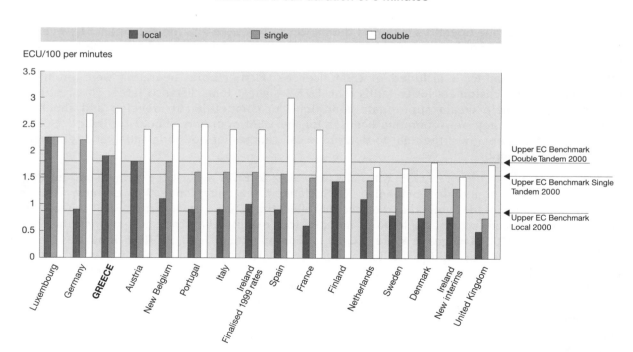

The third phase began with the transposition of the Interconnection Directive in 1999 and the publication by OTE of a Reference Interconnection Offer (RIO). OTE in its RIO for 1998 proposed interconnection charges for mobile operators of GRD 8.3 per minute. As this tariff falls within the best practice range that appears in the relevant EC Recommendation on Interconnection, it was approved by EETT. OTE's 1999 RIO is currently being reviewed and has not yet received EETT's final approval.

In the light of the upcoming full market liberalisation and according to the terms of the derogation given by the EC, it is the regulator's duty to determine a general framework for interconnection and prices before full market liberalisation. In this context, it is necessary for OTE to make known well in advance the terms and conditions of access to its network In June 2000 the regulator announced the interconnection rates for new entrants. However, several new entrants complained that the announcement came in too late and that OTE could benefit from a benchmarking exercise on how other operators design their RIOs. The major problem with OTE's RIOs so far was that they were addressed only to the mobile operators and not to a wider audience of new entrants. If for any reason such a framework cannot be implemented by the time new entrants enter the fixed PSTN market then the best recourse would be to adopt best practice EU interconnection prices as benchmarks until a costing methodology and a proper RIO is implemented by OTE. Given the importance of developing electronic commerce and Internet applications the EETT should also give consideration to developing a flat rate Internet access call origination product (FRIACO), which would facilitate the offer of unmetered Internet connections. The requirement imposed on BT in the UK has led to important changes in the UK Internet market and allowed for cheaper access and the development of an "always-on" environment.

As of March 2000 OTE's interconnection rates (peak time) exceeded by a considerable margin EU benchmarks for local, single transit and double transit interconnection (see Figure 1). For local and single transit interconnection Greece was the highest in Europe and the third highest for double transit. Since then improvements have been to the extent that for local interconnection Greece is the third most expensive in the EU, the second most expensive for single transit and the fifth most expensive for double transit.

2.2.3. Regulation of pricing

Decision 97/607/EC by which a derogation period was granted to Greece for the liberalisation of fixed telephony services and the underlying network infrastructure, states that OTE's fixed telephony prices should be aligned to costs no later than 1/1/2001. At the same time, law 2246/94 required that public fixed voice telephony tariffs be aligned to costs and that cross-subsidisation practices be avoided. Along with this requirement, since 1995 OTE has started re-balancing its prices. The enforcement of the above has been monitored by EETT, whilst the Ministry of National Economy generally consulted with OTE and gave its consent to price changes that are below or in line with increases in consumer price index. Overall, the tariff policy that has been followed since 1993 was designed so as to avoid negative reactions from subscribers. For example, in 1994 tariffs were not increased because of prior increases in 1993. Tariffs must also be approved by OTE's Board of Directors and published in the official government gazette.

The derogation granted to Greece was provided on the basis of a single justification, that is, to allow OTE time to rebalance its tariffs before market liberalisation. Such rebalancing should have been completed before full market liberalisation but it is unlikely that this will have been achieved. Existing evidence, and claims by OTE, indicate that further price rebalancing will be required. Overall, although monthly rental charges and local tariffs have increased over recent years (see Table 15), they continue to be below cost. Thus, local telephony continues to be subsidised by revenue generated from long distance and international services.[24] Further price rebalancing occurred in the second half of 2000, but it may be insufficient to attain cost-oriented prices. It is important for EETT, in consultation with OTE, to fix a schedule for completing rebalancing and ensuring that this schedule is transparent.

Currently there is no price cap regulation applied to OTE. However, for a period of three years beginning January 1, 1995, the Board of Directors of OTE was allowed to implement annual tariff increases up

Table 7. Changes in tariffs relative to the consumer price index (%)

	1995	1996	1997
CPI (% change from previous year)	10.9	8.2	5.5
Percentage points for price cap	0	2	3
Expected (permissible) increase	24	10	8.5
Actual weighted average tariff changes	15.6	5.6	4.6

Source: Ministry of Transport and Communications (MTC) and OTE.

to a maximum defined in OTE's Charter (Law 2257/94, article 2). More specifically, the maximum weighted average increase permitted for the calendar years were not allowed to exceed the increase in the annual consumer price index (the 'CPI') for the period March 1, 1993 to December 31, 1994 plus certain percentage points. Similarly, the maximum increases permitted for 1996 and 1997 were not allowed to exceed the increases in the CPI during the prior calendar years, plus certain percentage points. These percentage points were 3%, 2% and nil for 1997, 1996 and 1995 respectively. These increases were intended to allow OTE to readjust its tariffs to reflect the costs of providing the services. Table 7 shows the tariff changes in relation to changes in the CPI for the years 1995, 1996, and 1997.

The most transparent and effective way to regulate prices is through a price cap formula. The EETT should consider imposing a price cap as of 1 January 2001. In that the EETT has indicated that it intends to commission a study on price cap regulation the initial value for the productivity factor (the X in CPI-X) can be viewed as temporary.

2.2.4. *Accounting separation*

According to law 2246/94, OTE is required to keep separate accounts between its fixed voice telephony services and other operations. In particular, following the transposition of the Interconnection Directive into the Greek law, OTE as the incumbent telecom operator is required to follow accounting separation for interconnection services. In addition to the accounting separation issue, the cost accounting system developed by OTE follows the Fully Allocated Cost (FAC) model and is anticipated to further evolve to a cost accounting system based on LRAIC model. OTE presented this system to the Regulator in mid-2000 who is currently reviewing it with the help of independent academic advisors. It is expected that the IPO of COSMOTE will be helpful in ensuring arms length operation between OTE and its mobile subsidiary.

Accounting separation has weaknesses as a regulatory tool. For example, there are problems of "information asymmetry" concerning an incumbent's costs, as well as the ingeniousness of "creative accounting". Nevertheless, data provided on the basis of accounting separation will go some way in restricting OTE's cross-subsidisation. Moreover, sustained effort to analyse and calculate service costs will improve understanding of the costs that can be attributed to various activities.[25]

2.2.5. *Alternative infrastructure*

Unlike many OECD countries Greece is extremely weak in terms of the availability of alternative infrastructures. A particular weakness is that a cable television infrastructure does not exist, nor are there any plans to significantly improve the situation. In most OECD countries cable is viewed as providing an important means of access to high-speed infrastructure to support electronic commerce and multimedia applications, as well as providing the means to compete effectively against the PSTN. For this reason it is important that new broadband and narrowband technologies be allowed to enter the market as rapidly as possible, in particular wireless in the local loop technologies and third generation mobile technologies.

In principle, the Minister of Press and Mass Media grants the licenses for the provision of cable television/ broadcasting services (operators also need a telecommunication licence from EETT). Presidential Decree 123/98 (the transposition of Directive 95/51/EC), specifically states that cable operators are subject to approvals by the relevant authorities (including the municipalities) for using rights of way and they can use their infrastructure for the provision of telecommunication services. However, because of the lack of cable television infrastructure in Greece, the Decree has not been put to the test.

2.2.6. Numbering

Numbering has important implications for the development of competition as telecommunications operators need to have access to adequate numbers in order to achieve an effective provision of their services. In Greece, at present, the Ministry allocates numbers on the basis of individual requests from telecommunication operators and is responsible for managing numbering resources. However, upon passing of the new telecommunications law by the Greek Parliament, this responsibility will pass on to the Regulator who will be responsible for numbering and for managing numbering blocks.

Also important is the introduction of number portability, which refers to the ability of customers to keep their numbers even when they change their location, service provider, or type of service. When customers cannot keep their telephone number, they are often faced with substantial costs relating to, for example printing new letterheads, informing business partners and clients, etc. Thus the absence of number portability can put a new entrant at a disadvantageous position since the potential "switching costs" act as a strong disincentive for customers to switch from the incumbent to a new entrant. In this context, the relevant EC Directive requires the introduction of number portability in Member States as soon as possible as a means to enhance consumer choice and effective competition. Complying with the EC Directive and taking full advantage of the transition period offered,[26] the new Law sets as the latest date of introduction of number portability the year 2003, that is two years after the market is liberalised. This is too late. The government should empower EETT to oblige operators, and in particular OTE, to introduce number portability as soon as technically possible.

2.2.7. Carrier Selection and pre-selection

Carrier pre-selection is firmly in place in several OECD countries such as Australia, Denmark, Mexico, New Zealand, US, the Netherlands, etc. The EC requires member states to ensure that by 1 January 2000 fixed network operators with significant market power enable their subscribers to obtain access to the services of other interconnected service providers, by means of pre-selection with a call-by-call over-ride facility. OTE benefits from an extension of the deadline under EU regulations for the introduction of number portability and carrier selection and pre-selection to January 1, 2003. Greek officials argue that, in line with national and EU legislation, carrier selection will be introduced no later than 31.12.2002. The relevant EC Directive has already been transposed into the national legislation by Presidential Decree 165/99. However, no plans have yet been made for carrier pre-selection. With regard to mobile services, no provision exists for mobile service number portability, although it is perceived that number portability will be applicable in all services.

Carrier pre-selection should be in place as soon as markets are opened to competition. For this purpose, EETT should review these deadlines and try to accelerate the introduction of carrier pre-selection including local pre-selection. By deferring implementation the authorities are not trying to catch-up on the delay which the derogation has imposed on the Greek market and Greek users.

2.2.8. Spectrum allocation and the licensing of mobile operators (including UMTS)

To date, the Ministry has been responsible for spectrum allocation and planning. Spectrum is allocated according to the National Frequency Allocation Table, following the recommendations by the ITU and the European Radio-communications Commission (ERC). Ministerial Decision No. 61646/98 (OJ A 505) has determined that the calculation of charges levied for spectrum resources should be based on

329

a formula that takes into account, *inter alia*, the bandwidth of frequencies allocated, the technology used, the number of stations in operation, and the frequency zone in use. However, according to the new Law, all responsibilities with regard to frequency allocation and licensing of wireless operators will pass on to EETT.

The first two mobile operators, Panafon and STET Hellas, operate under licenses issued by the government on September 30, 1992 for the operation of mobile telephony services in the 900 MHz frequency band. The prevalent system at the time was that operators were paying for a license rather than for access to spectrum. STET Hellas and Panafon each began their operations in 1993.

In 1995, OTE was awarded an operating license paying a lump sum of GRD 160 billion. Its licence allowed OTE to provide mobile communications services using the DCS-1800 technology. In addition, it specified that OTE should pay an additional charge of GRD 90 billion, adjusted annually relative to the Consumer Price Index, for the use of all frequency spectrum allocated to the Organisation. The Ministry issued Decision 92093/1995 which granted OTE the right to use the radio spectrum of the 1710-1785 and 1805-1880 MHz frequency bands in the DCS 1800 system for mobile telephony. Subsequently, in 1996, COSMOTE was established for the purpose of providing mobile telecommunication services. Pursuant to Law 2465/97, OTE transferred its right to develop and provide personal communications services using DCS 1800 technology to its subsidiary COSMOTE. However, COSMOTE never paid for a mobile licence. Instead, OTE paid a lump sum of GRD 15.5 billion for the frequency bands required for the operation of the DCS 1800 system. Both established mobile operators complained to the Greek State and to the EC about unfair treatment since there was no open bidding procedure in the licensing of COSMOTE. However, there has never been a formal investigation to these claims.

According to its operating licence, OTE has also been enjoying certain privileges with respect to frequency allocation, including the right to request use of certain frequencies as part of its network expansion and modernisation programme. In the light of the upcoming new operating licence of OTE, these provisions should be reviewed and modified accordingly so as not to weaken competition in the market for wireless services.

A recent positive development that opened the way to new entrants in the market for wireless services has been EETT's decision in December 2000 to award six licences for fixed-wireless access (FWA) services in the local loop market.

With regard to the award of a fourth mobile licence, EETT sought the views of interested parties on a number of issues. These included, the type of services to be offered, the selected frequency bands, the expected number and duration of licences, the impact of the award of a fourth 2nd generation mobile licence upon the future award of UMTS licences, the role and rights of existing mobile operators regarding requests for use additional frequencies in the band they operate, the preferred mechanism for the allocation of licences (*i.e.* through a competitive tender procedure or through an auction procedure), etc. On 24 August 2000, EETT announced the results of the consultation process. In total, 10 companies participated in the process and all expressed interest in bidding for the fourth mobile licence. The majority of companies opted for the award of just one more operating licence in dual band through a competitive tender procedure.

No specific plans have yet been made regarding the introduction of the UMTS system. According to Greek officials, the granting of UMTS licenses is anticipated by June 2001. Given that FWA licences have been allocated by auction the same procedure should be used for UMTS. EETT needs to ensure that all licences are allocated on the basis of the same objective and transparent procedures.

2.2.9. *Rights of way*

Law 2246/94, as amended by law 2578/98, includes provisions for the granting of rights of way. Where the essential requirements or conditions related to environmental reasons are not met for rights of way to be granted, co-location and facility sharing are encouraged as second best alternatives. In particular, according to the Presidential Decree 165/99 that transposed the Interconnection Directive, the organisations that provide public telecommunications networks have the right to install own facilities on public or private land, or they can share the facilities and/or property with other organisations providing similar services following bilateral agreements among the parties concerned.

However, mobile operators and new entrants have reported several difficulties in getting access to rights of way which resulted in long delays in the installation of antennae for mobile services and the construction of alternative backbone infrastructure. The first company to obtain a license to build and operate a satellite network was granted the license in December 1999, almost three and a half years after it first filed an application in the summer of 1996. Company officials complained that delays were caused by the bureaucratic, uncoordinated procedures that required them to get permission from a range of public authorities for each earth station they installed.

Similar problems have been reported by Panafon and STET Hellas. The two mobile operators have filed a complaint with EETT accusing OTE of discriminatory behaviour for not treating them equally with COSMOTE in offering them co-locations in fixed facilities.

The new Law provides that EETT will establish procedures for 'one-stop-shopping'. These provisions are expected to facilitate new entrants in getting timely access to rights of way on public land. In addition, the new Law encourages negotiation of arrangements for facility sharing between operators, insofar as this would not impose an unreasonable economic burden or technical difficulty on facility-based operators.

2.2.10. Unbundling

In the last several years regulators have realised the importance of implementing policies to ensure that new entrants have access to unbundled local loops both as a means of stimulating competition for access, but also as a means of stimulating the roll-out of new technologies and stimulating the availability of broadband Internet access. For these reasons it is important that Greece ensure that unbundling policies, including the determination of prices for unbundled local loops, are in place.

EETT has looked at this issue and has published a consultative document seeking the views of industry players. A positive development in the implementation of unbundling policy has been the inclusion in the new Law of a condition that obliges operators with significant market power to provide competitors unbundled access to their local network at cost-based prices. In addition, the Law has taken an approach similar to the one adopted in Canada where unbundling of designated elements is mandated for a limited period of 5 years. The new Law in Greece provides for a limited period of compulsory unbundling of 4 years. These provisions are very positive as they will assist to compensate for the lack of alternative infrastructure in the country whilst giving an incentive to new entrants to deploy their own facilities. However, it is questionable whether the Law itself should specify the limited period during which unbundling will be required. Such detailed provisions should be left to the discretion of the regulator, who is in a better position to assess competitive and market developments and may need to impose a more flexible timetable. To be effective unbundling will depend on the price charged for wholesale access to unbundled local loops. If price rebalancing has not yet been completed, unbundling could well be ineffective so that the period during which unbundling provisions apply may need to be longer. Similarly, if an appropriate agreements between the incumbent and new entrants on technical and collocation issues have not yet been completed the full benefit of unbundling will not be available to new entrants.

2.3. Streamlining regulation

Greece is currently in the process of establishing a new regulatory framework for the sector. However, at the same time, officials responsible for the sector should question whether all regulations are necessary or whether the costs of establishing new regulations outweigh the benefits envisaged. No doubt that regulation will continue to be required in areas where the market mechanisms may fail, such as universal service, spectrum management, consumer protection and information and promotion of competition. However, in other areas, such as licensing streamlining could be rapidly implemented.

It is clear from the EU's 1999 Communication Review that during 2000-2003 there will be a new emphasis on streamlining regulations, including licensing procedures. Although Greece has only recently installed a new regulatory system, insufficient foresight has been given to implementing new best-practice regulations. Licensing is one area where the Greek authorities should take advantage of their delay and implement streamlined procedures that meet best practice regulation.

A number of OECD countries have introduced simple authorisation schemes that do not require explicit approval by the regulator for market entry. These market entry procedures have worked well and have facilitated the development of competition. The European Union is also in the process of proposing streamlined market entry procedures based on general authorisation.

In this context, the licensing regime in Greece needs to be streamlined to facilitate quick market entry at the expiry of OTE's exclusive provision period. This could best be achieved through a system of class licensing and eliminating the onerous requirements presently imposed.

2.4. Consumer protection and information

Greece has made important steps in the area of consumer protection. In particular, a relevant Ministerial Decree has been issued defining a procedure for public hearings and the resolution of disputes between consumers and operators. According to this Decree, EETT is responsible for examining unfair practices notified by consumers and for recommending appropriate action. EETT also maintains the right to require and obtain any information that is necessary in order to perform its duties. For example, it has the same powers as a taxation auditor, can make investigations on the premises of telecommunications operators, etc.

However, due to lack of human resources, EETT officials admitted that they have been unable to take drastic action in relation to consumer complaints. EETT has collected a 'package' of consumer complaints and has transferred them to the Ministry. In parallel, EETT has been collaborating with the Consumer Protection Authority, the body responsible for consumer affairs at the Ministry of Development, for the resolution of customer complaints against telecommunication operators.

A positive intervention by EETT on consumer affairs took place in June 1999 with the issue of a Recommendation addressed to both fixed and mobile operators. The Recommendation noted: (a) The need to provide consumers with sufficient information so as to enable them to make informed choices; (b) The provisions that telecommunication operators need to establish to resolve consumer complaints; and (c) The general provisions that need to be included in consumers' contracts with operators. The Recommendation referred to specific information that needs to be available to consumers, including information on tariffs, subsidisation schemes, quality of service indicators, etc.

A normal practice in the mobile market is for providers to impose on users a minimum subscription period of 1-2 years. This long subscription period is closely linked to the subsidisation of handsets since it allows operators to cover the subsidies for handsets through the monthly charges. EETT recommended that in their contracts with subscribers, mobile service providers should clearly state the exact amount of subsidies they provide for handsets. In this way, customers wishing to revoke their subscription before the end of the minimum subscription period will be able to refund the operator an amount equal to the subsidy provided by the mobile operator and be free to select a service provider of their choice. In addition, EETT recommended that mobile operators should not change the numbers allocated to customers if they move from one tariff package to another. However, so far mobile operators have not conformed to these recommendations.

Article 9 of the new Law further clarifies consumers' rights against telecommunication operators. What is still required is for EETT to establish a Consumer Complaints Centre where complaints about telecommunication operators will be collected, and for all operators to be report on the number of consumer complaints as part of their annual reporting duties to EETT. It is also important that EETT has, if necessary sufficient powers to enforce recommendations if they are not adhered to by industry.

2.5. Quality of service

OTE's license prescribes specific quality of service targets to be achieved in urban areas by the end of 2003 (see Section 3 for details). It also states that OTE should improve the quality of its telephony services each year between 1996 and 2003 and attain certain quantitative development objectives relating to the spare capacity of the exchanges, the level of network digitalisation, etc. Similarly, the licences of mobile operators issued in 1992 included specific geographical and population coverage requirements. In addition, specific quality requirements for the provision of leased line services were defined in relevant Presidential Decrees.

The law requires all telecommunication operators to provide EETT with data on their service performance in order to enable it to check compliance with quality of service targets. Furthermore, in a relevant Recommendation issued in June 1999 (see also Section on consumer information), EETT called operators to collaborate on the establishment of specific indicators to measure progress made in quality of service objectives.

EETT does not publish the results of its quality monitoring. EETT should monitor and publish quality of service data for the incumbent and other potential wire-based operators. It could also examine the possibility of publishing quality of service data for mobile operators and can benefit by examining similar initiatives of other regulators.

The earthquake in Attica in September 1999 led to a surge in mobile traffic by approximately 800% and created severe problems in the operation of mobile networks. In order to ensure that this problem would not occur in future emergencies, the EETT requested the incumbent and the three mobile operators to establish an action plan for emergency situations that would allow for the timely repair of faults on their networks.

2.6. Universal Service Obligation

Under the previous legal framework, OTE had total responsibility for the provision of universal service until 31/12/00. Article 5 of the Presidential Decree 165/ adopted a limited definition for universal service that includes provision of the following services:

- Voice telephony.
- Facsimile Group III communications in accordance with ITU – T Recommendation in the "T-Series".
- Voice band data transmission via modems at a rate of at least 9600 bps in accordance with ITU-T Recommendations in the "V-series".
- Operator assistance.
- Directory services.
- Provision of public pay phones.
- Free access to emergency services (112).

The previous telecommunications law provided that certain expenses incurred by OTE for the provision of services to remote geographical and uneconomic areas would be subsidised by the Ministry of Finance. These expenses could not exceed 2% of OTE's annual operating and capital expenditures. Up to now, OTE did not maintain an appropriate cost allocation method that would allow it to estimate the costs of providing these services. Thus, the compensation it has received so far is based on OTE's subjective estimates of the costs of providing services to uneconomic areas.[27] In the light of full opening of the market this practice should stop. The new OTE charter should delimit any form of subsidisation from the state and refrain any sort of favourable treatment to OTE that would put in danger the development of free and fair competition.

The new Law explicitly states that any telecommunication operator can undertake to provide universal service. At the same time, it extends OTE's obligations for the provision of universal service until 31/12/2001. Should market participants entrusted with the provision of universal service prove that it conforms an excess burden to them the law provides for the establishment of a universal service fund.

In the light of circumstances, it is unlikely that any initiatives will be taken before the end of 2000 to determine how universal service should be funded. Before such a decision is taken it is also important that a determination be made of the costs of providing universal service and to use this to decide whether it is a burden on the incumbent. Any such study should be based on a methodology that complies with the EC recommendations and is approved by all parties concerned.[28] If the cost of universal service provision constitutes a relatively small burden on the incumbent then it may be possible to require the incumbent to maintain the burden of universal service provision, recognising that there are also benefits to operators providing universal service.

The new Law also relates the concept of universal service to the development of an Information Society without, however, imposing any additional burden on telecommunication operators to subsidise educational, health, and other social policy objectives. This decision conforms to best policy practices and should be applauded. It is the Government's intention to fund the development of an Information Society directly through the structural funds allocated to the country from the 3rd Community Support Framework Programme.

2.7. Application of competition principles

The basic provisions of Greek competition law are set out in Law No.703/77 for the "Monitoring of Monopolies and Oligopolies and Protection of Free Competition". The law essentially incorporates the relevant EU regulations in the Greek legal context and applies to all sectors of the economy, except where it is provided otherwise.

In the telecommunication sector in particular, the relevant law 2246/94 entrusted EETT with responsibilities over the supervision and enforcement of competition principles in the sector. There is no exemption that prohibits the Competition Authority from playing a role in the telecommunication sector. In practice, it is the Competition Authority together with EETT who are the administrative bodies responsible for monitoring and enforcing competition policy. EETT often seeks consultation with the Competition Authority to restrain anti-competitive practices in the market, even though there has been no formal method of co-ordination with EETT. The Competition Authority remains severely understaffed and its officers have limited knowledge of the field of telecommunications.

The Competition Authority also approves mergers and take-overs where applicable. In addition, according to the previous telecommunication law (Law 2246/94), any significant change in the ownership of a telecommunication operator granted with an individual license has to be approved by the Minister for Transport and Communications. It is expected that the Competition Authority will play a larger role in the sector as competition emerges and a new statute on competition policy is adopted. It is important that, where there is some overlap in the jurisdiction and competencies of EETT and the Competition Authority that they establish agreed procedures for consultation and taking action based.

The new legislation on competition policy amends law 703/77 and provides for the re-organisation and empowerment of the Competition Authority. The law includes a provision that defines further the role of Competition Authority in sectors regulated by independent authorities like EETT. In particular, the law states that the Competition Authority should have sole responsibility over the enforcement of competition principles in all incidents reported to it by the independent authorities.

Further reference to fair competition practices is included in the new telecommunications law. Article 8, para 8 of the new Law transposes Directive 99/64/EC which calls for the legal separation between the telecommunication and cable television activities operated by a single operator. In particular, the new provision restricts a legal entity representing a telecommunication operator with significant market power from having control over a cable network. This is an important clause for the development of competition even though it is presently not relevant in Greece due to the lack of cable infrastructure.

There have been a few occasions where EETT, together with the Competition Authority intervened effectively and provided protection to new entrants against abusive market power of the incumbent. One example concerns a case in which two independent service providers, Forthnet and Telecom Dynamics, filed a complaint with EETT against OTE in connection with the provision of leased lines. The companies complained that OTE's considerable delay in providing leased lines was an abuse of its monopoly position. EETT initiated a formal inquiry in consultation with the Competition Authority. No decision has yet been issued, but if EETT finds there is ground to these allegations it is likely that OTE will be penalised. EETT has the authority to fine an organisation up to 15% of its annual turnover in the relevant sector.

On another occasion, EETT imposed a fine of GRD 80 millions against OTE for anti-competitive behaviour on the grounds that OTE did not provide independent Internet Service Providers with single access numbers as it had done with its own subsidiary OTEnet. Out of the GRD 80 million fine, GRD 50 million were imposed on behalf of the Competition Authority and the rest on behalf of EETT. Nevertheless, it should be noted that, so far, EETT has not taken a pro-active approach in monitoring the market and enforcing competition principles. Rather, it has waited for the industry to launch complaints before taking the initiative and responding to a market problem.

2.8. Greece and the WTO agreement

Greece has one of the 68 member-countries of the WTO that agreed to open their markets to competition in basic telecommunications services at pre-defined dates. The agreement also requires WTO members to allow foreign telecommunications operators to provide services in any member country as well as to have shareholding rights in telecommunications enterprises of that member country.

Greece is about to comply with the first commitment on 1/1/2001 when the market for public fixed voice telephony and network infrastructure will open to competition. In relation to the cross-border supply of telecommunications services, Greece permits foreign telecommunications service providers to operate in the market as long as they operate in the form of a *société anonyme* and are exclusively engaged in the provision of telecommunications services. As regards companies from non-WTO member countries, Greece will maintain the access restrictions to the market for public fixed voice telephony and network infrastructure until 1/1/2003.

2.9. The impact of convergence on regulation

The progressive convergence of telecommunications, broadcasting and information technology has led to the development of new types of applications and services that do not strictly fit into the existing service classification system set up for regulatory purposes. Such services stem from the deployment of Internet for business applications, including e-commerce, and the development of digital broadcasting platforms. Regulators across OECD countries have started to realise that technological and service convergence needs to be treated with care so that artificial regulatory barriers imposed do not inhibit the economic and social benefits it can generate. The main issue of concern has been how to facilitate the process of convergence, especially when each of the sectors involved is regulated by a different regulatory institution.

Greece has lagged behind its OECD counterparts in ensuring that regulators form the various sectors co-ordinate their actions to ensure efficient convergence between the various technologies and services. In Greece, the broadcasting and telecommunications sectors are still regarded as separate entities. The National Radio-Television Council supervised by the Ministry of Press and Mass Media regulates the broadcasting industry, and EETT supervised by the Ministry of Transport and

Communications regulates the telecommunications sector. There is a formal requirement for co-operation between the regulators and the Ministries in the case of licensing a broadcasting network. In particular, the relevant law stipulates that such a network should first obtain a telecommunications license. However, in practice market players are faced with an extended bureaucracy that causes delays in the launch of new services.

A plausible solution to the problem followed by many OECD countries is the unification of regulatory functions in broadcasting and telecommunications under a single independent organisation that will operate at arm's length from the relevant Ministries and the Government. The latter will still maintain their policy functions in the respective sectors.

Greece should consider the creation of a Telecommunications and Broadcasting Committee that would combine the regulatory functions of both the telecommunication and the broadcasting sectors.

3. PERFORMANCE OF THE TELECOMMUNICATIONS INDUSTRY

3.1. Introduction

The rationale for regulatory reform is the increase in the efficiency in the provision of services and the beneficial effects it is expected to deliver to users and consumers. This section assesses the performance of the Greek telecommunications industry in the delivery of those benefits to users and consumers, using indicators related to network penetration, investment, price, quality, and productivity.

The main elements of market performance examined below are:

- Network development and modernisation;

- Services based on leading edge technology and infrastructure;

- Lower prices;

- Improved quality of service;

- Increased customer choice; and

- Benefit to users.

The exclusive right retained by OTE for the provision of voice telephony and the establishment and provision of public telecommunications networks, arising from the European Commission's derogation,

Table 8. Main telecommunication indicators

	1995	1996	1997	1998	1999
Telecommunication Services: Operating Revenue (billion GRD)	680.6	832.9	1 048.0	1 273.8	1 597.4
Total Employment ('000)	25 381	24 758	23 841	23 733	24 000*
OTE's Operating Revenue per access line (GRD '000)	116.6	130.5	151.7	170.8	197.3
OTE's Operating Revenue per employee (GRD '000.)	24 498	29 206	36 224	43 116	51 275

Note:
Total employment includes mobile and fixed services.
* Estimate for 1999.
Source: OECD (1999), Telecommunications Database 1999 and OTE.

Table 9.   OTE's distribution of telecommunication service revenue

PSTN Service Revenue	1998		1999	
(incl. Revenue from fixed charges)	Drachmas (million)	Per cent	Drachmas (million)	Per cent
Basic monthly rentals	132 592	14.0	147 844	13.5
Local & long distance calls:	416 626	43.9	454 239	41.4
[of which fixed to mobile:]	112 325	11.8	177 779	16.2
Other	18 064	1.9	17 290	1.6
International	175 594	18.5	174 769	15.9
Mobile services	9 013	1.0	58 270	5.4
Total (fixed telephony & Mobile)	751 889	79.3	852 412	77.8
Leased lines & data communications	42 072	4.4	45 521	4.1
Other operating revenues	154 047	16.3	198 368	18.1
Total operating revenues	948 008	100	1 096 301	100

Source: OTE Annual Report 1999.

has limited customer choice with respect to the main telecommunication service offerings. Nevertheless, the indicators are important in the context of the incumbent's commitment, as well as that of the government, to use the breathing space given by the European Union's derogation to undertaken required structural changes and investments. The concern relating to network development and modernisation is also important since it is critical in the delivery of the benefits of the Information Economy.

The telecommunication service sector, as measured by telecommunication service revenues, in Greece has increased, as shown in Table 8, from 75.4 billion drachmas in 1985 ($546 million) to 1 597.4 billion drachmas by 1999 ($5 226.2 million). The telecommunication sector, one of the most dynamic in the Greek economy,[26] increased its share in GDP from 1.3% to 2.9% during this period. During the same period the number of telephone mainlines expanded significantly, from 3.1 million lines to 5.6 million or 53.4 per 100 inhabitants. Employment in the sector, which stood at 30 571 in 1985 has declined steadily to around 24 000. The incumbent, OTE, was ranked 43rd in 1999 among the major public telecommunication operators in the OECD area as measured by revenues.

Over three-quarters of operating revenue of OTE derives from public switched telecommunication services (Table 9). However, this share is in relative decline as new business areas are developing, mainly Internet access, and business services.

3.2. Network development and modernisation

The growth in telecommunication access lines in Greece has decreased from a compound annual growth rate of 5.3% during 1987-92 to 3.8% during the 1992-97 period.[30] This growth has been just above the average for the OECD during these two periods (see Figure 2). In terms of access lines per capita, Greece ranked 15th in the OECD in 1997 with a penetration rate of 52 lines per 100 population (compared to an OECD average of 49). By 1999 the penetration rate had increased to 53.4 per 100 inhabitants. The build-up of network capacity has eliminated the long waiting time for a connection, a common feature of the 1970s and 1980s. The waiting list which in 1994 stood at 210 930 had declined to 27 163 by 1998 and, at present, waiting time for a new connection is under a week.

The traditionally high penetration rate in Greece reflects the fact that more than one-third of subscribers have more than one home and about 14% of subscribers have more than one line. In addition, OTE has made an effort to equip the main tourist resorts with good telecommunication access. Data are not provided by OTE as to coverage in rural areas and small communities situated in areas not frequented by tourists.

Table 10. Public telecommunication investment as a percentage of revenue

	1986-88	1989-91	1992-94	1995	1996	1997	1998	1999
Greece	20.5	33.4	45.6	24.1	23.6	25.6	27.9*	29.5*
OECD average	25.8	27.5	25.0	24.4	25.1	24.4	25.1	26.6

* Only OTE Group investment.
Source: OECD (1999), *Communications Outlook* 1999, Paris, Table 4.10, p. 81.

Table 10 indicates that in Greece, public telecommunications investment (*i.e.* OTE's investment) as a percentage of revenue increased significantly in the early 1990s (when about 1 million access lines were added between 1991-1995). Increases in investment over the last few years reflect investment in mobile activities and OTE's international investments. OTE has also undertaken significant investments outside of Greece since 1997 (Table 11).

Table 11. International telecommunication investments by OTE

June 1997	20% in Telekom Srbija GRD 106 billion.
March 1998	90% equity in ArmenTel GRD 41 billion.
December 1998	35% in Romtelecom GRD 189 billion.
July 1999/July 2000	Failure to get agreement with KPN to purchase 51% of Bulgarian Telecommunications company USD 320 m (OTE share).
May 2000	Expression of interest in 51% of equity of telecommunication operator of FYR of Macedonia.
July 2000	Purchase of 85% of AMC (mobile operator in Albania) by COSMOTE USD85.6 m.

Source: OTE.

3.3. Digitalisation

In contrast to network expansion, Greece's performance in terms of network digitalisation has been rather weak. In 1997 Greece had the lowest rate of digitalisation among OECD countries at 47%.[31] As shown in Table 12 a number of smaller economies performed significantly better than OTE, even though during the last several years prior to full market liberalisation OTE has undertaken a significant improvement in network upgrading. By the end of 1999, 90.6% of installed access lines were connected to digital exchanges in Greece[32] and OTE has earmarked US$ 271 million over 2000-2002 for digitalisation of the switching network. The targeted rate of digitalisation for the end of 2000 is 95%.[33]

Table 12. OTE's rate of digitalisation

	1993	1995	1997	1998	1999
Greece	22.0	37.1	47.1	74.5	90.6
Czech Republic	10.0	17.0	54.6	64.1	74.4
Ireland	71.0	79.0	92.0	100.0	100.0
Poland	9.5	48.0	58.0	62.0	68.0
Portugal	59.0	70.0	88.3	98.0	100.0
OECD average	58.8	74.8	87.5	92.1	94.2

Source: OECD, *Communications Outlook* 1999, and *Communications Outlook* 2001, and OTE.

New technologies have emerged with digitalisation, in particular ISDN. National coverage for ISDN was achieved at the end of 1998. Penetration of ISDN increased from 4 184 subscribers in 1995 to 27 522 basic rate access lines by the end of 1999 or about 0.5% of main lines. By the end of the 1st quarter of 2000 the number of basic rate access line customers had reached 85 983 (or 1.5% of main lines). Commercial ADSL services had not yet been made available in mid-2000 although pilot trials were being held. The objective of the company is to have 2000 ADSL connections in service by the end of 2000. In this context there is concern by potential new market entrants that they will not be given sufficient time to be involved in trials before OTE begins offering ADSL commercially.

3.4. Cellular mobile services

Growth in fixed line infrastructure has been accompanied by rapid growth in cellular mobile infrastructure and markets where the benefits of competition to users can be clearly seen. As noted in previous sections, Greece, unlike most OECD countries, did not issue a licence for analogue mobile telephony. In September 1992, following a competitive tendering process, two GSM licences were provided to STET Hellas and Panafon. A third licence was given to the incumbent (as COSMOTE) in 1996. The first two licensees commenced service in mid-1993. However, significant growth and competition only began once the third licensee began commercial service in April 1998 (see Table 13). A fourth licence is expected to be awarded at the end of 2000.

Table 13.   Cellular mobile subscribers

	1997	1998	1999	2000*
Panafon	623 739	1 191 000	1 663 209	1 901 945
Telestet	391 000	688 614	1 182 751	1 414 812
Cosmote		299 000	1 058 000	1 515 235
TOTAL	**1 014 739**	**2 178 614**	**3 903 960**	**4 831 994**
Market penetration	9.7%	20.7%	37.1%	45.2%

*   June 2000.
Source: Company annual reports.

As of the end of 1999 the mobile penetration rate in Greece had reached 37 per 100 inhabitants climbing to 45% by mid-2000. This penetration rate was below the European Union average, but comparable to the OECD average. Market share was fairly evenly distributed among the three companies with the leader, Panafon 39%, Cosmote 32% and STET Hellas 29%. By the end of 1999 over 90% of the Greek population was covered by the 3 mobile networks[34] and the geographic area covered was, depending on the operator, between 45-56% of the country. The distribution of subscribers by type of subscription by the end of 1999 is shown below:

Table 14.   Distribution of subscribers by type of subscription

	Contract	Pre-paid
Cosmote	39.9	19.7
Panafon	36.3	45.5
Stet Hellas	23.7	34.8

The development of the cellular mobile sector and mobile revenue has resulted in its share in total telecommunications revenue increasing from 12% in 1995 to 31% in 1999 (Table 15). 3.5. Development of competition.

Table 15. Cellular mobile revenue (GRD million)

	1995	1996	1997	1998	1999
Panafon	40 700	82 100	130 500	205 500	221 800
Telestet	37 703	55 459	93 779	118 486	151 638
Cosmote	–	–	–	4 500	117 000
Total	78 403	137 559	224 279	328 486	490 438

Source: Company annual reports.

3.5. Development of competition

Although full liberalisation will occur only on 1 January 2001 in Greece, the potential threat of competition and the process of adjusting prices to reflect costs has brought some benefits to Greek consumers and users (see Section below). However, these have been mainly from digitalisation and the improvement in quality of service it brought, from the expansion in the network and, for relatively heavy users of long distance services. However, the delay in opening the market and the fact that Greece, unlike some other EU countries maintained a closed market for the full derogation period, has meant that most consumers and users have borne the cost of a monopoly market. The delay in awarding PSTN licences, which will inevitably occur given that 3 months before the scheduled market opening, no licensing framework had been put in place, will also reduce the cumulative benefits that would come from competition. The first effects of direct competition are unlikely to be felt before mid-2001 when new entrants begin service.

Greece, unlike a number of other European Union countries, lacks alternate communication infrastructures. Cable television infrastructure does not exist as a commercial service although some small pilot projects are underway. This may have the effect of slowing down the development of competition particular in terms of access to the local loop.

3.6. Price performance and rebalancing

OTE began in 1995 to rebalance its prices. Even though the derogation given by the European Commission to Greece in 1997, allowing it to maintain reserved services until 2001, was given in order to allow OTE to rebalance its prices, this process has yet to be completed. According to OTE monthly fixed charges and local charges are below cost.[35] The derogation (Decision 97/607/EC) specifically states that OTE's fixed network prices should be aligned with costs by 1 January 2001.

OTE's local telephony charges are shown below in Table 16. Two price adjustments took place in 1999 and one in 2000 and it can be expected that new price changes will be introduced either in late 2000 or the beginning of 2001 which will increase local call and fixed monthly charges. Local call charging has changed over the years from an untimed tariff rate for analogue lines to a duration-based tariff rate on digital lines (which now predominate). On 1 March 1999 the charge for one tariff unit was restructured to 6 drachmas per minute (subsequently raised to 7 drachmas on November 1999) compared to 13 drachmas per 3 minutes in 1998. This was a significant price increase, in particular for off-peak charges where the increase in the per minute price was from GRD 1.6 a minute to GRD 3.5 (the peak per minute charge applies for 2 minutes during off-peak). A further price adjustment took place in August 2000 increasing local call charges and monthly rental charges, while decreasing long distance charges.

Table 16.   Local telephony charges

	1995	1996	1997	1998	1999*	2000 (August)
Connection charges (GRD)	72 000	50 000	30 000	15 000	10 000	10 000
Monthly rental charges (GRD)	1 450	1 650	1 850	2 050	2 300	2 400
Charge for one tariff unit (GRD)	9.0	10.2	11.5	13.0	7.0	9.0
Duration of a tariff unit (minutes)						
Peak	3	3	3	3	1	1
Off-peak	8	8	8	8	2	2

* As of November 1999. The charge for one tariff unit was changed to GRD 6.0 per minute on 1 March 2000.
Source: EETT/OTE.

OTE in justifying the introduction of per minute charges argued that this is an advantage to consumers, because such a structure is fairer taking into account shorter calls,[36] but this is disingenuous in that under such circumstances OTE should have introduced per second charging, which has become the norm in competitive markets. OTE should move rapidly to implement local charges based on per second, rather than per minute charges. This would also allow for further rebalancing to be implemented while limiting the impact on consumers.

In line with changes in local charges, price changes have taken place in domestic long distance and international charges (Table 17). However, these price adjustments have not been consistent with price developments in other countries or with rebalancing. The period 1994 to 1997 was characterised by increases in long distance prices, whereas rebalancing would have suggested that these prices should have been reduced. The process of price reduction began only after the 1997 derogation. It was only in November 1999 that OTE made a significant effort to reduce long distance charges resulting in the ratio of the longest long distance call charge to the local charge falling from 21 to 8 (Table 17), and falling to 4 as a result of the August 2000 rebalancing. The shortest long distance call zone was all priced as a local call, thus effectively reducing the number of long distance zones to two. This is in line with practice in other OECD countries where pricing is becoming distance insensitive. Price rebalancing which took place in August 2000 merged the two remaining long distance zones into one. OTE, unlike many operators in OECD countries does not have different prices for residential as compared to business customers and does not provide any volume discounts.

Table 17.   Distance service charges (GRD per minute)

		1994	1995	1996	1997	1998	1999	2000
	Up to 45 km peak	23	25	27	37	30	7	9
Distance	45-80 km peak	56	63	68	70	60	45	40
	>80 km peak	78	90	94	99	90	54	40
Ratio of longest long-distance call charge to local call		55.7	30.0	27.6	26.0	20.9	7.7	4.4
International call charges per minute (weighted average in ecu)		0.56	0.57	0.57	0.56	0.52	0.49	0.44

Source: MTC/OTE.

Price levels in other countries provide an important source of price benchmarks. For these purposes the OECD collects the prices of a basket of telecommunications for residential and business customers in each of the OECD countries.[37] These price comparisons indicate that Greece's relative PSTN price performance has been within the lower third most expensive of OECD countries for residential prices (Figure 2). Performance for a business basket of calls was relatively better with Greece's performance just better than the OECD average (Figure 3).

Figure 2. **OECD Composite Residential basket, November 2000**

USD PPP

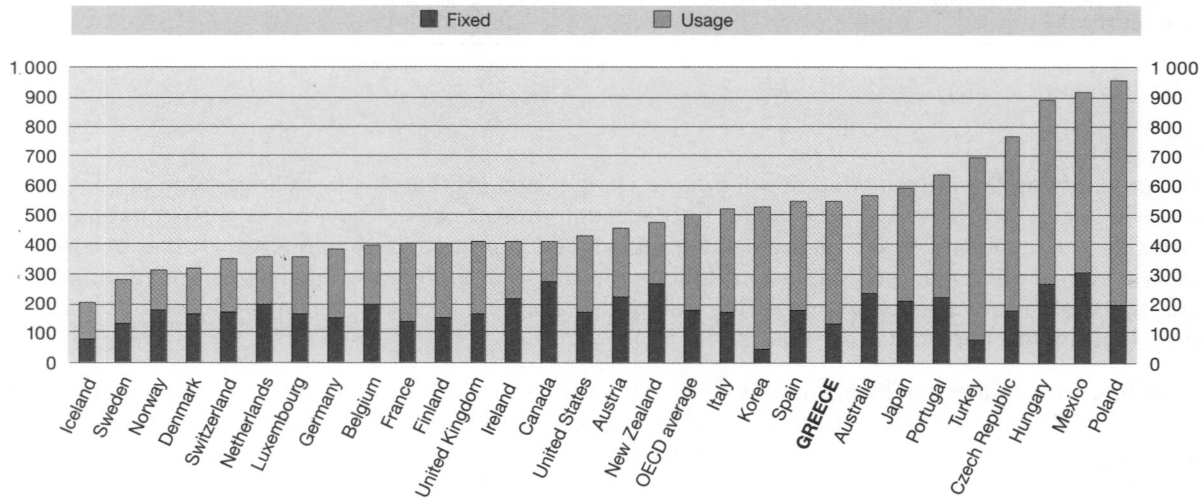

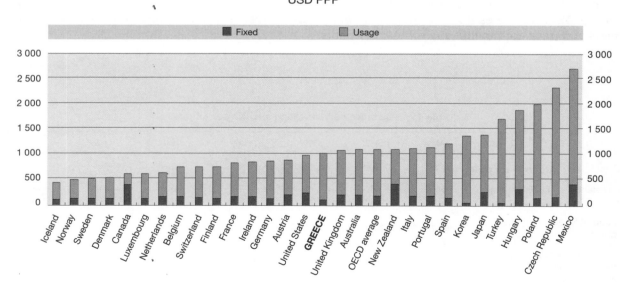

Note: VAT included, excludes calls to mobiles.

Figure 3. **OECD Composite Business basket, November 2000**

USD PPP

Note: VAT included, excludes calls to mobiles.

The trend in price rebalancing for OTE compared to some other OECD countries is shown in Figure 5. Significant increases in fixed charges (both monthly rental and connection) and in long distance charges (see above) after 1993 account for the exaggerated changes in prices between 1994-1997. The rental charge has been increasing since then, but mainly as a result of digitalisation, the connection charge has been reduced quite significantly.

3.7. International telecommunication prices

3.7.1. *International prices*

Greece in the past had relatively high international telecommunication prices[38] but recent price reductions have resulted in Greece's average collection charge (peak rate) to be well under the OECD average.[39] Significant adjustments have also been made in accounting rates, which in 1996 were considerably out of line with best practice (Table 18). Significant efforts have been made to reduce these rates, although there is still scope for further reductions. Given Greece's ambition to become a Mediterranean hub low international rates are important. A single price is now in effect for international calls to EU countries, Canada and the US.

Table 18.   Accounting rates with the United States (USD)

	1996	1997	1998	1999	2000
Greece	$1.01	0.86	0.55	0.30	0.26
France	$0.35	0.26	0.21	0.20	0.20
Ireland	$0.35	0.33	0.19	0.19	0.20
Italy	$0.52	0.33	0. 22	0.22	0.21
Portugal	$0.83	0.60	0.43	0.30	0.29
Spain	$0.64	0.48	0.26	0.27	0.27
United Kingdom (BT)	$0.36	0.20	0.21	0.21	0.20

Source: International Bureau, Federal Communications Commission, US.

3.7.2. *Mobile prices*

Greece is also performing relatively well in terms of mobile prices (Figure 4). Performance in this area has improved considerably due to the entry of the third licensee and their aggressive market behaviour.

Figure 4.   **Mobile consumer basket, November 2000**
USD PPP

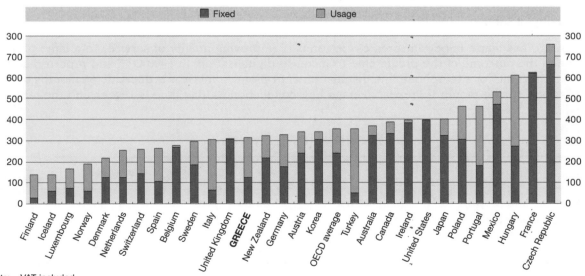

Note: VAT included.

3.7.3. *Leased lines*

The availability of leased lines and their price levels are important for the development of competition since new entrants initially will rely on these circuits to develop service. Leased circuits have also become important for the development of Internet services. Compared to other OECD countries, prices in Greece for leased circuits have been extremely high for 64kbit lines, on the basis of an OECD index of 100, Greece's index was at 168.[40] Since then price performance has improved but prices in this area remain above the OECD average (Figure 5). Prices for 1.5/2.0Mbit/s circuits were just under the OECD average for national lines and among the most expensive for international circuits.[41] In 1998 demand for leased circuits increased by 163% mainly as a result of mobile development.

Figure 5. **Leased lines charges, November 2000**
USD PPP

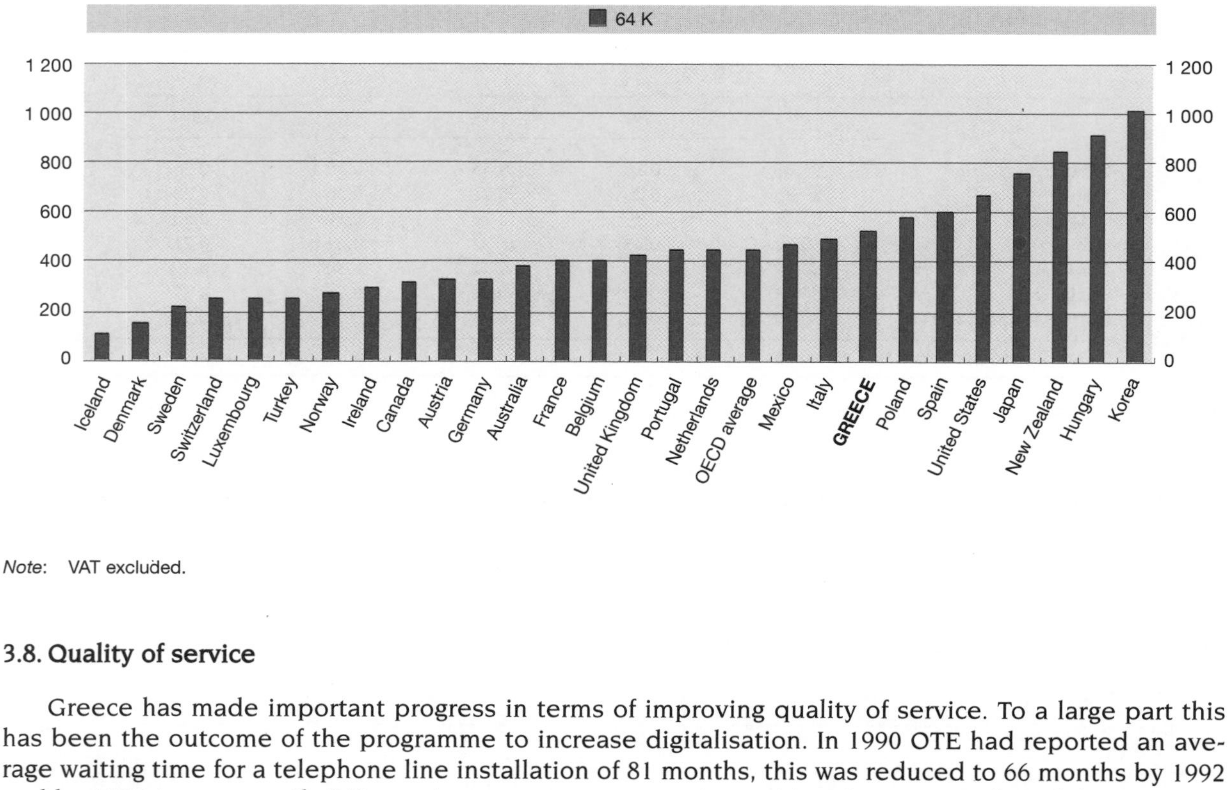

Note: VAT excluded.

3.8. Quality of service

Greece has made important progress in terms of improving quality of service. To a large part this has been the outcome of the programme to increase digitalisation. In 1990 OTE had reported an average waiting time for a telephone line installation of 81 months, this was reduced to 66 months by 1992 and by 1995 to one month.[42] Present average new connection waiting time is 1 week and the target for

Table 19. OTE's quality of service

	1993	1998	1999	2000 target	2003 Licence target
Faults per 100 lines per year	51.0	24	17	15	10
Percentage of faults repaired within 24 hours	57.0	83	90.5	92	95
Unsuccessful calls	n.a.	<0.9%	<0.8%	<0.8%	<1.0%
Calls waiting over 3 seconds for dial tone	n.a.	<5%	<4.8%	<4.5%	<1%

Source: OTE, OECD.

the year 2000 is for less than one week.[43] Table 19 provides data on the evolution of OTE's quality of service.

OTE is subject to quality of service targets to be met by 2003 (Table 19) which are imposed in its licence under the OTE Law. It has met several of these targets already. OTE's licence also requires it to install by 2003 7 public telephones for every 1 000 inhabitants (5 of these phones must be cardphones).

3.9. Employment and productivity

A simple measure of labour productivity is the number of access lines per employee. Although this measure has many shortfalls,[44] it is useful as a point of comparison. Labour productivity in telecommunications has increased rapidly in Greece as a result of the growth in infrastructure combined with a reduction of OTE's workforce (Table 20). The reduction in OTE's workforce has yet to be compensated through new employment creation in new entrants, for example, the mobile companies. As a result, net telecommunications employment has decreased in Greece and is unlikely to begin to show a net increase until the third quarter of 2001 as new entrants begin to develop a customer base.

Table 20.   Employment and labour productivity

	1995	1996	1997	1998	1999	2000 (31 March)
OTE employees	24 581	23 808	22 741	21 925	21 588	20 441
OTE lines per employee	210	223	238	252	260	275

Source: OTE.

Greece has had, historically, low ratios of revenue per employee (about half the OECD average). For example, in 1997 revenue per employee was USD 144 500 compared to an OECD average of USD 236 700.[45] Lack of competitive pressure resulting in high costs and over-employment account for this.

3.10. Internet developments and performance

As of the 1st quarter of 2000 the number of dial-up Internet subscribers in Greece numbered about 237 400 and permanent connections 1 709. The number of dial-up subscribers is extremely low amounting to about 2% of population, which places Greece among the lowest OECD performers in this area. Forthnet, is the leading commercial Internet Service Provider in Greece,[46] and OTE's ISP OTEnet holds second place.

Perhaps the main reason for this lag[47] is the low penetration of PCs estimated at about 5% of the population.[48] Pricing performance is slightly better than the OECD average for peak times (Table 21), however, because off-peak time starts at 22:00 hours, the comparisons for off-peak show Greece among the more expensive OECD countries. Internet usage does not follow PSTN usage patterns so that using the same off-peak rates as for telephony penalises Greek Internet users, and in particular children. Internet access tariffs should be adjusted by OTE to implement a more reasonable start for off-peak rates.

Most OECD countries have become concerned with the high cost of local call charges, especially for intensive use, such as for electronic commerce and Internet access. Regulators and incumbent operators, who view Internet as a new business opportunity, are therefore making efforts to readjust their call charges downward.

Table 21   OECD Internet access basket for 20 hours at peak times using discounted PSTN rates, September 2000, including VAT

	PSTN Fixed		PSTN Usage		ISP		Total	
	USD	USD PPP	USD	USD PPP	USD	USD PPP	USD	USD PPP
Australia	8.76	10.95	1.92	2.39	17.38	21.73	28.06	35.07
Austria	18.48	19.06	24.95	25.73	0.00	0.00	43.44	44.78
Belgium	14.65	16.09	26.90	29.56	5.59	6.14	47.13	51.79
Canada	16.76	20.44	0.00	0.00	12.37	15.09	29.13	35.53
Czech Republic	4.71	11.77	26.72	66.80	11.49	28.72	42.92	107.29
Denmark	18.24	15.33	0.00	0.00	18.07	15.18	36.31	30.51
Finland	11.55	11.41	11.44	11.30	7.26	7.17	30.25	29.88
France	10.66	11.11	0.00	0.00	21.64	22.54	32.30	33.65
Germany	13.31	13.72	0.00	0.00	19.79	20.40	33.10	34.12
GREECE	7.59	10.26	7.59	10.26	15.82	21.38	31.01	41.90
Hungary	7.88	18.75	25.18	59.96	9.55	22.74	42.61	101.45
Iceland	6.66	5.33	19.39	15.51	11.24	8.99	37.28	29.83
Ireland	15.17	17.05	19.01	21.36	13.89	15.61	48.07	54.02
Italy	10.48	12.63	16.25	19.58	0.00	0.00	26.73	32.21
Japan	16.17	9.86	24.02	14.65	18.02	10.99	58.20	35.49
Korea	2.47	3.98	10.67	17.21	3.85	6.21	16.99	27.40
Luxembourg	11.80	12.69	0.00	0.00	42.66	45.87	54.46	58.56
Mexico	17.20	24.57	0.00	0.00	8.98	12.83	26.18	37.40
Netherlands	16.68	18.53	28.39	31.55	0.00	0.00	45.07	50.08
New Zealand	16.16	22.77	0.00	0.00	11.13	15.68	27.30	38.45
Norway	20.47	16.91	23.61	19.52	10.94	9.04	55.02	45.47
Poland	7.00	13.22	32.15	60.66	0.00	0.00	39.16	73.88
Portugal	11.82	17.38	20.35	29.93	0.00	0.00	32.17	47.31
Spain	9.09	11.96	25.51	33.57	0.00	0.00	34.60	45.53
Sweden	11.32	10.02	26.02	23.03	2.59	2.29	39.93	35.33
Switzerland	15.83	12.77	32.66	26.34	0.00	0.00	48.49	39.10
Turkey	3.59	6.65	3.59	6.65	3.85	7.14	11.04	20.44
United Kingdom	14.87	13.64	29.55	27.11	0.00	0.00	44.42	40.75
United States	13.65	13.65	2.33	2.33	5.45	5.45	21.43	21.43
OECD	12.17	13.88	15.11	19.14	9.36	11.08	36.65	44.09
EU	13.27	14.21	16.10	17.82	9.34	9.96	38.71	41.99

Source: OECD.

4.   CONCLUSIONS AND RECOMMENDATIONS

4.1. General assessment of current strengths and weaknesses

The regulatory regime in Greece displays some strengths (see below). These strengths are, however, *potential* depending very much on the practical implementation of the provisions of the new Law by the regulator (EETT) and the extent to which the government takes an arm's length position towards the incumbent, OTE, and its new strategic partner. These strengths in the regulatory framework can position Greece for effective competition once the voice telephony market is open for competition in January 2001. They can also be expected to provide substantial benefits to consumers and users if further reforms are taken to complete the implementation of a transparent and neutral regulatory framework based on sound economic principles.

Greece has relatively high penetration rates for fixed telephony and a competitive mobile sector with good levels of penetration. The fourth mobile licence will ensure that the mobile sector become highly competitive and should boost penetration rates by a significant amount. Facilities-based competition, starting from 2001 should result in a rapid completion of digitalisation and begin to provide broadband access.

The new law, although it has some weaknesses, provides a good basis in which the EETT can begin to implement the necessary details of regulations. The enhanced role given to the EETT in the new law is important in this respect.

The incumbent, OTE, has made considerable gains in efficiency and improving quality of service over the last several years, but still requires significant changes in corporate culture laying stress on customer requirements and marketing. Prices, although relatively low, can be improved in terms of targeting specific customer groups more effectively, and by providing more suitable pricing structures for Internet access and electronic commerce applications.

An important initiative has been taken in this context of local loop unbundling. OTE is required to provide unbundled access (access to raw copper) to its local loop to other operators on reasonable terms, including any ADSL enhanced segments. To maintain incentives on new entrants to deploy their own infrastructure rather than depend indefinitely on the incumbent's, the requirement on OTE to provide unbundled elements of its network is restricted to a specific period (four years). Such policies will help enhance competition in the local loop if they are supplemented by regulatory oversight ensuring collocation, reasonable prices for unbundled local loops, and effective arbitration.

There are also a number of important weaknesses that characterise the Greek telecommunication scene.

The derogation provided to Greece can be characterised as a lost opportunity. The fact that the main objective of the derogation, to rebalance OTE's prices, was not achieved is indicative of the insufficient effort made to prepare for full market liberalisation. As well, the fact that the Greek government chose to maintain the full derogation, unlike some other EU countries, is indicative of the lack of commitment, during 1996-1999, to create a competitive telecommunication market. There are indications of a greater commitment to reform in the recent past. The new Law is a significant step forward relative to earlier drafts that had been under consideration. The decision to reduce the government's share in the incumbent is also an important step forward in the process of reform.

Yet, these positive signs have been marred mainly because of the decision to grant OTE a FWA licence without a requirement that they participate in the auction. The decision can only be explained by the wish of the government to add value to a company for which it seeking a strategic partner. As well, the new law provided an opportunity to use best practice regulations and to incorporate new EU thinking that has yet to be formally adopted. An example would be to streamline licensing procedures allowing market entry on the basis of class licences. The commitment to competition should also have been followed up by much earlier licensing of new entrants so that on 1 January 2001 they would have

---

Box 2.   **Strengths**

- Universal availability of infrastructure with high penetration rates.
- Competitive mobile sector.
- No line of business restrictions.
- Modern telecommunications law
- Unbundling of local loop to be implemented rapidly
- Low retail prices for many services
- Measures to cover consumer protection have been incorporated in new legislation

Box 3.   Weaknesses

- Delays in meeting the requirements of the EC derogation.
- Considerable delays in implementing necessary regulatory framework and lack of essential safeguards.
- Lack of expertise within the independent regulatory authority.
- Lack of advanced telecommunication services.
- Lack of alternate infrastructure.
- Discriminatory licence allocation for fixed wireless access.
- Relatively far behind in telecommunication market development compared to EU partners.

already been prepared to enter the market. As things presently stand, it is unlikely that new entrants will be in a position to compete before mid-2001 at the earliest. In turn this will retard the potential benefits to consumers from market liberalisation.

The independence provided to the regulator in the context of the new Law has still to be tested. However, the weakness of the regulator has characterised the period of transition. Attempts by the EETT to put in place required regulatory safeguards were constantly being undermined by the Ministry. The regulator was further weakened by being inadequately resourced. The regulator now needs to be given adequate resources so that it can attempt to catch-up on some of the lost time. A concerted effort to change behaviour through leadership and necessary institutional and structural change would quickly transform the Greek telecommunication scene into a leader and provide strong support in transporting the Greek economy into the information age.

A particular concern is the lack of a number of necessary safeguards to promote competition in the marketplace and a clear-cut timetable to implement these policies. This is the case for cost-based interconnection prices, price caps, cost-based prices, a methodology to calculate the cost of universal service, number portability, and licensing for third generation mobile services.

Greater emphasis on ensuring consistent decisions and on creating a strategic vision for the development of competition in the telecommunication service sector also would be of benefit to Greece. There should be greater reliance on competitive market forces to improve the competitive characteristics of the marketplace and benefit users. This would stimulate investment in new technologies and services, enhance industry competitiveness, and improve price performance.

4.2. Potential benefits and costs of further regulatory reform

Section 3 pointed to some early evidence that market liberalisation and competition are bringing significant benefits through:

- Lowering of national and international long distance prices;
- Competition stimulating investment, and innovation in the mobile service sector;
- Improving quality of service.

The immediate task is to ensure that PSTN competition develops and is translated into improved price structures and more advanced services when the market opens to competition in 2001. Early licensing of fixed wireless technologies has been an important step in this context as would be the encouragement of rapid development of cable television infrastructures in major cities. The fourth mobile licence will help improve price performance and increase penetration rates in that market segment. From a longer-term perspective, the most important impact of pro-competitive regulatory reform will be to accelerate broadband development and provide the foundations for electronic commerce and the information society. These developments can lead to important new growth (and employment) opportunities for the Greek economy.

4.3. Policy recommendations

The following recommendations are based on the above analysis, taking into account the "Policy Recommendations for Regulatory Reform" set out in the OECD *Report on Regulatory Reform* (OECD, June 1997).

1. **Ensure that regulations and regulatory processes are transparent, non-discriminatory, and applied effectively**

   - *Strengthen EETT in its role as an independent communications sector regulator and maintain a clear differentiation between MTC's policy responsibilities from regulatory responsibilities.*

   Creation of an independent regulatory body is of prime importance in Greece to ensure transparent and non-discriminatory regulations aimed at maximisation of consumer welfare through a market-oriented regime. The allocation of a number of important responsibilities to the independent regulator, as foreseen in the new law, should improve the effectiveness of regulation and help eliminate any potential conflict between the regulator and Ministry. An urgent effort needs to be made to rapidly increase the number of EETT's staff and improve its level of expertise.

   - *Implement a price cap system for OTE's PSTN prices effective 1 January 2001. Ensure an efficient system of prior approval of prices for prices outside of a price cap basket.*

   The regulation of prices through government authorisation is not appropriate for current competitive circumstances particularly since so far it has been driven by political considerations rather than the pro-competitive need for price flexibility. There has been insufficient competitive pressure in a number of market segments on OTE to increase efficiency and improve pricing structures. The independent regulatory body should implement price cap regulation rapidly. For prices outside the price cap basket a system of prior approval needs to be put in place which is efficient and rapid. OTE should also be required to implement 'per second' pricing for voice services.

   - *Implement an interconnection pricing framework using long-run average incremental cost (LRAIC) as the appropriate cost basis for pricing. and ensure that an agreed interconnection offer is available before full market liberalisation;*

   - *Ensure that prices are rebalanced as rapidly as possible providing a transparent target to the incumbent to achieve this goal.*

   Assuring interconnection to the incumbent's public switched telephone network is a key competitive safeguard. Such safeguards are particularly important where the incumbent carrier, like OTE, is vertically integrated into local, long distance and other services and therefore with strong incentives to hinder equal access. Progress in establishing an effective interconnection regime is important to assuring that the benefits generated from competitive market structures are fully realised. The current methodology used to determine interconnection charges forces new entrants to pay high interconnection charges. Efficient pricing needs to be based on forward-looking LRAIC costs, including a reasonable profit margin. An interconnection offer should have been made available for new entrants at a much earlier date than June 2000. It is important that such an agreed offer is available well before full market opening otherwise this will lead to delays. Consideration should also be given to introducing an interconnection offer to allow for unmetered interconnection services. The development of competition and local loop unbundling require that prices are rebalanced. OTE and the regulator need to agree on a target date to achieve rapid rebalancing.

   - *Implement number portability and full preselection as rapidly as possible and ensure that numbering allocation policies for both wireline and mobile carriers are competitively neutral.*

Local loop competition will not be able to develop effectively unless number portability and pre-selection allows customers to reduce the "transaction costs" of changing service provider and choosing the cheapest provider. The further delay that has been given to OTE to implement these requirements effectively strengthens its market power and slows down competition. OTE has had a sufficient lead-time to prepare for competition so that no further delays are necessary. This is important in the fixed telecommunication service market but should also be implemented for the mobile market.

- *Develop an adequate methodology to cost universal service.*

The government needs to establish a transparent universal service funding mechanism that is com-petitively and technologically neutral. Current universal service obligations on OTE will be maintained until the end of 2001.

- *Use auctions to allocate licences in the mobile sector and also to allocate licences for the 3rd generation mobile services. Ensure that the incumbent is required to participate for a fixed wireless access licence on the same terms and conditions as other potential licensees.*

Auctions allow for more transparency and increasing regulatory efficiency in spectrum allocation. The auction system chosen for wireless in the local loop licences should be maintained for all wireless licences. The incumbent should not be provided a FWA licence on an unfair and discriminatory basis, but should be subject to the same requirements as other potential new market entrants.

2. **Reform regulations to stimulate competition and eliminate them except where clear evidence demonstrates that they are the best way to serve the broad public interest.**

- *Reduce barriers to entry by introducing a system of general authorisations rather than individual licences. Conditions which need to be attached to licences can be through a general licensing framework*

In order to simplify and streamline regulations Greece could immediately adopt a class licensing system that relies on simple authorisation for market entry. This would accelerate market entry and reduce bureaucratic barriers to market entry. It would also be an important step in implementing best-practice regulatory models.

3. **Review, and strengthen where necessary, the scope, effectiveness and enforcement of competition policy.**

- *Review regulations in all areas of telecommunications regularly and systematically with a view to streamlining and where appropriate abandoning them.*

The government already reviews regulations, but these reviews need to be conducted more syste-matically and in depth to ascertain whether the regulations are still in the public interest, benefit users, and whether such regulation should be abandoned or modified. "Forbearance" procedures (or "sunset clauses") should be incorporated to ensure that regulations no longer necessary are eliminated and the industry should be given the right to request reviews of laws and regulation's to increase efficiency and reduce market barriers. EETT should be required in its Annual Report to examining the potential for streamlining regulations.

- *Ensure independent operation of the incumbent.*

Although subject to asymmetric regulation, it is important that the incumbent be allowed to act independently in the market without undue interference from the government, its major shareholder. The full privatisation of the incumbent should be accelerated and the government should not attempt to maintain control over its operation other than through transparent laws and regulations.

NOTES

1. Caloghirou, Y. and T. Darmaros (1994) in Bohlin, E. and O. Grandstrand (eds).

2. The initial responsibility of the EETT was only for telecommunications. Its responsibilities for postal issues were added in 1999.

3. Commission Decision 97/607 concerning the granting of additional implementation periods to the Hellenic Republic for the implementation of Commission Directive 90/388/EEC as regards full competition in the telecommunications markets. Published in the Official Journal: OJ L 245, 9/09/97, p. 6.

4. A new operating licence for OTE and the new providers of public voice telephony services has been drafted and was sent to the EC for approval on 31/12/99.

5. The net income margin is net income as a percentage of total operating revenues.

6. An Action Plan named 'Operational Programme for the Information Society' is currently being negotiated with EC officials in the context of the 3rd Community Support Framework for Greece in order for specific measures to be subsidised by the EC, in accordance with the terms and conditions approved by the EC.

7. OTE (2000), Annual Report Pursuant to Section 13 OR 15(d) of the Securities Exchange Act of 1934 for the fiscal year ended December 31, 1999, Commission file number 1-14876.

8. Interview with Forthnet, Athens, 21/6/00.

9. France Telecom's shares were floated on the Stock Exchanges of Athens and London.

10. Source: http://www.totaltele.com/view.asp?articleID=32096&Pub=TT&categoryid=627.

11. The EU's ONP Interconnection Directive allows for a regulator to notify an enterprise as having significant market power if that enterprise has a market share of more than 25% of the relevant market.

12. Interview at the Ministry of National Economy, Athens, 22.6.00.

13. No mention was made of renewal of the President in the first Telecommunications Law (Law 22 46/94).

14. Law has been under discussion since February 1998 and successive drafts have been presented to the interested parties since then. The view of most telecommunication service providers in Greece is that this is due to a conflict of interest between EETT and the Ministry. The latter wished to maintain the 'upper hand' and avoid the transfer tasks and powers to EETT. The same providers criticised the Ministry for acting 'at the last minute' and for loosing valuable time in preparing the new regulatory framework for competition.

15. So far, EETT's personnel was recruited by the High Level Council of Personnel Selection, known as ASEP. The new Law transfers responsibility over recruitment to EETT but any new recruitment has to be approved by the Council within 20 days.

16. It should be clarified that the installation, and/or operation of public telecommunication networks for the provision of liberalised services has been open to competition since October 1997.

17. In this context, it should be noted that a main argument used by the Greek government and OTE to request a derogation period was the necessity to invest substantially to upgrade the domestic network. OTE had argued that "digitalisation and modernisation would be prejudiced if full competition was introduced in 1998... This would deprive OTE of revenue needed both to finance the modernisation of the Hellenic Republic's telecommunications infrastructure and to provide universal service to dispersed customers in remote areas of the Hellenic Republic."

18. This is according to EETT's publication 'The provision of telecommunication services in Greece: Practical Guide'.

19. Ministerial Decision 78674/99 (B2117), amended by Ministerial Decision 29392/15.5.2000, (B' 6541, 22/5/2000).

20. Ministerial Decision 78794 (B' 2112, 3.12.99).

21. According to company officials they had submitted an application in February 1999 and were awarded a license in May 2000.

22. According to Ministry officials, for each application submitted to the Ministry for the installation of antennas, the Ministry is obliged to request the conduct of a study on the effects of electromagnetic waves to public safety, following the European Council Recommendation L199/1999/529/EC.

23. See Com(2000) 386 Final, Proposal for a Directive of the European Parliament and the Council on he authorisation of electronic communications networks and services, Brussels 12.07.2000.

24. OTE (2000), Form 20-F as filed with the Securities and Exchange Commission on June 28, Washington D.C., p. 17.

25. This was demonstrated for instance in the UK where Oftel considers that cost allocation efforts in various studies undertaken have succeeded in reducing the joint/common costs from about 30% down to some 10%.

26. Article1, para. 2 of Directive 98/61/EC with regard to operator number portability and carrier pre-selection allows for a maximum period of two years for the implementation of number portability in those countries which have been granted an additional transition period for full liberalisation of voice telephony services.

27. According to OTE's estimates these costs reached GRD 13.2 billion, 12.4 billion and 11 billion in 1997, 1998 and 1999 respectively. Source: OTE FORM 20-F (2000).

28. In 1998, EETT commissioned a study to determine the costs of Universal Service in Greece and to propose methods for financing any potential excess costs incurred. Although at that time OTE's role was critical because it could provide the team responsible for the study with detailed information on its network structure, its assistance has been rather poor. The Ministry commissioned a similar study on universal service that is currently under way and results are expected by December 2000.

29. See OECD (1999*a*).

30. OECD (1999*b*), Table 4.1, p. 97

31. OECD (1999*l*), Table 4.5.

32. The European Commission has assisted in investment by providing ECU 34.9 million as capital investment subsidies.

33. Presentation by OTE's Chief Executive Officer to the "Global Telecom Investor conference", New York, 13-16 March 2000.

34. The Greater Athens area accounts for 30% of the Greek population.

35. OTE (2000), Form 20-F as filed with the Securities and Exchange Commission on June 28, Washington D.C.

36. OTE has estimated that 49% of local calls are less than one minute long (SEC Form 20-F, June 2000), whereas in OTE News (May 31, 2000) data provided show the average call duration during the 1st quarter of 2000 as 190 seconds.

37. The basket includes a number of calls distributed at different times of the day, different days of the week and over different distances. The statistics are prepared in $US using both purchasing power parity (PPP) and current exchange rates. In general, it is considered that the PPP figures provide a more reliable comparison.

38. See, OECD (1999*b*), Table 7.9.

39. OECD (2001).

40. See, OECD (1999*b*), Table 7.18.

41. Op.cit. Tables 7.19 and 7.20.

42. See OECD (1993), OECD (1995), OECD (1997).

43. OTE.

44. See, for example, the OECD (1997), Chapter 8.

45. OECD (1999*b*), Table 9.5.

46. The Academic Net is the market leader in terms of number of addresses. See Open.gr domain survey.

47. Content in Greek does not appear to be a factor slowing Internet penetration. In fact Greece is fourth leading OECD country in terms of radio stations on the web per million inhabitants.

48. Flecher estimates for 1st quarter of 1999 putting Greece last among EU countries.

BIBLIOGRAPHY

Caloghirou, Y. and T. Darmaros (1994),
"Internationalisation of Telecommunication Service Provision and the Greek Privatisation Debate" in Bohlin, E. and O. Grandstrand (eds.), *The Race to European Eminence: Who are the coming tele-service multinationals?*, Amsterdam.

OECD (2001),
Greece, Economic Survey 2001, Paris.

OECD (1999*a*),
Greece, Economic Survey 1998, Paris.

OECD (1999*b*),
Communications Outlook 1999, Paris.

OECD (1997),
Communications Outlook 1997, Paris.

OECD (1995),
Communications Outlook 1995, Paris.

OECD (1993),
Communications Outlook 1993, Paris.

OECD PUBLICATIONS, 2, rue André-Pascal, 75775 PARIS CEDEX 16
PRINTED IN FRANCE
(42 2001 08 1 P) ISBN 92-64-18715-4 – No. 51921 2001